Gender and Islam in Africa

Gender and Islam in Africa

Rights, Sexuality, and Law

Edited by

Margot Badran

Woodrow Wilson Center Press
Washington, D.C.

Stanford University Press
Stanford, California

EDITORIAL OFFICES

Woodrow Wilson Center Press
Woodrow Wilson International Center for Scholars
One Woodrow Wilson Plaza
1300 Pennsylvania Avenue, N.W.
Washington, DC 20004-3027
Telephone: 202-691-4029
www.wilsoncenter.org

ORDER FROM

Stanford University Press
Chicago Distribution Center
11030 South Langley Avenue
Chicago, IL 60628
Telephone: 800-621-2736; 773-568-1550
www.sup.org

Library of Congress Cataloging-in-Publication Data

Gender and Islam in Africa : rights, sexuality, and law / edited by Margot Badran.
    p. cm.
    Includes index.
    ISBN 978-0-8047-7481-9
    1. Muslim women—Africa. 2. Muslim women—Political activity—Africa. 3. Women
in Islam—Africa. 4. Feminism—Religious aspects—Islam. I. Badran, Margot.
    HQ1170.G426   2011
    305.48′697096—dc22

                                               2011004127

 **Woodrow Wilson International Center for Scholars**

The Woodrow Wilson International Center for Scholars is the national, living U.S. memorial honoring President Woodrow Wilson. In providing an essential link between the worlds of ideas and public policy, the Center addresses current and emerging challenges confronting the United States and the world. The Center promotes policy-relevant research and dialogue to increase understanding and enhance the capabilities and knowledge of leaders, citizens, and institutions worldwide. Created by an Act of Congress in 1968, the Center is a nonpartisan institution headquartered in Washington, D.C., and supported by both public and private funds.

Conclusions or opinions expressed in Center publications and programs are those of the authors and speakers and do not necessarily reflect the views of the Center's staff, fellows, trustees, or advisory groups, or any individuals or organizations that provide financial support to the Center.

The Center is the publisher of *The Wilson Quarterly* and home of Woodrow Wilson Center Press and *dialogue* television and radio. For more information about the Center's activities and publications, including the monthly newsletter *Centerpoint,* please visit us on the web at www.wilsoncenter.org.

Contents

vii

Preface

I would like to share with readers the story of the origins of this book, which forms part of the foundational history of the Institute for the Study of Islamic Thought in Africa (ISITA). Since it was established by the eminent Africanists John Hunwick and Sean O'Fahey within the Program of African Studies at Northwestern University in 2000, ISITA has broken ground in institutionalizing the study of Islam in Africa—and with this, redefining African studies to include within its purview the entire continent. Now directed by Muhammad Sani Umar, ISITA continues to foster innovative research and connects a large international network of scholars with shared interest in Islam and Africa.

In each of its first four years, ISITA selected a theme for special focus and invited a preceptor to conduct a specialized seminar and organize a conference. I was honored to be asked to be preceptor the year that gender was the subject of focus. At the end of that year, I organized the Conference on Gender and Islam in Africa: Women's Discourses, Practices, and Empowerment. Scholars from Africa and elsewhere shared their research with a vast room full of participants, who engaged in intensely lively debate. This book presents a selection of papers from that conference, together with work from other scholars in the field. Most of the original conference papers have since been augmented with further research.

In this pleasurable moment of giving thanks, I first extend my deep appreciation to the contributors to this book for their impressive and innovative work, which provides inspiration for the ongoing study of gender and Islam in Africa. I express my gratitude for their cooperation and patience in our joint effort, which has been a collaboration across continents. It is with particular pleasure that I thank John Hunwick and Sean O'Fahey for inviting me to be an ISITA preceptor and for their warm collegiality during my stay. My special thanks go to Rebecca Shereikis, then ISITA's coordinator and now its associate director, for her manifold organizational skills in ensuring that the conference ran smoothly and for the extended assistance she has given in helping to see this book to completion. I thank Sylvia Washington Bâ, professor emerita in the French Department of the Université Cheikh Anta Diop de Dakar, for her help with translations. I thank Charlotte Weber for her fine editing and the sharp queries of a scholar-editor. I express my appreciation to the Woodrow Wilson International Center for Scholars and the supportive environment it provided while I was putting the finishing touches on this book. I thank the two outside readers, Barbara Cooper and an anonymous reviewer, for their suggestions and enthusiasm. Finally, I thank Joseph Brinley, the director of the Woodrow Wilson Center Press, and Yamile Kahn, the managing editor, with whom it has been a distinct pleasure to work.

Gender and Islam in Africa

Introduction: Gender and Islam in Africa—Rights, Sexuality, and Law

Margot Badran

This book looks at Africa as a continent where east and west, and north and south, have been historically connected by movements along vast networks of rivers and land routes and in more recent times by air. It does not view Africa as a vast space divided by the Sahara, as did the European colonizers in their transitory moment. In their script, so-called Sub-Saharan Africa was *Africa,* or "Africa proper," à la Hegel. They called the western rim of the north "the Maghreb," and they designated the eastern littoral as part of the Middle East. These colonial geopolitical categories were reflected and solidified in the academic division of labor, as expressed in area studies, and largely persist to this day.

Viewing the continent as a whole, as this book does, gives a complex, layered, and vibrant picture of Africa, of Islam, and of gender, and of the intertwined complexities that elude the truncated version. For example, the Senegalese philosopher Souleymane Bachir Diagne offers an eloquent and incisive mapping of Africa in its wholeness and rich diversity. Rejecting the fiction of a divided Africa, geographically cut in two by the Sahara and its people compartmentalized, he prods us to understand "African-ness as the South within the North and the North within the South."[1] Likewise, the Nigerien linguist and women's studies scholar Ousseina Alidou tells us in chapter 2 of this volume that Sahelian cultures, which are part of the Sudanic Belt running from Senegal in West Africa to the Red Sea in the northeastern part of the continent, are connected rather than separated by the Sahara.[2] And in chapter 1, the anthropologist Beverly Mack describes the routine exchange of knowledge that existed in past centuries across widely connected lands that we know today as nation-states. She speaks of the Greater Maghreb in referring to the intellectual and cultural connectedness of northern and western Africa. Such geographic and cultural flows speak of a dynamic, interconnected continent.

A corollary of bifurcating Africa is a cutting off of so-called Sub-Saharan Islam from Islam in the northern part of the continent. In this rendition, "Islam in Africa" (south of the Sahara) is hyperlocalized and made sui generis. Muslims first came to Africa during the time of the Prophet Muhammad, when troubles in Arabia prompted some to seek refuge in Ethiopia. In the seventh century, forces bringing Islam from Arabia swept across the continent's northern rim. The religion subsequently spread across the continent, especially starting in the ninth century, via land and river networks. Arabic, the language of the Qur'an, became an early and widespread lingua franca in Africa.[3] Now, in the twenty-first century, one-fifth of the world's Muslims are to be found in Africa, numbering some 5 million. There is a dynamic connectivity of Muslims throughout the continent, which has intensified in the past two decades with the continuing spread of information technologies.

The study of Islam in Africa is centuries old, with ancient centers of learning scattered throughout the continent from Timbuktu, to Sokoto, to Fez, to Kairouan, to Cairo.[4] Today, evidence unearthed by women scholars points to the presence of religiously learned women who have contributed to the corpus of Islamic knowledge in Africa, and, presumably, ongoing research will reveal much more. In contemporary times, centers of Islamic studies in Africa, as elsewhere, are found not just in seminaries but also in secular universities, and these centers incorporate the spectrum of modern disciplines. In 1996, for example, the University of Cape Town created the interdisciplinary Center for the Study of Contemporary Islam with an Africa-wide focus.

Women and gender in Africa as a field of research and academic inquiry goes back several decades. It was first institutionalized—with a focus on development and empirical research—with the founding of the African Training and Research Center for Women, headquartered in Addis Ababa, in 1975.[5] Meanwhile, in Africa, as elsewhere, the new fields of women's studies, and later gender studies, were being introduced into the academy. Women scholars at the University of Cape Town created the African Gender Institute in 1996, which became a pioneering focal point for gender and feminist studies Africa-wide. In 2002, the institute, together with the continental Feminist Studies Network, launched *Feminist Africa,* a journal for the study of gender, which was to serve as a "platform for intellectual and activist research, dialogue, and strategy," and has played a key role in generating and disseminating cutting-edge research, theorization, and analysis.[6]

This book brings together scholarship at the intersection of women's and gender studies, Islamic studies, and (continent-wide) African studies. The book's analytical framework, focusing on Africa in its entirety, opens up dynamic ways of comprehending the multiple expressions of Islam on the continent through the lens of women and gender. Although it starts off with an inaugural chapter that examines female intellectual production in the early nineteenth century, the book generally focuses on the late twentieth and early twenty-first centuries. This is a moment when the forces of patriarchal political Islam, or Islamism, are having an impact on Muslim women throughout the continent. Some Islamists come to Africa from Asia (including the Asian part of the Middle East). Some fan out from the continent's Arab-dominated northern rim, which has experienced both homegrown and foreign forms of political Islam. Women in very different parts of the continent turn their confrontations and connections with patriarchal Islamists to their advantage. It is striking how, with the spread of Islamism's gender conservatism across the continent, Muslim women are countering with their own readings of Islam, which articulate the principle of gender equality they find in the Qur'an and other religious texts. These women constitute the major forces in the promotion of an egalitarian Islam, one that affirms the equality of all *insan* (humankind), exposing the inequities in sustaining a patriarchal version of Islam.

This volume presents the work of both Africans and non-Africans, and Muslims and non-Muslims, all of whom but one are women scholars, ranging from established to newer scholars. These contributors, who have conducted extensive on-the-ground research, draw upon the methods and insights of a range of disciplines—cultural studies, religious studies, gender studies, feminist studies, linguistics, anthropology, sociology, history, literary criticism, film studies, political science, and the law. They examine thought and experience in northern, southern, eastern, and western Africa. Regional distribution, however, was not sought, but rather an emphasis was placed on themes and a cross-section of contemporary research.

The following twelve chapters include a rich array of carefully contextualized, innovative theoretical and empirical research on gender and Islam in Africa. These chapters are organized in three thematic parts: "Women Re/produce Knowledge"; "Re/constructing Women, Gender, and Sexuality"; and "*Shari'a,* Family Law, and Activism." As may be presumed, however, ideas and practices of gender, religion, and culture are not neatly contained—and indeed, in tantalizing ways, as the reader will see, transcend the organizing frames. Thus, particular subthemes that first appear in part I run throughout the book: the significance of orality and the intersections of the oral and the written, the meshing of public and private and the porosity of these categories, the insignificance or significance of the nation and the persistence of borderless cultural and religious flows, the volatile and intersecting constructions of "secular" and "religious," and fluctuating constructions of gender in the context of political, economic, and social change. In the book's vibrant kaleidoscope, readers can see continuities and ruptures, and commonalities and differences that move us beyond the thrall of stereotypes and stasis.

Women Perform as New Authorities in the Re/production of Religious Knowledge

Although this book focuses on the contemporary period, it should not be assumed that Muslim women have not had a prior history as reproducers and producers of religious knowledge and learned authorities; thus, this history is delineated in chapters 1 through 4, which make up part I. Women have been prominent historically in transmitting *hadith*s, starting with the Prophet Muhammad's wife, 'Aisha. Muslim women flourished in premodern times as religious scholars and were thus influential as teachers in the formation of male scholars, as the Egyptian specialist in Islamic history Omaima Abou Bakr and others have shown.[7] However, in more recent times, and especially under colonialism and in the processes of modernization and new state building (including different forms of institutionalizing knowledge), women religious scholars have largely disappeared from the public scene. Nonetheless, as we shall see, in more recent decades women have been returning to the fore and gaining visibility and respect as new dispensers of religious understanding.

Muslim women in contemporary Africa who have been entering into the arena of religious interpretation and activism find inspiration and can point to a female scholarly lineage on the continent in the person of Nana Asma'u, a religious scholar, Sufi, writer, poet, teacher, and social activist prominent in early–nineteenth-century northern Nigeria. Nana Asma'u's recognition by Muslims in other parts of the Islamic world is attested in the celebration of her life and work in *Great Ancestors: Women Asserting Rights in Muslim Contexts,* edited by the Pakistani feminists Farida Shaheed and Aisha Shaheed.[8] Likewise, in chapter 1 of the present volume, "Muslim Women's Knowledge Production in the Greater Maghreb: The Example of Nana Asma'u of Nigeria," Beverly Mack presents a thickly contextualized analysis of the prodigious output of this icon who embodied the spirit and practice of an egalitarian understanding of Islam. As the daughter of Shehu Usman dan Fodiyo, who launched a protracted struggle for religious and political reform in northern Nigeria and became the founder and head of the Sokoto Caliphate (1803–30), Nana Asma'u played a key role in supporting her father's religious, social, and political project. Seizing the opportunities such a position afforded, she became a revered religious intellectual in her own right, spreading her knowledge orally and through written texts. While serving as a model for women, she was also held in high esteem by men, and she played an important role in the life of the state.

A different kind of women's religious leadership is seen in the life and work of a woman in contemporary Niger, Malama A'ishatu Hamani Zarmakoy Dancandu, a poet, Sufi, teacher, and in later life a religious and cultural commentator on national radio and television. In chapter 2, "Rethinking Marginality and Agency in Postcolonial Niger: A Social Biography of a Sufi Woman Scholar," Ousseina Alidou contextualizes and analyzes the life and work of Malama ("teacher") A'ishatu, who, although of royal birth, spent her childhood and many of her adult years during the colonial era in modest circumstances. She finessed opportunities to acquire an education within the context of colonial and local patriarchal political and social systems. Her hard-won learning in a religious school (*makaranta*) serving only boys (the modern secular schools opened by the colonial authorities to prepare males for service in the lower echelons of state bureaucracy were even further out of bounds to her) gave her exposure to Islamic learning, which, along with her self-acquired knowledge and the abilities she honed as a poet, would later catapult her to national prominence in the era of Islamic resurgence. Alidou shows how Malama A'ishatu—who was offered a place on national radio and television, where she was to reach other women with a religious message—used her platform to convey a liberal understanding of Islam through verse and homespun commentary. At the same time, she impressed upon young girls and their mothers the importance of obtaining a secular education and seizing work opportunities. The broadcasts of a liberal interpretation of Islam by Malama A'ishatu, linked with her dispensing of practical advice to women and girls to claim their rights, especially to education, and to become productive members of their family and society in their everyday lives, can be seen as a kind of "populist Islamic feminism."

Around the time Malama A'ishatu was ascending the national stage in Niger, further to the north in Morocco, Fatima Mernissi was engaged in an investigation of misogynist *hadiths*, which she published in her book *Le Harem Politique* (translated into English as *Women and Islam: An Historical and Theological Enquiry* in the United Kingdom and as *The Veil and the Male Elite* in the United States), which is regarded as a seminal text of emergent Islamic feminism.[9] In chapter 3, "Deconstructing Islamic Feminism: A Look at Fatima Mernissi," Raja Rhouni offers an incisive analysis of the trajectory and complexity of her compatriot's corpus of secular feminist and Islamic feminist discourses. In so doing, she proposes a conceptual distinction between "secular," which she sees as connoting an open-minded critical engagement with religion concerning women's rights and gender equality, and "secularist," which she defines as presuming a priori that religion as such is inimical to women's rights and gender equality. She adds to our understanding of "secular" and how "the secular" and "the religious" are in conversation and mutually constitutive in ways Talal Asad and Elizabeth Shakman Hurd suggest, rather than the rigid and adversarial categories that Islamists make them out to be in the polarized world they seek to construct.[10] In her engagement with Mernissi, Rhouni takes the analysis of Islamic feminism into new territory. In seeing the limitations of classical Islamic tools or methodology, which Mernissi uses in her deconstruction of misogynist *hadiths*, Rhouni suggests the need to move beyond what she sees as foundationalism, along the lines proposed by Muhammad Arkoun and Nasr Hamid Abu-Zayd.[11] In place of "Islamic feminism," Rhouni prefers the term "postfoundationalist islamic gender critique," using the lowercased "islam" to indicate multiple interpretive possibilities.

The South African scholar Sa'diyya Shaikh, also among the new generation of feminist interpreters, makes a singular contribution to women's

Islamic knowledge production in chapter 4, "Embodied *Tafsir:* South African Muslim Women Confront Gender Violence in Marriage." She speaks of *"tafsir* (exegesis) through praxis" as a way women gain understanding of the Qur'an through their suffering as battered wives. Women have been socialized to accept as a religious truism the patriarchal model of the family, and with it male supremacy, and to believe the conventional notion that the Qur'an sanctions the physical admonishing of wives by husbands. The harrowing experience of domestic violence, Shaikh found, pushed some women to generate their own alternative understanding of their religion and its scripture. Their notion of a just God conflicted with the idea of religiously sanctioned violence. Through different routes, Mernissi and the battered women whom Shaikh encountered came to the same conclusion: that misogyny, whether expressed verbally or physically, and the consequent dehumanizing of women are not only un-Islamic but even anti-Islamic. In producing their own Islamic knowledge, Muslim women like these become the authors of their own lives and authorities for themselves and others.

Re/constructing Women, Gender, and Sexuality

Women as "Woman" have served as emblems of the nation and of Islam.[12] Women, in customary (secular) thinking, have also been repositories of honor—of men, families, and communities—deriving from their social decorum and sexual purity, that is, sexual relations confined to marriage, or "morality." The burden of maintaining and displaying individual and group morality lies with women, while men are exempted. In Islamic religious thought, however, sexual strictures are meant to apply to both men and women. Part II of this book, comprising chapters 5 through 8, offer insights into complicated mixtures of symbols and functions of "Woman"/women, gender, and sexuality in diverse settings.

Intersections between women, nation, and morality at a time of postindependence nation building are addressed by Lidwien Kapteijns in chapter 5, "Changing Conceptions of Moral Womanhood in Somali Popular Songs, 1960–1990." She shows how the modern popular song transmitted a new national narrative aiming to construct a modern nation in the move away from colonialism and primordial clan fragmentation. The popular song could serve as a vehicle for wide oral dissemination of the new discourse of *soomaalinimo* (Somali identity) that the state encouraged artists and intellectuals to articulate. The new popular song was an urban hybrid with roots in oral poetry and Islamic lore. In conveying notions of romantic love and self-chosen companionate marriages, such songs implicitly challenged the conventional authority of family and clan in the emergent national environment of constitutionally equal citizens. However, ideas and practices of equality faltered along the axis of gender. Women's lyrics, as Kapteijns shows, affirm personal freedom and the equality of women and men, whereas men's replicate traditional ideals of women's dependence upon and obedience to men. In short, gender tensions intrude in the construction of national identity. With the collapse of the Somali state in 1991 and the nation's descent into the fragmented chaos of warring clans, *soomaalinimo* has been replaced by a discourse of Islamic morality affirming strict gender prescriptions. In the newly disintegrated space, there has been a raw rupture between Somali identity and Islam. However, Kapteijins informs readers that the nationalist songs, and with them *soomaalinimo,* still live on in the Somali diaspora.

A very different constellation of cohesiveness and set of ideals are brought to our attention by Marloes Janson in chapter 6, "Guidelines for the Ideal Muslim Woman: Gender Ideology and Praxis in the Tabligh Jama'at in the Gambia." In her work on young Gambian women in the Tabligh Jama'at, Janson shows how, beginning in the 1990s, the adherents of this religiously and socially strict Islamic sect originating in South Asia have become agents in a new Islamization movement. These women, who see themselves as regular Muslims and the mainstream as deviant, have become key players in the creation and spread of new expressions of Islamic piety through increased access to public space, where, however, they maintain gender segregation. They spread their message more widely through their long-distance missionary tours. Through what might be called "internal proselytizing" work, Janson argues, Tablighi women acquire authority and mobility. Yet, as her research also shows, such authority and mobility are limited and subject to men's consent. Tablighi women, moreover, regard their domestic duties as the highest form of religious expression. The respect and public admiration that the women gain are thus acquired at a price, which they seem willing to pay.

Examining video production in northern Nigeria, Heike Behrend finds shifting, hybridic, and contradictory expressions of gender relations and sexuality. In chapter 7, "*Titanic* in Kano: Video, Gender, and Islam," she looks at representations of gender in a remake of the Hollywood film *Titanic,* which premiered in 2003 during the height of the politically motivated Islamic revival in northern Nigeria. The new turn to Islam was signaled in Kano and several other northern states by the so-called return to the *shari'a,* with the official codification of Islamic *hudud* (laws of crime and punishment) along with the imposition of puritanical rules of behavior in public. Behrend shows how *Titanic,* with its story of young love, passed through the new censorship board because the director adroitly pursued "a politics of culture that tried to avoid offensive sexual interaction while also affirming it," or, to put it differently, he created a film that oscillated between individual transgression and social conformity. The film, for example, affirms a woman's right to choose her husband (which is actually an Islamic right) but does not question the institution of marriage as such. Scenes reflect a cultural pastiche, with foreign elements heavily borrowed from India (i.e., from Bollywood), which is perceived as less threatening than the West, while the original of the *Titanic* remake was a Hollywood movie. Behrend observes that most Hausa video production in northern Nigeria, in Kano—dubbed Kallywood—has been sponsored by women who are at the same time great consumers of videos. Films, like songs, often convey the complexities and contradictions that constitute life itself, which censors, whether as officially constituted boards or informal cultural vigilantes, often face difficulty policing in societies swirling in the vortex of change where people are caught up between forces of ambivalence and desire.

In northern Nigeria, a new form of policing sexuality came with the codification of the *hudud,* whereby sexual relations outside marriage (*zina*) were criminalized, and if the accused were proven guilty in a *shari'a* court, he or she would be condemned to death by stoning. Whereas women have often paid the price for what is deemed illicit sex in Islam, or even the mere appearance of impropriety, men have typically gone free. In chapter 8, "*Shari'a* Activism and *Zina* in Nigeria in the Era of *Hudud,*" Margot Badran shows how attempts to apply the new *hudud* ordinances to women alone, and, moreover, to poor women, backfired. When two poor women were tried and condemned to death for committing *zina,* activist women, Muslims and Christians together, through their nongovernmental organizations supplied the accused with legal teams comprising lawyers and specialists in *fiqh* (Islamic jurisprudence), to appeal the sentences before the higher *shari'a* courts in their respective states. The legal teams gained success through their scrupulous attention to conditions laid down in books of classical *fiqh.* Citizens, seeing that only women and the poor were summarily dragged before the law, rejected the blatant assault upon social justice and exposed the hypocrisy of *hudud* politics and patriarchal machinations. Women and poor people, Badran shows, thus became the touchstone of humanity's cry for justice.

Shari'a, Civil Law, and the Family

In Muslim societies in general, the family is the last frontier of gender inequality, or, to put it another way, the family is the last bastion of patriarchy. In Muslim-majority countries in Africa, there are found both religiously grounded family laws and secular family laws. Both these types have exhibited patriarchal influences. Efforts to reform or to recast family laws, whether secular or religious, and to acquire legal recognition of Muslims' religiously conducted marriages bring to the fore contesting political forces that manipulate secular and religious arguments to achieve their desired ends. Chapters 9 through 12, which make up part III, deal with matters related to marriage and the family and illustrate different approaches and problems. Three focus on Muslim-majority countries—Mauritania, Mali, and Morocco—and one looks at a Muslim-minority community, South Africa.

Specialists in *fiqh* have traditionally been religious scholars who have mastered the written corpus of Islamic jurisprudence and who then, in their capacity as experts, are called upon to apply it. Corrine Fortier, however, shows how ordinary women in Mauritania apply their knowledge of *fiqh,* as expressed in the Maliki school and passed down orally from mother to daughter, to obtain the right to a monogamous marriage. In chapter 9, "Women and Men Put Islamic Law to Their Own Use: Monogamy versus Secret Marriage in Mauritania," she notes that when in 2001 Mauritania acquired its first official personal status code (or family law), which recognized woman's right to monogamy, it was simply enacting in state law what women had been practicing all along. She links monogamy in marriage not only to women's use of *fiqh* arguments but also to the social realities of a society that was traditionally nomadic and whose patterns of male honor were connected with men's chivalrous treatment of women rather than expressed through menacing controlling mechanisms such as threats of polygamy. However, she also shows that the widespread concurrent custom of secret marriages subverted the reality of monogamous marriage. In more recent times, with increased sedentary living patterns accompanying socioeconomic change, secret marriages have declined and divorce has become more prevalent.

The family law in Morocco, called the Mudawana, is a religiously backed code. In Morocco, as generally in western and northwestern Africa, the Maliki school of jurisprudence prevails. Different laws and practices, ostensibly based in Maliki jurisprudence, indicate divergent interpretations. The Moroccan Mudawana was dramatically recast in 2004. The confirmation of husband and wife as dual heads of the family and other provisions—such as making polygamy virtually impossible, enhancing women's abilities to initiate divorce, and eliminating the necessity for women to be represented by an agent (*wali*) in order to effect a marriage—make the Mudawana the most egalitarian marriage law based in *fiqh* anywhere on the books today. The successful reform followed recent decades of activist women's use of both secular and Islamic feminist arguments and relentless campaigning. At a moment that was politically ripe, following the Casablanca terrorist attacks in 2003, the king, in his role as commander of the faithful, took charge and sent a draft family law reform to parliament, which was quickly endorsed. With the new Mudawana, the conflict between the equality of citizens guaranteed by the Constitution and the inequalities embedded in the original family law of the late 1950s was effectively removed. Half a century later, Islamic language was deployed to affirm an egalitarian model of the family. Reflecting on the state in chapter 10—"Islam, Gender, and Democracy in Morocco: The Making of the Mudawana Reform"—Julie Pruzan-Jørgensen regards the new law more as a manifestation of political liberalization than as evidence of a democratic transition. She demonstrates how timing and complex politics, which included adroit political maneuvers by secular and religious women activists and their broad bases, were crucial in affecting the new family law in Morocco.

In Mali, the civil family law (called the Code du marriage et de la tutelle) of 1962 is a secular code, which, as the 1950s religiously based Moroccan family law had done, upholds gender inequality in contradiction to the Constitution of the state, which enshrines the principle of the equality of all citizens. In the second half of the 1990s, during the era of political liberalization, there were serious efforts in Mali on the part of the state and other actors to reform the family law in order to bring it into alignment with the Constitution and the international conventions that Mali had signed and to meet the demands of activist women's groups and other liberal segments of society. As Benjamin F. Soares recounts in chapter 11, "Family Law Reform in Mali: Contentious Debates and Elusive Outcomes," the proposed reform of the family law sought greater gender equality, which attracted both religious and secular critics, while the failure to include legal recognition of religiously performed marriages (marriage in the existing statutory law is defined as secular) attracted widespread popular outcry. Soares notes that the derailing of the proposed reform (the bill was eventually shelved) was attributable less to opposition by Islamists and other religious conservatives to the increase of women's rights than to the disaffection of the wider population, for whom religion is central in everyday life. The key factor in the broad opposition, Soares argues, was the failure to include official recognition of religious marriages in the reform package.

In South Africa, where Muslims constitute a religious minority, Muslim religious marriages have never been officially recognized. The Constitution of South Africa, enacted in 1996 following the end of colonial rule and demise of the apartheid regime with its horrific injustices and inequalities, affirms the equality of all citizens, unequivocally acknowledging the equal rights of all individuals to culture, religion, and tradition. The mandate of the Constitution, which has been applauded worldwide as a state-of-the-art instrument, is transformative justice in order to redress historical wrongs. The South African Commission on Gender Equality was created to provide machinery for ensuring the implementation of gender equality and rights. The interface between freedom of religion (including individuals' freedom to choose the way they interpret and practice their religion) and equality is complicated. Rashida Manjoo reveals some of these torturous complications in chapter 12, "Legal Recognition of Muslim Marriages in South Africa." She points out that the Muslim Marriages Bill was problematic from the start because of the flawed process involved in its production. The bill reflected one particular and patriarchal understanding of Islam that violated the principles of (gender) equality and freedom of religion and belief that the Constitution of South Africa mandates. In advancing a single version of Islam, the bill does not represent the wide spectrum of religious understanding within the highly differentiated Muslim communities of South Africa. Manjoo is sensitive to the many constitutional problems raised by the attempt to achieve codification of religious laws in a secular democracy, and she thus points out that the "norms and values underpinning Islamic laws and jurisprudence are also embodied in the [South African] Constitution." What needs to be done, she argues, is to gain legal recognition of all religious marriages, including Muslims' religious marriages. The Commission on Gender Equality, of which she was formerly a member, has proposed a (secular) draft bill to that effect. The South African debates around the subject of instituting Muslim family laws in a secular democratic state have resonance for other countries in Africa as well as the West. In Canada, for example, some Muslims clamor for the creation of Muslim family laws, while other Muslims are vehement in their opposition.

Envoi

The chapters in this book offer a tantalizing introduction to the growing scholarship on women, gender, and Islam in Africa. They reveal the breadth of historical experience, contemporary practices, and interpretive and theoretical work under way by scholars from and focusing upon Africa. The book reveals how much can be learned about the range and nuances of religious interpretation and lived experiences of Muslims by examining gender and Islam in an Africa-wide frame and by breaking through the confines of intellectual compartmentalization that are perpetuated by area studies such as those on so-called Sub-Saharan Africa and the Middle East. It demonstrates the reverberations of theoretical breakthroughs and the implications of shared empirical work for charting and analyzing issues related to women, gender, and Islam throughout the continent. The scholarship presented here makes unique contributions to Islamic studies and gender studies, both within Africa and beyond, and adumbrates future directions.

Notes

1. Souleymane Bachir Diagne, "Northern Africa and the 'Sudan': Reading Identities on the Map," presentation at Domain Dinner, Northwestern University, Evanston, Ill., fall 2003.

2. See Ousseina D. Alidou, *Engaging Modernity: Muslim Women and the Politics of Agency in Postcolonial Niger* (Madison: University of Wisconsin Press, 2005), 8–11.

3. See John Hunwick, "Arabic as the Latin of Africa," in *West Africa, Islam, and the Arab World: Essays in Honor of Basil Davidson* (Princeton, N.J.: Markus Wiener, 2006), 49–58.

4. On Timbuktu, see Alida Boyle, John Hunwick, and Joseph Hunwick, *The Hidden Treasures of Timbuktu: Rediscovering Africa's Literary Culture* (London: Thames & Hudson, 2008).

5. The very first Africa-wide center for research on women was the development-oriented African Training and Research Center for Women (AFTRCW) established in 1975, the first year of the United Nations Decade for Women, as part of the UN system, to conduct research that would help promote women in development. See Margaret C. Snyder and Mary Tadesse (the first director of AFTRCW), *African Women and Development* (Atlantic Highlands, N.J.: Zed Books, 1995).

6. See Amina Mama, "Editorial," *Feminist Africa,* issue 1, 2002, http://www.feministafrica.org/index.php/edition_one_editorial.

7. See Muhammed Akram Nadwi, *Al-Muhaddithat: The Women Scholars in Islam* (Oxford: Interface Publications, 2007); and Omaima Abou-Bakr, "Teaching the Words of the Prophet: Women Instructors of the Hadith (Fourteenth and Fifteenth Centuries)," *Hawwa: Journal of the Middle East and the Islamic World* 1, no. 3 (2003): 306–28.

8. Farida Shaheed with Aisha L. Shaheed, *Great Ancestors: Women Asserting Rights in Muslim Contexts* (Lahore: Shirkat Gah, 2004).

9. See Fatima Mernissi, *Women and Islam: An Historical and Theological Enquiry* (Oxford: Blackwell, 1991), and this book's U.S. edition: Fatima Mernissi, *The Veil and the Male Elite* (Reading, Mass.: Addison-Wesley, 1991).

10. See Talal Asad, *Formations of the Secular: Christianity, Islam, Modernity* (Stanford, Calif.: Stanford University Press, 2003); and Elizabeth Hurd, *The Politics of Secularism in International Relations* (Princeton, N.J.: Princeton University Press, 2008).

11. See Mohammed Arkoun, *Islam: To Reform or Subvert?* (London: Saqi, 2006); and Nasr Hamid Abu-Zayd, *Reformation of Islamic Thought* (Amsterdam: Amsterdam University Press, 2006).

12. See miriam cooke, "Deploying the Muslimwoman," in "Roundtable Discussion: Religion, Gender, and the Muslimwoman," *Journal of Feminist Studies in Religion* 24, no. 1 (Spring 2008): 91–99; and Margot Badran, "Between Muslim Women and the Muslimwoman," *Journal of Feminist Studies in Religion* 24, no. 1 (Spring 2008): 101–10.

Part I

Women Re/produce Knowledge

Chapter 1

Muslim Women's Knowledge Production in the Greater Maghreb: The Example of Nana Asma'u of Northern Nigeria

Beverly B. Mack

Patriarchal bias has been as true for Islamic cultures throughout history as for others. Yet Islam was founded on the dual mandates of human equality and the pursuit of knowledge. At its inception in the seventh century, Islam carried the promise of equality for all, regardless of gender, race, nationality, or any other characteristic that might differentiate privilege or right.

Much of the research on which this study is based was funded by a Carnegie Fellowship, for which I am grateful. Where there is discussion concerning Nana Asma'u and her works, the reader is referred to Jean Boyd and Beverly Mack, eds., *The Collected Works of Nana Asma'u, bint Shehu Usman dan Fodio* 1793–1864 (East Lansing: Michigan State University Press, 1997). I thank Jean Boyd for reading and commenting on an earlier version of this chapter. I also appreciate the readers' comments for this volume; an anonymous reader suggested that I clarify the context at the outset, which I have endeavored to do. Barbara Cooper's thoughtful questions have deepened our longstanding friendly debate about the historian's need for tangible evidence in opposition to the literary/cultural analyst's inclination to trust triangulation. We do, however, appreciate our common ground.

This premise is repeated clearly throughout the Qur'an (literally, "the [divine] recitation), which guides Muslims in decisions about daily living and the ultimate purpose of one's life. This chapter argues that even with the imposition of patriarchal restrictions on women's equitable roles in Islamic contexts, many Muslim women have pursued scholarly endeavors, basing their right to do so on the ideals of equality contained in Qur'anic language. The chapter considers the example of a nineteenth-century Muslim woman scholar in West Africa whose work was founded on religious precepts of equality that were accepted by the ruling male elite as inarguable in her time and place. This study notes that her scholarly endeavors were not considered an exception, but were understood to reflect a history of women's involvement in the pursuit of knowledge in Islam, and a common canon. It further argues that orality is central to a definition of scholarship in the Islamic context, and that facility with the oral recitation and transmission of modes of knowledge is not restricted by gender.

The Primacy of Women's Roles in Islam

The importance in Islam of the pursuit of knowledge as a path to God was evident from the first revelation recorded in the Qu'ran, in which the angel Gabriel conveyed to Muhammad God's command, "Read! Recite!" (Q96:1). Confused by this command, the unlettered Prophet Muhammad sought solace and clarity from his wife, Khadija. She recommended that he understand and revere this message as a benevolent communiqué from a merciful God. Muslims throughout history have known this story well, and they understand from youth the importance in this message of both reverence for the word and Khadija's supportive role in the prophet's life. She was the first convert to Islam. Although neither Khadija nor Muhammad was literate in the way of contemporary scholars, they held the conviction that attention to God through the intellect was as important as love of God through the heart. Islam has since its founding advanced "knowing" as a means of praying. A famous *hadith qudsi* conveys God's explanation for creation:[1] "I was a hidden treasure, and I created the universe that I might be known." If the universe is indeed God made manifest, then it is reasonable that learning all one can about the universe is a means of moving toward God. This is true regardless of one's gender.

Assessment of Muslim women's scholarship requires consideration of Islam's founding ethics. Ideally, in Islam women are not only allowed but are also encouraged to study. In practice, many Islamic societies have denied women such rights, and colonialization only reinforced such oppression. Despite this, it remains true that exemplary Muslim women throughout history have been engaged in the pursuit of knowledge, though often secluded from public view and unacknowledged beyond their own communities. In the Maghreb, Muslim women have been engaged in intellectual pursuits for centuries, but their scholarly activities remained virtually unknown in the West until scholarship toward the end of the twentieth century began to bring their activities to light.[2] Education in Islamic settings involves much more than studying books; it also includes memorizing passages of the Qur'an for a multiplicity of purposes, not only for developing literacy but also for internalizing a divine message for further use in intellectual discourse. Although Muslim women have participated in educational activities in the Maghreb within a religious framework throughout history, the nature of the canon of works on which they rely remains largely unexplored. Any analysis of such a canon must begin by taking into account the fluidity of scholarly interchange within the Maghreb region, the concept of gender equality set forth in the Qur'an, and the oral nature of the Qur'an as a model for scholarly sources.

Scholarly Exchange in the Maghreb

Muslim scholars historically have communicated without restriction across what are now fixed national borders. They had access to common philosophical perspectives, which were grounded in the Qur'an, and they shared Arabic as their lingua franca, regardless of distinct cultural traditions and languages. The fluid spread of knowledge throughout the Maghreb region, which continues in contemporary times, suggests that works of scholarship would have been broadly distributed in the region and altered through such dissemination. Thus, consideration of a canon of works needs to address the broadest regional expanse of communiqués among Islamic scholars in the Maghreb.

Precolonial caravan routes, unbounded by polity borders, facilitated cultural and educational exchange over a wide swath of northern and western Africa, creating an intercommunication zone extending beyond the Maghreb to include regions now known as Algeria, Tunisia, Libya, Morocco, Mauritania, Mali, and northern Nigeria. Principal desert paths linked Tripoli and Tunis to Kano, Nigeria, and Fez, Morocco, as well as to Cairo in the northeast. At least among Sufis, active intellectual interchange in the region during the eighteenth and nineteenth centuries established a complex network of communications among scholars of both genders.[3] As Mervyn Hiskett writes, "Sufi devotees were constantly going to and fro between Hausaland and Cairo or Fez and bringing back accounts of wondrous visions experienced by saintly personalities in the metropolises. The Shehu [in Sokoto, Nigeria] had cordial relations with Shaikh al-Mukhtar al-Kunti, the leader of a Sufi community centered around Timbuktu, who also had [Sufi mystical] visions."[4] Intellectual production was vital throughout the region, unlimited by political borders, and transmitted by itinerant scholars.[5]

Such cross-fertilization of ideas continues in contemporary times. The Tijaniyya brotherhood network in the Maghreb, a more recent moving force in Nigerian experience, inspires many Nigerian Tijaniyya adherents to travel to Fez, where the brotherhood's founder, Ahmed al-Tijani, is buried in the medina, which dates to the tenth century.[6] The link between Sufi scholars in northern Nigeria and Morocco existed centuries before the imposition of country designations by Western imperial powers, during which the region operated as an integrated region of fluid cultural, commercial, and intellectual exchange. In this milieu, women's roles were defined through Islamic values variously influenced by indigenous patriarchies, but the intellectual climate of the region likely meant that women were active scholars far more regularly than recent histories allow.

Gender Equality in Qur'anic Language; Inequality in Education

In this context, gender equality was integral to both the form and content of intellectual exchange, based as it was on the message of the Qur'an in a common language, Qur'anic Arabic. The Qur'an constitutes a foundation of ethics that provides a potentially level playing field. At its revelation in the seventh century, the Qur'an guaranteed equal rights and opportunities for women. Where these are respected, women find their right to pursue education in the authority of the divine word, not in human-made laws flowing from patriarchal polities. As the main source of faith among Muslims, the Qur'an repeatedly emphasizes equality between men and women, through language that specifies each group.[7] The salient feature in Qur'anic language is the spiritual, not biological, nature of the individual; the gender-neutral exhortation, "Oh you who believe!" is found repeatedly throughout the Qur'an.[8] Similarly, the importance of pursuing knowledge as a means of knowing God is stressed to all: "He causes those given knowledge to realize that this Revelation is your Lord's Truth, so that they may believe in it and humble their hearts to Him: God guides the faithful to the straight path" (Q22:54). Because the pursuit of all kinds of knowledge in the world is the basis of moving closer to knowledge of God, it is mandated for every individual.

Although the Qur'an repeatedly urges the pursuit of knowledge,[9] the influence of patriarchal systems on the social organization of Islamic societies has privileged the education of boys and men. Formal schools are more likely than informal study groups to be segregated by gender and narrow in their interpretation of Islam's message. Indigenous Islamic education systems often focus on rote memorization of the Qur'an and repress the exercise of intellectual investigation. The most severely patriarchal societies also limit girls' and women's public educational opportunities.

In Islamic societies today, as they have in the past, educational activities unfold in a variety of settings, both public and private. State-run schools provide primary and secondary classes for both boys and girls; whether boys outnumber girls in these classrooms depends on local perspectives concerning the value of girls' education. As they reach the secondary-school level, adolescent girls may be expected to leave their formal educations in favor of marriage; such trends depend on many factors, including the socioeconomic level of the family, their own attitudes about education, and circumstances determined by the opportunities and obligations of urban and rural life. Depending on the family circumstances, a girl may continue to pursue her education after marriage, but this is by no means guaranteed.

Private education programs, especially those operated by Sufis, are more likely to be conducted in an egalitarian manner, although this may not be immediately evident. Classes among Sufi adherents may be offered for both girls and boys, but in this context educational activities for females often are hidden; in the Maghreb, girls' daily religious education classes are held in private settings. Women who are members of Sufi brotherhoods meet separately from the men, gathering in informal settings for discussions and education sessions. Groups of these adult women meet voluntarily on a weekly or twice-weekly basis to learn from one among them who preaches informally in private study groups. Their sessions involve wide-ranging discussions on topics from current events and politics to religious issues. In these settings, discussion is the basis of educational dialogue. The absence of written works is no gauge of the quality of their intellectual activities; in Fez, Sufis are reticent to produce written works, feeling that the material that is most important should be internalized and kept safe from possible compromise by others. These informal seminars are not meant for indoctrination or document production, but for the enlightenment of those who attend.

Orality

Defining a canon must therefore take into consideration the oral nature of the Qur'an itself. Although secular works written by and for Muslims exist, any canon of religious works in Islam must be founded on interpretation (*tafsir*) of the Qur'an and studies relating to it, which include orally transmitted works as well as written ones. Written documents are essential to the definition of contemporary Western canons, but Islam's dependence on the spoken word has meant that Muslim cultures esteem the orally conveyed message to a degree unrecognized in the Christian West. This is also true for Judaism. Orality has been an integral part of Talmudic learning among Jewish scholars throughout the world, and Orthodox religious scholars committed the Talmud to memory and objected to its being written as late as the nineteenth century. The nature of orality and the respect it is accorded is central to Islam, and needs to be considered in any discussion of intellectuality among Muslims.

The issue of orality is also central to an analysis of Muslim women's scholarship. For many reasons, women's educational activities depend on the flexibility and portability of the oral transmission of knowledge.[10] The Qur'an—God's own "recitation"—is the foundation of both Islamic thought and literacy. Memorization of the Qur'an traditionally has been a hallmark of a Muslim child's religious and general education, which includes classical works as well as contemporary ones.[11] Classical works in the traditional context range from those that are wholly religious in nature to works that would be considered secular in the West. Muslim scholars were renowned for their erudition in areas as diverse as mathematics, history, sociology, philosophy, geography, geometry, literature, grammar, linguistics, and aesthetics.[12] Works on such topics are typical in the private family libraries that have been the source of education for generations of female and male scholars.

The Qur'an is described as the "foundation of the religion . . . [and] the source of Arabic grammar";[13] for scholars who contemplate its messages, it is an infinitely accessible font of wisdom that can be comprehended at whatever level best suits the student, whether literate or not. In northern Nigeria, women singers and poets to this day perform material that is replete with Qur'anic references, despite a popular consensus that their work as entertainers is un-Islamic.[14] For the average Muslim woman in northern Nigeria, Qur'anic perspective is integral to every aspect of daily life; it is not surprising that entertainers, as products of their culture, incorporate this personal immersion in the Qur'an in their performances. Even the illiterate are likely to be familiar with passages of the Qur'an and the spirit of its message from the five daily prayer sessions incumbent upon Muslims. That the orally transmitted word is revered implies the need for a reconsideration of what constitutes a canon.

In contemporary Sufi circles in Fez, written material is of only secondary importance to intellectual advancement; scholars there express reticence to rely on the written word, or to publish. Instead, one advances one's knowledge through contemplation of the spoken word, memorization of Quranic passages, and discussion of concepts in a variety of venues, including in Qur'anic schools at the lowest to the most advanced levels, in community study groups in the Sufi centers known as *zawiyas* (learning circles), and in dedicated affiliation with particular brotherhood study groups. Examples abound among Muslims in the Maghreb of oral materials that complement written versions in the contexts of women's educational experience. What this means for contemporary historians and chroniclers of Maghrebi scholarship is that what is written constitutes merely a portion of the evidence and product of the region's intellectual activity.

The Fodiyo Community

A good example of Muslim women's precolonial scholarship in both oral and written form in the northern Nigeria region is the work of Nana Asma'u bint Shehu Usman dan Fodiyo (1793–1864), who was born into a Fulfulde-speaking Fulani family of Qadiriyya Sufi intellectuals.[15] Until her biography was published at the end of the twentieth century, she was mentioned only in passing in historical works concerning the period.[16] An examination of some of her works offers a sense of the nature of and inspiration for her scholarly activities. In addition, attention to her various audiences demonstrates that women of many levels of educational preparation and degrees of literacy were lifelong learners. Asma'u was an impressive scholar, teacher, and poet, but it would be a mistake to dismiss her as an exception. Several of Asma'u's sisters, equally well educated and erudite, remain unknown because their works are unpublished.[17] Similarly, elsewhere in the Maghreb, family archives are said to be repositories of unpublished works by other women scholars, whose productivity remains to be discovered.[18]

The Fodiyo clan was made up of devout Muslims in the region now known as northern Nigeria. They were Fulfulde speakers who also communicated in Hausa with the majority Hausa population around them. The lingua franca of scholars in the wider region of the Maghreb has long been Arabic. By the late eighteenth century, Shehu Usman dan Fodiyo had gained a significant following through his preaching until the local Hausa king began to restrict the Shehu's freedoms. Disturbed by the lack of orthodoxy demonstrated by the Hausa populace, the Shehu sought to institute reform. His quest evolved into a political campaign, because the freedom to practice Islam depended on prevailing law. At the time of Asma'u's birth, the Shehu was beginning to receive Sufi mystic revelations. Although she was a twin and the Shehu named her brother Hassan, one of the traditional names for a twin, the Shehu called his daughter Asma'u (meaning beautiful) rather than the expected Husseina.[19] Asma'u's experience as a woman scholar was both extraordinary and representative. Her life was unusual in being intensely politically and intellectually focused. She was raised in a climate of crisis caused by the nominally Muslim king's suppression of her father's preaching. Years of such suppression led the Shehu to launch a jihad (literally, struggle, often glossed as "holy war") of reform (the Sokoto Jihad, 1803–30) that changed profoundly the nature of Islam in the region. It established a region united in greater orthodoxy. Local kings (*sarki* in Hausa) were replaced by more orthodox leaders known by the Arabic term *amir;* regional leadership passed from the Shehu to his son Muhammad Bello, who became the caliph. Asma'u was a determined teacher of the masses, alternately teaching men and women scholars, training women as itinerant teachers of secluded women, and creating works for use in teaching illiterate Hausa-speaking refugees.[20]

Asma'u believed fervently in the Qur'an's message of equality, as is evident in her written works. Clearly, her family shared and fostered these views. Her father had been educated by his mother and grandmother. Asma'u was quadrilingual, speaking Fulfulde (the language of her clan), Hausa (the language of the Hausa majority in the region), Arabic (the language of scholars), and Tamshek (the language of the region's Toureg/Berber desert dwellers). She wrote in Fulfulde, Hausa, and Arabic, and she wrote much of her poetic teaching material in Hausa so that it would be immediately accessible to the illiterate masses taught by the itinerant teachers she trained. She studied a traditional set of materials, relying on books from her father's library. She began with the Qur'an and classical works of Qur'anic interpretation, continuing in a program of collaborative activity with her elder half-brother Muhammad Bello, her father, and other scholars of the day.

Nana Asma'u's writings reveal that her education, like that of others on her level of learning, regardless of their gender, included the study and imitation of classical works as well as collaborative activity with her family members and peers using literary techniques common to her time.[21] Her education must have followed the traditional patterns of learning evidenced for others in the region from Mauritania and Mali to Kano, as her written works reflect familiarity with the topics of such a program of study. Subsequently, her own works became part of the corpus of materials later used in educating both men and women in the Sokoto Caliphate, which extended across what is now known as the northern half of Nigeria.

A Kano man born in Asma'u's old age attested to her renown in the region. Alhaji Umaru (b. 1858 in Kano) knew of Nana Asma'u, and commented in his writings that she was well known in the region.[22] His education would have been typical of rigorous instruction of the time, and it thus also tells us something about Asma'u's likely program of study. Umaru began Qur'anic school at the age of seven and spent five years learning the Qur'an and Arabic literacy. At the age of twelve, he began a program of advanced learning with several different teachers that was to continue for twenty-one years, ending in 1891. The areas of study he pursued included the Islamic religion, history, law, and the Arabic language. He also devoted two years of study to Qur'anic commentaries and history, and eleven years to the study of religion and language.

In addition, Umaru studied *hadith,* Maliki law, the historical traditions of Islam, the history of the Prophet Muhammad's life, world history, West African authorship, Arabic grammar, and pre-Islamic and Islamic poetry.[23] It is likely that this course of study was influenced by the intellectual movement that began in Sokoto and spread throughout northern Nigeria during the nineteenth century in the course of reformation following the Sokoto

Jihad. And although Umaru does not cite works by any of the Fodiyos, it would not be surprising to find evidence that the poetry and prose produced by the Shehu, his brother Abdullahi, Bello, and Asma'u was an integral part of the Islamic education system at the end of the century.[24]

Influences on Asma'u's Works:
The Qur'an and the *Sunna*

Asma'u was the daughter of a man who felt compelled to follow in the footsteps of the Prophet Muhammad, and this must have caused her to consider her own role in the community. Her collection of poetic works in many categories was influenced by the Qur'an and the *Sunna.* These include mnemonic guides to facilitate memorization of the Qur'an, stories based on the *Sunna,* elegies, and poems about medicines of the prophet. Her historical works reflect influences from the *sira* (biographies of the prophet) and also include eulogies and panegyrics.[25] Her Sufi-inspired works convey experiences of *khalwa* (mystic retreat) and *dhikr* (remembrance), and include an account of Sufi women. These different kinds of production exemplify collaborative creativity, particularly the reworking of commonly known poems, including some directly related to tenth-century manuscripts, some influenced by thirteenth-century panegyric, and others focused on the Abbasid Caliphate's (c. 750–1258) concepts of the state.

Asma'u's didactic work, in the form of a poem titled "The Qur'an,"[26] is extraordinary for compressing into thirty verses the names of every chapter of the Qur'an, which made it a compact mnemonic device for the teaching of the Qur'an.[27] Any qualified teacher would have been able to unpack each chapter title, teaching the entire chapter over one or more lessons. Asma'u wrote this poem nearly simultaneously in all three major local languages—Arabic, Fulfulde, and Hausa—obviously intending it to have wide appeal.[28] This work skillfully guides an organized study of the Qur'an for students at both beginning and advanced levels. Its usefulness as a mnemonic device for oral transmission and teaching purposes is evident in its efficient design.[29]

Asma'u's brother, Bello, held an important role in the Sokoto Caliphate as his father's chief aide and first caliph. Bello and Asma'u were extremely close, sharing intellectual interests and collaborating on many works. In *Tanbih al-Ghafilin* (The Way of the Pious, 1820), Asma'u uses her brother Bello's *Infaq al-Maisur,*[30] a story of the Sokoto Jihad, as a model for a discussion of the Shehu's intellectual focus, teaching methods, and materi-als.[31] This work is imitative of the *Sunna,* and it would have been familiar to anyone raised in the tradition of the *hadith.* A similar work is Asma'u's *Godaben Gaskiya* (The Path of Truth [in Hausa, hereafter H], 1842), which advises listeners to follow the path of right behavior, warning explicitly against sin by describing the pains of hell and the rewards of heaven as de-picted in the Qur'an. *Sharuddan Kiyama* (Signs of the Day of Judgment [H], n.d.) is also imitative of the *Sunna* and derived directly from the Qur'an. In this work, Asma'u's sense of her authority is clear; she remarks that "I, daughter of the Shehu, composed this song—you should follow her" (v. 126). She claims authority as the daughter of a man who represents both leadership and scholarship, traits that she shares.

That Asma'u was a Qur'anic scholar is evident in her mastery of its con-tent in the composition of her own works. She had to have studied the Qur'an to be able to draw on its content for her own compositions. In *Sharuddan Kiyama,* Asma'u outlines in graphic detail the punishments of hell as they are described in the Qur'an. This work allows Asma'u to draw a metaphorical parallel between the price of sin and the cost of disobedi-ence to local authority. As most of her other works, Asma'u's perspec-tive is grounded in the belief that divine moral authority guided the Sokoto Jihad. Her works emphasize the importance of conforming to its reforms. The Islamic court of the Sokoto Caliphate enforced public behavior through statutory punishment, but Asma'u chose to impress upon the masses the im-portance of obedience at a spiritual level as well as a civil one. As with all her works, the aim of this piece was to instruct. If people were not inclined to follow political authority, the fear of eternal punishment instilled by the poem was an effective means of promoting right living on a moral level.

Perhaps the most frightening of her works outlining the perils of hell is *Hulni-nde* (Fear This [in Fulfulde, hereafter F], n.d.). Interestingly, this work was written in Fulfulde, indicating that it was not intended for the masses but instead was addressed to her clansmen to bolster their convic-tion in the rightness of their cause in waging jihad. The work's origin is in a poem in couplets by Muhammad Tukur, one of the earliest composers of warning (*wa'azi*) verse in the nineteenth-century community of Sokoto scholars.[32] In creating a *takhmis* form by adding three lines to each origi-nal couplet, Asma'u transformed the poem into one of quintains while main-taining the original sense of the work.[33] Asma'u was also familiar with the Shehu's sermon on the fear of hell, which her brother Bello later incorpo-rated into his own *Infaq al-Maisur.*[34] Each of these works demonstrated the

authors' familiarity with Qur'anic descriptions of hell that would have also
been known, and in many cases memorized, by their listeners. Incorporating Qur'anic injunction was a way to increase the authority of one's message; repetition helped drive it home.

Asma'u's *Tabshir al-Ikhwan* [in Arabic, hereafter Ar] (literally, Message
to the Brethren / working title, Medicine of the Prophet, 1839) reflects both
her immersion in the *hadiths* and comparable works by her clansmen. Written in Arabic, it was meant to be appreciated by scholars, especially those
who specialized in the spiritual healing system outlined in the Shehu's trea-
tise *Tibb al-Nabi* (Medicine of the Prophet), which he derived from relevant
commentary in the *hadiths*. The Shehu wrote (in *Ihya' al-Sunna* [Revival of
the *Sunna*]) that medical treatment with verses from the Qur'an was advis-
able and had been advocated by the Prophet Muhammad. The Shehu's
brother, Abdullahi, wrote about the conduct of physicians and the procedures they should follow (in *Masalih al-Insan al-Muta'alliqa bi-l-Adyan*
[Benefits for Human Beings Related to Religions] and *Diya al-Qawa'id wa
Nathr al-Fawa'id li-Ahl al-Maqasid* [The Rules for Spreading the Benefits
of the Peoples' Intentions]).[35] But as with other works, it was Asma'u's
brother Bello who most influenced her in this piece on medicine. He was
noted among writers throughout the Sudan as an authority on medicaments.[36]
Among Bello's ten books on medicine is his *Talkhis al-Maqasid al-Mujar-
rada fi-l-Adwiya al-Farida* (Summations of Objective Unique Remedies),
a summation of al-Kastallani's fifteenth-century book on religiously oriented healing. Bello's other works on medicine include *Tibb al-Hayyun*
(Remedies for Eye Disease), *Al-Qual al-Sana' fi Wujuh al-Taliyan wa-l-
Tamashshi bi-l-Sana* (Purgatives), and *Al-Qual al-Manthur fi Bayan Ad-
wiya 'Illat al-Basur* (Remedies for Piles). In 1837, in his old age, he wrote
Tibb al-Nabi following a visit by Egyptian scholar and Qadiri Sufi Qamar
al-Din, who passed his medical knowledge on to Bello.[37] It was characteristic of both Bello and his sister Asma'u to frame their works in terms of
benefit to the masses, a deviation from the focus of classical writers on the
topic, who composed their works as gifts to royalty. Certainly the oral form
was a common vehicle of transmission.

In addition to these works, Asma'u cites her contemporary, the scholar
Muhammad Tukur, as a source for her own work. Tukur was encouraged by
Bello to write a 22,000-word book in 1809, *Qira al-Ahibba' fi Bayan Sirr
al-Asma* (The Medical Benefit of Reciting the Names of God).[38] Tukur's
Mu'awanat al-Ikhwan fi Mu'asharat al-Niswan focuses on the use of
minerals and herbs with prayer for the purpose of curing.[39] In her version,

Asma'u focuses on *suras* 44–108, although it is unclear why she did so. Although protection during pregnancy, childbirth, and weaning are mentioned in this long piece, women's ailments are not at all the focus. Among the directions for healing through prayer, it is mentioned several times that if a person cannot read the prescribed verses, spiritual benefit may nevertheless be realized by drinking the water used to wash the ink from the words. Thus, the benefit is available to all in the community, not just those who are literate.

Asma'u's *Tabbat Hakika* (Be Sure of God's Truth, [H] 1831) harkens back to the Abbasid concept of the state (c. 750–1258), which was the subject of books by Asma'u's father, (*Bayan Wujub al-Hijra 'ala al-'Ibad* [Communication of What Is Necessary Concerning the *Hijra*], 1806),[40] her uncle (*Diya al-Hukkam* [The Light for Governors], 1806), and her brother (*Al-Gaith al-Wabi fi Siral al-Imam al-Adl* [Explanation of the Requirements for the Upright Imam], 1821). Bello's work parallels the seventeenth-century work of the Ottoman historian Mustafa Naima (1687), with identical wording concerning the Neoplatonist concept of the "circle of equity," which confirms the need for royal authority.[41] The work juxtaposes earthly and divine truth—truth versus Truth—to raise the metaphorical meaning of the content to a spiritual level and remind both listeners and leaders that there is a higher power than the mortal authority figure who rules.[42]

Tabbat Hakika emphasizes the need for rulers to keep in mind divine law. Because divine law never strayed from the concept of gender equality, as human law did beginning in the ninth century, this message was important for all women, without regard to social status, ethnicity, or degree of literacy. Asma'u's *Tabbat Hakika* also demonstrates the degree to which she collaborated with other writers. In another *takhmis,* she expanded the Shehu's version of this work, creating a new poem whose recurring rhyme is the final phrase *tabbat hakika* (be sure of God's Truth). This poem highlights the interdependence of Islamic scholars in creating works that may now list only one author. Indeed, the authorship of Asma'u's poem—a new work generated by her own ingenuity—rightfully belongs to Asma'u herself, despite its origins in her father's text.

The issue of authorship is complicated by the fact that women usually did not sign their compositions. A bookseller in Fez showed me many old works of *hadith* and *fiqh,* all attributed to male authors. When I asked if it were possible to find works by women, he said it was not, but added that this did not mean that women did not write. He insisted that it was quite common for women to compose, but for propriety's sake they would never sign their own name; they would sign their husband's name instead.[43] Whether it is a matter of women veiling their identity or a question of valid authorship in collaborative pieces, this practice of women omitting their signatures suggests that the individual ownership of a written work is less important than the message in a tradition that values the benefit of the word over the fame of the author.

Sufi Works

At the end of the eighteenth and beginning of the nineteenth centuries, Sufi students and scholars traveled regularly between Hausaland in northern Nigeria, Fez, and Cairo. In northern Nigeria, the Fodiyo clan's affiliation with Qadiriyya Sufism was strong.[44] In addition, the newly formed Tijaniyya brotherhood (c. 1780) affirmed a linkage with Fez, where Ahmed al-Tijani is buried in the medina. Asma'u's *Mimsitare* (Forgive Me [F], 1833) is written in Fulfulde, indicating that it was not intended as a teaching tool for the larger, Hausa-speaking audience but rather was aimed at the Fodiyo clan. This work, along with *Tawassuli ga Mata Masu Albarka/ Tindinore Labne* (Sufi Women [H/F], 1836) and *Sonnore Mo'Inna* (Elegy for my Sister Fadima [F], 1838), underscores Asma'u's Sufi activity. *Mimsitare* indicates Asma'u's own entry into *khalwa,* while the other two works mention Bello's mother Hauwa, and her daughter Fadima, respectively, having gone into retreat frequently. Asma'u was forty when she wrote this poem, about the same age as her father when he began to practice *khalwa* and have visions establishing his connection to Shaikh 'Abd al-Qadir al-Jilani, founder of the Qadiriyya Sufi order.[45] His recollections about Sufi experiences are related in his *Wird* (Litany).

Asma'u's later work, *Mantore di Dabre* (Remembrance of the Shehu [F], 1854), is modeled on a work written by the Shehu early in his life, perhaps as early as the age of ten, in 1765. That poem, *Afalgimi* (Litany [F]), is a simple Sufi litany, whose style she "copied . . . from the Shehu" (*Mantore di Dabre,* v. 10) nearly a century later. Both works appeal to God for strength in following the *Sunna* and for generosity. Asma'u's imitation of her father's early work was intended to honor him, following the Arabic poetic tradition of imitating another author's style.

The only poem in which Asma'u mentions her health is one that is clearly in a Sufi context. A mere dozen lines, this piece is untitled, but was given a working title in translation: "Thanksgiving for Recovery" (1839). Although no other known poems concerning recovery exist, this one is linked in context and tone with one by Rabia al-Adawiya of Basra, the eighth-century Sufi of renown. Rabia's poem concerns praying all night and fasting in appeal for the healing of her broken wrist. In Asma'u's work on this same topic, she indicates both a reliance on classical sources and creativity in the Sufi mode.

Asma'u's *Sufi Women* was written with the aim of endowing with respectability the Muslim women of the Sokoto Caliphate, both members in long standing and new converts alike. Its origins indicate the historical depth of the canon upon which Asma'u drew. The bases of the work include a prose work by Muhammad Bello, *Kitab al-Nasihah* (Book of Advice, 1835)[46] (which he asked Asma'u to translate into Hausa and Fulfulde and versify), and the poet al-Jawzi's twelfth-century poem *Sufi Women,* based on a work by his predecessor, as-Sulami's tenth-century poem of the same name.[47] An overwhelming majority of names in the original and twelfth-century version appear in the same order and with comparable descriptions in Asma'u's poem. Her poem differs from the originals, however, in her addition of women from the caliphate to the list of revered Sufi women, thereby elevating their status to that of historical Sufi women.

Asma'u's poem also differs from Bello's prose version in that she omitted his admonitions to women, which he had included as a means of controlling irreverent behavior. Instead, she focuses on women's accomplishments and contributions to the Muslim community, emphasizing capabilities that parallel those of women of the Prophet Muhammad's community: the ability to teach, preach, adjudicate, and model ascetic piety. By using existing works as the basis for new material, Asma'u gained the credibility associated with works well established in Islamic intellectual circles and used it to convey different messages relevant to her place and time.[48] Thus, her single manuscript represents but a moment in the continued variation of materials used for study. Some of these new creations in turn became part of a new, ever-changing canon of works in a fluid context of learning.

That *Sufi Women* appears in Hausa as well as Fulfulde affirms that it was targeted to Hausa-speaking women of the masses as well as members of Asma'u's Fulfulde-speaking family members. It was intended as a teaching tool to promote women's education in an Islamic way of life. Toward that end, Asma'u crafted a poem that focuses on exemplary women in the Sokoto Caliphate community, merging their names and stories with a litany of historically established Sufi women whose reputations were well known.[49] This is further evidence that it was intended for women of the local community.

Collaboration with Male Scholars

Asma'u's collaborative activities are evident in other works as well.[50] She and other scholars in the Sokoto Caliphate community felt linked to the wider Islamic world. Her father, the Shehu, wrote only in Arabic. Her uncle, Abdullahi, favored pre-Islamic poetry and that of seventeenth-century North African poet Abu 'Ali-Hasan b. Mas'ud al-Yusi.[51] Asma'u's elegies bear a striking similarity in tone to those of al-Khansa, a woman poet who was a contemporary of the Prophet Muhammad,[52] so it is likely that Asma'u knew of al-Khansa's works.[53] Asma'u's *Dalilin Samuwar Allah* (Reasons for Seeking God [H], 1861) is rooted in Bello's *Infaq al-Maisur,* which clarifies the content of the Shehu's sermons. Examples abound of the close collaborative bond among several generations of Fodiyos, and their reliance on classical works.

Prophetic panegyric has long been associated with Sufism.[54] Asma'u's *Kiran Ahmada* (In Praise of Ahmada [H], 1839) is a panegyric to the Prophet Muhammad in the form known as *madih,* which functions to provide an outlet for emotional needs in worship. Asma'u would have been familiar with panegyrics to the prophet, which were well known by the thirteenth century, especially al-Busiri's *Burda* (The Cloak), al-Fazazi's *Al-Ishriniyyat* (The Twenties), al-Lakhmi's *Al-Qasa'id al-Witriyya* (Supererogatory Odes), and al-Tawzari's *Simt al-Huda* (The Necklace of Guidance), all of which were well known in the region. Asma'u's emulation of the subjects and styles of these works is evident in her own poems, so it is known that she was familiar with them.[55] Another example of panegyric is Asma'u's *Mantore Arande* (Remembrance of the Prophet [F], 1843). In this work, she drew parallels between selected details of the Prophet Muhammad's life and those of the Shehu, as she had in "Yearning for the Prophet."

Fa Inna ma'a al-'Usrin Yusra (So Verily . . . [F], 1822) is a prime example of collaborative authorship between Nana Asma'u and her brother Muhammad Bello, with whom she was very close. Her poem is a response to an acrostic poem left for her by Bello as he headed into battle. The initial letters of each of the poem's fourteen lines are coordinated to form the verse *"fa inna ma'a al-usrin yusra"* (So verily with every difficulty there is relief) (Q94:5) when read vertically. Bello's poem was written as comfort to a worried sister; hers was composed as support—a prayer for victory and his safe return.

Asma'u's *Gawakuke Ma'unde* (The Battle of Gawakuke [F], 1856) is also highly collaborative; Bello described this battle, as did al-Hajj Sa'id, a follower of al-Hajj Umar, and Asma'u would have known those works. Despite its apparent historical theme, this work is actually an elegy, describing Bello's character, his *baraka,* or blessedness, charismatic leadership, and miracle working, setting him in the context of Sufi devotion.[56] By combining these styles and addressing a topic already covered by other poets of her time, Asma'u created a work of wide appeal at the same time that she endowed a political figure with specifically Islamic significance.

Nana Asma'u's role as a scholar was multivalent: She was multilingual, an author of both oral and written works, a scholar known throughout West Africa and the Maghreb, and a teacher of women and men, and of scholars and students, as well as a trainer of teachers. Her life was dedicated to the premise that the accumulation of knowledge was of prime importance. She acknowledged no limits of intellect, gender, nationality, or creed. In contemporary times, she is the model for women throughout the Maghreb who choose to study; they note that her life gives legitimacy to their pursuits.

Conclusion: The Question of a Canon

Considering Islam's origin in the scriptural promotion of equality and the pursuit of learning, it should come as no surprise that Muslim women scholars have long been active in Islamic cultures, learning for themselves and teaching others. The seeming diminution of this practice during colonialism resulted from the colonialist assumption that the production of written documents solely constitutes evidence of scholarship, and the privileging of boys' education over girls'. The (falsely) presumed dearth of scholarly activity in the Maghreb, especially on the part of women, reflects this legacy.[57]

The Qur'an is the basis for an extended education, as the student moves from a rudimentary understanding of this ultimate source to the discovery of increasingly deeper levels of meaning, according to the development of his or her intellectual abilities over a lifetime. With skillful guidance, an Islamic scholar can rely on the Qur'an to acquire both literacy and a grounding in religious precepts; these can be the basis for the study of other classic works that depend on a deep understanding of the Qur'an as a primary source of wisdom. Further educational pursuits depend on regional and social opportunities, which often occur in local, gender-segregated upper-level schools with wide ranges of curricula.[58]

Determining a canon of Muslim women's scholarship requires a redefinition of intellectual currency. It is impossible to compile an authoritative list of works—such a list would involve far too many diverse works, and would vary from region to region. Further, a fixed canon would militate against the fluidity of learning and composition evident in the examples described above. In addition, the oral nature of Islam means that a great deal of what is central to the process of education is not held in written repositories but instead is committed to memory.[59]

Thus, though it is not possible to identify a static, finite canon of works from which Asma'u—or any other writer—drew inspiration, it is important to confirm that each poet establishes her own canon by drawing from the vast array of materials that have remained accessible to Muslim scholars since at least the tenth century. The canon changes with the needs of a particular scholar; the emphasis of a given work varies according to the needs of the moment. Many of the newer works, created on the foundations of earlier ones, become classics for subsequent generations, joining the ranks of those that have heretofore constituted the "canon."

Nana Asma'u relied on both her own educational background in classical Islamic works and her familiarity with works by her kinsmen for the creation of her own poems. Many of her poems are collaborative works that honor the poems of her contemporaries by reworking them to her own effect. Echoing a traditional program of study, her works include descriptions of the Qur'an, panegyrics, elegies, and biographies of the Prophet Muhammad. Asma'u transforms some of these into works more pertinent to her own context; her biography of the Shehu parallels her biography of the prophet, and her description of the prophet's endeavors parallels her description of the Shehu's campaigns. Asma'u's devotion to Sufism also figures prominently in her works, which include litanies and *dhikr.* Her poem on medical cures of the prophet reflects traditional works on religiously based healing, and her work on Sufi women not only imitates the classic tenth-century work of the same name by al-Sulami but also weaves in the names of local women, whose status she elevates by associating them with historical women of note.

Beyond the collection of written documents, an investigation of oral sources is especially central to an understanding of scholarship in Sufi circles. Many Sufis in Morocco note that the most important material is written on the heart, not on paper where it can be destroyed. All Muslims begin with the same source, the Qur'an, whose multivalent nature ensures that it is accessible to all, regardless of intellect, literacy, talent, or gender. Beyond that, a combination of circumstances—education, interests, and ability—will lead an individual to focus on law or history, on Sufi concepts, or on another aspect of interpretation. Thus, a woman scholar's canon will vary depending on her interests and needs, just as one's understanding of the Qur'an depends on individual circumstances.

If women scholars and their works are sought in settings beyond schoolrooms, it becomes clear that they are common in the Maghreb. The concept of intellectual engagement is widespread and commonly pursued; those who are intellectually engaged are not necessarily connected to formal schools of higher learning, and in fact may not even be literate. Those whose intellectual relations are limited to their own communities meet in private neighborhood groups. They organize themselves into groups of teachers and students by consensus, according to their abilities, and meet as voluntary study groups simply for the assimilation of knowledge and mutual support. On a broader scale, the historical evidence demonstrates intellectual linkages between individual scholars in historic Mauritania, which covered a wider area than the contemporary polity of Mauritania. The region included much of contemporary southern Morocco, as well as the Islamic intellectual communities of northern Nigeria.[60] Religious scholars and Sufis moved throughout this region, a highway of intellectual productivity, communicating with one another directly or through messages carried by others. Not every Muslim is an intellectual or a scholar, and not every Muslim studies the Qur'an. But Muslim scholars and intellectuals who spend time teaching, writing, and preaching inevitably begin with the Qur'an, the source of their worldview. Women who choose to extend their investigation of Qur'anic wisdom through individual study and regular seminars are much more numerous than the evidence of written documents can indicate.

Notes

1. A *hadith qudsi,* a sacred or holy tradition, is distinct from other *hadith*s in that it conveys God's own words to the Prophet Muhammad as opposed to the prophet's own words.

2. Julia Clancy-Smith's observation about women in Algeria was true in the early twentieth century for the entire Maghreb: "Women, whether European or indigenous, are notably absent from the enormous literature both colonial and recent on nineteenth-century Algeria. Aside from a few brief references in the literature to extraordinary females—holy, learned women like Zaynab or heroines such as Lalla Fatima, who led the 1854 Kabyle resistance—the history of women in colonial Northern Africa or in earlier periods constitutes a virtually blank page." Julia Clancy-Smith, *Rebel and Saint: Muslim Notables, Populist Protest, Colonial Encounters, Algeria and Tunisia, 1800–1904* (Berkeley: University of California Press, 1994), 338 n. 71. More recently, Margot Bad-

ran and miriam cooke's *Opening the Gates: A Century of Arab Feminist Writing* (London: Virago, 1990) and Fatima Mernissi's own work and extensive support of other Muslim women writers have made significant contributions to the field.

3. Asma'u's easy correspondence with the mysterious Mauritanian scholar (al-Hajj Ahmed Muhammad al-Shinqiti) implies a longer-standing network of correspondences and familiarity that likely dates to at least one if not several previous generations, which would put the connection well into the eighteenth century. More work on the Shehu's writings is required to demonstrate this linkage.

4. Mervyn Hiskett, *The Sword of Truth* (Oxford: Oxford University Press, 1973), 63–64.

5. People in contemporary Fez know of Asma'u's historic Fodiyo family in northern Nigeria and demonstrate easy familiarity their many written works. The erudition of the Shehu Usman dan Fodiyo, his brother Abdullahi, his son Caliph Muhammad Bello, and his daughter Nana Asma'u is especially well known, even when their writings are not available. Murray Last notes that in 1964 a "text based on copies [of Bello's *Infaq al-Maisur*] from the Moroccan Archives, Rabat, and from Sokoto was printed in Cairo." Murray Last, *The Sokoto Caliphate* (London: Longman, 1967), xxxi. This gives some sense of the breadth of intellectual networks, even into the twentieth century.

6. Ahmed al-Tijani (1737–1815) established the order in 1780.

7. See, e.g., Qur'an 24:30–31: "[Prophet], tell believing men to lower their glances and guard their private parts: that is purer for them. . . . And tell believing women that they should let their headscarves fall to cover their necklines, and not reveal their charms except to their husbands." *The Qur'an,* trans. M. A. S. Abdel Haleem (Oxford: Oxford University Press, 2005).

8. See, e.g., chaps. 49, 58, 59, 60, 61.

9. See, e.g., Qur'an 29:44, 45, 49, 51; 34:9, 35:28, 53:30.

10. Women's domestic work and child care activities preclude the luxury of quiet, focused time for reading and writing. The songs and poems that can be performed while they are engaged in other tasks are the best means of education for women during their intensely domestic years. For more on this topic, see Beverly B. Mack, *"Wa'ka 'Daya Ba Ta Kare Nika* [One Song Will Not Finish the Grinding]: Hausa Women's Oral Literature," in *Contemporary African Literature,* edited by Hal Wylie et al. (Washington, D.C.: Three Continents Press, 1983), 15–46.

11. Formal Islamic education programs of study parallel those of the West, well beyond the postgraduate level. These include intensive programs of courses including a wide range of topics like the natural and physical sciences, history, geography, sociology, medicine, and mathematics, often at renowned institutions like al-Azhar University in Cairo and the Karaouine Medrasa in Fez (one has only to consult fourteenth-century Ibn Khaldun's *Muqaddima* to gain a sense of the breadth of traditional Islamic learning). As library holdings in Mauritania demonstrate, more advanced fields of study included "Qur'anic sciences, Arabic language, mysticism (Sufi literature), jurisprudence, scientific manuals (including medicine, astrology and mathematics), general literature, . . . historical accounts (genealogies, biographical dictionaries, chronologies, pilgrimage memoirs), political material, . . . [and] general correspondence"; Ghislaine Lydon, "Inkwells of the Sahara: Reflections on the Production of Islamic Knowledge in *Bilad Shinqit,"* in *The Transmission of Learning in Islamic Africa,* edited by Scott Reese (Leiden: Brill, 2004), 62. Nana Asma'u's nineteenth-century collection of her own poetic works demonstrates comparable breadth; it includes histories, memoirs, political

treatises, eulogies, and instructional verses. Nevertheless, in addition to these works in formal settings, many more oral sources contribute significantly to Islamic education in the Maghreb, and many more women engage in study than those enrolled in formal programs.

12. E.g., to name a few, al-Kindi (d. 866), an encyclopedic scientist, and the author of 270 books on mathematics, physics, music, medicine, pharmacy, geography; al-Farabi (d. 950), an authority on music and master of Greek philosophy, and the author of the *Bezels of Philosophy* and *The Perfect State* (later used by Thomas Aquinas); Ibn Sina (d. 1037), a physician and psychologist, and the author of *Canons of Medicine,* commentator on Aristotle; al-Ghazzali (d. 1111). a theologian, and the author of *The Revival of the Religious Sciences in Islam;* Ibn Rushd (d. 1198), a physician, scientist, linguist, and philosopher; Fakhr al-Din Razi (d. 1209), a mathematician, physicist, physician, and philosopher, and the author of a multivolume encyclopedia of medical science; and Ibn Khaldun (d. 1406), a historian and philosopher, and the founder of the history of science and sociology.

13. Reza Aslan, *No God but God: The Origins, Evolution, and Future of Islam* (New York: Random House, 2005), 57.

14. See Beverly B. Mack, *Muslim Women Sing: Hausa Popular Song* (Bloomington: Indiana University Press, 2004), esp. chap. 2.

15. It is certain that there are many other women scholars largely unknown or unacknowledged throughout the world, both in Muslim and non-Muslim contexts. Their writings and stories of their lives can be found in family archives, not public holdings, where men's works are showcased.

16. The biography is by Jean Boyd, *The Caliph's Sister* (London: Frank Cass, 1989). Asma'u is mentioned by Last, *Sokoto Caliphate;* and Hiskett, *Sword of Truth.*

17. It is likely that other manuscripts exist in private family libraries, but these are closely guarded because they are so highly prized.

18. Lydon, "Inkwells of the Sahara."

19. Lalla Zaynab, the daughter of the nineteenth-century Sufi Algerian resistance leader Sheikh Abu Ziyan, was "trained [by her father] from childhood to fill the role that awaited her"; Cecily Mackworth, *The Destiny of Isabelle Eberhardt* (London: Quartet Books, 1977), 157, as cited by Clancy-Smith, *Rebel and Saint,* 233 n.77. The parallel to Nana Asma'u's experience is noteworthy. It would not be surprising to learn that the Abu Ziyan knew of the Shehu and his illustrious daughter, who lived earlier in the same century.

20. Margot Badran notes that Huda Shaarawi (1884–1918) speaks of Sayyida Khadija al-Maghrabiyya, an itinerant poet who used to visit Shaarawi in the course of visits to the grand houses, reciting poetry and discussing intellectual matters. Her name indicates her origins. Shaarawi reported that this woman poet would oblige a request for a recitation, but when Shaarawi asked the poet to teach her how to compose, she responded that it was impossible, because it required a "knowledge of grammar, morphology, and prosody." This literate, knowledgeable itinerant woman poet could not have been unique in the culture. Huda Shaarawi, *Harem Years: The Memoirs of an Egyptian Feminist,* edited and translated by Margot Badran (New York: Feminist Press, 1986), 42, 140n.

21. E.g., she wrote works modeled on others' poems by adding three lines (*takhmis*) to each couplet of the original poem, thereby creating her own new work in quintains. The challenge of this approach was in keeping consistent the original author's rhyme

scheme and thematic tone. Nana Asma'u also collaborated with her brother Caliph Bello by writing poetic responses that mirrored his poems structurally on a specific topic; an example of this is her work "So Verily, . . ." in response to his poem with the same title. See Jean Boyd and Beverly Mack, eds., *The Collected Works of Nana Asma'u, bint Shehu Usman dan Fodio 1793–1864* (East Lansing: Michigan State University Press, 1997), 28–31.

22. Stanislaw Pilaszewicz, *Housa Prose Writings in* Ajami *by Alhaji Umaru from Mischlich H. Solken's Collection* (Berlin: Dietrich Reimer, 2000), 86.

23. Ibid., 10–11.

24. Six of Asma'u's sisters also wrote—Hadiza, Habsatu, Fadima, Safiya, Maryam, and Khadija. I have seen some of their manuscripts in the archives of the Sokoto History Bureau. There is a collection of twenty-two works by nine of Asma'u's close women relatives in the Boyd Collection, PP MS 36, School of Oriental and African Studies Archives, University of London.

25. Another classic Arabic poetic genre focusing on biography, *sira,* is evident in Asma'u's *Filitage/Wa'kar Gewaye* (The Journey [F/H], 1839, 1865) (concerning the Shehu's campaigns of reform) and *Begore* (Yearning for the Prophet [H], n.d.). In the first, Asma'u draws clear parallels between the Shehu's nineteenth-century campaign to reform Islam and the Prophet Muhammad's efforts to establish the religion in the seventh century. In the second, Asma'u focuses on aspects of the life of the prophet that can be easily compared with the Shehu's life. See Boyd and Mack, *Collected Works,* 133–54, 304–45; detailed parallels are drawn in this volume. By drawing parallels between the Prophet Muhammad and the Shehu, Asma'u underscores the Shehu's credibility and confirms her own role as instrumental in the completion of God's intentions for Islamic reform through the Sokoto Jihad. Credibility was central to the effective transmission of her message to the masses.

26. English titles given here, it should be understood, are at best loose interpretations of the general meaning of the works and should be considered merely working titles to facilitate identification. The works are untitled in the original manuscripts, indicating that Asma'u intended them more for pedagogical use than for personal renown.

27. The late Mervyn Hiskett's dismissal of this poem as being of "little literary interest" is typical of the degree to which Asma'u's works were ignored by twentieth-century Western male researchers, who focused on men of note in the region. Mervyn Hiskett, *A History of Hausa Islamic Verse* (London: School of Oriental and African Studies, 1975), 44.

28. The three versions were written in 1850, 1829, and 1838, respectively, appealing (chronologically) to Fulfulde speakers, then the Hausa majority, and finally to Arabic speakers.

29. Several of Asma'u's works are in the classic Arabic poetic mode of elegy; they focus on aspects of character familiar from studies of the *Sunna* and *hadith.* These include elegies for those well known, like her brother the caliph, as well as for named individuals of no historic note. In *Alhinin Mutuwar Halima* (Elegy for Halima [H], 1844), Asma'u comments on the virtues of an ordinary woman, a neighbor, who is remembered especially for her patience and mediatory skills among family members; Boyd and Mack, *Collected Works,* 195–96. Asma'u's sixty-one collected works include fifteen elegies, and three more that may be considered as such; two mourn the loss of 'Ayesha, a close friend, and one is a deeply felt commemoration of Bello's character, written after his death, indicating the depth of her loss. In her remembrance of her brother, Asma'u

noted none of his political or historical achievements. Instead, she outlined the moral and ethical qualities that distinguished him as a person who followed the *Sunna* with his heart. Asma'u was in the habit of emphasizing what for her were the most noteworthy characteristics of those she eulogized. Staying true to Bello's values, Asma'u emphasized the state of Bello's character, rather than his position in the state.

30. This title, like many that follow in this context, is rendered in English only with difficulty. Murray Last refers to *Infaq al-Maisur* as "the most detailed and factual account of the jihad" available; Last, *Sokoto Caliphate,* xxxi.

31. Sections include attention to barriers dividing man from paradise, discussion of dangerous habits, redeeming habits, and distinguishing features of those who follow the *Sunna.*

32. Hiskett, *A History,* 41.

33. This is known as adding *takhmis* for the production of a new poem based on an earlier one.

34. Note that Asma'u's piece as discussed here is a prime example of collaborative work.

35. Thanks to Naima Boussofara for translating these titles.

36. Ismail Abdalla, "The *'Ulama'* of Sokoto in the Nineteenth Century: A Medical View," in *African Healing* Strategies, edited by Brian DuToit and Ismail Abdalla (New York: Trado-Medic Books, 1985), 8–19.

37. Last, *Sokoto Caliphate,* cited by Boyd and Mack, *Collected Works,* 100.

38. Ismail Abdalla notes that Tukur's sources for this work "are not practitioners from the high period of Islamic civilization, but some lesser known Sufis and theologians who flourished in the medieval period." Ismail Abdalla, "Islamic Medicine and Its Influence on Traditional Hausa Practitioners in Northern Nigeria" (PhD diss., University of Wisconsin, 1981), 158. I thank Ismail Abdalla for the title and its translation (personal communication, September 29, 2006).

39. "The title translates as "The Means of Helping Brothers toward Legitimate Social Relationships with Women" (Al-Hajj Sheikh Ahmed Lemu, personal communication with Jean Boyd, September 21, 1994). Abdalla writes that in the *Ma'awanat al-Ikhwan fi Mu'asharat al-Niswan,* emphasis is placed on *material media* for the treatment of various illnesses and as aphrodisiacs; Abdalla, "Islamic Medicine," 163. As far as we know, there is no translation of the work." Boyd and Mack, *Collected Works,* 101 n. 209.

40. The translation for this work is not available, but Jean Boyd indicates that F. H. al-Masri says "it was composed to elucidate the law on the *hijra,* and the subsequent jihad" (personal communication, September 26, 2006). I am grateful for her help on this and many other translations of titles in this study. I thank Naima Boussofara for her translation of the title.

41. See Boyd and Mack, *Collected Works,* 45–46. Abdullahi emphasizes the role of a leader in administering justice to the disenfranchised, while the Shehu affirms the role of scholars in enjoining Truth, the *Sunna,* and justice.

42. For a discussion of controversy concerning authorship of this poem, see Boyd and Mack, *Collected Works,* 46.

43. Other scholars have commented on the reluctance of women to sign their own names. See Badran and cooke, *Opening the Gates;* and Margot Badran, *Feminists, Islam, and Nation: Gender and the Making of Modern Egypt* (Princeton, N.J.: Princeton University Press, 1995). Badran notes that in nineteenth- and early-twentieth-century

Egypt, it was considered improper, and almost immoral, for a woman's words, name, or home to appear in public.

44. In addition to Asma'u's involvement in mysticism, the Shehu's wife Aisha was a devout mystic, and his wife Hauwa and her daughter Fadima regularly went into *khalwa.* See Hiskett, *Sword of Truth,* 61–69; and Boyd and Mack, *Collected Works,* 60. Early in his education, the Shehu studied Ibn 'Arabi's *Al-Futuhat al-Makkiyya* (Meccan Revelations), c. 1238.

45. Hiskett, *Sword of Truth,* 64.

46. Thanks to Naima Boussofara for this title translation.

47. See Boyd and Mack, *Collected Works,* 68–82. At the time of our writing, we reported that she had modeled her work on that of Ibn al-Jawzi's (d. 1200) work of the same name. Examination of Rkia Cornell's 1999 translation of Abu 'Abd ar-Rahman al-Sulami's tenth-century work, *Dhikr al-Niswa al-Muta 'abbidat al-Sufiyyat* (Memorial of Female Sufi Devotees), demonstrated that al-Jawzi's own work was modeled on the earlier one by al-Sulami; the same women are listed in the same order as in al-Sulami's earlier work. See *Early Sufi Women:* Dhikr an-niswa al-muta 'abbidat as Sufiyyat *by Abu 'Abd ar-Rahman as-Sulami,* translated by Rkia Cornell (Louisville: Fons Vitae, 1999).

48. She used "Sufi Women" extensively in training "extension teachers" of secluded women in the community; thus it provides a window to an Islamic world in which women were recognized as important to the community.

49. Boyd and Mack, *Collected Works,* 68–82.

50. Ibid., 133–34, indicates a degree of collaboration that makes tracing an "original" difficult.

51. Hiskett, *Sword of Truth,* 10.

52. Boyd and Mack, *Collected Works,* 84.

53. The citations in Boyd and Mack, *Collected Works,* 84, include two works by al-Khansa; one cited by A. J. Arberry, *Arabic Poetry* (Cambridge: Cambridge University Press, 1965), 38; and one translated by Arthur Wormhoudt in *Diwan al-Khansu* (Oskaloosa, Iowa, and High Wycombe, U.K.: William Penn College and University Microfilms, 1973), 96. See also Charis Waddy, *Women in Muslim History* (New York: Longman, 1980), 70.

54. Abdullahi wrote such panegyrics to the Prophet Muhammad, and the Shehu wrote *Ma'ama'are* (In Praise of the Prophet) in 1805, which Isa, Asma'u's brother, translated into Hausa in 1864. See also Hiskett, *History,* 43.

55. Hiskett, *History,* 43–44, 48–50.

56. Boyd and Mack, *Collected Works,* 231.

57. It is hoped that contemporary projects for the preservation of scholarly materials, like that which is under way in Timbuktu, will redress this legacy.

58. Depending on the setting, such schools may incorporate courses modeled on Western curricula, in foreign languages that remain the legacy of colonial presences.

59. The question of literacy is separate from the issue of education. For a Muslim, the recitation of passages from the Qur'an is primary in importance, discussion of the Qur'anic meaning is secondary, literacy is tertiary, and the production of documents is by no means prime evidence of scholarship.

60. These connections are indicated in a letter written by Asma'u to a Mauritanian scholar, with whom she evidently was well acquainted. See "Welcome to the Mauritanian Scholar," in *Collected Works,* ed. Boyd and Mack, 282–83.

Chapter 2

Rethinking Marginality and Agency in Postcolonial Niger: A Social Biography of a Sufi Woman Scholar

Ousseina D. Alidou

The democratization process of the early 1990s in the Republic of Niger not only paved the way for the expression of political pluralism, with both secularist and Islamist articulations, but also encouraged the emergence of Muslim women spiritual leaders and Islamic authorities in this francophone West African setting. Under French colonial rule, women were excluded from political participation and barred from subordinate positions that were open to colonized men. In the early period after independence was granted in 1960, women continued to play more ancillary, restricted roles in politics. However, as Barbara Cooper and Hadiza Djibo have rightly pointed out, in spite of the gender imbalance, women's political roles in government-authorized associations grew under successive regimes.[1] With Niger's democratization era beginning in the early 1990s and the advent of political pluralism, women began to play prominent leadership roles as members of Parliament and political parties as well as in religious organizations.[2] During this democratization process, grassroots Muslim women educationists used support from Islamist organizations to fund and expand educational

41

options for women in marginalized communities who did not have access
to a mainstream French education. The new Islamist-sponsored education
in these communities, in both urban centers and semiurban regions, has
been providing both Arabo-Islamic schooling and the range of courses offered in a typical French curriculum and includes building skills in information communication technologies.[3] This phenomenon in Niger, I argue,
displays significant similarities to the experiences of contemporary Sahelian Islamic (cultural-cum-religious) women leaders, who are known as
muqqaddamat in northern Nigeria[4] and the *shaykhat* in Senegal.[5]

By "Sahelian," I refer to cultures located in the Sudanic Belt, a region
that geographically covers the entire area from Senegal in West Africa to
the Red Sea in East Africa. This region has a rich history and remarkable
linguistic, cultural, and ethnic patterns of interactions among populations
on the southern fringes of the Sahara, commonly referred to as the Sahel,
as well as the central and northern fringes of the Sahara, which are dominated by Arabs and Amazigh (Berber) peoples. It was also through the interactions of Muslim Arab-Berber populations with Sudanic Belt populations that Islam made its historical imprint on the cultures and societies of
the region, resulting in a distinctive Afro-Islamic identity. The Sudanic Belt
has served for thousands of years as a link between so-called Sub-Saharan
Africa and the world of so-called North Africa (both Western colonial
terms) and the entire southern Mediterranean shore (this would of course
include Egypt, as the term "North Africa" would not), leading to the cultural and ethnic blending commonly referred to as *brassage sahélien*. Even
after the colonial delimitation of national borders, populations in the Sahel
continued to maintain strong ties among themselves. A full understanding
of Hausa Islam must include the historical contributions of Sahelian Muslim traders and scholars from Mali, Senegal, and Sudan as well as those
from the northern regions of Africa.

In the francophone context of Niger, one of the most prominent Muslim
women is Malama A'ishatu Hamani Zarmakoy Dancandu,[6] a Sufi believer
in her eighties who is a public figure on national television and radio in her
role as an Islamic commentator. She is also an accomplished poet and has
made vital contributions to Qur'anic neighborhood literacy projects for
Muslim women and girls. The intervention of a Sufi woman in public space,
contrary to the life of privacy and asceticism traditionally associated with
Sufism, needs to be understood against the historical background of postindependence political regimes' violation of the freedom of religious expression in the country. This new face of "public female" Sufism must be

read as a conscious inscription of religious pluralism in the new democratic space of Niger. The denial of religious expression in the modern public sphere under both French colonial rule and postindependence military regimes eventually led, with the coming of democratization, to an urgent quest for a public voice—even by the ascetic, private Sufis. By looking at the gender implications of French and Qur'anic literacies, this chapter provides a social biography of Malama A'ishatu with the aim of demonstrating how the conjuncture of different historical and contemporary forces determines both women's marginality and agency in the postcolonial dispensation.

In the following pages, through an account of Malama A'ishatu's life and work, I illustrate the strategies by which Muslim women of the periphery rise from marginality—a sociocultural and political condition of institutional exclusion resulting from the conjuncture of patriarchy, colonialism, and hegemonic class ideologies—to place themselves at the center of public leadership when, to use Saba Mahmood's words, "the conditions of exercising their agency are overtly met."[7] Marginality should not be confused with a lack of consciousness. Once one becomes cognizant of one's status as "marginal," one is in fact displaying a degree of consciousness. The question that remains is whether or not conditions are ripe enough for an individual, or a group, to act on that consciousness. With the opening up of political space, especially as the society became increasingly intolerant of the tyranny of militarism, active women of the periphery began to engage in public transformative acts in the cultural, political, and economic domains through social networks in religious or secular spaces.

As I show here, it is not unusual for agency to be exercised in overlapping boundaries of identity as defined by ethnicity and class affiliations. Class often determines whether a Muslim has, or has had, access to Western or non-Western types of education. Muslim women of the periphery, like Malama A'ishatu, took advantage of the democratization process of the early 1990s to emerge from silence, and they implicitly or explicitly forced French-educated urban elite activists to form a broad coalition with them in the struggle to achieve women's rights within the context of a pluralistic vision that included both secular and religious space. Women's new collective, public, and political activism has been remarkably successful in mobilizing lower-income and lower-middle-class urban Muslim women in Niger's largest cities, such as Niamey, Maradi, and Zinder. Malama A'ishatu's work is one example of women's intervention on behalf of religious rights in a public sphere hitherto reserved for men. Of course, the intervention of these new female constituencies in the public arena should not be read as initiating a homogenous political consciousness across class divides or even within the same organization. As with secularist women, Islamist women in Niger in urban and semiurban spaces range from traditional conservatives to modernist liberals who draw on an understanding of Islam that is compatible with Nigerien liberal secularist ideologies on a number of issues.

In examining the public intellectual work of Malama A'ishatu, I consider two legacies associated with Islam in the popular imagination throughout the Sahelian region—the seclusion of women (*kuble* in colloquial Hausa, or *kulle* in standard Hausa); and the Arabic-derived literacies commonly referred to as *ajami* in Hausa and other West African languages—and how they have defined the lives of the women who came to embrace Islam.[8] In Niger, the practice of *kuble* has both extreme and moderate manifestations. In the extreme instance, found mainly among the Hausa, Fulani, and nonethnic Hausa-assimilated communities, the womenfolk are subject to total seclusion within the domestic space. This phenomenon is particularly prominent among the families of Sufi *marabout*s (local Sufi clerics), aristocrats, and merchants. The more moderate version of *kuble* is one that allows women some measure of mobility outside the domestic space, but only with the permission of the male head of the household. This latter form of *kuble* is found throughout urban Niger, usually across boundaries of ethnicity.

There is an important class dimension to the various expressions of *kuble*. As indicated above, on one hand, the stricter seclusion is found among the families of chiefs and *amir*s (aristocratic leaders), merchants, and *marabout*s who constitute the aristocracy and the rich among the "traditional" communities. Among the urban middle class, on the other hand, the less rigid form of *kuble* is most prevalent. In the lives of poor people, both in urban and rural spaces, however, there is no room for either form of *kuble*. The severity of the material conditions of families at this lower end of the social hierarchy requires the active engagement of men, women, children, and the elderly in seeking a livelihood "unencumbered" by the cultural limitations of the laws of seclusion, be they religious or secular.

The new Islamist groups that have emerged with the rise of political Islam are very much influenced by recent Arab and Iranian Islamist models of bodily (re)presentation for both men and women. In Niamey, Maradi, and Zinder, women within "modern *kuble*" who exhibit this new Islamist fashion with full-body coverage, including the hands, are popularly referred to as *ninja* women (drawn from the Chinese film *Ninja*). The contemporary Islamist *kuble* in Niger also displays a similarity to purdah as practiced among traditional communities in Pakistan and in general in Afghanistan. This is especially evident in the households of Nigerien Islamist men who have contact with these countries.

The recent democratization process in Niger has both linguistic and educational dimensions, represented by the emergence of the hitherto marginalized elite of the Arabo-Islamic educational track as important political players backed by funding from international Islamic organizations. These new political elite, called "Arabisants" in Niger, have elevated the prestige of Arabic-language- and Arabic-script-derived literacies as a crucial symbolic expression of the "modernity of one's Muslim-ness" and the legitimacy of the new Islamist political and cultural discourses. The tradition of Arabic-based literacy can take the form of reading and writing either directly in Arabic or in the indigenized versions of the Arabic script called *ajami* in Niger and other Sub-Saharan African Muslim societies. In recent times, Arabic literacy and *kuble* have become expressions of both material well-being and cultural Islamic modernity among the aristocracy and Islamist traders as well as among the Islamist lower and middle classes.

Though both Arabic-based literacies and *kuble* were used historically by men to keep Muslim women in "their place" and domestic seclusion was reinforced by the patriarchal policies of French colonial rule, this chapter demonstrates that Muslim women were not merely passive recipients of the ideological values bequeathed by this dual heritage. At specific historical junctures, some women have made use of new openings in political and cultural space, as in the democratization era of the 1990s, to transform the received traditions of literacy and *kuble* by registering women's religious voices in the public arena. These voices have varied from those expressing strong allegiance to conservatism to those offering more liberal interpretations of the meaning of Islam in women's lives.

Research Methodology

Much of the data for this study, which were collected between the summers of 1996 and 2001, were based on qualitative participant observation. In the summer of 1996, I traveled to Niger to begin my research on literacy among women in Niger. Because I had already transcribed several religious poems recited by Malama A'ishatu on radio or television, I decided to begin my research with her. I regularly attended Malama A'ishatu's home-based Qur'anic school, known as *makaranta* in Hausa, for girls and women. She conducted lessons for two hours every morning except Thursdays and Fridays to accommodate her students, who included homemakers and their daughters who assist them in house management. I also followed her twice-weekly, nationally broadcast television and radio programs, in which she offered Islamic religious commentaries in addition to reciting religious poetry, often with her students. Finally, I had personal meetings with Malama A'ishatu on Friday afternoons after her activities at the main mosque and headquarters of the Islamic Association of Niger.

During my fieldwork, I became close to the female members of Malama A'ishatu's family, who were also her students and who often assisted her in teaching. My regular participation in the *makaranta* activities facilitated my interaction with Malama and her students. This situation also created an environment of trust that was conducive to negotiating possibilities for interviewing Malama about her life history and her students about the various aspects of their lives that led them to her *makaranta*. Except for the rare occasions when she used Zarma language—the majority language of Niger after Hausa, to which it is linguistically unrelated—all my interviews with Malama were conducted in Hausa, the language of her Islamic intellectual formation. In this chapter, I provide my own English translations of her oral history, poems, and interviews.

The Rise of Malama A'ishatu Hamani Zarmakoy Dancandu

Malama A'ishatu Hamani Zarmakoy Dancandu rose to national prominence in Niger in her seventies as a result of her Islamic radio and television programs. Malama was the first child of the chief of the Zarma-speaking village of Dancandu in southwestern Niger. At age two, this daughter of Zarma royalty moved to Magaria in eastern Niger with the rest of her family when her father was appointed by the French authorities to serve as a "native" clerk in the colonial administration. In this new location, she made her entry into the linguistic and cultural space of Hausa identity by acquiring the new local language, Hausa, and she made her entry into the world of Islamic literacy through the training she received from her Hausa Muslim religious teachers. Her Islamic training involved mastery of the Qur'an, development of Qur'anic and *ajami* literacy skills, and Qur'anic interpretation (*tamsir* in Hausa), as well as *wa'azi* or sociopolitical and cultural counseling that drew on Islamic canonical texts and teachings such as the *hadith*s (the sayings and traditions of the Prophet Muhammad).

The resettlement of Malama's family in Hausaland began a process of "biculturalism" for Malama that is manifested by her fluency in two languages, Hausa and Zarma. The former belongs to the Chadic branch of the major Afro-Asiatic language family and is totally unrelated linguistically to Malama's mother tongue, Zarma, which she retained in spite of her family's relocation more than 800 kilometers away from their native Zarmaland and her eventual marriages to Muslim Hausa men.

Malama married twice, in both cases not to Zarma royalty but to prominent Hausa *malam*s (*marabout*s), who moved from place to place throughout eastern Niger and all the way to northern Nigeria, making a living through religious instruction, healing services, and the composition and performance of Islamic poetry. Travels across colonially divided Hausaland provided Malama with new opportunities not only to expand the scope of her Islamic knowledge but also to enrich her cultural experiences and her understanding of the dynamic interplay between womanhood, ethnicity, and religious identity. Eventually, in the 1980s, she settled in Niamey, the capital of Niger. At the time of my research, she was living with her younger sister, whom she had raised from infancy. She had begun her new life in Niamey in her midsixties as a teacher in a home-based Qur'anic school for girls and women.

It was in the 1980s in Niamey that Malama A'ishatu heard a radio recitation of a religious poem, *Imfiraji,* by the late Aliyu na Mangi, the famous composer of classical Hausa Islamic poetry in Nigeria.[9] She had committed this poem to memory while married to a *malam* and living in a town near Sokoto called Dan Lima in northern Nigeria. She explained: "When I lived in Dan Lima I recited the poem with my co-wives and the other neighbors. I did not know it at the beginning. So I decided to call a younger brother of our husband who happened to own the book with the original poem. I asked him to teach it to me because any type of studying requires *'usuli* [the authentic or original text] from which to learn. So he instructed me." What is significant here is not only Malama's description of how she learned Aliyu na Mangi's famous poem but also the importance she accorded to the power of memory as a way to master the written text. For her, as Beverly Mack has also observed, orality and literacy are not dichotomous entities but processes that constantly feed each other.[10]

Given her knowledge of the original poem, Malama A'ishatu was convinced that the version she heard on Nigerien national radio had been misrendered. She thus took it upon herself to approach Sheikh Alfa Ismael, the chairperson of the Islamic Association of Niger, to express her opinion on the subject. To convey her point, she produced a copy of the original text of the poem from her rich collection of Islamic material from Hausaland and beyond. This quest for truth and knowledge as an aspect of intellectual Islam led Malama A'ishatu to transgress the boundaries of *kuble* and address the highest religious male authority in the country in order to correct the rendition of a popular religious poem. Sheikh Alfa Ismael and his association were extremely impressed by Malama A'ishatu's demonstrated knowledge of Islamic poetry and Qur'anic learning in general, so they proposed that she host a program catering to Muslim women on national television and radio. Thus began Malama's emergence from the confines of *kuble* to the public arena of national electronic media commonly known as Tele Sahel and Radio Niger.

Gendered Spaces: Between Indigenous Tradition and French Colonialism

From her early childhood, Malama A'ishatu had been trapped between the forces of "tradition," on the one hand, and French colonialism, on the other. This was particularly evident in the area of education. She was born into a tradition that privileged boys' education over girls', and men over women, with respect to access to Islamic literacy and scholarship. Therefore, it was not uncommon for girls and women to be restricted to a limited body of Qur'anic texts sufficient only for the performance of mandatory rituals like *salat* (prayers). This, of course, is not to deny the fact that some Sahelian women of aristocratic background did have the opportunity to pursue Islamic learning to relatively advanced levels. The experiences of women from British-occupied Hausaland like Nana Asma'u (1793–1864), the daughter of the legendary Sheikh Usman dan Fodiyo, and her female siblings are striking cases in point, as Jean Boyd and Beverly Mack have demonstrated.[11] For the majority of Sahelian Muslim women, however, access to Islamic learning was limited to a narrow and usually ritualistic segment of Islam. Women's Islamic learning generally took place in the household—domestic space. Most local Qur'anic schools (again, known locally as *makaranta* in Hausa), therefore, tended to be exclusively male, especially at higher levels of instruction.

At the same time, the French colonial government had just introduced its own schools, partly to promote its policies of cultural and linguistic assimilation and partly to produce subaltern male clerical support for its local administration. Because the French colonial system was bent on delegitimizing the Afro-Islamic schools then in vogue, it undertook to train mainly males of the Muslim elite in the French language to produce an exclusive educational elite in this predominantly male Muslim polity. The French educational system, influenced by the European tradition of female domesticity, proceeded to marginalize girls and restrict their access to French-based education. Restrictions on Islamic learning, even within domestic spaces, due to the potential threat of subaltern subversion, also reduced girls' and women's access to religious literacy and Arab-Islamic culture. Initially, the chiefs recruited the sons of their slaves and other lower-class subjects to attend the French schools. However, as newly educated Africans began to assume roles of colonial authority, traditional power relations among social classes began to change. To prevent threatening incursions upon their traditional (patriarchal) power and to garner the benefits associated with the French educational system, the chiefs began to enroll their own sons while still denying access to girls. This colonial pattern for the education of girls in Niger is similar to that documented by Barbara Callaway and Lucy Creevey with regard to Senegal and Mali.[12]

It was against this backdrop that, as a child, Malama A'ishatu witnessed boys in her neighborhood attending the *makaranta* while her own male siblings, being children of a "native" colonial clerk who was also royalty, were enrolled in the newly established French colonial school. As a girl, her designated role was to provide support for the women of the household in their (re)productive roles and domestic tasks. But early completion of her daily domestic chores left Malama idle and lonely in a world of adult female homemakers. In the meantime, she kept overhearing the chanting of male children from the *makaranta* next door. Eventually, as she told it, her yearning to transcend her confines led to a window of opportunity:

> When we were taken to Magaria [a town bordering Nigeria and eastern Niger], it was decided that I would not be sent to *lakkwal* [*école*, "French school"], even though I was the eldest child and had to help my mother with their chores. My younger brothers were sent to *lakkwal*. After finishing my chores, I was left to play by myself. My mother then asked my father if he would allow me to attend the *makaranta* next door. She said to him, "Take her to the *malam* [male teacher] so that she can learn what is necessary for prayers." My father agreed, and I was admitted to the *makaranta*. I was the only girl in the *makaranta*. People were amazed at how quickly I memorized the *sura*s [Qur'anic chapters] and how well I retained everything in my head. [Laughs.]

Though intended to provide her with no more than basic training for purposes of prayers, this initial childhood experience became an important foundation for Malama's lifelong learning within an Islamic paradigm. As she commented with respect to her parents' hope, "Yes, I did learn what was necessary for prayer. *Alhamdulillah* [thank God]. Isn't that right? [Laughs.] I say I got what was necessary for prayers. But today I can also teach others. [Laughs.]" What began as an accidental or fortuitous occurrence precipitated by the segregated educational system ultimately led to a cherished profession for Malama A'ishatu in the postcolonial period. Malama's use of *lakkwal* is also significant, for it signals her ties with French-occupied territory. This word, as noted above, derives from the French word *école* and is not used in British Hausaland, where *boko,* a derivative of the English word "book," is used for "school."

There is no doubt that the prevailing ideology during the colonial period was hegemonic, articulated in gendered policies that circumscribed women's participation in the production and consumption of knowledge and promoted patriarchal biases that accompanied those processes. Malama A'ishatu did not escape the ideological contradictions of her time and place. Her espousal of patriarchal thinking is particularly evident in her comments about the role of the husband in a woman's access to knowledge: "It is required that husbands instruct their wives. If a man is not a learned one or is not literate, he must look for someone to instruct her. He must look for someone who can come to instruct her privately, or [otherwise] she must go to a safe place [i.e, to a woman teacher, *malama*] to learn." It is important, however, to realize that within these patriarchal confines, Malama A'ishatu nevertheless found room to inscribe a relatively progressive position for women in Islam by insisting on their right to knowledge, even if men determined the specific path of their access to that knowledge.

In her advocacy work for women's education, Malama A'ishatu invoked the tradition of the Prophet Muhammad, who is reported to have said: "The search for knowledge is mandatory for all Muslims, male and female alike." It is in this regard that Malama continued to explain:

> Well, isn't it during the old day of *ijtihad* [rational (religious) inquiry] that the Prophet endeavored to call for knowledge and the end of *jahilci* [i.e., *jahiliyya,* the period of ignorance]? In fact, his talk on the importance of *ilimi* [knowledge, education] was a recurrent one. And he did not say that women should not seek it. In fact, it is on women that the Prophet bestowed the greatest responsibility for acquiring knowl-

edge. . . . Knowledge, therefore, is *wajibi* [compulsory], and a woman must be allowed to seek it. Isn't that right?

Malama A'ishatu's adaptation of Arabo-Islamic concepts into Hausa reflected her competence in religious metalanguage and her deep familiarity with the Prophet Muhammad's early intellectual struggles to establish the quest for knowledge as a crucial component of the believer's duty and responsibility. Such qualities positioned her as an authoritative voice in Islamic matters and a knowledgeable Muslim woman scholar who used the same strategy employed by male Muslim scholars and religious authorities. She reasoned that the primacy of women's education lies in the recognition that women, as mothers and nurturers, are the ones who give shape to the early cultural and intellectual formation of both male and female children. The transmission of Islamic and other values important to the early development of the "Muslim" child is part of women's critical role in society. As she explained once again:

When a woman is knowledgeable, her children will learn before attending school. They [the women] will make use of it [their knowledge] from the beginning. That is why a woman's knowledge is not like a man's knowledge. . . . You see my children here, no matter how young they are, I teach them the Qur'an because we are Muslims and we have to teach them this at home. That is why it is *wajibi* [compulsory] for women to seek knowledge.

Therefore, in spite of her traditional conservatism, Malama A'ishatu drew on aspects of what is understood to be Islamic doctrine to press her campaign for the right of girls and women to education.

It is also significant that Malama's understanding of the realm of knowledge went beyond the religious. Here, too, she benefited from her understanding of Islam by drawing on one of the *hadith*s of the Prophet Muhammad, which exhorts Muslims "to seek knowledge even unto China" (a rather distant land at that time, where obviously no Islamic learning existed). Thus, she came to appreciate the value of both the religious education that she herself was privileged to receive and the secular modern learning to which she had been denied access:

As far as knowledge is concerned, it is not said that one must not acquire Western knowledge or Islamic knowledge. Qur'anic learning is for knowing how to prepare for the world to come and learning to live a harmonious Islamic social life. As for the other one, God grants it to us so that we can assist ourselves; you help yourself and help others. Now what can daughters do for their own parents that a man can object to? The way female children assist their parents—there are men who do not do that. Haven't they sent their mothers and fathers on haj [pilgrimage to Mecca]? Hasn't a daughter built a house for them? Hasn't she bought them a car? Is it what they are saying? This is what is valued, isn't it? Which one of all these things hasn't a woman done? And without *lakkwal* [laughs], how could she have achieved this?

Elsewhere, Malama A'ishatu observed:

Now, for our sake, . . . our children are educated in both *Mahammadiyya* [Qur'anic or Islamic schools] and *lakkwal.* Even now, there are some who attend madrassas and others who attend *lakkwal.* All our children attend *lakkwal.* They do both—they attend *lakkwal* and attend *Mahammadiyya,* our own children. So, could you tell someone's child not to attend? Seeking knowledge is a wonderful thing.

Malama A'ishatu thus saw modern secular education as important, especially for girls, not only in terms of the material benefits it provides for them and their families but because it enables parents to fulfill their religious obligations, like the haj, which also require material means. By fusing the material and the religious, she made her argument for girls' and women's education both compelling and urgent. She embraced those aspects of European education that enhance a Muslim's abilities to fulfill the material duties and responsibilities of an Islamic life.

In other words, Malama A'ishatu celebrated the educational hybridity that shapes Nigeriens as francophone Muslims, a hybridity that combines the Qur'anic schooling of a predominantly Islamic tradition with the formal state schooling inherited from the French colonial legacy. This complementarity is crucial in addressing both the need to be spiritually grounded, as required by Islam, and to satisfy, through the knowledge and skills acquired in formal school, individual as well as communal material obligations. Malama's position seemed to be in conformity with the saying of the Prophet Muhammad: "Work for the hereafter as if you will die tomorrow. And work for this world as if you are going to live forever."

Sheikh Hamidou Kane's *Ambiguous Adventure* (1963) poses a question about the process of acquiring knowledge thus: "Can one learn *this* without forgetting *that,* and is what one learns worth what one forgets?"[13] The concern of the community here was whether initiating their young to the newly introduced French colonial education might result in their estrangement from the knowledge they had acquired in their traditional Afro-Islamic training. Obviously, Malama A'ishatu suffered no such anxiety. Even as a young person, she did not seem to have been bothered by being the only girl in the masculine space of the *makaranta* she attended. She saw the possibility of combining the old and the new in the construction of a new francophone Afro-Islamic modernity that necessarily hinges on the integration of women.

Equally important in Malama A'ishatu's observations is the connection between women's education and women's role in the economic well-being of the Muslim family. In the urban "traditional Islamic" patriarchal arrangement, it is the man—as husband, father, and son—who is defined as the primary breadwinner and provider. However, it is important to point out that even for Muslims, religiosity and its gendered ideologies are experienced differently by different socioeconomic classes. For example, for the materially less privileged Muslim classes, especially in rural agricultural or pastoralist environments, every member of the family—regardless of gender and, at times, age—helps provide for the family, often in a gendered structure of labor; thus, skills and mode of production are specified and performed according to gender and age. But with the intrusion of French colonialism and its aftermath, the responsibility of providing for the family had increasingly been assumed by the daughters and women of the household, even in urban centers. It is true, of course, that growing economic hardships in society now require that both men and women contribute to the family income. Yet, ironically, it is precisely at this juncture that more and more men are failing to fulfill the requirements of their traditionally prescribed roles as providers while nominally occupying that status.

The 1980s was commonly known as *la période de conjuncture économique* (era of economic stress). It was precipitated by the collapse of the uranium market, followed by the World Bank's and International Monetary Fund's structural adjustment programs. Shortly afterward, the devaluation of the francophone currency, the Communauté Financière Africaine franc, plunged the country into a devastating economic depression with severe sociopolitical and other consequences.[14] Some of the negative consequences included an educational crisis characterized by students' and teachers' strikes followed by government repression and school closures over the

years, juvenile delinquency, prostitution, and high unemployment rates that
often led to broken families.

As men began to lose their jobs, their sense of masculinity, which was
tied to their role as breadwinners, was also damaged. The unavailability of
the male wage, which was fundamental to the patriarchal conception of the
family, along with women's active struggles to materially support themselves and their families, created a new societal crisis that led men and
women alike to seek new ways to negotiate both gender and power relations, not only within the private domain but also in the public sphere.[15] In
Beyond the Veil (1987), Fatima Mernissi noted how the modern world order caused a similar disruption of traditional class and sex privileges in
other Muslim societies.[16]

In previous eras, marriage had been considered a form of material security for Muslim women during times of economic crisis. However, given
the increasing rate of divorce and the more and more common failure of
husbands to provide for their families (whether due to polygamy, absen-
teeism, alcoholism, prolonged migration, or unemployment), women began
to see that they had no alternative but to become income generators. Under
these uncertain circumstances, it became normal, especially in urban areas,
for mothers to counsel their daughters to invest in education to ensure the
acquisition of the skills necessary to sustain themselves and their children
in the event of a failed marriage. The result of this conjunction of forces has
been a steady rise in the proportion of female-headed households in Niger,
in both rural and urban areas.

These new realities, then, have reinforced Malama A'ishatu's efforts to
advocate the maximizing of educational opportunities, both secular and religious, for girls and women. In this endeavor, Malama has sometimes
locked horns with conservative Muslim men—Western-educated as well as
non-Western-educated ones, from the lower middle class upward—who
have opposed, either openly or in more subtle ways, the provision of secular Western education for their girls, which they believe would turn them
into "bad" women. Malama A'ishatu has often exposed such beliefs as hypocritical. Observing how the young themselves have to come to appreciate
the benefit of secular education, she comments on the songs and poems
aired on her radio and television programs:

Well, you see, today's children see it for themselves, and they articulate
this understanding on their own. Moreover, if their parents are sitting and
listening, they too hear the message in the songs: "For God's sake, send

your children to school regardless of their number." And you see, this [message] is not too much, you see. From this, children will understand and know that illiteracy is not good. *Lakkwal* is not a sin. This is what some say. But those in *wannan zamani* [these times] who tell us that *lakkwal* is not good have their children attending *lakkwal*.

The general cultural opposition to Western secular education for girls was particularly pronounced during the initial phase of the colonial period. Since the rise of political Islam in the 1990s, the rejection of Western education has acquired a new momentum with the resurgence of Islamic conservatism. Some of its adherents have taken a public stand against Muslim women's secular education. Much of their reasoning is based on a conception of Islamic morality that, as Malama A'ishatu argues, is not necessarily in conformity with what is culturally understood as Islam. At the same time, however, some of these conservative new Islamist men are quick to exploit every opportunity to enroll their own children—male and female alike—in modern schools, both locally and internationally. It is this double standard as well as the undervaluing of women's education that Malama A'ishatu criticizes as both hypocritical and detrimental to a "modernist" vision of Islamic society that incorporates women as agents in nation building. This modernism is the essence of Malama A'ishatu's allusion to *wannan zamani* [these times], displaying a consciousness of tradition as malleable, one that constantly reconfigures itself to adapt to new circumstances and demands, notwithstanding the conceptual purity that its patriarchal guardians and ideologues seek to ascribe to it.

Poetry, Piety, and Identity

Poetry has long been an important didactic mode of religious expression in Afro-Islamic societies throughout the continent, as Mack amply illustrates.[17] It is thus natural that Malama A'ishatu would seek to make poetry a tool of her advocacy work, especially when she was called upon to launch Islamic programs for Muslim women on radio and television. With her efforts focused on the theme of education (*tarbiyya*), she made her students' recitation of her own poem *Ilimi* (literally meaning "knowledge/education/science/intelligence") the signature opening of all her media programs. The eighty-two verses of the poem are reproduced in full below to show how they lend themselves to memorization. As an important process of learning, students are expected to practice memorization on a regular basis. The goal is to cultivate a high level of concentration and focus, essential to successful learning in any field.

Ilimi[18]

Mun gode Allah mun yaba ma ma'aiki	We're grateful to God and we worship his messenger
Za ni jawabina ga 'yem *makaranta*	This is my advice to the students of Qur'anic school
[Chorus:] Mun gode Allah mun yaba ma ma'aiki	We're grateful to God and we worship his messenger

[After each line below, the chorus chants "Mun gode Allah mun yaba ma ma'aiki."]

Za ni jawabi wun iyayen yara	This will be my advice to the children's parents
Don Allah mai yaro shi sa *makaranta*	For God's sake, whoever has a child send him/her to school
Don sai da *ilimi* duniya ke k'aruwa	Because it is with knowledge that the world progresses
In babu *ilimi* ya ake a wadata?	If there is no knowledge, how can we have comfort?
Shi *ilimi* dad'inshi ba shi masantuwa	The good of knowledge is that it does not vanish
Yara ku sa himma zuwa *makaranta*	Children, focus your energy on attending school
Abin da ke sawa a samu *karatu*	What can allow one to gain knowledge (or to acquire literacy)
Su shidda ne farko zuwa *makaranta*	There are six. First, attend school
Sanad da ka y [(ka yi)] fa hankali ga lura	Enlightenment, diligence, and observation
Ga ladabi gum malamim *makaranta*	And good behavior toward the schoolteacher
Sanan da daurewa da yi ba fashi	Then patience and endurance
Yaro shi bar fashin zuwa *makaranta*	The child must not give up going to school
Sanad da samun malami mai hali	Then identifying and getting a teacher with character

Mai iya tarbiya ga 'yem *makaranta*	One who knows how to educate pupils
Abin da ke sawa a samu *karatu*	What allows one to gain knowledge
Su shidda ne farko zuwa *makaranta*	There are six. First to attend school
Abin da ke sawa mutum shi wadata	What allows one to be fulfilled
A duniya farkonshi yim *makaranta*	In the world (life), first is schooling
Abin da ke sawa mutum shi talauta	what can make a person poor
A duniya farko rashin *makaranta*	In the world, first is the lack of schooling
In ka yi *ilimi* ka tsaya ka gane	If you gain knowledge and you are critical
Ba yanda za a y [(a yi)] duniya ta talauta	There is no way for the world to be poor
Shi *ilimi* na maida yaro babba	(It) Knowledge can transform a child into an adult
Shi maida bawa d'a saboda gabata	It can transform a slave into a noble son because of enlightenment
Ni dai ina fata iyayen yara	I do pray that the children's parents
Su gane amfanin zuwa *makaranta*	Would understand the importance of attending school
Sun sannya 'ya'yensu su yi ta *karatu*	They ought to enroll their children in school
Komi yawan'ya'yenka ka sa *makaranta*	Whatever the number of your children, do send them to school
Shi *ilimi* farkonshi ga shi da dad'I	Knowledge is first of all sweet
D'aci ga rai [(ga re shi)] d'acinshi ya wuce gauta	It is bitter, and its bitterness is beyond the taste
Amma fa in ya samu ga shi da dad'I	However, once acquired, it is sweet
Dad'i ga rai dad'inshi ya wuce tsinta	Its sweetness is beyond an unexpected treasure
Shi *ilimi* tamkar uwa da uba ne	(It) knowledge grants sustainability for one's mother and father
Mai *ilimi* shi bai zama da talauta	A person with knowledge is never poor
Shi *ilimi* ka k'ara dub'e basira	Knowledge is what increases wisdom
Shi kau da jahilci shi kau da makanta	It chases away ignorance and it chases away blindness
Yara ina jan hankalinku ku gane	Children, I am calling on your attention to understand
Ba ku da aikin yi kamar *makaranta*	You don't have a better task than school

Shi *ilimi* dad'inshi in ya samu	The sweetness of knowledge once gained
Komi wuyad da ka sha ta ba ka ganinta	Whatever hardship you underwent, you would learn from it
Daure da yawan shanta ya zama doli	Endure the hardship, for acquiring it has become a must
In dai karatu za ka yi ka sha ta	If you are to study, you will absorb it
Allah Ta'ala duniya shi ya yi ta	God the Almighty is the one who created the world
Komi kake son duniya ka bar ta	However you love the world, you will leave it
Allah Ta'ala in ya ba ka *karatu*	God the Almighty, if he granted you knowledge
To in da more ka more zamanta	Well, if there is rejoicing, you will rejoice
Nina ga halin duniya halinta	I see the way of the world
Kuna cikin dad'i ku ce kun b'ata	As you enjoy its sweetness, it spoils
To shi ya sa tilas mutun shi yi *ilimi*	This is why a person ought to search for knowledge
Don shi kad'ai ke maganin cutatta	Because it is the only remedy to illness
Yara ku sa himma ga neman *ilimi*	Children, do put your effort to the quest for knowledge
A bar kasala nan da nan an huta	Do not be playful, and decide to rest
In ko ana nemanshi a yi ta biyayya	And then, if one must seek it, one must do it with obedience
Gum Malammai shi ne mabud'I nata	Toward the teachers who hold the key to it
Ita *makaranta* ba ta son mai fitina	School does not want someone who is troublesome
Mai rena kowa nan da nan an b'ata	An arrogant person who can easily mess with everybody
Ita *makaranta* cin kashinta ga yaro	School does challenge a child
Babu kamar fashin zuwa *makaranta*	There is no such thing as missing school
Ita *makaranta* ba'a sonta da k'iwya	One does not embrace schooling with laziness
Kuma ba'a son wauta cikin sha'aninta	Moreover, one does not want silliness in its undertaking

Yaro ana son tunda safe ya tashi — One needs a child to wake up early in the morning

Cikin nisha'i za shi je *makaranta* — Full of inspiration, he/she heads to school

Ya dena wasa mai yawa kan hanya — He/she must stop playing a lot on the way to school

Shi maida himma tai [(ta shi)] wajen *makaranta* — He/she must focus his energy toward school

Yaro ana son zuciyarsa ta saba — One would like a child to engage full-heartedly

Ko za shi yawo wajen *makaranta* — Even if all his/her outings be to school

Yara ana son hannuwansu su saba — One would like the hands of children to become used to

Da yin *rubutu* kun ji 'yen *makaranta* — Writing. Do you hear students!

Su yi ta tunanen yanda za su yi *ilimi* — They must keep on thinking about how to gain knowledge

Ku maida himma kun ji 'yen *makaranta* — You must focus your energy. Do you hear students!

Ku dena k'osawa ku dena kasala — You must stop being rigid; you must stop fooling around

Rago abin k'i ne wajen *makaranta* — The lazy one is not desired in school

Wuyar karatu mai yawanci ku sani — The difficulty of studying is to know the most

In babu himma ya ake a rabauta — If one does not put in effort, how could one gain?

In dai ana son duniya da kiyama — If we wish the world and the afterlife

Su samu tilas ne a je *makaranta* — To be reached, we ought to attend school

Babbar muk'ami ba kamar mai *ilimi* — There is no greater stature than that of the knowledgeable

In ya yi aiki yanda duk ya kamata — If one works hard as it is required

In ka yi *ilimi* mai yawa ya samu — And you gain a lot of knowledge

In babu aiki sai a fara *makaranta* — If there is no other activity, then one must start to teach (or study)

The word *makaranta* ("school"), on one hand, appears 24 times in the main poem and 80 times in the chorus verses, making a total of 104 occurrences. *Ilimi* (knowledge) and *karatu* (reading/studying), on the other hand, turn up a total of 16 and 4 times, respectively. In this poem, repetition, a common strategy of the oral tradition, serves to emphasize the importance of education. Furthermore, the verses *shi ilimi tamk'ar uwa da uba* ([It] knowledge grants sustainability for one's mother and father) and *inda son duniya da kiyama* (if one desires this world—in practical, moral, intellectual realms—and the hereafter) imply the religious, intellectual, and material value of *ilimi*.

For Malama A'ishatu, then, the power of poetry lies not only in its aesthetic appeal but also in its didactic utility. Through the poem *Ilimi,* she seeks to raise the consciousness of her audience, a constituency characterized mostly by both religious and nonreligious illiteracy. As a social commentator, public educator, and religious authority figure, she uses her new role and power to speak about the crucial importance of literacy in the life of the community.

Although Malama A'ishatu uses a variety of written poetic compositions in her programs and speaks of her gift for committing them to memory, she underscores the place and role of Hausa language as a transethnic language through which Qur'anic learning, teaching, and artistic performances are mediated. Hausa has come to define her personal and public identity even though she was born into the royal Zarma family of Dancandu. As explained above, she grew up and lived to an advanced age in Hausaland in both Niger and Nigeria, and she speaks Hausa primarily at home in Niamey, where I interviewed her in that language. On only a few occasions did she use Zarma during our interview sessions, such as when discussing the danger of some overt ethnocentric current she observed in politics. In the process of travel and resettlement, Hausa became the lingua franca for immigrant families from neighboring countries, such as Mali, Burkina Faso, and Benin, who settled in the urban centers of Niamey where Qur'anic education is provided. As Malama A'ishatu relates:

> As for the songs, they are so many of all sorts. I love songs. . . . Everywhere, I hear songs. . . . I don't even know where the written records of some of the songs are. But I retained them in my head. The songs I sing are in Hausa, and this is why people say I am Hausa ethnically. So this is the language in which I lived my life in Dan Lima, Kano, and now here. And this is what I teach the children. They are all fluent speakers of Hausa, and they are learning. All the female children can speak Hausa. Those who are literate and those who are not are all part of it.

Thus, Malama A'ishatu draws attention to the complexity of her "hybrid" linguistic and cultural identity, reemphasizing her Islamic Hausa-Zarma biculturalism. In addition, by saying that she does not know where she placed the written records of the songs, she draws our attention to the fact that the songs were oral renditions of written poems, which in Hausa are referred to as "written songs," *wak'a rubuce,* as opposed to original orally produced songs, *wak'ar baka* (literally, song of the mouth).[19]

Furthermore, Malama A'ishatu's training in Qur'anic schools in both Arabic and Hausa by Muslim Hausa teachers, and her subsequent marriages to Hausa men from Niger and Nigeria, which drew her more deeply into "Hausaness," have created confusion in the minds of people with a narrow understanding of the processes that shape complex individual sociocultural identities. In other words, unlike most people, Malama A'ishatu does not view ethnic identity as biologically transmitted.

Malama A'ishatu's shift from Zarma to Hausa suggests how language can offer, in transethnic and transnational urban milieus, a powerful means of inclusiveness and a path to new ethnicities as well as serving as a key marker of ethnicity and medium of instruction in Qur'anic schools. Increasingly, Hausa came to define her intellectual life as a religious teacher, poet, and television and radio religious commentator. Furthermore, she has chosen the transethnic Hausa as a medium for instruction because her current students come from a variety of ethnic and linguistic backgrounds. As Malama points out, "So this is how I lived my life in Dan Liman, and now here [in Niger]. And this is what I teach the children [students]. Some of them can speak [Hausa]. Those who are literate and those who are not are all part of it. . . . This is what we do." By pointing out that some of her students are children from Marka and Bambara in Mali, Malama underscores the salience of Hausa for the children of immigrants to Niger, for whom the issue is beyond one of "national" identity or ethnic affiliation because they are neither citizens of Niger nor do they belong to any of the groups that supposedly constitute the "original" ethnic makeup of the country.

The question of language and identity also concerns Malama A'ishatu with respect to current issues that have arisen in the wake of political democratization and the reemergence of multiparty politics. She challenges the ethnicization of politics evident in the nationalist expressions of the middle- and upper-class political elite, who make opportunistic appeals to ethnocentric regionalism. Their political orientation is reflected in their request that she run her programs on public radio and televise them in Zarma to assert her "Zarma roots." In response to such subjective postcolonial politics, she has retorted:

[Switching from Hausa to Zarma.] One day I went to visit a teacher at Garbaa-do, and he told me, "For God's sake, A'ishatu, speak in the Zarma language for my *komi* [from French *commis*, "clerical officer," a term used to refer to Westernized elite] to hear that you are a Zarma person." So I said this is a problem. . . . I then decided to greet him and his company in Zarma by saying, "Did you sleep well? In peace? [Laughs, then switches to Hausa.] I said [back to Zarma], "Did you sleep well?" They replied in Zarma, "In peace. So you are Zarma?" I replied in Zarma, "I am a Hausa." [Back to Zarma.] "Please, leave me alone with this business of Zarma-Zarma." [Back to Hausa.] My people, the Zarma, are too proud, my people, . . . in the past, they forbade me to do what I am doing now. They didn't want me to do it. . . . But now that they derive pride in seeing me in national Muslim programs, they want me to run the program in Zarma [laughs]. . . . Now, people see everything through the lens of ethnic pride. . . . This is ignorance. We are all Muslims at the mosque, and in my family, some are married and have children with non-Zarma, like my sister, with whom I now live. . . . Do you hear me?

In this respect, Malama A'ishatu belongs to the same school of thought as some leading Islamists who see the relationship between Islamicity and ethnicity as mutually exclusive and even conflictual, and the resort to ethnicity in modern-day politics as belonging to the world of *jahilci* (ignorance). As F. Dale Eickelman and James Piscatori have written: "The idea that Islam and ethnicity are antithetical and antagonistic also appears in the thinking of Islamist such as Egypt's Sayyid Qutb, who consigns ethnicity, tribalism and nationalism to the category of the *jahiliyya*. In using this term, which originally refers to the pre-Islamic 'age of ignorance,' he powerfully criticizes the validity of particularistic ties."[20] Within the same logic, Malama A'ishatu also transcends ethnocentrism by clarifying that as a Zarma woman, her Islamicity is also rooted in transethnic "Hausaness," which transmits Arab/Islamic values with their strong focus on the acquisition of knowledge.

On the question of poetry, piety, and identity, then, unlike the traditional griottes (female praise singers of West Africa), whose relationship to song or verbal art performance in general is located in the realm of orality and is most commonly a skill inherited through ancestral blood ties, Malama A'ishatu's relationship to religious songs—most commonly identified as religious poetry in Hausa, when written—reveals an interplay between literacy and Islamic identity. Hence, unlike the griotte, Malama's love for songs is not rooted in ancestral tradition. It emanates rather from her personal artistic attraction to songs and her initiation into Islamic poetry recitation, as her reference to some of the lost papers of her collection suggests. Malama A'ishatu might be called a "griotte of Islam."

Transitional "Digraphia": From Hausa *Ajami* to Arabic Script

For Malama A'ishatu, the Hausa language is not only important with respect to questions of identity and ease of communication; it is also central to the methodology of her Qur'anic literacy work, which I describe as "transitional digraphia." Applied linguistics offers the concept of "transitional bilingualism," in which one language, usually the native one, is used as a bridge to the acquisition of another, usually a foreign language. I also use the term "transitional digraphia" to refer to an educational process in which a script tied to the students' native language is used transitionally to help them acquire the script and literacy skills of a second or foreign language. In the context of this research, the locally used script, called *ajami,* itself an adaptation of Arabic script for writing the Hausa language, became more indigenous. Hausa *ajami* differs from the original Arabic alphabet in that it includes some modifications to accommodate Hausa sounds that do not exist in Arabic. The "foreign" script, conversely, is the original Arabic script, which students may acquire later in life either in a limited way for religious purposes, for broader studies of the arabophone context, or for general communication needs.

Malama's educational efforts and methodology raise the broader issue of epistemological contrasts among different societies and cultures. It is now widely known that global imbalances of power, which define Western hegemonic relations with non-Western cultures, have been successful in privileging Western epistemologies over non-Western ones. Western-educated elites in non-Western countries have generally been the main promoters of this imbalance in the postcolonial dispensation, which has resulted in the marginalization and devaluation of other indigenous/native modes of knowledge. The hierarchization of the different forms of epistemologies in accordance with their cultural origins signals the unequal relations between Western-trained scholars (whether of Western or non-Western origin) and other non-Western-trained scholars and intellectuals whose scholarship and intellectual products are grounded in more independent, "organic/native"

discursive paradigms. This state of affairs, combined with indigenous patriarchal culture(s), means that the contributions of organic intellectuals and
scholars, especially if they are women, are not registered in most accounts
of literacy and intellectual production in countries such as Niger, where
globalization has stiffened the competition between *francophonie* and *an-
glophonie.*

Studies dealing with Islamic education or literacy in Islamic cultures
in Africa often depict Islamic education in a negative light because
their authors fail to recognize—whether through bias or ignorance—the
particularity of Western modes of instruction.[21] Belying such studies, my
discussions with Malama A'ishatu about her teaching reveal a well-
rationalized curriculum designed for her students. She understood when
to use rote learning and memorization, and for what purpose. She knew
when to introduce writing in *ajami* and when to switch to classical Arabic. She was conscious about when to promote critical skills and which
Islamic texts to use for that purpose, and of the importance of fostering a
competitive spirit, not with other fellow students but with one's self. Consider the following:

> When they [the students] reach *Alamtara kaifa* [Qur'anic verse from
> chapter 105, "The Elephant"], I introduce them to the slate [writing]. Or
> when they reach *Sabbi* [chapter 87, "The Most High"] in reading the
> Qur'an, I introduce them to the consonants and vowels, whether the Ara-
> bic ones or the Hausa ones. You know there are the Hausa consonants
> and the vowel markers, for example, when you write the subscript (-) un-
> der the consonant marker; you have the syllable *bi;* you keep moving
> until the end. And if it is the Arabic ones that we will do, it goes *a, ba,
> ta, sa ja. . . .* But ours [*Ajami*] is much easier for the minds of the chil-
> dren to grasp. Once he or she understands it, then one introduces the Ara-
> bic one. . . . But usually this comes around the fifth *izb.*[22]

What Malama's comment suggests is a great understanding of the cognitive implications of learning a new language, becoming literate simultaneously in one's mother tongue and a foreign language (Arabic), and
mediating mother-tongue literacy through a foreign alphabet and mediating
the learning of the foreign language through literacy in the mother tongue.
My constructive engagement with Malama gave her the opportunity to explain her methodology as a teacher and to provide a rational account of her
teaching approach that demonstrates her intellectual understanding of what

in Western epistemology is located within the discipline of psycholinguistics, a concept that she herself might never use.

The Qur'anic text itself is replete with verses calling on those who are reading it to engage, at the same time, in a reflective physical exercise about the relationship between the physical and the divine: "This conception of nature finds its appropriate place in the overall context of Islamic cosmology, which acts as a bridge connecting pure metaphysics with the physical world."[23] It is difficult to understand how such an approach to learning that takes into account the full scope and stages of the learners' linguistic and cognitive abilities can be described only in terms of rote memorization.

Malama A'ishatu: Between Womanhood and Motherhood

The question of epistemologies is relevant to Malama A'ishatu's public work as a teacher as well as to a more intimate part of her personal life as a woman who did not bear a child in a society that accords high value to a woman's capacity to bear children. Her childlessness took an emotional toll. Even in this very private domain—which Malama A'ishatu addressed without my prompting—she makes a clear connection between the personal and professional dimensions of her life: "A person who can read this paper and another who can't, we are not the same. I have told you about my happiness, reading, the quest for knowledge and teaching young girls and composing songs and that I used to cry for not having children. Haven't I told you? However, since the day I completed my *saukar Qur'ani* [Qur'anic training], . . . when I realized that I knew now that even this smallest piece of paper has someone to take it, . . . that bitter yearning [for children] left me. Since that day, I forgot the subject of childbearing." Like her male counterpart, a woman intellectual can also claim her scholarship and her ability to bequeath this knowledge to posterity as prime determinants of her identity and value in society.

The absence of childbearing does not mean an absence of mothering. As Malama A'ishatu herself reminded me in the course of our interviews, she mothered her younger siblings until they came of marriageable age. Her Qur'anic school is now located in the home of one of her younger siblings, whom she raised as her daughter. Malama A'ishatu also assisted in mothering the children of her co-wives and other relatives. And in her own mind, the boundary between teaching and mothering her students was often blurred, as shown by her references to them at times as "my students" (*d'alibaina, almajirraina*) and other times as "my children" (*yarana*).

Conclusion

The life of Malama A'ishatu Hamani Zarmakoy Dancandu demonstrates how, for a long time, indigenous patriarchal traditions and colonial modernity colluded to marginalize her in the realm of knowledge. Although she had some opportunity to acquire Qur'anic knowledge in her early life, the forces of Afro-Islamic patriarchy prevented her from entering the advanced spheres of Islamic knowledge and from engaging in the public exchange of ideas in public, even on issues related to Muslim women, until the political democratization of the 1990s.

Malama A'ishatu's current status is that of an elite Sufi scholar and leader. In many ways, her aristocratic birth parallels those of the legendary Nana Asma'u Dan Fodiyo of the Sokoto Caliphate and the twentieth-century Sufi women leaders (*muqqadamat*) of Kano (Nigeria), who are described by Alaine Huston and by Balaraba Sule and Priscilla Starratt,[24] and their Senegalese counterparts known as the *mouride shaykhas*.[25] Unlike these other Muslim women leaders in the Sahelian region, who ascended to the highest religious ranks through the patronage of their male kin, Malama did not attain the status of a Sufi woman leader of the Tijaniyya order as a result of patrilineal inheritance. Although Malama comes from a family of devout Muslim parents, she was the only female child to attend Qur'anic school, while her male siblings were sent the newly established French school. Now, as an electronic media figure, a teacher of a women's home-based Qur'anic school, and a transmitter of Islamic literacy to her female kin, Malama has built a new and significant legacy, especially for womenfolk. Ironically, the very gender ideology that discouraged her enrollment in French schools enabled her rise to prominence. Although young women are at the forefront of the struggle to create an alternative modernity for Muslim women within indigenous traditions, Western secular education and the new Islams in Niger have opened up new spaces for women of their mothers' and grandmothers' generations, such as Malama A'ishatu Hamani Zamakoy Dancandu.

Notes

1. Barbara Cooper, "The Politics of Difference and Women's Associations in Niger: Of Prostitutes, the Public, and the Politics," *Signs* 20, no. 4 (1995): 851–82; Hadiza

Djibo, *La Participation Politique des femmes africaines à la vie politique: Les exemples du Sénégal et du Niger* (Paris: Harmattan, 2001).

2. Ousseina D. Alidou, *Engaging Modernity: Muslim Women and the Politics of Agency in Postcolonial Niger* (Madison: University of Wisconsin Press, 2005).

3. Ibid., 56–81; Zeinabou Hadari, "Muslim Women in the Age of Information Technology," paper presented at African Studies Association conference, Washington, December 5–8, 2002.

4. Beverly Mack, "Muslim Women's Educational Activities in the Maghreb: Investigating and Redefining Scholarship in Morocco and Northern Nigeria," *Maghreb Review* 29, nos. 1–4 (2004): 165–85; S. Muhammad Umar, "Profiles of New Islamic Schools in Northern Nigeria," UCLA Fellows Paper, 2004; Alaine S. Huston, "We Are Many: Sufis and Islamic Scholars in Twentieth-Century Kano, Nigeria" (PhD diss., Indiana University, 1997); Alaine S. Huston, "The Development of Women's Authority in the Kano Tijjaniyya, 1874–1963," *Africa Today* 46, nos. 3–4 (Summer–Autumn 1999): 42–64; Balaraba B. M. Sule and Priscilla E. Starratt, "Islamic Leadership Positions for Women in Contemporary Kano Society," in *Hausa Women in the Twentieth Century,* edited by Catherine Coles and Beverly Mack (Madison: University of Wisconsin Press, 1991), 29–49; Jean Boyd and Murray Last, "The Role of Women as 'Agents Religieux' in Sokoto," *Revue Canadienne d'Études Africaines* 29, no. 2 (1985): 283–300.

5. Christian Coulon, "Women, Islam and *Baraka,*" in *Charisma and Brotherhood in African Islam,* edited by Donal Cruise O'Brien and Christian Coulon (Oxford: Clarendon Press, 1988), 113–30.

6. In Hausa, "Malama" refers to a female *marabout* or Sufi religious leader, and can also refer to a woman religious teacher.

7. Saba Mahmood, "Feminist Theory, Embodiment, and the Docile Agent: Some Reflections on the Egyptian Islamic Revival," *Cultural Anthropology* 16, no. 2 (2001): 202–36.

8. The system of female domestic seclusion (called *kuble* in Niger, *kulle* in Nigeria, and *purdah* in Afghanistan and South Asia) was not practiced during the life of the Prophet Muhammad, nor during the period of the four caliphs who succeeded him. Female domestic seclusion and Arabic literacies appeared in various parts of Africa with the spread of Islam.

9. The works of Aliyu na Mangi, the most prolific Hausa poet, are discussed in detail by Graham Furniss, *Poetry, Prose and Popular Culture in Hausa* (Edinburgh: Edinburgh University Press for International African Institute, 1996), 208–9. *Imfiraji* is his most famous poem, consisting of twelve cantos. He composed it for his daughter, intending it to replace frivolous songs and impart a serious religious ethos.

10. Mack, "Muslim Women's Educational Activities."

11. Jean Boyd, *The Caliph's Sister: Nana Asma'u, 1793–1865, Teacher, Poet, and Islamic Leader* (London: Frank Cass, 1989); Jean Boyd and Beverly Mack, *Collected Works of Nana Asma'u* (East Lansing: Michigan State University Press, 1997).

12. Barbara Callaway and Lucy Creevey, *The Heritage of Islam: Women, Religion, and Politics in West Africa* (Boulder, Colo.: Lynne Rienner, 1994), 61.

13. Sheikh Hamidou Kane, *Ambiguous Adventure* (London: Heinemann, 1963), 34.

14. Myriam Gervais, "Niger: Regime Change, Economic Crisis, Perpetuation of Privilege," in *Political Reform in Francophone Africa,* edited by F. John Clark and David E. Gardinier (Boulder, Colo.: Westview Press, 1997), 86–107.

15. Alidou, *Engaging Modernity,* 13.

68 OUSSEINA D. ALIDOU

16. Fatima Mernissi, *Beyond the Veil: Male-Female Dynamics in Modern Muslim Society* (Bloomington: Indiana University Press, 1987).

17. Beverly Mack, *Muslim Women Sing: Hausa Popular Song* (Bloomington: Indiana University Press, 2004).

18. *Ilimi* (knowledge/education/science/intelligence) was recited by Malama A'ishatu's students; this transcription is from a recording I made from the Niger National Radio Broadcasting System in the summer of 1996.

19. Dalhatu Muhammad, "Individual Talent in the Hausa Poetic Tradition: A Study of Ak'ilu Aliyu and His Art" (PhD diss., University of London, 1977), 9–14; Mack, *Muslim Women Sing,* 33.

20. F. Dale Eickelman and James Piscatori, *Muslim Politics* (Princeton, N.J.: Princeton University Press, 1996), 100.

21. Callaway and Creevey, *Heritage of Islam,* 61. The authors cite scholars who provide a definition of Islamic learning in comparison to Western understandings of learning, but do not include other researchers whose definitions of the same subject matter suggest alternative understandings, e.g., Brian V. Street, *Cross-Cultural Approaches to Literacy* (Cambridge: Cambridge University Press, 1993); Stefan Reichmuth, "Islamic Learning and Its Interaction with 'Western' Education in Ilorin, Nigeria" in *Muslim Identity and Social Change in Sub-Saharan Africa,* edited by Louis Brenner (Bloomington: Indiana University Press, 1993), 179–97; and Fatima Mernissi, *Beyond the Veil, and Doing Daily Battle: Interviews with Moroccan Women* (London: Zed Books, 1989).

22. The Qur'an is divided into sixty equal-length sections to facilitate memorization.

23. Zahra al Zeera, "Paradigm Shifts in the Social Sciences in the East and West," in *Knowledge across Cultures,* edited by Ruth Hayhoe and Julia Pan (Hong Kong: University of Hong Kong Press, 2001), 55–74, 67.

24. See Huston, "We Are Many"; Huston, "Development of Women's Authority"; Sule and Starratt, "Islamic Leadership Positions," 29–49.

25. Coulon, "Women, Islam, and *Baraka.*"

Chapter 3

Deconstructing Islamic Feminism: A Look at Fatima Mernissi

Raja Rhouni

As observers have pointed out, the term "Islamic feminism" first appeared in the 1990s as a reference to the struggles for equal gender rights in "Islam" under way in various geographical locations, whether in Africa, Asia, Europe, or America.[1] The designation, as they note, also came to identify the scholarship of a growing number of women, but also men, who have been engaged in a new reading of the foundational and canonical texts of Islam from a gender perspective, the distinctiveness of which is its distance from secularist (rather than secular) approaches that reduce Islam to a mere patriarchal ideology. A "secularist" position in this particular instance refers to a perspective that considers Islam as inherently opposed to women's human rights. Those who adopt such a stance approach Islam only to demonstrate its essential opposition to women's rights. They do not envision Islam as a source of women's empowerment and often refer to universal human rights as the only guarantee of equality. The term "secular," conversely, refers to the position of scholars who reject the project of the "Islamic state" but nevertheless engage religious issues in order to "discover" and "invent" means of women's empowerment. This is the position of a number of "feminist" scholars with Muslim backgrounds, like the Moroccan sociologist Fatima Mernissi, who is the subject of this study, and others. Some of its observers and practitioners define "Islamic feminism" as a new type of feminism, although the feminist label is often at the heart of the controversy over the term, which takes its legitimacy from the Qur'an itself or from what is often referred to as "Qur'anic ethics" or the "Qur'anic ethos of social justice."[2]

In fact, one can argue that utilizing a religious idiom to claim women's rights is a tradition that can be traced as far back as the seventh century CE, when Umm Darda, for instance, a prominent female jurist in Damascus, "shocked her contemporaries by praying shoulder to shoulder with men— a nearly unknown practice, even now—and issuing a fatwa [ruling on Islamic law], still cited by modern scholars, that allowed women to pray in the same position as men."[3] This is far from being an isolated case, or exclusive to some "eccentric" female jurist. In Morocco, for example, a sixteenth-century *faqih* (male religious scholar) named Ibn 'Ardun issued a fatwa saying that women should have the right to compensation after divorce.[4] These examples are only a few from a larger history of what can be identified as a "women-friendly *ijtihad* [independent legal reasoning]."

However, and beyond this broad definition that allows us to see "Islamic feminism"—in the sense of using Islamic arguments to advance a gender-egalitarian reading and practice of Islam—as a long-standing tradition rather than a novelty, the term also refers to the growing body of scholarship since the 1990s that has undertaken a revision of Islamic thought and a new reading of foundational texts from a fresh perspective. The main distinctions of this emergent scholarship are the use of feminist categories of analysis like "gender" and "patriarchy" by most of its practitioners and the self-proclaimed Islamic feminist position some of them adopt. Generally, and especially in Muslim-majority countries, this scholarship emerged at a moment of late postcoloniality, usually in contexts of widespread postindependence social disillusionment and the rise of Islamism, a trend that presents both challenges and promises.[5]

At least two major factors explain the emergence of this growing body of revisionist scholarship. On the one hand, it emerged as a strategic response to rising Islamist movements, which have become more and more vocal in Muslim-majority societies since the late 1970s, with their often conservative discourses on women's rights and gender relations. In this respect, these scholars have realized that Islamists, in the words of Islamic studies scholar Abdullahi An-Na'im, "have already succeeded in islamizing the terms of reference of public discourse in most Islamic societies."[6] The new scholars have realized that the struggle has to be waged within a religious framework and that there can be no advancement of women's rights if the model of the family and gender relations constructed by classical *fiqh* (Islamic jurisprudence) is not seriously questioned and openly debated. Thus in Muslim-majority societies, which are witnessing an evident Islamization of public discourse, the secularist standpoint is not only intellectually untenable but also, and more important, politically obsolete.

Mernissi shifted her position on Islam in the late 1980s from what I have called a "secularist feminist" standpoint to what has been identified as an "Islamic feminist position." The 1980s in Morocco witnessed not only the growing popularity of Islamism as an oppositional discourse but also the failure of efforts to amend the Mudawana, or personal status code. This was also a period during which Mernissi began to mingle with Moroccan scholars of Islamic studies and jurisprudence within the framework of a multidisciplinary research group concerned with issues of family and women. Among these progressive scholars were Ahmed Khamlichi and Aberrazak Moulay Rchid, whose respective positions on the Mudawana may have influenced Mernissi's perspectives on Islam and gender. Khamlichi's main argument is that *fiqh,* on which the Mudawana is based, is a human rather than divine creation, being a product of simple *ijtihad,* and may therefore be subject to revision. It is significant to note that Khamlichi is a member of the Moroccan Council of the 'Ulama'. Moulay Rchid is a jurist who wrote the first thesis on the status of women in a Moroccan university.[7] He advocates amending the Mudawana by appealing to what he calls "the spirit rather than the letter of Islam," by which he means Islam's egalitarian ethos.

"Islamic feminism" also emerged quite surprisingly from within Islamism itself, usually from female militants who were reacting against the patriarchal politics and discourses of Islamism. This was the case, for instance, with the female militants of the Rafat Party in Turkey, who felt marginalized within the same party they had worked to bring to victory.[8] However, in the case of the Moroccan Islamist militant Nadia Yassine, spokeswoman of the Islamist group al-'Adl wa al-Ihssan, it is the misogyny of *fiqh* rather than political marginalization within her group that leads her to express what might be described as an Islamic feminist position, though she has rejected that label. Yassine declared in 2003 that *fiqh* is "macho."[9] To my mind, Yassine's critical distance from the almost sacralized *fiqh*—indeed, her capacity to hold a critical view of the early jurists, or *fuqaha*—is enabled by the Islamist discourse of her own group, which is critical of a number of religious scholars on the basis that they have historically been agents of power and a corrupt group, whose role since the Ummayad Dynasty has been to legitimize authoritarianism. This demystification of the *fuqaha*'s pious image, which recognizes their political partiality, paves the way for criticism of their gender biases.

The two tendencies that explain the emergence of Islamic feminism as either a *reaction* to Islamism or a trend emerging from within its midst, as described above, may give full sense to Ziba Mir-Hosseini's statement that "Islamic feminism is the child of political Islam."[10] However, "Islamic feminism" cannot be seen exclusively as the offspring of Islamism—first, because some of these scholars see their work and activism not as a mere strategic or tactical response to political Islam but rather as emanating from a "spiritual imperative," to use Sa'diyya Shaikh's phrase.[11] It is also important to understand the emergence of Islamic feminism as a reaction to the secularism of feminism as practiced by some feminists with Muslim backgrounds. Indeed, some of these scholars insist on demarcating their own position from that of some feminist scholars with Muslim backgrounds whose work has often portrayed Islam as one of the major obstacles to gender equality.[12]

"Islamic feminism," like black feminism, may indeed be seen as a revision of the universalism of feminism, a new kind of reappropriation of feminist language, or, to use Marnia Lazreg's phrase, a "decentering of feminism" from the Western location where it is often thought to have originated.[13] It claims its own modality of "doing" feminism by staying away from the trajectory of secularism, often equated with Western feminism, and by refusing to forsake "a faith position," especially with the stigmatization of Islam after the terrorist attacks on the United States on September 11, 2001, and the bombings of Madrid and London in subsequent years. To sum up, the motivation behind this new gender critique is often the awareness of the irrelevance of the secularist discourse given the centrality of religion in the public spheres of Muslim-majority societies today as well as the deep conviction in the very power of "Islam" to enhance gender equality rather than restrict it.

This brief account of the emergence of Islamic feminism allows us to see the designation as an umbrella term encompassing various positions ranging from those of secular intellectuals like Fatima Mernissi and Nasr Hamid Abu Zayd, who support the separation of religion and state, to the positions of the Islamist proponents or militants like Nadia Yassine in Morocco and

Zaynab al-Ghazali in Egypt.[14] It also allows us to see that Islamic feminists may write either from a position of faith, reflecting a deep conviction in the egalitarian global ethics of the Qur'an, or from a strategic or scholarly position that often seeks to contextualize what have been considered "Islamic gender norms" in order to reveal the historical contingency and the cultural constructedness of these norms. I should say here that "strategic" should not be always distrusted as denoting an opportunistic or hypocritical attitude that simply instrumentalizes religion. Strategy can also be dictated by a given situation and can actually emanate from the salutary position of scholars we might designate as "organic intellectuals" in the Gramscian sense, who in order to continue influencing their societies cannot but follow its moves and engage in its issues, refusing to stay in the elitist ivory tower of so-called enlightened secularist intellectuals.

Islamic Feminist Hermeneutics: The Case of Mernissi

With this general background on the rise of what is called Islamic feminism in mind, I now undertake a discussion of what we might call "Islamic feminist hermeneutics," though the phrase is inadequate to describe the various hermeneutical models used by scholars labeled "Islamic feminists." I focus on the case of Fatima Mernissi, one of the main exponents not only of feminism in Muslim societies but also of what is called Islamic feminism today. I place particular emphasis on her influential book *Le Harem Politique: Le Prophète et les femmes,* published in 1987, which miriam cooke and Margot Badran, two important observers and theoreticians of this new trend, consider to be one of the pioneering texts of Islamic feminism. I consider Mernissi's essay one of the most advanced and original contributions to the study of gender and Islam, given its contextual approach to canonical religious texts.

The originality of Mernissi's work stems from the fact that she engages with "traditional" religious disciplines like *tafsir* (exegesis) and *hadith* collections in a way that creates interesting conversations with this tradition. Her work engages with one of the most important collectors of *hadith,* al-Bukhari, and offers new readings of various verses of the Qur'an dealing with women that take the historical and sociological context of their production into account. This approach departs from the simplistic methodology of selectively invoking passages that support gender equality and providing interpretations (or *tafasir*) that are more women friendly. However, despite its novel approach, the book is also, to my mind, limited by its tendencies toward the retrieval of "truth," the search for authenticity, and compliance with foundationalism. I argue that these limitations are often endorsed by some conceptions of the term "Islamic feminism" itself, which is one of the main reasons I find the term rather problematic. I suggest a way out of the search for authenticity and foundationalism by putting forward what I call a "postfoundationalist islamic gender critique."

I write the adjective "islamic" in this particular instance with a lowercase "i" in order to avoid constructing this field of research in hermetic terms, as well as to foreground the element of methodological cross-pollination that characterizes Islamic feminist scholarship(s). This practice follows Mohammed Arkoun's transcription of "islam" (with a small letter), by which he opposes or problematizes the essentialist construction of "Islam" (with a capital letter) by what he refers to as "Orientalist Islamology" and political science, on the one hand, and the canonical construction of "Islam" (with a capital letter) by orthodox Muslim theologians and jurists who refuse to consider its plurality and open-endedness, on the other.[15] Arkoun argues that the two ideological constructions do not take into consideration the sociocultural construction of belief and its metamorphosis throughout history. He thus prefers writing "islam" with a small letter to designate a "religious formation among others and its diverse manifestations in history."[16] Therefore, the transcription of the adjective "islamic" in my term "islamic gender critique" refers to the double critique that "Islamic feminism" represents: that is, a simultaneous critique of both an Orientalist, essentialist construction of "Islam," written with a capital to underscore its alleged fixity and eternal dogmatism, and a fundamentalist, gender-biased construction of "Islam," also written with a capital, which stresses its orthodoxy.

Why read Mernissi as an "Islamic feminist" and what are the assumptions underlying the theorization of this term? Indeed, I read Mernissi's standpoint in *Le Harem Politique* as an example of an "Islamic feminist" position, despite the fact that Mernissi, like many other scholars, has never self-identified as an "Islamic feminist." In fact, most of the prominent figures of this critique have, at some moment, refused the label for different reasons. In most cases, it is the "feminist" part of the phrase that prompts their reluctance to adopt the label. The African American scholar Amina Wadud, for instance, was reluctant to use the label to describe her position and work, even though she acknowledges a debt to feminist theory. She seems to prefer the more religious or theological term "gender jihad," which is also part of the title of her second book, *Inside the Gender Jihad: Women's Reform in Islam*.[17] The Pakistani American Asma Barlas is another critic who rejected the label on the grounds that she first encountered the radical idea of women's full humanity in Qur'anic discourse itself rather than in feminist scholarship, though she acknowledges her debt to feminist tools of analysis.[18] One of the main reasons why both Wadud and Barlas have resisted the label "Islamic feminist" is their sense that it does not give sufficient primacy to Islam as the principal source of their struggle for gender equality. Margot Badran's definition of Islamic feminism, however, has alleviated this problem and helped to reconcile some of these scholars to accepting the designation.

Fatima Mernissi resists labeling in general and the feminist label in particular, which she associates, rightly or wrongly, with the feminist discourse of the 1970s that she encountered during her stay in the United States, with its (according to her) hostility toward men and patronizing tendencies toward other women.[19] However, like Badran, the reason I retain this identification or description is "not to impose a label of identity upon those who refuse it but simply as a way of *identifying*"[20] Mernissi's "speaking position," in miriam cooke's sense.[21] From Mernissi's writings, particularly in her earlier work, we can see her as a (secular) feminist and in her later work, especially *The Veil and the Male Elite: A Feminist Interpretation of Women's Rights in Islam*,[22] as an Islamic feminist.

With respect to Islamic feminism, I concur with cooke, who attempted an early theorization of the term in her book *Women Claim Islam: Creating Islamic Feminism through Literature*: "Whenever Muslim women offer a critique of some aspect of Islamic history or hermeneutics, and they do so with and/or on behalf of all Muslim women and their right to enjoy with men full participation in a just community, I call them Islamic feminists."[23] In this sense, we can see Mernissi as an Islamic feminist.[24]

I agree with cooke, Badran, and others who to their credit have defended the term "Islamic feminism" against the charge that it constitutes an oxymoron. Surprisingly, resistance to the term came from both fundamentalists and secularists. The strongest rejection came indeed from among the ranks of Iranian expatriate feminists, who could not envisage how "Islam" could be the basis for feminist claims.[25] This indicates that fundamentalists and secularists can at times represent two sides of the same coin, because both groups tend to reify religion and often carry implied or unstated assumptions about either feminism or "Islam." Along with cooke, I believe that feminism in the sense of resistance to patriarchy is quite obviously not culture-specific; neither is Islam gender-specific. I also consider Islam not an ideology but a religion with such semantic richness that it has invited multiple readings and significations, which are still not exhausted today.[26] Most important here, these multiple meanings have yielded what amounts to different *islam*s for women, as the gender studies scholar Leila Ahmed argues.[27] I also consider feminism not an ideology to be followed but a theory that provides a cluster of indispensable categories of analysis, like gender and patriarchy.

However, I must confess that I find both the term "Islamic feminism" and its theorization problematic because of its Eurocentric connotation, however misguided it may be, and, more important, because of its often essentialist conceptions, which support foundationalism. One might ask, for instance: Why give center stage to the term "feminism"? Does not the insistence on this term suggest the idea that feminism is conceived more as a master narrative than as a theory that offers analytical tools? Does not the term "Islamic feminism" somehow overshadow the affiliation of this gender critique with Islamic thought, which in its dynamic form, as represented by the Islamic modernist discourse of the Nahda (the Arab cultural and intellectual "awakening" that began in Egypt in the late nineteenth century), began to rethink the status of women as early as the nineteenth century,[28] or with contemporary thinkers who are engaging in a critique of Islamic thought?[29]

One might contend that this affiliation to Islamic thought is precisely what is meant by the adjective "Islamic"; however, this is not always the case. For instance, cooke's theorization of the term, despite its undeniable value in stressing the importance of this new trend in feminism, tends to define the qualifier "Islamic" in rather reductive terms. For cooke, the adjective "Islamic" is related to the *defense of a faith position.*[30] Of course, one should acknowledge that cooke was describing the position of many scholars with Muslim backgrounds in the aftermath of 9/11. However, this conceptualization may be problematic. First, it risks being exclusionary because it seems to leave both non-Muslims and secular scholars out of this critical project. Second, it seems to ignore the complexity of the concept of faith in contemporary Islamic thought and the way "Islamic feminists" (wittingly or unwittingly) challenge, or redefine, the concept.

One might ask, for instance: *Who* determines the parameters of faith, and *how?* If most gender critics legitimately believe social and gender justice to be the core of the Qur'anic message, their "faith" is nevertheless often questioned. In fact, if, following cooke, Mernissi wrote from a position of faith in *Le Harem Politique,* her historical readings of some verses and refutation of some *hadith*s were nonetheless considered heretical, because she was personally subject to a death fatwa, and her book was subject to censorship. Even the Islamist activist Nadia Yassine has been subject to a fatwa declaring her an apostate after her criticism of *fiqh.*[31] The consignment of both Yassine and Mernissi to apostasy logically means that in the eyes of those issuing the fatwas, both women had renounced their faith. This leads to questions about the parameters of faith in Islam. As Nasr Hamid Abu Zayd explains, in Islam, *iman* (faith) is defined as the combination of both *aqida* and what the Qur'an refers to as *shari'a,* divine law.[32] However, *shari'a,* referred to in the Qur'an in broad terms, is often confused with Islamic jurisprudence, *fiqh.* The fact that *fiqh* is only an interpretation of *shari'a* and is of human origin (it was undertaken by mostly men in the ninth and tenth centuries) is often forgotten. This confusion may explain the two fatwas. It also indicates that Islamic feminism is necessarily inscribed within a problematization or redefinition of the concept of faith itself within contemporary Islamic thought.[33]

But what is more problematic, I think, is the tendency to put forward the project of "Islamic feminism," or what I prefer to call an "islamic gender critique," as essentially one of *retrieval* rather than critique and deconstruction. Cooke identifies Islamic feminism as the task of "Muslim women," who are "speaking out against patriarchal *distortions* of the values and norms of the founding *umma.*"[34] This definition suggests that the project of Islamic feminism is to retrieve "pure" founding norms and values, "untainted" by pre-Islamic patriarchal culture, seventh-century Arabian patriarchy, or contemporary androcentric discourses. Of course, cooke is aware that the task is more complex than simply retrieving "a lost truth" or "extracting" more egalitarian laws. Besides, one might acknowledge that cooke's definition is drawn from the very practice of scholars like Mernissi, who also at times (if not always) define their task as part of a project of "recovering the truth of Islam." However, such conceptions may lead to foundationalism—in the sense of the search for "truth—which I find to be one of the limitations of this emergent scholarship, as I indicate below by considering the example of Mernissi.

But before illustrating this tendency, I first need to explain my preference for the term "islamic gender critique." To my mind, the adjective "islamic" is not an essentialist qualifier—there is nothing intrinsic to the term per se, because I believe that there is no such a thing as a monolithic "Islamic paradigm" or an "Islamic methodology." It is also not a hermetic qualifier, which would preclude interdisciplinarity and cross-pollination, namely, with other "religious feminisms." Indeed, the new gender critics are using fresh approaches and reading tools. If Margot Badran writes that Islamic feminism is speaking from an "exclusively Islamic paradigm," she hastens to add that "even this is complicated." This is because, as she argues, scholars of Islamic feminism often use methodologies borrowed from both "classical" Islamic methodologies and the human sciences.[35] Some of these scholars, like the South African Sa'diyya Shaikh, declare that they borrow reading tools from Islamic modernist scholars, secular feminists, and feminist biblical scholars.[36]

To further clarify my point and define the content of the qualifier "islamic," I address what is often considered to be its "other," the term "secular." In my conception, the two adjectives are not necessarily conflicting or mutually exclusive. As Badran argues, "The terms religious and secular are not hermetically sealed terms; there are, and always have been, imbrications between the two."[37] This is to say that writing from an islamic gender position does not preclude writing from a secular position, as in the case of Abu Zayd or Mernissi. I must repeat here that I make a fundamental distinction between "secularist" and "secular."[38] I use "secularist" to describe a militant anti-religious stance that takes an ahistorical, literalist approach to religious texts and rejects what is seen as the misogynist essence of Islam. The term "secular" suggests an antidogmatic position, which does not approach religious texts apologetically or fail to consider their historicity. In this I am influenced by Edward Said's model of the "secular critic," who, as Bruce Robbins succinctly puts it, is characterized by "the refusal of orthodoxy and dogma . . . who submits to no authority."[39] The distinction is key in my conceptualization of an islamic gender critique because as I see it as open to non-Muslims and secular scholars alike, as well as to those who claim to be writing from a position of faith. Indeed the adjective "islamic," as I see it, does not fundamentally describe an identity or a faith position.

But why retain such a qualifier? What is Islamic about it? Or to use cooke's question: "Why call Islamic feminism Islamic if it is not a matter of *defending* a faith position? You might as well call such a critique a feminist critique of Islam that could apply to any kind of religion."[40] Why not call it, for instance, a "religious feminism," to use Nasr Hamid Abu Zayd's salutary phrase?[41] Basically, the adjective "islamic" serves to describe an intellectual commitment, as opposed to an intellectual distance or detachment, to redynamize islamic thought by posing new questions, which are enabled by new analytical tools along with traditional ones. Besides, I retain the adjective "islamic" while bearing in mind that there is no such a thing as "Islam" in the sense of a uniform and singular body of thought. If "Islam" must be defined, I prefer Talal Asad's useful concept of a "discursive tradition,"[42] which, in this dynamic sense, is neither inherently inimical to women's equality nor fundamentally impervious to the analytical tools provided by feminism, for instance. I also retain the term to stress that this gender critique is not alien to Islamic thought but actually represents a new engagement with it, and to foreground its affiliation with the Islamic reformist critiques of the Nahda. Hence also the word "critique," which suggests deconstruction and revision rather than simply or exclusively the retrieval of women's rights in the name of "the true egalitarian message of Islam." The term "gender," as a matter of fact, owes an undeniable debt to feminism, because it was feminist scholars who first appropriated and refined it. However, my preference for the phrase "gender critique," as opposed to "feminism," is related to my suggestion that Islamic feminism should amount to more than a "feminist *ijtihad,*" per se; that is, it should move beyond merely offering more liberal interpretations (*tafasir*) to generate a critical history that seeks to dismantle the mechanisms by which gender was constructed in orthodox scholarship in fixed terms. This task has already been undertaken by many scholars like Mernissi and others; but, as in the case of Mernissi, the critique has sometimes deviated from the deconstruction of truth as constructed by *fiqh,* toward the search for truth. Furthermore, the phrase also captures the broad gender issues with which most Islamic feminist scholars are concerned, beyond the exclusive concern for women's legal status.[43]

Le Harem Politique: Between the Subversion of Truth Claims and the Search for Authenticity

I now discuss the perils of Islamic feminist hermeneutics by undertaking a brief reading of Mernissi's important book *Le Harem Politique,* in which she investigates the authenticity of some misogynous *hadith*s, or statements attributed to the Prophet Muhammad, and offers a new reading of some Qur'anic verses. Her approach combines subversive elements with a more "mainstream" methodology. She foregrounds a refreshing contextual reading of some verses considered problematic regarding gender equality. As I noted above, her book is one of the first initiatives to offer a new reading of the Qur'anic verses dealing with women in the context of their production, rather than simply highlighting the egalitarian moments of the Qur'an to rhetorically argue that "Islam" is compatible with gender equality.

Mernissi starts by reminding her audience that the Qur'an originated in the form of oral statements that were subject to the immediate reactions of the first actors and the particular concerns of the Arabian society of the time. She stresses this interactive character of the Qur'an by showing how at times it responded to the questions of the first female converts, even the most feminist ones, in the jargon of the day. She also presents the Prophet Muhammad in his full humanity, as a lover and as a leader, who could be vulnerable to his social environment and the pressures of his companions and entourage, a price he had to pay for his desire to be as close as possible to his community. She then moves on to explore the broad context and atmosphere in which the verses dealing with the issue of the *hijab* (veil) came into being by explaining how the Qur'an defines *hijab* and the different requirements for Muhammad's wives. The aim is to suggest the historical contingency of what are often perceived as eternal divine prescriptions.

By considering the political, social, and psychological context in which those verses were produced, Mernissi's hermeneutics moves beyond the methodology of classical exegesis, or *tafsir,* to what is called *asbab al-nuzul,* "occasions of the revelation," which is a tool limited to the consideration of the immediate events that occasioned the revelation of a particular verse. Her work can also be seen as *building on* this tradition because *asbab al-nuzul* is a tool of historical analysis, even though it is not typically applied to the broader historical, social, and psychological environment. Her engagement of this tradition as a gender critic is noteworthy.

Another interesting instance of this productive interchange is Mernissi's critique of the work of one of the most important collectors of *hadith* in Sunni Islam, al-Bukhari. Mernissi follows the same methodology of verification that al-Bukhari and others have elaborated, that is, the *isnad,* which is basically concerned with authenticating statements attributed to the Prophet Muhammad by verifying the reliability of their transmitters, in order to prove the untruthfulness of some misogynous *hadith*s. In her inquiry, Mernissi asks the same questions posed by *isnad* methodology, yet with particular attention to the gender dimension. Once again building on a traditional methodology (in this case, *isnad*), Mernissi casts doubt on the authenticity of some of the *hadith*s contained in al-Bukhari's canonical text *Al-Sahih* (The Authentic) by questioning the credibility of the persons who reported them. The results of her inquiry may be seen as questioning the truth claims of *Al-Sahih* and highlighting the flaws of al-Bukhari's *isnad* methodology. By problematizing the truth claims of one of the most important sources of *hadith*s in Sunni Islam and one of the most significant references of *fiqh,* Mernissi's investigation can also be considered a problematization of *ta'sil,* the methodology behind the science of *fiqh*—that is, *usul al-fiqh*—which derives laws from passages found either in the Qur'an or the *Sunna,* the prophet's tradition.

Nevertheless, Mernissi's critique of authenticity and *ta'sil* is soon weakened by her own conclusion, which urges her Moroccan readers, or to use her own expression, "every good Maliki Muslim,"[44] to discard the *hadith*s she investigated as unsound and their transmitters as unreliable. This conclusion reveals her ambition, which is indeed fraught, to uncover and establish "new religious truths," an exceedingly difficult task. As mentioned above, a death fatwa was pronounced against Mernissi, and her book was subject to censorship, which suggests the ineffectiveness of her efforts to bestow legitimacy on her methodology and findings. To my mind, the kinds of conclusions she reaches serve only to undermine her methodology of problematizing truth claims. Indeed, she makes the inauthenticity of those particular *hadith*s an end in itself rather than a means for highlighting the inadequacy of the methodology of authentification as practiced by al-Bukhari, which relies on literalist and legalist readings of *hadith*s without considering their context. By so doing, Mernissi settles within the foundationalist logic and unwittingly reinforces the methodology of *ta'sil,* in which the Prophet Muhammad's statements and Qur'anic texts—regardless of their historical context—are considered statements of law that are binding upon all Muslims in all times. In sum, she does not challenge the essential goal of *isnad* methodology, which is to establish *hadith*s as authoritative sources of law alongside what are believed to be Qur'anic *prescriptions.* Here her conversation with the tradition gets short-circuited. She ends up affirming the principle of authenticity or authentification rather than leading the discussion toward the necessity of new reading methodologies like the contextual approach.

In my view, the methodology of the South African scholar Sa'diyya Shaikh, for instance, avoids some of the pitfalls of Mernissi's methodology. In her article "Knowledge, Women and Gender in the Hadith: A Feminist Interpretation," Shaikh presents new readings of some *hadith*s in order to counter androcentric theological interpretations without falling prey to authenticity claims.[45] One of the assumptions of Shaikh's study is that the

Prophet Muhammad came to reform and "ameliorate aspects of patriarchy without bringing the entire paradigm into question."[46] Shaikh admits that these *hadiths* reflect the patriarchal assumptions of their formative context, but she opposes "contemporary Muslim proponents of patriarchy [who] often look to those *hadiths* . . . as the justification for supporting sexism in Islam."[47] Rather than seeking to prove that misogynous *hadiths* are not authentic, she instead offers new readings of them in light of the historical, social, linguistic, and cultural context in which they originated.

Against Mernissi's approach, one can logically ask: What if the revision of *isnad* did not provide for the desired objective, which is here the unreliability of the transmitter? In other words: What if the *hadiths* are found to be authentic? One can also ask whether Mernissi's methodology, which may have succeeded with the particular *hadiths* she investigated, is likely to succeed with *all hadiths* voicing a patriarchal worldview. I am here especially thinking of the argument made by Abu Zayd and others regarding Qur'anic discourse, which is also applicable to the *hadith*. Abu Zayd suggests that because gender differentiation was an important feature of the society first addressed by the Qur'an, it is only natural that such differentiation would be reflected in Qur'anic dialogue with that society. This does not, however, mean that the Qur'an *espoused* this differentiation. Abu Zayd also contends that it is mistaken to consider dialogical or polemical expressions as *legislation* per se that Islam brought about or invented. He points out that the so-called legislative verses do not constitute more than one-sixth of the whole Qur'an.[48]

To my mind, one way to transcend the limitations of the search for authenticity is to ask new questions, such as those actually posed on occasion by Mernissi: What are the cultural, social, and ideological elements that inform religious texts? What do they tell us about the society of the time? What was the original tone in which a statement attributed to the Prophet Muhammad was uttered? But most important, were these texts or statements meant to be prescriptive or rather descriptive, as Abu Zayd would ask?

In his article "Qadiyyat al-Mar'ah bayna Sindan al-Hadatha wa Mitraqat al-Taqalid" (The "Woman Question" between the Hammer of Modernity and the Anvil of Tradition), Abu Zayd argues that, regarding the issue of "women in Islam," Islamic thought is unable to transcend what he refers to as "the crisis of interpretation and counterinterpretation."[49] Both opponents and proponents of gender equality employ the same strategy to bolster their respective positions, interpreting those Qur'anic passages that serve their interests as *asl,* the most original or truthful, and those that contradict their interests in such a way as to eliminate the undesired meaning.[50] Abu Zayd suggests that such selective readings reflect an inability to transcend the prevailing paradigm of Qur'anic exegesis, which does not consider the text's historical context, its communicative or dialogical aspect, or its descriptive dimension. To consider these dimensions of Qur'anic discourse, he insists, is not to deny its divine provenance.

Abu Zayd's criticism of the tendency to present one's own reading as *asl,* or the foundation, parallels my argument about the tendency toward foundationalism in "islamic feminist hermeneutics." This tendency not only results in the manipulation of the meaning and ideologization of the religious text, as Abu Zayd argues, but, most important for me here, ultimately reifies —by not subverting—the canonical approach to and understanding of these texts.[51] This is especially significant for a gender critique that aims to challenge the conception of Qur'anic passages as exclusively prescriptive and/or permanent statements of law that stand apart from the context of their emergence. In fact, Abu Zayd's goal in this article is to underscore the necessity of the contextual approach.

In addition to Abu Zayd's critique of what can be called "the *asl* reading methodology," or the foundationalist approach, Mohammed Arkoun's problematization of *ta'sil* or foundationalism in Islamic thought has also influenced my thinking on islamic feminist hermeneutics. Arkoun's problematization of the concepts of *asl* and *ta'sil* is deployed in a book published in Arabic with the provocative title *Al-Fikr al-Usuli wa Istihalat al-Ta'sil: Nahwa Tarikin Akhar li al-Fikr al-Islami,* which may be roughly translated as *Foundational Thought, or Foundationalism, and the Impossibility of Providing for Foundations/Foundationalism.*[52]

To briefly summarize Arkoun's argument, he deplores the way that *ta'sil,* the search for a given law's *asl* (origin or foundation) by relating it to God, ceased to be a genuine practice of *ijtihad* after the "classical" age of Islam ended in the thirteenth century. For him, the classical age (c. 632–1258) was an era of intellectual ferment characterized by the spirit of *munazara* (disputation, or *disputatio*), involving different scholars with different tendencies who used all the tools of analysis available to them.[53] It saw the reasoned debate between advocates of literal readings of the sources, such as the Ahl al-Hadith, who preferred adding the *Sunna* of the Prophet Muhammad as a second source of *ta'sil,* and proponents of reason and philosophy like the Mu'tazila.[54] The end of *ta'sil* as a scholarly quest and the beginning of *taqlid* (imitation), which is referred to in Sunni Islamic thought as *ighlaq bab al-ijtihad* (the closing of the gate of independent rea-

soning), is what Arkoun identifies as the beginning of "the dogmatic closure" (la clôture dogmatique). He illustrates how the acceptance of al-
Shafi's classification of usul al-fiqh in his Al-Rissala led to the constraints
on ta'sil and the marginalization of philosophy and the human sciences that
we see today in Islamic thought. He points out in this respect that we cannot be content with the imitation of early scholars' ta'sil, because every
statement uttered by a scholar referencing ta'sil was informed by the social,
historical, linguistic, and political framework within which the scholar
operated.[55] A contextual approach to the early scholarship would reveal
what has been silenced and "un-thought" in the process of ta'sil itself.[56]
Arkoun's project of applied Islamology (islamologie appliquée) aims to subvert this dogmatic closure through the incorporation of human sciences
methodologies.[57] Although some of Arkoun's pronouncements on ighlaq
bab al-ijtihad and taqlid are questionable,[58] his problematization of ta'sil
and emphasis on the need to apply social science methodologies to the study
of Islam remain valuable for an islamic gender critique that employs new
analytical categories and approaches.

Conclusion

To conclude, despite Mernissi's promising methodology, her failure to
claim the legitimacy and even primacy of the contextual approach and her
inability at times to move beyond the methodology of fiqh, or to create a
more productive conversation with it, ultimately reinforce foundationalist
thinking. I argue that so-called islamic feminism as formulated by Mernissi
and others should move beyond the search for truth and authenticity, beyond the search for the asl and the methodology of ta'sil. This is what I
mean by a "postfoundationalist islamic gender critique." I use "post" rather
than "ante" because such a gender critique engages the tradition as opposed
to simply ignoring or refuting it. Contextual readings of the Qur'an, which
some gender critics adopt, can be seen indeed as expanding rather than de-
parting from or opposing the classical methodologies of exegesis.

Notes

1. On the history of the emergence of "Islamic feminism," see Margot Badran, "Toward Islamic Feminisms," in Hermeneutics and Honor in Islamic/ate Societies, edited
by Asma Afsarrudin (Cambridge, Mass.: Harvard University Press, 1999), 166–67; Margot Badran, "Between Secular and Islamic Feminism/s: Reflection on the Middle East

and Beyond," *Journal of Middle East Women's Studies* 1, no. 1 (2005): 6–28; Margot Badran, "Islamic Feminism Revisited," February 10, 2006, http://www.countercurrents .org/gen-badran100206.htm; and Margot Badran, "Islamic Feminism: What's in a Name?" *Al Ahram Weekly Online,* January 17–23, 2002, http://weekly.ahram.org.eg/ 2002/569/cu1.htlm. See also miriam cooke, *Women Claim Islam: Creating Islamic Feminism through Literature* (New York: Routledge, 2001).

2. The phrase "Qur'anic ethos" is used by the African American scholar Amina Wadud in *Qur'an and Woman* (Kuala Lumpur: Penerbit Fajar Bakti Sdn. Bhd, 1992). The South African scholar Sa'diyya Shaikh uses the phrase "Qur'anic ethos"; see Sa'diyya Shaikh, "Exegetical Violence: *Nushuz* in Qur'anic Gender Ideology," *Journal for Islamic Studies* 17 (1997): 49–73, http://www.rightsathome.org/docs/dv/Saadiya.doc. In defining Islamic feminism, Badran argues that Islamic feminism, "which derives its understanding and mandate from the Qur'an, seeks rights and justice for women, and for men, in the totality of their existence"; Badran, "Islamic Feminism: What's in a Name?"

3. These findings concerning Umm Darda come from research undertaken by a scholar at the Oxford Center for Islamic Studies in Britain, Mohammad Akram Nadwi, who is writing a biographical dictionary of female *hadith* scholars. On this research, see Carla Power, "A Secret History," *New York Times,* February 25, 2007, http://select .nytimes.com/gst/abstract.html?res=F00916FE395A0C768EDDAB0894DF404482.

4. See Abdessamad Dialmy, "Un fiqh marocain et les droits de la femme du XVIe siècle," *Prologues: La réforme du droit de la famille cinquante années de débats* 2 (2002): 71–83. One of the changes introduced by the 2004 amended family law in Morocco, which pertains to the separation of property in the case of divorce, can be considered as a consecration of this fatwa, known as *al-Kad wa al-si'aya.*

5. See Badran, "Between Secular and Islamic Feminism/s," esp. 8.

6. Abdullahi An-Na'im, "The Dichotomy between Religious and Secular Discourse in Islamic Societies," in *Faith and Freedom: Women's Rights in the Muslim World,* edited by Mahnaz Afkhani (Syracuse: Syracuse University Press, 1995), 51–56; the quotation here is on 59.

7. Abderrazak Moulay Rchid, *La Femme et la loi au Maroc* (Casablanca: Le Fennec, 1991).

8. See Nilufer Gole, *The Forbidden Modern: Civilisation and Veiling* (Ann Arbor: University of Michigan Press, 1996); and Badran, "Toward Islamic Feminisms," 166–67.

9. Nadia Yassine is the daughter of Shaikh Abdessalam Yassin, the leader of the banned (but tolerated) Islamist group al-Adl wa al-Ihssan. She has declared that *fiqh* is misogynous, but also that her positions are not necessarily that of the group; see Nadia Yassine, "La jurisprudence musulmane est machiste," 2003, http://www.nadiayassine .net/fr/thema/11.htm. For more details on Yassine's position and views, see her Web site, at www.nadiayassine.net.

10. Ziba Mir Hosseini, discussion at the international workshop, "Reconsidering 'Islamic Feminism': Deconstruction or the Quest of Authenticity," Wissenshaftskolleg zu Berlin, Berlin, April 26–28, 2007.

11. Shaikh, "Exegetical Violence."

12. See, e.g., Asma Barlas, "Qur'anic Hermeneutics and Women's Liberation," paper presented at International Congress on Islamic Feminism, October 29, 2005, Barcelona, http://www.asmabarlas.com/TALKS/Barcelona.pdf.

13. Marnia Lazreg, "Decolonizing Feminism, " in *Feminism and Race,* edited by Kum Kum Bhavnani (Oxford: Oxford University Press, 2001), 8.

14. Cooke describes Zaynab al-Ghazali as an Islamist female militant who adopted a flexible position that allowed her to speak as a feminist in her prison memoirs and as an Islamist militant when opposing the Egyptian regime; cooke, *Women Claim Islam*, 86–92.

15. Mohammed Arkoun, *Humanisme et islam: Combats et propositions* (Paris: Librairie philosophique J. Vrin, 2005), 82–83.

16. Ibid., 82. Arkoun also states that, counter to the prevalent trend in Islamic studies and political science, he prefers to speak about "societies moulded by the Islamic fact" rather than "Muslim" or "Islamic" societies. Mohammed Arkoun, "Present-Day Islam between Its Tradition and Globalisation," Institute of Ismaili Studies, 2003, http://www.iis.ac.uk/view_article.asp?ContentID=101216; orig. pub. in *Intellectual Traditions in Islam,* edited by Farhad Daftary (London: I. B. Tauris and Institute of Ismaili Studies, 2000), 179–221.

17. Amina Wadud, *Inside the Gender Jihad: Women's Reform in Islam* (Oxford: Oneworld Publications, 2006).

18. Barlas, "Qur'anic Hermeneutics."

19. See Mernissi, interview by Serge Ménager, *Le Maghreb littéraire* 2, no. 4 (1996): 87–119.

20. Badran, "Between Secular and Islamic Feminism/s," 15.

21. Cooke argues that Islamic feminism is "not an identity but rather one of many possible speaking positions" which can be adopted by Islamists as well as secular intellectuals; cooke, *Women Claim Islam*, xxvii.

22. Fatima Mernissi, *The Veil and the Male Elite: A Feminist Interpretation of Women's Rights in Islam.,* translated by Mary Jo Lakeland (New York: Addison-Wesley, 1991); orig. pub. as *Le Harem Politique: Le Prophète et les femmes* [The Political Harem: The Prophet and women] (Paris: Albin Michel, 1987); and also available in a British edition: *Women and Islam: An Historical Enquiry* (Oxford: Basil Blackwell, 1991).

23. Cooke, *Women Claim Islam*, 61.

24. Though cooke's definition might be interpreted as excluding male scholars, she nevertheless acknowledges that there are also male scholars whom one can include in this typology. She offers the example of Abdullahi An-Nai'm (email message to the author, January 27, 2003).

25. See cooke, *Women Claim Islam;* and Nayereh Tohidi "'Islamic Feminism': Perils and Promises," *Middle East Women's Studies Review* 16, nos. 3–4 (Fall 2001–Winter 2002): 13–15, 27. See also Val Moghadam, "Islamic Feminism and Its Discontents: Towards a Resolution of the Debate," *Signs: Journal of Women in Culture and Society* 27, no. 4 (2002): 1135–71.

26. On the difference between religion and ideology, see, e.g., Arkoun's interview with Yves Lacoste, "L'Islam et les islams," *Hérodote* 35 (1984): 19–34, 20.

27. See Leila Ahmed, *Women and Gender in Islam: Historical Roots of a Modern Debate* (New Haven, Conn.: Yale University Press, 1992), 91.

28. See, e.g., Nasr Hamid Abu Zeid, "The Nineteenth Century" and "Rifaat Hassan and Others: Feminist Hermeneutics" in *Reformation of Islamic Thought* (Amsterdam: Amsterdam University Press, 2006).

29. Indeed, a number of scholars of "Islamic feminism" use the hermeneutical models, tools of analysis, or intellectual insights of "modernist" scholars of Islam. Amina Wadud and the South Africans Sa'diyya Shaikh and Naeem Jeenah declare, for instance,

their intellectual debt to Fazlur Rahman's scholarship. In the Maghreb, the Tunisian historian of Islam Latifa Lakhdar cites the influence on her methodology of Mohammed Arkoun's "applied Islamology." See Wadud, *Qur'an and Woman;* Shaikh, "Exegetical Violence"; Na'aeem Jeenah, "Towards an Islamic Feminist Hermeneutics," *Journal for Islamic Studies* 21 (2001): 36–70; and Latifa Lakhdar, *Imra'at al-Ijma'a* [The Woman of al-Ijma'] (Tunis: Cérés Edition, 2001).

30. For cooke, the adjective "Islamic" describes the commitment of Islamic feminists to *defend* their faith position. She asks the interesting question: "Why call Islamic feminism Islamic if it is not a matter of *defending* a faith position? You might as well call such a critique a feminist critique of Islam that could apply to any kind of religion" (email message to the author, July 30, 2003; my emphasis). The present chapter is also in a way a response to this question.

31. Yassine was declared an apostate by the Salafiya al-Jihadiya, an extremist Islamist organization repressed by the Moroccan state, especially after the terrorist attacks of May 16, 2004, in Casablanca. See her interview with Radio France Internationale, "Toutes Voiles Dehors," October 2, 2003, http://nadiayassine.net/fr/thema/11.htm.

32. *Aqida* is defined mainly as the belief in, among other things, the one God (*al-wahid al-ahad*), the angels, God's scriptures (*kutubihi*), his prophets, and the day of judgment.

33. On the subject of the constructedness of the concept of faith in contemporary Islamic thought and especially in Islamism, see Nasr Hamid Abu Zayd, "Qadiyyat al-Mar'ah bayna Sindan al-Hadatha wa Mitraqat al-Taqalid," in *Gender and Knowledge: Contribution of Gender Perspectives to Intellectual Formations,* edited by Ferial J. Ghazoul, *Alif: Journal of Comparative Poetics* Series (Cairo: American University in Cairo Press, 2000).

34. Cooke, *Women Claim Islam,* 153.

35. Badran, "Islamic Feminism: What's in a Name?"

36. In her article "Exegetical Violence," Shaikh cites her borrowing of the feminist hermeneutical model proposed by the biblical scholar Gerald West, as well as the influence of Fazlur Rahman. The title of a recent conference paper suggests that cross-pollination between the ideas of Islamic feminist scholars and biblical feminists goes in both directions; see Franz Volker Griefenagen, "Reading the Bible with Islamic Feminists Reading the Qur'an: Comparative Feminist Hermeneutics," paper presented at the annual meeting of Feminist Hermeneutics and the Bible, Toronto, 2002, http://www.projects.ex.ac.uk/fem.bible/toronto_2002.htm. The author describes his paper as arguing for the way "feminist hermeneutics of the Bible can fruitfully be informed by Islamic feminist readings of the Qur'an."

37. Badran, "Islamic Feminism: What's in a Name?"

38. See also Badran, "Between Secular and Islamic Feminism/s," which explores the intersections between what are often believed to be antithetical entities, secular feminism and Islamic feminism in the Middle East.

39. Bruce Robbins, "Secularism, Elitism, Progress, and Other Transgressions," *Social Text* 40 (1994): 25–37, 28.

40. This is from an email message to the author, July 30, 2003.

41. Abu Zayd, discussion at the international workshop "Reconsidering 'Islamic Feminism.'" Abu Zayd speaks from a position of the idea of fundamental commonality of religions.

42. Talal Asad, *The Idea of an Anthropology of Islam,* Center for Contemporary Arab Studies Occasional Paper (Washington, D.C.: Georgetown University Press, 1986), 14.

43. E.g., Amina Wadud is concerned with the issue of AIDS. See Wadud, *Inside the Gender Jihad,* chap. titled "Vulnerabilities: HIV and AIDS," 233–44.

44. Mernissi, *Harem Politique,* 81. The Maliki school is one of the four main schools of Islamic law, and the source for Moroccan family law.

45. Sa'diyya Shaikh, "Knowledge, Women and Gender in the Hadith: A Feminist Interpretation," *Islam and Christian-Muslim Relations* 15, no. 1 (2004): 99–108.

46. Ibid., 104.

47. Ibid., 100.

48. Abu Zayd, "Qadiyyat," 43.

49. Ibid., 60.

50. Ibid, 37.

51. For Abu Zayd, Islamic feminist scholars do not go beyond a certain ideologization of the Qur'an. See Zeid, "Rifaat Hassan and Others," 91.

52. See the introduction to Arkoun, *Al-Fikr al-Usuli wa Istihalat a-Ta'sil:Nahwa Tarikh Akhar li al-Fikr al-Islami,* translated by Hachem Saleh (Beirut: Dar Al Saqi, 1999), 7–16. This book is an Arabic translation of texts originally written by Arkoun in French.

53. He often argues that contemporary Muslims should imitate the example of these early scholars by using all the analytical tools available in the modern era, especially those provided by the human and social sciences.

54. Arkoun insists that the triumph of the first faction was more political than intellectual. In fact, during the caliphate of al-Ma'mun (783–833), the Mu'tazila's thought and doctrines were mainstream and dominant. However, under his successor, Caliph al-Mutawakkil, the Mu'tazila were persecuted.

55. Arkound, *Al-Fikr,* introduction.

56. Ibid., 11.

57. See Arkoun, "The Answers of Applied Islamology," *Theory Culture Society* 24, no. 2 (2007): 21–38.

58. E.g., the Islamic studies scholar Wael Hallaq has demonstrated that there has never been an *ijma'* (consensus) on *ighlaq bab al-ijtihad;* see Wael B. Hallaq, "Was the Gate of Ijtihad Closed?" *International Journal of Middle East Studies* 16, no. 1 (1984): 3–41. Mohammed Qassim Zaman suggests, moreover, that *taqlid,* often dismissed as "blind imitation," historically served as a framework for *ijtihad* and as a platform for change. See Mohammed Qassim Zaman, "Ijtihad and Religious Authority in Modern Islam: The Discourses of the Sunni 'Ulama'," paper presented at Zentrum Moderner Orient, Berlin, May 24, 2007; and Mohammed Qassim Zaman, *The Ulema in Contemporary Islam: Custodians of Change* (Princeton, N.J.: Princeton University Press, 2002).

Chapter 4

Embodied *Tafsir*: South African Muslim Women Confront Gender Violence in Marriage

Sa'diyya Shaikh

And among Allah's signs is this: that Allah created for you mates from among yourselves, that ye may dwell in tranquillity with them, and Allah has put love and mercy between your (hearts): verily in that are Signs for those who reflect. (Q30:21)[1]

In engaging with the challenges, joys, and trials within marriage, many Muslims derive inspiration from the Qur'anic teaching quoted above. According to this verse, cultivating a marriage based on love, mercy, and tranquillity brings to fruition a divine gift. More important, intimate relationships that embody these qualities also allow for the partners to reflect on the

This is a slightly altered version of an earlier paper published under the title "A *Tafsir* of Praxis: Gender, Marital Violence, and Resistance in a South African Muslim Community," in *Violence against Women and World Religions,* edited by Daniel Maguire and Sa'diyya Shaikh (Cleveland: Pilgrim Press, 2007), 66–89. I would like to thank both the reviewers of this chapter for their very helpful feedback.

very nature of God. Attaining and sustaining harmony in a marriage thus becomes a profound spiritual exercise for the believer. Another Qur'anic verse that echoes related notions of reciprocity as well a shared humanity for all men and women within the Muslim religious community is Qur'an 9:71: "And the believers, men and women, are protecting friends [awliya] one of another; they enjoin the right and forbid the wrong, and they establish worship and they pay the poor-due, and they obey Allah and Allah's messenger. As for these, Allah will have mercy on them. Lo! Allah is Mighty, Wise."[2]

Here the Qur'an defines friendship and unity as the basis of gender relationships more broadly. More especially, it states explicitly that moral, social, and religious agency is exactly the same for men and women alike, thereby articulating a fundamental assumption of gender equality as intrinsic to this supportive relationship between men and women. For many contemporary Muslims, these Qur'anic teachings resonate with Islam's deepest spiritual imperative for gender ethics. Because these Muslims are committed to gender egalitarianism, they find problematic the ways in which patriarchy pervades many of their communities around the world and, consequently, the dominant interpretations given to their holy scripture. They would argue that hierarchical gender power relations are fundamentally opposed to mutuality, genuine intimacy, and justice between men and women.

The Qur'anic verses quoted above also provide some of the scriptural basis for feminist critiques of hierarchy and nonegalitarian gender relations in Muslim societies. Many Islamic feminists approach the Divine Word as an active and dynamic hermeneutical encounter.[3] Revelation speaks to human beings who are constantly striving to reach a progressively deeper understanding of God and the nature of human realities. Within this view, tafsir (i.e., Qur'anic exegesis) incorporates human conceptions of justice and equality that continually reshape the dynamic and emerging social texts of Islam. Traditional and religious epistemological tenets are thus in a state of continuous creation and re-creation. In this manner, religious ethics emerge as a process of human interpretations of and engagements with the Divine. An approach of this nature also acknowledges that Islamic principles, as expressed in Qur'anic verses, have always been interpreted in light of contextual realities dictated by specific social structures, cultural norms, and the forces at play in specific historical moments.[4]

A rival view in some Muslim communities, however, sees Islam as a useful ideological abettor of patriarchy.[5] Proponents of such a perspective may cite alternative Qur'anic verses that appear to highlight hierarchy between men and women as the foundation for their views, and thus they call attention to this verse: "Divorced women shall wait concerning themselves for three monthly periods. Nor is it lawful for them to hide what God has created in their wombs, if they have faith in God and the Last Day. And their husbands have the better right to take them back in that period, if they wish for reconciliation. And women shall have rights similar to the rights against them, according to what is equitable; but men have a degree [of advantage] over them. And God is Exalted in Power, Wise" (Q2:228). The following verse is also used to justify polygyny: "If you fear that you shall not be able to deal justly with the orphans, marry women of your choice, two or three or four; but if you fear that you shall not be able to deal justly [with them], then only one, or [a captive] that your right hands possess, that will be more suitable, to prevent you from doing injustice" (Q4:3).[6]

Debates among proponents of religious views that showcase gender hierarchy and male dominance over women on one hand, and those that support gender equality and social justice on the other, are present in most religions of the world. The fact that many of the scriptures of various faiths themselves exhibit a tension between gender hierarchy and gender egalitarianism is also a salient feature of this debate. That gender ethics are also dynamic and contextually determined invites believers to constantly engage these tensions within the text.

Within many traditions, those who oppose patriarchy have critiqued male dominance in their religion. Feminist scholars in particular have shown that many normative religious ideas pass as objective and neutral theological knowledge, while in fact they represent the cumulative product of male interpretations of social reality.[7] Indeed, these interpretations represent primarily the views of elite male scholars living in societies in which patriarchy is and has been the norm. By engaging in efforts to challenge the overwhelming male biases inherent in much religious scholarship, feminist theory has focused on the lived experiences of women as a conceptual category to redress the historical gender imbalance.[8]

Methodologically, contemporary Islamic feminist exegetes, such as Amina Wadud and Asma Barlas, have argued against patriarchal perspectives on gender within the Qur'an by bringing into focus the fact that, despite a seeming ambiguity, the Qur'an's overall ethos strongly supports gender equality.[9] Thus, these Islamic feminists and others have shown that verses reflecting patriarchal norms are symptomatic of the historical moment in which they were revealed.[10]

The biases inherent in these verses represent a descriptive dimension of the Qur'an that speaks in relation to the existing gendered assumptions of seventh-century Arabia. These scholars have argued that such contextual biases do not reflect the central ethical teachings of the Qur'an. On the basis of these important hermeneutical principles, it appears that there is space for a perspective to be more fully developed within contemporary feminist exegesis of the Qur'an. I propose a Qur'anic hermeneutics that purposefully takes into consideration the lived experiences of Muslim women when seeking to understand gender ethics in the Qur'an. Such a view amplifies the growing awareness that intellectual labor addressing the development of Islamic ethics needs to accept direction from and remain responsive to the contextual lived realities of marginalized and alienated sectors of Muslim communities.

In light of the high levels of gender violence internationally, I hold that Qur'an 4:34 particularly demands reinterpretation from the perspective of women's experience. This verse reads as follows:

> Men are [qawwamun] protectors and maintainers of women,
> because God has given the one more [strength] than the other,
> and because they support them from their means.
> Therefore the righteous women are devoutly obedient,
> and guard in [the husband's absence]
> what God would have them guard.
> As to those women on whose part you fear
> [nushuz] disloyalty and ill conduct.
> Admonish them [first], refuse to share their beds [next]
>   and [last] [wa adribuhunna] strike them [lightly].
> But if they return to obedience
> seek not against them means [of annoyance]
> for God is the most high, Great [above you all].[11]

That this verse reflects the gender mores of the seventh-century Arabian context should be quite clear. Yet it may and has been used in the contemporary era to support patriarchal ideologies. In this manner, the verse seems to provide the scriptural basis for a general marital hierarchy and may be interpreted as permission for men to assault their spouses. From the perspective of feminist theory, exegetes have suggested that such interpretations are isolated from the historical and sociological context and culture in which Qur'anic revelation occurred, as well as its approach to social reform.[12] Stripped of context, such interpretations reflect an approach to the text that is naive and simplistic, and consequently often results in the suffering of women and children, which paradoxically is what the Qur'an tries repeatedly to halt.

Here I discuss the results of a feminist qualitative research project. I conducted in-depth, lengthy interviews with eight Muslim women between the ages of twenty-eight and forty-three years in the greater Cape Town area in 1994–95. I recruited participants through local community social service centers. They were all survivors of violent physical abuse by their husbands or ex-husbands from Indian or Malay communities. Seven of the eight participants were either separated or divorced, while one was still married at the time of the interviews. Respondents were asked open-ended questions from a semistructured interview schedule that I had jointly constructed with two counselors who had worked extensively with battered women. One of these counselors was herself a survivor of a violent previous marriage.

In the pages that follow, I examine the manner in which ordinary Muslim women, who have survived violence at the hands of their husbands, consider the ethical dimensions that surround interpretations of Qur'an 4:34. By doing so, I engage Qur'anic hermeneutics in a way that is informed by the lived realities of Muslim women. In effect, I examine the social world of the Qur'anic text in a contemporary South African Muslim context. I call attention to the way in which ordinary women engage, interpret, contest, and redefine the dominant understandings of Islam. I also place emphasis on the ways in which their engagement might inform some of the ethical conundrums that emerge from interpretations of the Qur'an that are ahistorical and decontextualized. This often invisible community of the text, through its explicitly experiential grappling with Qur'anic ethics, offers us a "*tafsir* through praxis."

My approach is an alternative to the standard conceptions of *tafsir* or exegesis that emphasize a distant, cerebral, and dispassionate engagement with scripture that is characteristic of male scholarship. Such conceptions obscure the fact that dominant interpretations are reflective of male experiences of reality. Rather, my approach explicitly brings into focus the manner in which a group of Muslim women reflect on and discuss the text and engage God, ethics, and religion via *their experience* of suffering and oppression. They emerge with an understanding of Islam that often has a very different ethical perspective from that of traditional male scholars, their husbands, and male clerics in their communities. I argue that the experiences of these women and how they relate these to their understandings of Islam constitute a legitimate form of *tafsir*. On the basis of this argument, it then becomes necessary to transform and redefine traditional boundaries of what qualifies as Qur'anic exegesis.

Exegetical Glimpses of Verse 34 in the
Qur'an's Chapter on the Woman (al-Nisa')

Here, I offer a selective review of various approaches to the exegesis of verse 34 in the Qur'an's chapter on "the Woman" (al-Nisa'). These approaches range from the interpretations of classical male scholars to those of contemporary women exegetes. Although these approaches exhibit different understandings of gender, they all commonly assume that *tafsir* or Qur'anic exegesis is essentially a scholarly, hermeneutical enterprise. My review provides a broader historical context for understanding the diverse ways in which Muslims have interpreted the ethics of Qur'an 4:34.[13]

In the classical tradition, the *tafasir* (plural of *tafsir*) of Abu Jafar al-Tabari (839–922), Abu Qasim al-Zamakshari (1075–1144), and Fakhr al-Din al-Razi (1149–1210) are regarded highly in the community of Islamic scholars.[14] However, despite the great richness, diversity, and sophistication of their contributions to Qur'anic exegesis, their interpretations of Qur'an 4:34 were heavily influenced by the gender norms characteristic of their cultural and historical contexts.[15] By focusing on how each of these scholars interpreted two particular concepts in this verse—namely, *qawwamun* (men as "protectors and maintainers" of women) and *wa adribuhunna* ("to strike" one's spouse)—I illustrate the impact of context on exegesis.

The first part of the verse makes a broad statement about the nature of marital relations by stating: "Men are the protectors and maintainers [*qawwamun*] of women, because God has given the one more strength than the other." In Tabari's view, the relationship of *qiwama* (men's role as protectors and maintainers of women) was a material preference that God granted to men with regard to their spouses.[16] He read this "preference" to imply the financial duty of men to give their wives a marriage dowry (*mahr*) and material maintenance (*nafaqa*).[17] Thus Tabari saw the relationship of *qiwama* as hinging on a socioeconomic phenomenon instead of some inherent quality of a man or woman per se. Two hundred years later, also during the rule of the Abbassid Caliphate, Zamakshari reinterpreted *qiwama* as simply the rule (*musaytirun*) of men over women.[18] In his opinion, the male-female relationship paralleled the relationship between a sovereign political leader and a male citizen. Thus, in the same way that a political leader commands his subjects to perform or abstain from particular acts, so men regulate the behavior of women.[19] This analogy was largely derived from the context of twelfth-century Muslim society, in which autocratic monarchs wielded extensive power and authority over male citizens. Zamakshari's *tafsir* accordingly reflected the prevailing political and social realities of his time.

Further, Zamakshari asserted that the relationship of *qiwama* was premised on "natural" preferences that God had granted to men over women.[20] Writing a generation after Zamakshari, Razi, the Asharite, held a similar view.[21] Both Zamakshari and Razi believed that men were naturally gifted with several superior attributes, ranging from intellect and determination to literacy and horsemanship.[22] and by virtue of such superior attributes, these scholars argued, men should be natural leaders in the areas of religion, politics, the judiciary, and marriage.[23] In deriving a set of criteria for determining differences between men and women, Zamakshari and Razi conflated biology and social construction. For them, the notion of intrinsic and natural differences between men and women was at the core of their assumptions about human nature. Such a religious understanding of intrinsic differences between men and women reflected the normative gender ideology and roles that characterized the social, cultural, and historical realties and experiences of these exegetes.

The second element of the verse relating to *adribuhunna,* the notion of a husband physically striking his wife, reads: "As to those women on whose part you fear [*nushuz*] disloyalty or ill conduct, admonish them [first], refuse to share their beds [next] and [last] strike them [*wa adribuhunna*]." Tabari interpreted *wa adribuhunna* as a measure of last resort in disciplining a disobedient wife. He stated that it involved striking her "without hurting her [*gayr mubara*]."[24] Razi was far less inclined to offer an endorsement of violence. In his interpretation of this part of the verse, he noted that that while hitting is permissible, it was much better to refrain from this.[25] The pronouncement from Razi that abstaining from wife beating is desirable was accompanied by a quote from the *hadith* in which the Prophet Muhammad said that men who beat their wives are "not among the better men."[26] Razi suggested that this *hadith* was a clear admonition against hitting women. He suggested that the raison d'être for the three-step resolution of conflict process—first to admonish, then to separate beds, and finally to strike—was to curb (existing) male violence.[27] Even though Razi accepted that men may ultimately, as a last resort, engage in *darb* (striking), he tried to minimize its potentially violent aspects by stating that only a folded handkerchief or *miswak* (a small twig used as a toothbrush) could be used to this effect.[28] This recommendation implies that *darb* merely symbolizes male authority, a point that Razi seemed quite willing to accept. He made concerted attempts to substantially reduce the violent potential of *darb* by means of interpretation.

Unlike Razi, Zamakshari unapologetically condoned violence in his interpretation of *darb*. He quoted a *hadith* in which the Prophet Muhammad is reported to have told a husband, "Hang your whip in such a place that the family can see it."[29] However, Zamakshari conceded that this *hadith* has a weak chain of narration, which implied that it is likely to be inauthentic. This type of interpretation and narrative provides theological legitimacy for a perspective that sanctions male violence against women. Even Razi, who suggested practical alternatives to violence, still maintained—albeit at a symbolic level, and actually as the third step of last resort—that husbands had the right to physically discipline disobedient wives. Despite the fact that they clearly differed on the question of the acceptability of male violence, these exegetes' interpretations of the Qur'an were based on a gender ideology that was hierarchical and masculinist. It is evident, therefore, that the classical *tafasir* reflect premodern, patriarchal assumptions that systematically served to silence women's voices.

Contemporary Muslim women scholars—such as Amina Wadud, Asma Barlas, Maysum Faruqi, Riffat Hassan, and Azizah al-Hibri—have also conducted Qur'anic exegesis.[30] Their interpretations of Qur'an 4:34 draw on the classical *tafasir* but at the same time contest much of the premodern gender ideology. Despite varying interpretive nuances, these contemporary female exegetes place a special emphasis on visions of gender justice and universal human dignity in their understanding of the Qur'an.

These feminist-oriented exegetes usually interpret Qur'an 4:34 in relation to other Qur'anic verses that address relations between men and women. Scholars such as Wadud and Barlas have argued that Qur'an 4:34 was an attempt to ameliorate highly specific and contextually based seventh-century gender norms, and as such it is not universally applicable. In keeping with Tabari's position, many of these scholars suggest that *qiwama* should be limited to the material support roles that men have occupied regarding women, given the latter's role in childbearing. Yet, these scholars argue, such gender relations are not static but reflect one of many possible ways to establish equitable roles and responsibilities.

Regarding the question of striking one's wife, these scholars have suggested that Qur'an 4:34 introduced a pragmatic three-step solution in an ef-

fort to phase out spousal violence in seventh-century Arabia, where such violence against women was considered acceptable. The view of these interpreters is that the verse is descriptive of the gender norms that characterize
the context in which the revelation occurred, rather than a prescription for
how men and women should relate to each other. It is noteworthy that both
the premodern Razi and contemporary feminists share a *descriptive* rather
than a *prescriptive* interpretation of violence in their readings of Qur'an
4:34. However, contemporary feminists have insisted that spousal violence
is contrary to the logic and spirit of the Qur'an. They propose a reading of
the Qur'an that is holistic, arguing that all verses should be read in terms of
the abiding Qur'anic concern for creating social justice. Where there are
tensions about gender issues, the argument is that the Qur'anic themes of
justice, moral agency, and human equality should be unconditionally prior-
itized. Wadud, for example, argues that by means of the various gender reforms that the Qur'an put into place in seventh-century Arab society, the
Qur'an began a trajectory of gender transformation that Muslims should
continue to develop.[31] In a similar fashion, Barlas asserts that the Qur'an
holds within it possibilities to envisage gender equality that are progressive
and expansive.[32]

Despite the various perspectives reflected in both premodern male and
contemporary feminist exegeses, all exegetes bring their own experiences
and knowledge of women's experiences in general, including ideas of gender relations, to their interpretations of the Qur'an. To this extent, my focus
on the perspectives of women who have endured marriages characterized
by violence expands the range of experiential perspectives that inform understandings of Qur'anic ethics as it relates to marital relations and practices. More important, the unique positioning of these women brings to the
tafsir discourse a contemporary social world of the text and the urgent imperative of engaging gender ethics in Islam.

Negotiating Gender and an "Embodied *Tafsir*"

The women I interviewed revealed that they had been socialized and educated to accept that traditional gender roles and marital hierarchy were
religiously ordained. Although they were married, many in their social
constellation—including their families, communities, and religious leaders
—had offered no active support in resisting their husbands' violent behavior or in condemning such behavior. For many participants, Islam was of-

ten presented as the rationale for women to remain in their marriages, regardless of how difficult it was. Nonetheless, my findings suggest that these women actively contested the dominant patriarchal perspective of Islam. By experiencing violence, these participants developed their own sense of religious identity that challenged gender hierarchy in religious terms. Their lived responses to violence present a different mode of exegesis and interpretation of Qur'anic ethics. I call this lived response a "*tafsir* through praxis" or an "embodied *tafsir*" that emerged from experiences of pain, marginality, and oppression—realities that the Qur'an itself constantly seeks to address.[33] I now explore and analyze some of the themes that emerged from the women's realities in more detail.

Men's Role as Protectors and Maintainers of Women

All the women interviewed had grown up in families that considered traditional gender roles and male authority as the religious norm. When asked to define a good Muslim woman, many participants referred to themes of virginity before marriage, sexual fidelity during marriage, appropriate Islamic dress that included covering of the hair, being a good mother, and ensuring education of the children. Only a few of the women also stated that regular prayer was characteristic of a good Muslim woman.

Chastity was strongly connected to religious identity for many participants. When they were girls, it had been impressed upon them that virginity was a religious virtue for women. One interviewee, Fatima, told how her parents' concern about her sexuality had caused them to pressure her into an early marriage rather than pursuing further studies: "As a young Muslim girl, my parents feared for me. . . . I suppose it's natural for any parent to fear for their daughters. But I still feel that they knew what kind of person I was, and that I could look after myself, like you know, I was never really interested in boys, I was more interested in my studies." Another interviewee, Shayda stated: "There was only one thing I was taught by my mother about sex when I was young. She said that when a man uses you, there's a first time, then he breaks you and he takes your *izzat* [honor] away, so always look after yourself. So I always looked after myself, I never let any boys touch me. . . . You know how strict the Indian community and the Indian culture is, especially where a woman's *izzat* is concerned, where the pride is concerned. My mother brought us up very strict."

These quotations show the centrality of sexuality—associated with anxiety, danger, and honor—in defining women's value. Shayda's mother's description of sexual relations contains strong images of male aggression and violation: Men "use" and "break" women's bodies. In response to male sexuality that is framed by women—especially responsible adult women—as predatory, a woman's honor and worth are made dependent on her remaining a virgin. Yet not one member of the sample spoke of the religious importance of male chastity. In fact, in many of the narratives there was an implicit assumption that women were required to be vigilant because men were sexual opportunists who prey on women. Thus, in these narratives, men and women are considered to be accountable to very different standards of sexual ethics.[34]

For all the participants, the definition of a "good Muslim woman" was consistently associated with modest dressing and chastity. As such, female religiosity was collapsed with sexual propriety. Many respondents also said that being a "good mother" and a "good wife" was integral to their religious life, suggesting a relational and familial notion of religious identity. For these women, religiosity was related to the quality of one's interpersonal relationships, especially those that relate to the domestic and social spheres. The participants tended to respond to formal questions regarding their religious identity with gender-stereotypical statements. Yet, from their stories it was clear that they responded to real-life situations by challenging traditional gender stereotypes, sometimes in explicitly religious terms. In actual situations, as we will see, the women presented an articulation of Islam that demanded justice and contested traditional gender constructs. Their need to challenge the prevailing gender ideologies becomes especially clear when examining their marital experiences.

Marital Violence, Female Subjectivity, and Family Responses

The participants described their marriages in ways that revealed extremely hierarchical power dynamics. The women reported extremely controlling behavior by their husbands that included restricting their movements, randomly searching their bags, restricting them from pursuing further education, and keeping them isolated from friends, family, and other potential support networks.

The participants described being forced to endure excessive levels of violence and aggression in their marriages. One respondent told how her husband had brandished a gun at her. Others reported being hit in the face with the butt of a gun, being beaten with lead wires, and being partially strangled. Another participant told of being attacked with a knife and sustaining injuries of such severity that she required stitches on her face. The extremely violent nature of these relationships was expressed in the form of fear among all participants that they might be killed by their husbands. Their experiences are a record of the everyday brutality and violence that some women experience in their marital relationships.

Many of the participants reported that they were taught as part of their religious upbringing to remain married, regardless of the difficulties they experienced with their spouses. These religious teachings had been a central influence on their decision to remain in their marriages despite the marriages' violent nature. Jaynub, a thirty-year-old woman with three children, stated that remaining married even though she suffered physical abuse was in keeping with her understanding of the Islamic virtues of patience and female obedience: "Islamically, you are brought up to be obedient as a girl, taught to make *sabr* [patience], so I took the beatings as much as I could. . . . And finally, when I couldn't take it anymore, I did run to my parents' home. My mother used to tell me to go back and me, being the obedient child, used to listen and go back. . . . As for my father, when I go home he never ever wants to know what's going on in my marriage. Even now, when I go home with a problem, he walks past like he doesn't hear me—like he doesn't *want* to hear me and he doesn't *want* to listen."

As was the case for many of the others, members of Jaynub's family played a role in facilitating her husband's abusive behavior. She had been socialized into believing that as a Muslim woman, she was expected to be obedient and submissive. Despite being an adult married woman, she described herself as the "obedient child" who followed her mother's advice to return to her husband after being assaulted by him. Her father's lack of involvement and failure to intervene in this situation reflect his complicity in and possible indifference to his daughter's plight. It may also reflect his powerlessness to act, given that a patriarchal power structure dictates that once authority over a woman passes from her father to her husband, her father no longer has any influence. In effect, whatever the underlying rationale, his behavior sustains an abusive patriarchal structure. The fact that her parents failed to intervene served to legitimize and normalize her husband's abuse. Their silence ultimately denied their daughter her claim to physical safety and her complete value as an individual human being.

Several participants also called attention to their family's silence in response to the abuse they suffered. Jaynub stated:

After the abuse, when I went back to my family's home, he would come to my mother and apologize for his behavior. She would say to him [the husband], "Come and sit here." She said that he is another person's child and she will always listen to him. That was the problem as well. She shouldn't have done that. If that happened to my daughter, I won't say come and sit down here, I'll really give it to him. That's the problem— it was almost like he was encouraged.

Anisa said:

> I used to feel anger inside me when he use to come to my people, and they all talked to him so nicely and they forgot what he's done and what he is doing to me. I used to ask them, "Why are you so nice to him and you don't even ask him why he is doing that to your daughter?" They did nothing at all!

Several participants reported that their families did not hold their husbands accountable for his violence. On the contrary, their congeniality and tolerance toward the aggressive husband appeared to actively enable his behavior. In this study, battered women expressed their experiences of acute alienation from their family that stemmed from a lack of social and family support. Religious and cultural constructions that idealize female obedience and submissiveness, premised on assumptions of marital hierarchy, thwarted collective social resistance to abusive marital power relations.

Women's Agency and Religious Contestations

Even though they received little support from people in their social constellations, almost all the participants in the study contested their husbands' violence in ethical and religious terms. Often they directly challenged their husbands. Shayda said:

> After he hits me, he doesn't even say "I am sorry for the way I hit you." He just goes on to ask Allah *ma'af* [forgiveness]. I say, "How can you ask Allah *ma'af* when you didn't even ask me for *ma'af*? You think Allah will accept your *ma'af*? He won't accept it!"

Farida said:

> When I ask him "How can you hit me and then go to the mosque and pray?" then it ends up with him hitting me again for just saying that because it hurts him.

Fatima said:

> As the years went by, I could never get myself to make *salat* [prayer]
> with this man. I couldn't let him stand in front of me [i.e., lead me in
> prayer], knowing that he is not a leader that I could respect, not even as
> a husband. . . . And it's just because he ill-treats me so badly.

For all the participants, ideals of being close to God and upholding Islamic principles are incompatible with spousal violence. By proclaiming
that God will not accept an abusive husband's petition for forgiveness before the husband seeks forgiveness from his wife, Shayda implicitly argued
that ethical human relationships are integral to one's relationship with God.
Farida brought into focus the ethical contradiction between her husband's
physical abuse and his subsequent attendance at the mosque to pray. Fatima
stated that she felt unable to pray behind her abusive husband. She rejected
both the leadership and the religious integrity of a man who was violent with
her. For these women, physically abusing others without genuine repen-
tance was never justifiable according to Islamic principles. They believed
that God took their humanity seriously enough so as not to forgive those
who consistently abused them. For these women, Islam offered an ethical
framework that demanded a social covenant among believers as a prereq-
uisite for a meaningful God-human relationship.

In conversation with the participants, an "embodied *tafsir*" emerged in
which violence on the part of men was viewed as incompatible with the
practice of Islam and the conduct expected of believers. In the process of
recounting their experiences, the women revealed their understandings of
the nature of God, which suggested that God is just and demands that human beings account for the injustices they perpetrate against one another.
Moreover, God is the antithesis of violence, and it is unacceptable for believing men to supplicate God after violating another human being. In their
discussions, an image emerged of God as an omniscient being who witnesses the suffering of the oppressed and who will not accept the brutality
and religious hypocrisy of the violent oppressor. By experiencing physical
and psychological trauma, the participants believed that they had engaged
in an existential struggle in coming to know God, understand human behavior, and uphold religious ethics. Their experience of spousal abuse as an
extreme form of patriarchy caused them to think deeply about what it meant
to be a human being. What emerged from this existential engagement was
an Islamic ethical and theological framework that presents a challenge to

misogynistic and opportunistic religious perspectives on women and explicitly interrogates the legitimacy of spousal abuse on the basis of religion. Their interpretations, or "embodied *tafsir*," amount to a feminist contestation of patriarchal understandings of Qur'anic teachings and a clear indictment of an interpretation of Qur'an 4:34 as a license to physically abuse women.

The women also objected more broadly to the religious justification of nonegalitarian marital relationships and what they perceived as the mismatch between beliefs and practices in their communities. Maryam said:

> I accept Islam and I respect it very much as my religion. So Islam is not the excuse just because these men have got Muslim names and use Islam for their own purposes. . . . It's an individual person himself actually that is to blame. But I will think twice before I marry a Muslim man again; . . . maybe it's the way we are brought up in an Islamic culture. At work I've heard the white girls speak of their husbands, how they work together, how they respect each other and how they help one another, while both are working. . . . We don't get that support from our Muslim men; for Muslim men, their wives . . . are like maids—we are like slaves.

Farida said:

> Muslim men, especially religious ones, have the idea that they are above women. . . . But it is also the kind of person I am. I am very proud of being Muslim, although I am not very religious.

The view of these women was that Muslim men were socialized into believing that they were superior to women. Maryam attributed the gender power imbalance partially to what she called "Islamic culture." She had been exposed to non-Muslim ("white") couples and admired their marriages because they appeared to be based on mutuality, shared responsibility, and partnership. This presented a stark contrast to her personal experience of male domination in a Muslim marriage. By stating that her ethical ideals for relationships were reflected in marriages between non-Muslims, she clearly implied criticism of the dominant mode of gender relations within the Muslim community.

Farida stated that "especially religious" men assumed that they were "above" women. She indicated that she believed that Muslim men considered hierarchical modes of gender relations as the religious norm. Her refusal to accept these norms led her to consider herself "not very religious." Thus, in her understanding, her rejection of patriarchy meant that she was located outside the circle of religiosity. Yet she stated that she felt proud of her Muslim identity, despite being unable to accept hierarchy and inequality between men and women. The dissonance she experienced was a direct consequence of the harmful impact of sexism in her experience of Muslim social practices. Her ambiguity was a reflection of a broader tension experienced by many Muslim women. On the one hand, Islam calls for treating human beings in a just, fair, respectful, and egalitarian manner. On the other hand, Islam also appears to be characterized by an underlying hierarchal gender ideology. Farida's position indicates the need to popularize among Muslims feminist articulations of Islam that contest discriminative gender practices and prioritize the Islamic emphasis on gender justice and women's equality.

One participant, Shamima, indicated an engagement with Islam that reflects a more singular and problematic internalization of patriarchy. She said:

I must try and adapt to him, start living like a proper Muslim. . . . He lives like a good Muslim should, and if I live like that too, there will be less hassles because I will be praying five times a day, and if you do it every day, it will be on your mind, and I'll be a different person; . . . then you say to yourself, I shouldn't get angry because I just prayed five minutes ago. . . . Before, I said what I wanted to say and did what I wanted to do. I'll be more careful now, communication will be better, and there will be less violence, but it has got to also come from inside of me.

While Shamima was also considered ending her marriage, she was the only participant who stayed with her husband despite severe conflict and violence. She maintained that her husband was a good Muslim because he prayed regularly, and she saw no contradiction between his violent behavior and his purported religiosity. Unlike other participants, her idea of being a good Muslim did not necessarily mean that her husband was compelled to engage in a fair and basically decent, respectful relationship. In fact, she took responsibility for the abuse by saying that if she changed her behavior and became a better Muslim, her husband would not be compelled to assault her. In Shamima's view of Islam, women ideally acquiesced, endured, and persevered, and did not express their needs. The internalization of religious constructs of this nature inevitably undermines resistance to male violence and supports conditions under which patriarchy may flourish.

Community, Imams, and Religious Authority

All the participants stated that they had consulted Muslim scholars ('*ula-ma*') or clerics to play a mediating role in situations of marital conflict. Two themes occurred repeatedly in conversations between these women and the '*ulama*'. First, these '*ulama*' made consistent attempts to keep the marriage together at the expense of the women's well-being. This practice was in keeping with a "reconciliation at all costs" approach. Shayda stated:

> They [the '*ulama*'] don't care about the pain and abuse that the women are experiencing because even now, even after all this abuse, this imam said "I am not performing any *talaq* [divorce], I'm not doing anything, because I believe in reconciliation." Even after what I told him, even after what he knows I'm going through, what my children are going through, that's the answer I got.[35]

Second, a consistent theme in these conversations with clerics was that the responsibility for the abuse rested with the women themselves. For example, Maryam described her visits to the local '*ulama*' offices in the following manner:

> I use to sit there for hours waiting to see one of them. Finally, when they did see me, all of those imams said the same thing: "What do you do to make him so angry?". . . They always said "You and your husband must come together and you must talk."[36]

Farida noted:

> The imam's attitude is like I am the one at fault. At the end of the day, it was my husband. It's like the violence and abuse meant nothing to them. And it *was* a big thing.

It is apparent that the responses from the '*ulama*' reflected in these excerpts abet male violence. By refraining from criticizing, challenging, or explicitly condemning the husband's behavior, the '*ulama*' actually facilitated and enabled the systems of male violence. Maryam stated that she thought this clerical bias was due to their male subjectivity. She stated: "The problem with these *shaykhs* [religious leaders] is that because they are men, they often side with the husband." Anisa noted that the '*ulama*' were unable to empathize with her experience:

To tell you honestly, because of all the beating, there's something inside that happened to me. . . . Even though there was love originally, that love turns to hatred and disgust and all these horrible feelings toward that person. You just can't help it, but when I speak to the imam and I tell him how I feel, he says, "Oh, but you mustn't say these things, it is not Muslim and it's not Islamically right." Then I tell him, "But I'm telling you how I feel. This is how I feel, it's the truth, why must I lie, because that's how I feel and it's this man that's caused this feeling inside." It's just natural I suppose, because of the way I've been ill treated. That's another thing about these imams, I don't know, because I think they are not also trained in that way to really help the people.

Anisa's remarks highlight an important gap in the education of the 'ulama'. In their religious training, they were typically not schooled in counseling, mediation, or communication skills. The assumption was that because they had studied the Arabic language and the premodern Islamic legal and exegetical canon, this somehow had equipped them to offer pastoral services. In reality, the converse was true. The fact that their training emphasized an intellectual legacy formed in the context of premodern gender norms tended to suggest that patriarchy was intrinsic to Islam. What was not included in their studies was an active engagement with Islamic gender ethics as a living, dynamic, and contextually unfolding phenomenon. This omission was a serious aporia in their discourse and also served to present "official" Islam as embodying a stagnant, ahistorical perspective on gender that emerged from patriarchal readings of the text. This static and male-centered perspective was reflected in the interview with Anisa, where the alim (religious scholar) showed no sensitivity to her pain and condemned her negative feelings toward the batterer as "un-Islamic." He did not denounce the husband's violence as "un-Islamic." As such, he used "Islam" to silence the woman's emotional response to the abuse she suffered. Anisa, however, asserted that her feelings were important and could not be dismissed in this context. By insisting, "But that is how I feel!" she powerfully maintained that her emotional and affective reaction to violence could not be altered by external judgments about ideal Muslim womanhood.[37] Her response suggested that that there was something basic to Anisa's subjective sense of human-ness, something innate that made her feel deeply that justice had to mean something different from what the dominant voices of religious authority were claiming.

Another participant, Fatima, was married only in accordance with Muslim rites. At the time the interviews were conducted, the legal framework in South Africa did not recognize Muslim marriages. Thus children from such unions were regarded as illegitimate. The law at the time also stated that the mother had sole custody of children born out of wedlock.[38] Thus, after Fatima was granted a divorce in terms of an uncodified Islamic ruling, custody of the children reverted to her rather than her husband, as stipulated by South African common law. Her now-former spouse had a history of physical abuse toward her and their children, and she was determined to deny him visitation rights. In response, the ex-husband, with the assistance of the imam, compiled a set of pseudolegal documents in order to secure his rights of visitation and access to the children. As an ally of the ex-husband, the imam then visited Fatima and informed her that it was her Islamic duty to sign the documents. She reported the following exchange to have taken place:

> I told the imam that I don't have to sign that document, which also included property rights. He told me "*Shari'a* says that the father has rights over the children," and "*Shari'a* says this, . . . and *shari'a* says that. . . ." I said "*Shari'a* is fine, I'm not arguing with *shari'a,* but I have a valid reason for not wanting to allow him rights to the children. He's the father, but he is violent. I'll never sign something like that." This imam just wanted me to sign, so then he says to me, "*Ja jou kop is deurmekaar* [literally, your head is confused], *kom maak istikhara*" [perform your *istikhara* prayer]. I said, "Fine, I'll go make *istikhara*." The next day, I phoned him back. I said, "Please, throw that document in the dirt-bin, because I didn't sign it." He said, "No, but you don't have to sign because your husband signed already and it's legal." How can one partner only have the rights to sign concerning properties and maintenance and custody?! I don't have any rights??! As for the imam, how can he, who is supposed to be Islamically inclined, how can he help my husband to take away my rights just like that? . . . When I took the document to lawyers for human rights, they said to me that the document was not legal; even if I had signed, it was not legal.

The self-evident manipulation and dishonesty of the cleric in question aside, it is apparent that Fatima's response was extremely powerful. She remained undaunted by the cleric's efforts to blackmail her psychologically and emotionally. By stating that she did not disagree with *shari'a,* she implicitly suggested that an ethical interpretation of Islamic law would not in-

validate her claims. Thus, she contested the cleric's invocation of *shari'a*
on the basis that this invocation was unjust and opportunistic. She also challenged the religious authority of the cleric, who claimed to represent an
ethical Islamic position but in reality behaved in an unjust manner and con-
nived to disempower her.

The efforts of the clerics who ministered to the participants were mostly
counterproductive. Their lack of helpfulness is reflected in their use of
Qur'anic teachings in the context of marital violence. In most cases, Qur'an
4:34 was invoked by the violent spouse subsequent to the mediation of the
marital conflict by the clerics. Jaynub stated:

> In times of problems, I have told the imam about the way my husband
> beats me up. He [the imam] spoke to him, and after that, he [the husband]
> told me that the Qur'an states that he should not lift his hands on his wife,
> but if his wife doesn't want to listen to him, then he is allowed to hit her.
> Where in the Qur'an does it state that? I don't believe that it can say that
> in the Qur'an, but my husband, after talking to the imam, tells me that.

Anisa said:

> They [the clerics] say that the Qur'an says that the husband can hit his
> wife with the *miswak*. . . . But I don't accept that. You can't hit your wife
> with the broom the way he does. He really whips me. That man is cruel,
> really cruel.

For these women, male religious leaders have interpreted and used
Qur'an 4:34 as a justification for spousal abuse. It is noteworthy that in all
cases except one, the abusive husbands had not invoked Islam or the Qur'an
as a rationale for their behavior on their own. Instead, the imams minister-
ing to these husbands had, perhaps inadvertently, provided them with a
Qur'anic rationale for their behavior. By doing so, the imams added to the
problem rather than solving it.

A salient theme that emerged from the data was the participants' refusal to
accept that it was the Qur'an's intention to condone cruelty and violence
against them. One participant, whom I had initially consulted for assistance
in constructing the interview schedule, was herself a lay counselor and survivor of a violent previous marriage. In responding to Qur'an 4:34, she stated:

> Recently, I gave the Qur'an as a present to an agnostic friend who was
> interested in Islam. Before I gave it to her, I struck out that verse [Q4:34].

I did this because I think that this verse is open to misinterpretation. After my experiences, I just refuse to accept that Allah allows or condones violence against women.

Her comment was a reflection of the deep pain and sense of betrayal she experienced in knowing that the Qur'an could be interpreted in a manner that condoned violence against women. Yet she continued to be deeply committed to Islam and the Qur'an. In her view, any interpretation of Qur'an 4:34 that condoned violence against women represents a misunderstanding of Islamic ethics. Similar to the other participants in the study, she rejected the idea that the Qur'an intended harm or condoned violence against them. Through their experiences of abuse, their encounter with Qur'an 4:34 resulted in their actively contesting violence against women. In doing so, they constituted an alternative interpretive community of the text. Similar to the contemporary feminist exegetes of the Qur'an, the women in the sample considered Qur'an 4:34 in terms of a broader Islamic framework, whereby the principles of justice and fair treatment are regarded as integral to the revelatory message. Hence their experiential *tafsir* abrogated the literal and patriarchal readings of Qur'an 4:34 reflected in the approach of some of the clerics.

Two participants found alternative voices among the traditional clerics. These atypical imams, after unsuccessfully intervening with the husbands of the study participants, advised the women that their marriages were harmful to them and that Islam did not require them to accept such abuse. Shayda reported:

He [the *shaykh*] said that because my husband is beating me and then he was messing around with other woman, in the end I am going to sit with AIDS. He told me straight to leave the marriage. . . .

While religious leaders who expressed concern about the health and well-being of battered women were a minority voice among the Cape Town area *'ulama'* at the time, it is nonetheless noteworthy that such opinions were voiced. Such perspectives illustrate the potential for egalitarian voices to emerge from traditional religious authorities. However, the fact that these voices were in the minority brings into focus the need for broader clerical bodies to examine the way they view gender relations and adopt approaches that are more justice based. This need is especially urgent, as imams have central roles in their communities as mediators in marital disputes and are seen to be religious authorities.

Women as Transformers

Despite the difficulties they faced, the participants in the study displayed a remarkable resilience and resistance to common stereotypes of female passivity. They often acted as agents of transformation. In one particular case, a participant showed remarkable courage and uncanny survival skills in life-threatening situations. Anisa stated:

> You know the first time I retaliated physically was after fifteen years of marriage. When he was hitting me with the stick, I grabbed it from his hand and hit him. . . . I was so scared that I had hit him, but I realized that when I pulled back and defended myself, he actually backed off, and then I was shocked at myself. I thought, "Why didn't I do it long ago, because he got scared?" After that, I thought to myself, "Now I'm going to put my foot down." I was nervous and I was scared, and I tried not to show it, and I said to him, "Don't ever lift a finger on me again or I'm going to kill you!" I said, "Don't ever do it again." And since then, he has not done it. Sometimes, when I thought he wanted to hit me, I went right up to him and I said: "Don't! Don't ever try to do it! I'm going to kill you. Don't try it with me again, you're not going to start that nonsense again, I'll kill you." I just say that all the time.

In the context described above, being continuously assaulted by her husband caused Anisa to rebel against religious and cultural socialization. Breaking out of the traditional model of femininity by physically defending herself, she rejected the model of a submissive wife. As she unexpectedly found herself successfully opposing her husband, she remained psychologically and physically vigilant against him by issuing death threats whenever she suspected he might again become violent. Her response was unique. In another situation, a woman who adopted this approach could have been murdered by her husband. Although Anisa did not intend to transgress traditional gender roles in a consciously religious sense, the way she dealt with her husband was in reality a critique of normative assumptions of femininity presented by her religious socialization.

The agency of other women is reflected in their active search for alternative understandings of Islam and gender relations. Fatima stated:

> I went to the library and took out these cassettes by Jamal Badawi, and he spoke in general about all the rights of Muslim women. I thought,

"Gosh! I *do* have rights as a Muslim woman," and that also helped in slowly changing my approach, and I stopped accepting this relationship.

In this case, Fatima actively educated herself about religious faith, rejected the status of a victim, and embraced teachings that focused on Islam's heritage of gender justice. Another participant stated that alternative types of religious socialization and education were imperative to help transform society. Shayda stated:

We need to teach our children to behave differently. My son does domestic chores. When he started to bully my daughter, I stopped him and told him that just because he is a boy does not mean he can treat his sister badly. I always tell the boys that one day, when they get married, they must never do what they father does to me. It's wrong and very un-Islamic.

Shayda pointed to a crucial issue alluded to by a number of respondents, namely, the destructive impact of children being exposed to family violence. Witnessing a mother being beaten up by a father, even when the children are not themselves physically abused, constitutes long-term psychological and emotional scarring. It is a poignant and painful moment when a mother attempts to undo the damage of her abusive husband, telling her son *not* to be like his father. This also incisively points to the critical juncture where a woman needed to prioritize the virtue of providing a good and healthy example for her children over and above the normative virtue of female submission to male authority. By leaving her marriage and opposing stereotypes that are oppressive and sexist, Shayda sought to teach her children healthier modes of interaction between men and women. She pointed to the urgent moral and religious responsibilities of positive family role models and nurturing relationships. Shayda has embodied the potential for transformation in societal and religious constructs. In these instances, empowering and liberatory Islamic constructs about gender relations provided resources for female agency and transformation.

Conclusion

The present study suggests that a variety of factors informed the participating women's understandings of Islam. These included their religious socialization in families and communities in which traditional gender roles and male religious authority were considered normative. Until these women married spouses who abused them, none had actively contested the belief in male supremacy prevalent in their communities. However, their experiences of being on the receiving end of male violence introduced crisis situations that made them confront the most extreme form of patriarchy. These experiences created the conditions for a kind of ideological rupture with the power structure of patriarchy that the women had previously accepted. This mismatch between the way in which the participants in the study had been socialized and their experiences in their marriages brought the dominant ideology into question.

Here the Gramscian theory of hegemony is illuminating. For an ideology to effectively maintain its hegemony, both the oppressed and the oppressor need to accept the given power structure as natural. The ideology that enjoys hegemony portrays itself as providing the maximum good to all parties concerned.[39] In the narratives provided by the participants, the dominant ideology of male authority and power, articulated in religious terms, was based on the unstated claim that it was beneficial to all members of society. Yet the participants' experiences of violence were evidence that this was not the case. Spousal abuse was an explicit violation of the participants' sense of safety, protection, and value that the status quo of male hegemony purported to provide.

Of particular importance, the participants in the study were not ultimately defeated by their experiences of dissonance and rupture—nor did they reject Islam. Instead, they were active in reconstructing their sense of self, of Islam, and of Islamic ethics. This reconstitution involved, inter alia, contesting patriarchal ideology that promoted their docility and submissiveness in the face of violence. Through their experiences of spousal abuse, the participants in the sample brought into focus the contradictions between patriarchal versions of Islam that claim to speak for the greater good of all humanity, on one hand, and the lived brutality that is symptomatic of patriarchal religious ideologies, on the other. By practicing Islam in empowering ways, they were able to destabilize male-centered religious perspectives in their own lives. They assumed the capacity and the authority to act in their own best interests and invoked notions of Islamic ethics and gender relationships in ways that were different from the dominant power structures. Through their struggles and lived experiences, they engaged in a performative encounter with Qur'anic revelation that constituted a "*tafsir* through praxis" or "embodied *tafsir*." Their approaches reflected understandings of Islam and the Qur'an that consciously oppose violence against women and assert women's full humanity in religious terms.

Through their mode of *tafsir,* the participants in the study showed that the contemporary social world of the Qur'anic text is an arena of engaged, dynamic, and polysemic encounters. This chapter has critically reflected on fundamental theoretical questions of religious authority and interpretation, showing that Islamic ethics and Qur'anic exegesis are not only the purview of those considered authoritative in the traditional power structures, such as Tabari in the ninth century, or even of Islamic feminists, such as Amina Wadud and Asma Barlas in the twenty-first century. By thus challenging dominant perspectives that limit the creation of religious meaning and knowledge production to a male religious scholarly elite, I have focused instead on the perspective of those who live outside the centers of social power, whose very lives embody meaning-making in relation to religion, gender ethics, and the Qur'an as social text. Women engage in Qur'anic *tafsir,* as an embodied praxis, in their private and domestic spaces. They may practice it by rejecting their husbands' violent behavior as contrary to the true Islam, or by teaching their sons or daughters to become different kinds of Muslim men and women from previous generations. This study thus exemplifies the feminist theory that posits women's experience as a source of understanding and knowledge production within religious traditions.

Notes

1. Abdullah Yusuf Ali, *The Holy Qur'an* (Brentwood: Amana, 1989).

2. Mohammed Marmaduke Pickthall, *The Meaning of the Glorious Koran: An Explanatory Translation* (New York: New American Library, 1930).

3. See, e.g., the exegetical works of Amina Wadud, *Qur'an and Woman: Rereading the Sacred Text from a Woman's Perspective* (New York: Oxford University Press, 1999); and Asma Barlas, *"Believing Women" in Islam: Unreading Patriarchal Interpretations of the Qur'an* (Austin: University of Texas Press, 2002).

4. For a discussion on the relationship between context and Qur'anic revelation, see Fazlur Rahman, *Islam* (Chicago: University of Chicago Press, 1979).

5. See, e.g., Barbara Daly Metcalf, *Perfecting Women: Maulana Ashraf 'Ali Thanawi's Bihishti Zewar* (Berkeley: University of California Press, 1990).

6. Ali, *Holy Qur'an.*

7. See, e.g., Rosemary Radford Ruether, *Sexism and God-Talk* (Boston: Beacon Press, 1983); and Barbara Stowasser, *Women in the Qur'an, Traditions, and Interpretation* (New York: Oxford University Press, 1994).

8. For varying feminist discussions on the category of experience and female subjectivities, see, e.g., Sandra Kemp and Judith Squires, eds., *Feminisms* (New York: Ox-

ford University Press, 1997); Ursula King, *Religion and Gender* (Oxford: Blackwell, 1995); and Judith Plaskow and Carol P. Christ, *Weaving the Visions: New Patterns in Feminist Spirituality* (San Francisco: HarperSanFrancisco, 1989). There is a growing number of theoretical discussions on Islamic feminism, including the works of Margot Badran, miriam cooke, Shahrzad Mojab, Anour Majid, Valentine Moghadam, and Sa'diyya Shaikh.

9. See Wadud, *Qur'an and Woman;* and Barlas, *"Believing Women."*

10. The term "Islamic feminism" is not universally embraced by Muslim gender activists. For a discussion of some of these contestations and complexities, see Sa'diyya Shaikh, "Transforming Feminisms: Islam, Women and Gender Justice," in *Progressive Muslims: On Justice, Gender and Pluralism,* edited by Omid Safi (Oxford: Oneworld Publications, 2003), 147–62.

11. In this verse, like many others, the challenge of translation becomes apparent. Terms like *qawwamun* and *nushuz,* particularly, are open to several interpretations. For discussions on terminology, see Barlas, *"Believing Women,"* and Wadud, *Qur'an and Woman.* I have chosen to use the Yusuf Ali translation here because it conveys the popular interpretation of the verse.

12. See Barlas, *"Believing Women,"* 184–89.

13. In a previous work, I examined in depth some of the *tafasir* of the authoritative classical exegetes of Q4:34. See Sa'diyya Shaikh, "Battered Women in Muslim Communities in the Western Cape: Religious Constructions of Gender, Marriage, Sexuality and Violence" (MA thesis, University of Cape Town, 1996).

14. For a more detailed analysis of their positions on Q4:34, see also Sa'diyya Shaikh, "Exegetical Violence: Nushuz in Qur'anic Gender," *Journal for Islamic Studies* 17 (1997): 49–73.

15. For an excellent discussion on women in the Qur'an, *hadith,* and *tafasir* literature, see Stowasser, *Women in the Qur'an.*

16. Abu Jafar al-Tabari, *Jami' al-Bayan 'an ta'wil al-Qur'an,* 30 vols. (Beirut: Dar al Fikr, 1948), vol. 3, 57–59.

17. Ibid., 57.

18. Abu Qasim al-Zamakshari, *al-Kashshaf 'an haqa'iq ghawamid al-tanzil wa-'uyun al-aqawil fi wujuh al-ta'wil,* 4 vols. (Beirut: Dar al-Haqq, n.d.), vol. 1, 505.

19. Ibid.

20. Ibid.

21. Fakhr al-Din al-Razi, *al-Tafsir al-Kabir,* 32 vols. (Makkah: Dar ul-Fikr, n.d.), vol. 9, 90.

22. Al-Zamakshari, *al-Kashshaf,* vol. 1, 91.

23. Ibid.

24. Al-Tabari, *Jami' al-Bayan,* vol. 3, 68.

25. Al-Razi, *al-Tafsir,* vol. 9, 93.

26. Ibid.

27. Ibid. Indicative of the "normality" of violence against wives is a *hadith* quoted in the exegesis of al-Zamakshari. Asma bint Abu Bakr is reported to have said that "I was one of four wives of Zubair ibn al-Awwam. If he got angry, he would hit us with a stick, on which clothes are hung, until he broke it." Her husband is reported to have responded by saying that "if her sons were not around then I would hit her more"; al-Zamakshari, *al-Kashshaf,* vol. 1, 507. Hence, it appears that violence against wives was prevalent among some sectors of the Prophet Muhammad's society.

28. Al-Razi, *al-Tafsir,* vol. 9, 93.

29. Al-Zamakshari, *al-Kashshaf,* vol. 1, 507.

30. Barlas, *"Believing Women";* Maysum al-Faruqi, "Women's Self-Identity in the Qur'an and Islamic Law," in *Windows of Faith,* edited by Gisela Webb (Syracuse: Syracuse University Press, 2000), 72–101; Azizah al-Hibri, "An Introduction to Muslim Women's Rights," in *Windows of Faith,* 51–71; Riffat Hassan, "An Islamic Perspective," in *Women, Religion and Sexuality,* edited by Jeanne Becher (Philadelphia: WCC Publishers, 1990), 93–128; Wadud, *Qur'an and Woman.*

31. Wadud, *Qur'an and Woman,* xiii.

32. Barlas, *"Believing Women,"* 133.

33. E.g., Q107:1–7 explicitly admonishes worshippers who perform ritual prayer while being heedless of the suffering of orphans, the hungry, and other marginalized groups of people around them.

34. As reflected in a study in the United States, these types of sexual double standards are not restricted to Muslim societies but are also reflected in varying forms in other societies. See Mary Crawford and Danielle Popp, "Sexual Double Standards: A Review and Methodological Critique of Two Decades of Research," *Journal of Sex Research* 40, no. 1 (2003): 13–26.

35. According to traditional Islamic law, the *'alim* (singular for *'ulama'*) cannot perform the *talaq* because this is the husband's prerogative. An *'alim* can, however, pronounce a *faskh,* that is, dissolution of the marriage, the conditions for which vary in different legal schools.

36. In popular terms, the *'ulama'* are often referred to as imams.

37. I want to sincerely thank reviewer Barbara Cooper for this and other very thoughtful insights. I am equally indebted to the helpful comments of the other, anonymous reviewer.

38. South African law has changed since that time. In 1997, the Natural Fathers of Children Born out of Wedlock Act was passed, which granted unmarried fathers legal rights regarding custody and access to their children.

39. David I. Kertzer, "Gramsci's Concept of Hegemony: The Italian Church-Communist Struggle," *Dialectical Anthropology* 4, no. 4 (1979): 321–28.

Part II

Re/constructing Women, Gender, and Sexuality

Chapter 5

Changing Conceptions of Moral Womanhood in Somali Popular Songs, 1960–1990

Lidwien Kapteijns

Social struggles over conceptions and definitions of moral womanhood—of what it means in any time or place to be a "proper" woman—often develop in dialectical relationship with other social and political movements and institutions. Thus, discourses about women's rights and emancipation in the nineteenth- and twentieth-century Middle East and elsewhere in the Islamic world were both enabled and circumscribed by the anticolonial nationalist movements for independence of which they were a crucial part. Both movements—nationalism and women's emancipation—were characterized by their will to be modern while "preserving" their notions of cultural authenticity and authentic morality, and by their goal of ending Western colonial rule while emulating aspects of liberal Western philosophies and institutions.[1] Although it has been well established that nationalist victories rarely gave feminists what they had hoped and struggled for, it was not until the

An earlier version of this chapter was published under the title "Discourse on Moral Womanhood in Somali Popular Songs, 1960–1990" in the *Journal of African History* 50 (2009): 101–22. I acknowledge Cambridge University Press for permission to reprint.

deep failure of the nationalist projects and their displacement by other social and political movements, such as the Islamist ones, that new conceptions of moral womanhood started to increasingly become normative.

Somalia is no exception to these developments. However, there are several reasons why the Somali case is of particular interest. First, in few countries was the popular discourse about nationalism and nationalist moral womanhood as articulate and lively as in the Somalia of the 1960s through the 1980s. Second, in few countries was the failure of the nationalist project as absolute as in the Somalia of the early 1990s, when the state and the social order themselves collapsed in communal (clan-based) violence that took many Somalis completely by surprise. This cataclysm, which had been in the making for more than a decade and gave rise to diasporic communities of Somalis throughout the world,[2] has transformed (and is still transforming) the discourses about Somali communal identities and moral womanhood, as well as the discursive sites in which these are debated and propagated. The genre of Somali popular culture that is central to this chapter is increasingly being produced outside Somalia and reaches Somalis, wherever they are, through the electronic media.

The Somali popular songs analyzed here were part of the nationalist project of "modernity" of the Somali nationalist movement and independent state from 1955 to 1991.[3] After giving a brief overview of this period, I analyze the contradictory impulses in the visions of moral womanhood expressed in the songs, as poets and songwriters articulated a desire for "modernity" in tandem with a particular notion of Somali "tradition" (i.e., cultural authenticity and traditional religious morality) to mark and anchor the communal identity or collective self-understanding of the new Somali nation and national state. In conclusion, this chapter touches upon the dramatic changes in Somali common public identity and the new gender norms that have been developing since the collapse of the state in 1991, as Islamist discourses of different kinds have gained power in both Somalia proper and its diaspora. However, given that the (discursive) battle about the form and control of a new Somali state is in full swing, and the sites and genres of popular culture are multiplying as you read these words, this analysis can only be partial and provisional.

The Nationalist Ideals of Unity and Modernity

The nationalist movement that fought for Somali independence from colonial rule emerged in the years during and following World War II, when all the Somali territories were united under British military rule. Although Western Europe's colonial empires were on the decline, international competition was still acute, with Italy, in spite of its defeat in the war, vying with Great Britain for the control of its former colony of southern Somalia. Moreover, the Soviet Union and the United States, then squaring off to confront each other in the Cold War, were also influential and jealous players, while Egypt maintained a strong interest in Somalia throughout. It fell to the Somali nationalist movement of the 1950s and 1960s and a new configuration of international realpolitik to shape the emerging national consciousness and propel the Somali nation and state toward taking (in nationalist terms) its rightful place among the nations of the world. Although some Somali parties objected to the establishment of a unitary (rather than federal) centralized state, on July 1, 1960, on a wave of popular enthusiasm, the former British and Italian Somalilands came together to form the independent Somali Republic.[4]

In terms of political program, the nationalist movement organized and called upon Somalis to leave sectarian and exclusive clan identities behind and embrace *soomaalinimo,* a national Somali identity.[5] They regarded ignorance (i.e., a lack of education) and the smaller-scale communal identities based on clan and subclan as their main internal obstacle to unity, but they hoped that, under their own youthful, educated, modern, and urban leadership, the commonalities of language, culture, religion, and territory could form the basis for an independent, modern state for a unified Somali people. Of course, Somali society had significant cultural differences and social inequalities beyond those most explicitly addressed by the nationalists.[6] However, gender had a modest place in their discourse about the future, about which more below.

The obstacles to the goal of unity were daunting.[7] First, in spite of geographical contiguity, it turned out that colonial boundaries could not be undone, and thus the Somalis of the Northern Frontier District, French Somaliland, and the Ethiopian-occupied Somali territory remained outside the Somali Republic. This caused an irredentist program whose failure was to have huge political costs for the new country. Moreover, whatever the commonalities between Somalis might be, in reality, the nationalist movement and the civilian administrations (1960—69) inherited a country that had been deeply marked and divided not just by colonial rule but, what was more, by differential (British, Italian, Ethiopian, and French) experiences of colonial rule. In both British and Italian Somalilands, nationalist ideals ran up against the suffocating administrative legacy of a system of governance that had largely failed to build modern institutions and that, to the extent that it had institutionalized Somali administrative practices at all, had made clan (and thus clan rivalry) into the only mode of access to the colonial state and the primary focus of administrative interaction with the people. In other words, at independence, the nationalists, buoyed by the unconditional support of the people, had to hitch their project of inclusion, unity, and modernization to deeply tribalized administrative habits, institutions, and popular attitudes toward the state.[8]

There is no doubt that the desire to become modern, in Donham's sense,[9] was an integral part of the Somali nationalist project of the 1960s and after. Many of the dimensions of this discourse are well known. They included a liberal belief in constitutional democracy and representative, accountable government; individual rights and freedoms, including equality before the law and freedom from government oppression; social progress derived from formal, modern education, based on European models; and economic development inspired by scientific and technological progress. Here, too, the nationalists faced major obstacles to their hopes for modernization, and the gap between discourse and reality remained vast. Before World War II, public educational institutions in both Somalilands had been practically nonexistent, with private schools few and far between and limited to small numbers of students.[10] The economic policies the nationalists inherited were equally undeveloped. Apart from a small plantation sector in the south, which even after independence continued to be in Italian hands, the colonial state had not seriously invested in, or developed, the economic sectors on which the majority of the population depended: livestock herding and farming. Beyond heavy import and export taxes (and smaller levies, e.g., tax stamps on legal documents), the colonial powers had not developed a system of taxation on which the new state could draw. Thus, independent Somalia inherited an economically deeply underdeveloped state.[11] The dependence on colonial handouts and, after 1960, foreign aid made the new state vulnerable to international manipulation and, in the end, during the second half of the Mohamed Siad Barre regime (1969—91), not accountable to its own subjects.[12]

However, if the nationalist project was intrinsically modern, in that it wanted to catapult Somalia into the ranks of other modern nation-states, it also had to distinguish Somalia from the latter by articulating a uniquely Somali national identity—a communal identity that drew on the past in order to mobilize Somalis for a modern future. In Somalia, as in other (post-independence) nationalist contexts, modern articulations of culturally authentic communal identities proved to be deeply intertwined with conceptualizations of gender relations and moral womanhood and personhood. Indeed, it was in this area, about which more below, that the tensions between modernity and traditional culture (*hiddiyo dhaqan*) became most contested. The task of articulating much of the public and popular discourse about *soomaalinimo* fell to the (organic) intellectuals and artists,[13] who took this on themselves and were also actively encouraged to do so by state institutions. Undoubtedly, the schoolbooks, scholarship, literature, and journalism that were produced in Somalia in this era also contributed to the construction of a national identity. However, given the context of very limited literacy,[14] at the popular level, this discourse about *soomaalinimo*—about how to be a modern yet moral (or culturally authentic) Somali—took shape particularly in a new, modern genre of oral poetry, that of the popular song (*hees* or *heello*).

Somali Popular Song: Mobilizing the Past for a Nationalist Future

The Somali popular song developed in post–World War II Somalia both in interaction with older forms of oral literature and in response to Somalia's self-conscious encounter with the world. The popular song was born as a love song in the social space opened up by those who moved and mediated between the countryside and the town (e.g., truck drivers and schoolteachers), but it came of age as a genre—that is to say, it gained wide social acceptance and importance—when it became a vehicle for nationalist, anticolonial sentiment and argument.[15] Moreover, as political parties used songs to spread their message and appeal to the masses, as the towns of Hargeisa in the north and Mogadishu in the south established radio stations, and as—after independence, and especially after 1969—state institutions (e.g., the Ministry of Information) put increasing numbers of Somali artists and bands on their (however meager) payroll, the popular song gained a strong institutional basis.[16] The popularity of the popular song was paralleled by that of plays (*riwaayad, masrax*), which, at least into the mid-1970s, often combined a focus on major political and social issues confronting Somali society with simple, and sometimes bawdy, comedy.[17] After these plays premiered in the new National Theatre in Mogadishu, or in Hargeisa, they then toured the country, often for months at a time. Songs both marked the major episodes of the plot and articulated the underlying political, social, or philosophical themes of these plays. Both because of their compelling artistry and social relevance and the new mass media technology of radio broadcasting and audiocassettes, they thus gained wide popularity in the urban areas and the countryside alike. To this day, most Somalis who grew up anywhere in Somalia during the era 1955–91 remember and often have memorized hundreds of these songs, and still listen to them in their cars and homes, growing nostalgic when they do so. During its heyday in the period 1960–90, the popular song provided a major site of public discourse in Somalia and helped fashion the ideals of a modern Somali national consciousness or nationalist "imaginary."[18]

To understand the social significance of the popular song in Somali society from 1960 to 1990, one must understand how it used the power of the past to mobilize Somalis for a particular vision of the future, namely, a modern, nationalist vision. According to Said Samatar in his book *Oral Poetry and Somali Nationalism* (1982), oral poetry in (pre)colonial, Somali society had three characteristics relevant to us here: It was "utilitarian," in the sense that the poet aimed "to inform, persuade or convince" others of a particular point of view or proposal; it was "committed," in the sense that it was "composed and chanted in relation to a specific occasion or for the purpose of achieving a specific end"; and it aspired to have an impact on two kinds of moral universe, that of the immediate present and the timeless one of larger, universal moral truth.[19] The popular song inherited from traditional oral poetry the utilitarian urge and commitment to persuade, inform, educate, and bring about action and change. Moreover, and this perhaps explains how deeply the songs moved (and still move) contemporary Somalis, the popular songs often had multiple layers of meaning—from the anecdotal to the symbolic, from the particular to the general, and from the "immediate" to the "transcendental." Like Samatar's "good poem," the well-conceived and well-crafted popular song, "once its immediate point is appreciated, passes into a secondary phase whereby it . . . becomes a part of the people's spiritual heritage."[20]

However, the new genre of the Somali popular song also incorporated radically new features. First of all, they were accompanied by an increasing range of musical instruments, among which the lute, drums, and flute initially figured most prominently. Second, they were sensual and sometimes risqué, with romantic passion and physical desire constituting a major theme. Although *tatrib* (being transported, or ecstasy) was nothing new to traditional Somali dances (which almost always had a verbal dimension), unlike the latter, the modern song was not restricted to specially demarcated social occasions and were performed and enjoyed by men and women, privately, in mixed company, with people sitting down. It was socially simply a very different phenomenon. Even if it derived many aspects of form and function from traditional, and thus rural, genres, the Somali popular song was a child of urban life that was raised on the heady diet of nationalist popular fervor. As such, it came to mark the youth culture of the new era. In a context of limited literacy, and with the support of formal institutions, the popular song came to constitute a social commentary that captured the mood of its time.[21]

It was in this context that Somali popular songs—more than any other genre or discursive site—came to express and shape the popular debates about how to be a "modern and yet moral" Somali. In this search for moral and modern *soomaalinimo,* traditional cultural concepts, which included aspects of religious morality, took on the power of a legitimizing discourse, while women and gender roles became a major focus.[22]

Gender and Nationalist Conceptions of Modernity

Although there are no comprehensive and detailed histories of Somali women, it has been well established that women played a crucial part in the nationalist movement for independence and the political parties that competed in the political arena after independence. They became members en masse and held office, recruited new members, sacrificed their scant personal financial resources such as jewelry, raised funds from friend and foe alike, fed and housed young nationalists who were denied jobs because of their affiliations, organized and helped find resources for major congresses and demonstrations, composed poetry to raise awareness and keep up spirits, translated the lofty words of party programs into action, and, at times, even paid for their convictions with prison terms and death.[23]

Women did gain the vote, a major milestone and reward, first in the municipal elections of 1958 and then in the general elections to the Legislative Assembly in 1959.[24] However, while male nationalist leaders of various parties appealed to women for support, depended on them, and acknowledged their contributions, they regarded women largely as supporters and, when independence and unity were achieved—as happened in Egypt and elsewhere—no woman was given a major position in the new administrations.[25] Partly this was because women generally had even lower educational qualifications than men, although for men such lack of formal education turned out to be much less of an obstacle to obtaining positions of political leadership. If it proved difficult for the generation of men who inherited the mantle of leadership in 1960 to regard and treat the women with whom they actually collaborated as equals, their vision of modernity encompassed such equality in theory and in the long run. This was evident, for example, from their support of education for Somali youth of both sexes. Although, in the 1960s, women were politically active alongside men, to what extent an organized women's movement spearheaded changes in gender ideology is still unclear and requires further research.

In the popular songs of this era, both the concept of greater equality in gender relations and that of modern personhood, in Abu-Lughod's sense, are strikingly evident.[26] The idea of a "modern subject," with intense personal emotions and desires, is a core feature of the genre of the modern song and gives rise to two intrinsically modern themes: the ideal of romantic love—with all its symptoms and outcomes and all its variations and degrees—and that of a companiate marriage, that is to say, marriage based on romantic love, mutual respect, partnership, and shared decisionmaking.[27] By emphasizing the mutuality of love and desire, the concept of the love match differed radically from traditional marriage—or at least from public articulations and constructions of traditional marriage—which was presented as a marriage that was often arranged by (and in the best interest of) the families of the couple and in which the husband's authority over (the labor of) his wife, or wives, and children was paramount. These were revolutionary, modern ideas at the time, because they challenged the traditional authority and conventions of family and clan, challenged narrow definitions of Islamic morality, and constructed new self-representations and selves. In the songs at least, romantic love and companiate marriage became the ideal of the Somali youth of the nationalist era, and they inspired many young people to defy their families in order to marry whom they wanted.[28]

This is reflected in the popular songs, which legitimized these new social institutions of love match and companiate marriage by imbuing old cultural concepts with new meanings and applying them to new contexts. Thus the old concept of *nabsi* (or "avenging fate"), the leveling force ensuring that all human beings get their share of fortune and misfortune, became in the songs the social sanction an ill-starred lover invokes against the one who does not return his or her love. The word *axdi,* meaning solemn pledge or agreement, became in the love songs the private agreement reached by two young lovers, often irrespective of the wishes of the parents. Many more examples exist.[29]

An example of the use of traditional cultural concepts to legitimize and sanction the modern ideals of love marriage is the song "The Yearnings of

Our Love," from the play *Xuskii Jacaylkii* (The Celebration of Love), which became, and continues to be, a popular wedding song. Three things are worth noting about this song. First, the text makes clear that the wedding it celebrates is a love match. As the bride puts it in the song, "The memory of our love and our long-standing desire . . . make me shiver, make me bite my lips, my fingers." Second, the song states that this love match is sanctioned by both Somali tradition, in the form of customary law and the approval and blessing of the couple's fathers and family elders, and the religion of Islam, in the form of the sheikh, religion, and God. Third, it is worth noting that Islam and Somali tradition are mentioned in one breath and regarded, if not as mutually constitutive, at least as inseparable. Here are the song's lyrics, with a translation following:

"The Yearnings of Our Love."[30]
Sung by Mohamed Ahmed and Saaddo Ali.
Words by Mahmud Abdullahi "Sangub."

She: Xiisaha kalgacalkeenna, xaasha ee guurkeenna, beryo samu ku waarkeenna. Sidii Xaawo iyo Aadan, Rabbi baa isu keen xulay. Waa xaal innaga weynoo, xagga samada laga qoray. Duqay xeer aqoon-liyo, xer cilmiyo sheekh baa, xirsigana inoo xidhay. Rabbigeenna Xaakim ahee, xilo iga kaa dhigay baan kun jeer ku xamdiyayaa.

He: Is xaqdhawrka labadeenna, xuralcaynta quruxdeeda, xabiibkii u helay qaybta. Sidii Xaydar iyo Faduumo, Rabbi baa isu keen xu-lay. Waa xisaab dhammaatiyo, xad aan laga tallaabayn, xuquwaalid ducadiyo xaajo odayo gooyeen baa, xurma lagu muteystaa. Rab-bigeenna Xaakim ahee, xilo iga kaa dhigay baan kun jeer ku xam-diyayaa.

She: The yearnings of our love, this wonderful marriage, and our living together ever after. Like Adam and Eve, the Lord has chosen us for each other. [Our marriage] is a condition more powerful than us, written for us in heaven. The elders who know customary law as well as the sheikh and his students have given us their protective blessing. Because our Lord, the Judge, has made me your spouse, I thank Him a thousand times.

He: The way we respect each other and the angelic beauty of which the Prophet had his share. Like [the legendary Somali lovers] Haydar and Faduumo,[31] the Lord has chosen us for each other. It is an ac-count that has been settled, a limit that cannot be overstepped. It is

our fathers' rightful authority and blessing and the decision reached
by the elders, which deserve respect. Because our Lord, the Judge,
has made me your spouse, I thank Him a thousand times.

In a number of popular songs of this era, modern, "feminist," or emancipatory articulations of gender roles and relations can be seen to hold their
own against more conservative ones, with the latter basing themselves on
Somali cultural tradition. The following three famous songs take the form
of a poetic debate between men and women. The first two texts are part of
the play *Shabeelnaagood* (Leopard among the Women), produced in 1968
by Hassan Sheikh Mumin.[32] In the first fragment, a debate between two
teachers, who represent modernity in the play, the female teacher raises the
issue of male/female inequality, while the male teacher soothes her with references to the unique love and closeness that characterize a couple:

"By God, Men Are. . . ."[33]
Sung by Hibo Mohamed and Abdi Muhumed.
Words by Hassan Sheikh Mumin.

She: Nagaadiga adduunyada qayb ku ma leh naaguhu
      Xeerkii sidaa naqay nimankaa sameystee
      Alla, Alla, nimanku waa nacab aan korinnoo
      naaskeenna nuugoo naafeeyay dumarkoo
      nabad lama wadaagee.
He: Nimanka iyo naaguhu waa laba nafood oo
      nuday qudh ah ka beermoo nolosha wadaagee
      Naa hoy, naa hoy, nimanku waa naq iyo raaxiyo
      nafaqada haweenkoo. Waxaan nahay hal iyo nirig
      midba mid u nuurtee.
She: Women have no share in the arrangements of this world
      and the laws governing it were made by men to their own
          advantage
      By God, by God, men are the enemies we ourselves raised
      and nursed at our breasts, but they have crippled us
      and we cannot share peace with them.
He: Men and women are like two beings
      that grew from the same first cell and share life
      Listen, you women, men are the green grass, the comfort,
      the sustenance of women. We are like a she-camel and its calf
      that share in the same radiance.

In the second song, the same two teachers blame the other sex for the sorry state of marriage. In the scene of which the song is a part, these accusations include seducing, deceiving, and being unfaithful, with women allegedly giving their favors to the highest bidder and men impregnating innocent girls. In the song quoted here, however, he attributes the decay of marriage to women's modern and indecent dress and nontraditional social freedom, while she asserts the rights and freedoms of all women and blames the problem on men's abusive treatment of women. Striking in this song is how the male teacher associates modernity with indecency and frivolity, while she bases her argument on women's rights and solidarity:

"Is This Just?[34]
Sung by Hibo Mohamed and Abdi Muhumed.
Words by Hassan Sheikh Mumin.

She: Annagu xorrownoo xaqayagii midhaystay. Inaad na xakamaysaan aadna xidhxidhaan, xaq miyaa, xeer miyaa, ma idiin xalaal baa? Idinka xujooboo xuduudkii ka talaabsanaayee. Xubin na siiya!

He: Inaad marada xayddaan, xaglaha na qaawisaan, xuub caaro huwataan, xeradii ka baxdaan, xaq miyaa, xeer miyaa, ma idiin xalaal baa? Idinka xujooboo xuduudkii ka talaabsanaayee. Naa xishooda!

She: Xilagube haddii uu hanan waayey tiisa, xaawaley dhammaanteed, in nala xumeeyaa, xaq miyaa, xeer miyaa, ma idiin xalaal baa? Idinka xujooboo, xuduudkii ka talaabsanaayee. Xubin na siiya!

She: We have gained our freedom and achieved our rights. That you should bridle us and tie us down—is this just, and do custom and religion permit you to act this way? You have committed a punishable offense and are overstepping the limit—concede a point to us!

He: That you should tuck up your dresses, bare the backs of your knees, put on clothes as transparent as a spider's web, and break all moral bounds—is this just, and do custom and religion permit you to act this way? You have committed a punishable offense and are overstepping the limit—you, women, shame on you!

She: If a controlling husband cannot stomach [our newly found freedom], [it is] all women [who are hurt]. That we should be abused— is this just, and do custom and religion permit you to act this way? You have committed a punishable offense and are overstepping the limit—concede a point to us!

The third song, called "In the Old Days," also takes the form of a debate between a man and a woman, this time explicitly about moral womanhood. To the male, a good woman is a traditional woman: beautiful and well groomed, quiet to the point of being invisible to men, obedient, and accepting of a marriage arranged for her by men. Modernity stands for cultural transgression, characterized by untraditional dress, mobility and visibility in the public sphere, and the rejection of familial authority. But she has other ideas, and the songwriter lets her gain the upper hand. Unafraid to couch her ideas in untraditional, modern terms, she asserts the importance of leaving backward customs behind, actively participating in leadership and public life, and getting an education. She suggests that God created men and women as different but not unequal beings and depicts men who marry off girls as thieves handling stolen property. Although in the three songs presented here women's morality and modernity are not represented as contradictory terms, the conservative equation of moral womanhood with traditional womanhood is powerfully articulated.

"In the Old Days."[35]
Sung by Mohamed Jama Joof and Maryan Mursal.
Words by a poet currently unknown (late 1960s).

He: Beri hore waxaa jiray, inan timaha diibtoo, baarkana u tidhicdoo, boqorkiyo dhaclaha iyo, maro baylah xidhatee.
Wax beddelay kuwii hore, balo geesa dheeroo, buul madaxa saarto, suuqa baratamayee.
Naa bi'ise dhaqankii, sharcigii ka baydhoo, diintii burburisee, hablow maad is badh qabataan?
She: Boqol sano horteed iyo, beri hore wixii jiray, ee layska baal maray, budulkii dib ha u qaban, laga soo baqoolee.
Hadda baratan iyo orod, bisha iyo cadceeddiyo, beesha loo horseedoo,
aannu beegsanaynaa.
Horta baro tacliintiyo, buuggiyo dhigaalkoo,
badowyahow dib ha u celin dadka soo baraarugay
He: Beri hore waxaa jiray, inan aan bil iyo laba, hadal kaaga bixinoo raggu baadiggoobaa, beri arag ku weydaa
Wax beddelay kuwii hore, casarkii dar baxayoo, kiish buuran qaatiyoo
budhcad dibedda meertee.
Naa bi'ise dhaqankii, sharcigii ka baydhoo, diintii burburisee,

hablow maad is badh qabataan?

She: Ilaahii bad iyo webi, biyahooda dhaarshee, meel kula ballamayee,
dhulka baaxaddaliyo, buuraha rakibay baa
bani aadmigiisana, ruuxba cayn u beeree
waad baafiyoodee, cidi kulama baydhinee.
Horta baro tacliintiyo, buuggiyo dhigaalkoo,
badowyahow dib ha u celin, dadka soo baraarugay

He: Beri hore waxaa jiray, inan baarax geeliyo, faraskii Baxdow wada,
yarad looga bixiyaa, bunduqana la raacshaa.
Wax beddelay kuwii hor, isu bogan badh maqanoo,
bahdii ay ka dhalatiyo, baylihisay waanee.
Naa bi'ise dhaqankii, sharcigii ka baydhoo, diintii burburisee,
hablow maad is badh qabataan?

She: Baarax geel iyo faras, iyo boqonyaraha adhi
hablihii lagu beddeli jiray, diintaynu baraniyo
ma bannayn kitaabkuye, booliqutiyaashii
beecsan jiray haweenkiyo, baaxadsoorihii tegay,
maanta loo ma baahnee.
Horta baro tacliintiyo, buuggiyo dhigaalkoo,
Badowyahow dib ha u celin, dadka soo baraarugay.

He: In the old days, it was custom that a girl perfumed her hair and braided it. She wrapped around her waist a wide cloth belt with fringes and an ornamental cord, and wore a white dress. But something has changed. Something weird with long horns they wear as hats on their heads and run all over the market. [Refrain:] You women have destroyed our culture. You have overstepped the religious law and destroyed our religion. Girls, won't you behave?

She: What was custom in the old days and a hundred years ago and what has been left behind, don't make us go back to that well-worn road, for we have turned away from it with effort. Now we expect to run and compete for the sun and the moon and to lead people. [Refrain:] First get some education and learn how to read and write. Don't try to turn back, you country hick, people who have woken up!

He: In the old days, it would happen that a girl would not address you for one or two months, and the men who went out looking would not see her for days. But something has changed. In the evening, a whole gang of them goes out, carrying fat purses, wandering about outside like robbers. [Refrain]

She: God calmed the waters of sea and river and made them flow together. Then he put in order the wide Earth and the mountains and created his human beings each in a different way. You are a loser. No one is asking you to come along. [Refrain]

He: In the old days, it was custom to pay as bridewealth for a girl a whole herd of camels and the most exceptional horse, and a rifle on top of that. But something has changed. You are self-absorbed and ignore the advice of the family in which you were born. [Refrain]

She: Girls used to be exchanged for a herd of camels and short-legged goats. But the religion we learned and the Qur'an do not allow this. Today we have no need for those who deal in what they do not own and for this old-fashioned dividing up of women. [Refrain:] First get some education and learn how to read and write. Don't try to turn back, you country hick, people who have woken up!

However, although the poets and songwriters of the popular songs—and the society they reflected and tried to shape—had a vision for women that had modern aspects, the concept of moral womanhood that was articulated and legitimized in terms of authentic cultural tradition came to be more and more constrained by such constructions of tradition. Thus, as occurred in other nationalist contexts,[36] when applied to women, the traditional legitimacy that was constructed left little room for modernity. In the songs, and thus in public, popular discourse of this postindependence era, women's modernity became increasingly synonymous with inauthentic, untraditional, Western immorality and frivolity, while women's morality was articulated in terms of "traditional" dress, limited freedom of movement, respect for male authority, and a deemphasized sexuality.

The following songs are an example of this narrowing of the public discourse about women's roles and gender relations. The first song, "Truly Marriage Causes Hardship," is sung by three women. Each describes her favorite way of being treated by the other sex. The first woman likes men to indulge her senses through music, dance and (indirectly) sex. The second singer likes rich men who can keep a woman in luxury. But the third one advocates for a proper (although, nevertheless, companionate) marriage, engaged in with the approval and support of the family:

"Truly Marriage Causes Hardship."[37]
Sung by Maryan Mursal, Faduumo Ali "Nakruuma," and Hibo Mohamed.
Words: Mahmud Tukaale, from the play *Girls, When Will You Get Married?* (Hablayohow, hadmaad guursan doontaan?).

Maryan: Guurkii runta ahaa waa lagu rafaado. Reer lamaba dhaqan karo.
Raalliya kuu noqon karaa qayrkaa lagaa reeb
Waxaa aniga ila roon, ninka aad is rabtaanee
fiid kastaa is raacdaan, Roog iyo Jaas la tumataa,
waqtiga isla riixdaan, keligiin wada riyaaqdaan.
Bal aadna?

Faduumo: Qofba wuxuu jeclaystiyo, dookhii dada kala reeb
Qofba awr u raranee, raynta aan la garan
Waxaa aniga ila roon, ragga taajiriintee kala rogaya
maalkiyo raasamaaliyiinta, rug intaad ninkaas la joogto,
raar weyn ku geeyoo, raaxana kula aroosaa
Bal aadna?

Hibo: Ruuneey, walaaleey, hiddaha yaan dhalan rogin, laga roorin dhaqankii,
raaskii awowgeen, bohol yaanan lagu ridin,
waxaan anigu ila roon, ninka kugula koray raas,
reerkiinu kuugu daro, ducana laguugu raacshaa,
iskula dhaqantaan run, Rabbina kuugu dar khayr.

Maryan: Truly marriage only causes hardship. It is impossible to build a family. To become an obedient wife means being left behind by one's age group. What I prefer, when you and a man want each other, is to go out in the early evening and dance to rock and jazz, hang out together and enjoy yourselves, just the two of you. What do you think?

Faduumo: Everyone has his own preference and taste is what sets people apart. One cannot tell who is wealthiest from how someone presents himself. I prefer rich men, who turn over lots of wealth and have capital; who, while you live with them, put you in a huge house and give you a luxurious life. What about you?

Hibo: Dear sister, Ruun, don't get rid of the culture in which you were born or run away from your cultural heritage. Don't throw away the ways of your ancestors. What I prefer is a man who establishes a home with you, receiving you from your male relatives, with their blessing. You will live together honestly, blessed by the Lord. (Book, 199–200)

A second song deals explicitly with women's clothing. Four girls are singing here, two favoring modern and two traditional dress. In this song, traditional dress is associated with beauty, morality, virginity, dignity, and authenticity, while modern dress is represented as the opposite of all this.

"History Has a Direction."[38]
Sung by Kinsi Adan, Adar Ahmed, Khadija Hiiraan, and Fadumo Elbai "Haldhaa."
Words by Hasan Gini (1982).

Kinsi: Taariikhdu wax bay hagtaa, dadkuna u haybsadaa.
           Adduunkuna waa hayaan hir dooglaa lagu socdaa.
           Hoggaanku waa casriga. Naftaadana lama hagrado
           Qayrkaa ka hadh waa habaar. Heeryadan aad sidatiyo
           haylahan waa laga ilbaxay. Sallaanka aad halabsatidee
           ma kuu gacan haadiyaa? Haaneedka ma kuu qabtaa?
           Hoobaanta ma kuu guraa?
Adar: Habeenooy hebedka geel, hashaan maqasha iska celin
           harraatiyin kaanay dhalin, markay hiigaamisooy,
           jilaalkii bay hadhaa. Hambana waa layska nacay.
           Higgaaddana igu afqaro. Dharaartii ninkaan ka helo,
           habeenkii kuma dhaxee. Hantidu waa ii dhantahay.
           Xishood hodan baan ka ahay, xayihii baan soo huwaday
           hablaha Soomaaliyeed
Khadija: Hanyari waa loo dhintaa, hagoogtana waxaa lahaa
           kuwii waa heermi jiray, dharka hayruufayana,
           sidaan sheekada ku helay, hafsi lama qaadan jirin.
           Ruuxii kuu hiiliyana inaad yeeshaa habboon.
           Haraaga nin la dedee. Hurdaay reerkeenni guur
           horseed kuu baaqayo, ku soo helay baan ahee.
           Ma kuu gacan haadiyaa? Hoobaanta ma ku guuraa?
Faduumo: Haldhaa baa la i yidhaah. Heensigii baan weli sitaa.
           Hiddihii la i wada yiqiin, asluubtii hooyaday
           hormood baan dhaqan u ahay, inaan hirgashaan jeclahay.
           Huf iyo been kuma luggo'o, xirtaaqa wanniga dhalay
           in lagu hoobtaan ogahay. Habowdayee waxaan ku idhi
           hugaadiyo kan aan xidhnahay, abada kee haybad wacan,
           hilbana keennee astuuran?
Kinsi: History has a direction people try to catch on to. The world
           is a journey toward a beautiful dream that is guided by

modernity. Don't shortchange yourself. It is a curse to stay behind one's age group. People have emancipated themselves from these rags and heavy clothes you wear. Follow us on this path. Shall I help you move forward and show you the way to the benefits it will have?

Cadar: Foolish one, a docile camel that does not protect itself from [other] sucklings and does not kick away calves that are not its own is left behind in the dry season when its udders run dry. No one likes leftovers. Know the meaning of my words. I do not spend the night with any man I may like in the daytime. My treasure is untouched. I am a paragon of modesty and represent the decency of all Somali girls.

Khadija: Putting yourself down is fatal. Even those who covered themselves used to get into trouble, while those who disliked this clothing—as I have heard tell—did not go wrong. It is better that you follow the person who takes your side. One covers things only if there is something bad. Sleepy one, the encampment has moved on. I am beckoning you to move forward. Follow us on this path. Shall I show you the way to the benefits it will have?

Haldhaa: They call me beautiful like the male ostrich. I still wear the finery and am the leader of the tradition everyone knows is mine, of the ways in which my mother reared me, of our cultural heritage. I love to support this way of life. Contempt and dishonesty cannot undermine me, for I know these always cause problems and destruction. You, lost soul, I tell you, of your dress and mine, which of the two is more respectful, which one covers the body best?

Thus, the modernity of the nationalist vision and the public discourse about moral womanhood had its limitations. Definitions of authentic tradition and notions of moral womanhood became more and more mutually constitutive. Articulating national identity in terms of cultural authenticity (sanctioned by Somali tradition and Islam), cultural authenticity in terms of women's morality, and women's morality in terms of women's behavior and dress in public space (and thus their sexuality and obedience or respect for authority) severely foreclosed—on the level of public discourse—the possibility for Somali women to be modern.[39]

Political Violence and New Struggles over
Communal Identity and Moral Womanhood

Although, at the level of popular discourse, achieving moral modernity thus became more difficult for women, the Barre regime's introduction of the Family Law of 1975, which brought women equality with men in divorce, inheritance, custody, and other personal status laws, turned out to be a mixed blessing for the cause of women's emancipation. When the regime, fortified by strong Soviet support, proved itself ready to brutally oppress any opposition, by executing ten religious sheikhs who had spoken out against the family law, the concept of women's emancipation—already controversial in this period of rapid change—became associated with a regime that was ever more obviously oppressive.

Nevertheless, throughout the period 1960–90, many women, especially those who, in spite of the deteriorating political and economic conditions, managed to get an education and aspire to middle-class status, led modern and moral lives. Especially under the Barre regime, women received government scholarships to study abroad, obtained graduate degrees, and found work in practically all sectors of government, even if rarely at the highest levels. Women also played key roles in voluntary and state-mandated community organizations at all levels, in which they worked with, and often outperformed, men. However, as occurred in many military regimes, the government created and used a national women's organization for its own ends.[40] Thus a narrowing of the public discourse about women's social freedom did not foreclose their economic and educational, or even political, opportunities. It did, however, mark a social moral unease and fortified conservative critics then and later.

The nationalist project foundered well before the state collapsed in January 1991. However, the violence incited by power-hungry warlords masquerading as national leaders and perpetrated by many ordinary Somalis marked its demise, at least for the foreseeable future. With it went the collective self-conception and gender discourse that had been part of it. Although many Somalis resisted the call to commit violence in the name of clan, during the civil war, there were many lapses of morality—traditional or modern—with Somali women paying an especially high (and gender-specific) price. Women became victims of abduction, sexual abuse and assault, maiming, and murder, as well as the hunger and disease that resulted from the war. This was true in Somalia, as well as during the massive exodus and in the refugee camps in neighboring countries. Though there were women among the initial perpetrators of violence, and though many women, after the violence had started, supported it in word, deed, or thought, it was through their leadership in saving others that women distinguished themselves. Somali families in the diaspora often comment on how Somali women—young and old, in or outside Somalia—came to the rescue of their family, friends, and neighbors. "Which daughterless family even survived?" is the hyperbolic, rhetorical question often asked.[41]

There are still very few studies of how Somali women's lives changed in Somalia in the wake of the civil war. As happened elsewhere in parallel circumstances,[42] it is reported that Somali women continued to take on exceptional leadership roles. They often became the breadwinners of their families and restored the basic institutions of communal life and survival. They also participated, jointly, as women, at all levels, in peacemaking, as has been attested to by a number of recent reports and publications, including a book largely written by Somali women themselves: *Somalia: The Untold Story—The War through the Eyes of Somali Women.*[43] However, neither in Somalia nor in the diaspora have women as yet developed a common agenda and a public voice.[44]

It is perhaps too early to discern the full impact of the new gender ideologies that have begun to take shape since the civil war. However, it appears that the common conceptualization of a moral public identity in terms of Somali tradition described above has fallen casualty to the fratricide. *Soomaalinimo,* the shared sense of being Somali, proved unable to protect Somalis from each other—not even Somali women from Somali men. Moreover, during the war, unscrupulous agitators resorted to clannist instrumentalism and a denial of the validity of *soomaalinimo* to incite people to violence, while some postwar writings have denied that national feeling and a nationally minded, inclusive state project ever even existed.[45] Therefore, the sectarianism (clannism) in whose name people had been incited to violence and that is currently an organizing principle of the new Transition Federal Government is a powerful challenge to *soomaalinimo,* even though it is highly questionable whether it can provide a moral common and public identity for Somalis in their interactions with each other and the world.[46] As the discourse on the solidarity of *soomaalinimo* broke down, appeals to an Islamic morality became increasingly explicit. Therefore—this chapter posits—although Islam was always an integral part of *soomaalinimo,* and although *soomaalinimo*—especially if it can respond to the rightful critiques from the minorities—is far from a spent force among Somalis—the articulation of a common public identity in Islamic terms has gained strength, including in the context of prescriptions for moral womanhood.

As we saw above, when the popular songs and public discourse of the 1960–90 period legitimized moral modernity in terms of authentic Somali tradition, this did not mean that Islam was absent, for it was ever present, both implicitly, because traditional Somali morality was seen as coterminous with Islamic morality, and explicitly, as the discursive sanctions of Islam and tradition were invoked in tandem. Moreover, while the nationalist generation of the 1950s and 1960s had not isolated or foregrounded Islam in its emphasis on cultural commonalities, they had remained, with very few exceptions, strongly rooted in Islam. As was the case for many of their contemporaries, their Islam was a strong, liberal Islam, constituting an intrinsic part of their hopes of modernity. However, after the civil war, this shifted dramatically—so dramatically that one might argue that the bifurcation of Somali culture and Islamic religion in the discourses legitimizing Somali moral personhood is a significant marker of the end of the nationalist era and the beginning of a new one.

The bifurcated view of culture and religion as legitimizing discourse and the shift to Islam as the focus of a new, common, public morality predates the civil war and was, from its inception, closely related to women and gender ideology. Though this shift was part of the emergence of Islamist and jihadist movements worldwide,[47] in Somalia, it may be traced back to 1975, when, as mentioned above, ten religious sheikhs were executed because of their opposition to the Barre regime's Family Law. The 1980s, when large numbers of Somalis became labor migrants in the Middle East and were directly exposed to Islamist trends and regimes, also formed an important milestone. However, popular awareness of the contradictions between *dhaqan* (Somali traditional culture) and *diin* (the religion of Islam) appears to have become acute and general only after the intense civil war violence of 1988, 1991, and after. Thus, the violence of the civil war, including the experiences of refugee camps that often became rape centers, marked the most dramatic transformation of Somali—including Somali women's—self-understandings and self-presentations.[48] As has been argued above, Islam was an intrinsic part of the legitimizing discourses of Somali communal identity and the contestations about moral womanhood. It is just that the nature of Islamic discourse and its relationship to the discourse on tradition has been changing. For women, adopting—or being forced to adopt—a Somali *Muslim* identity, with an emphasis on *diin* or *islaannimo,* instead of a Muslim *Somali* one, with an emphasis on *dhaqan* or *soomaalinimo,* allows for new constructions of social space for Somali women. This has, theoretically, as Salma Ahmed Nageeb has shown for the Sudan, the potential of being emancipatory (especially where alternative models of moral womanhood retain power and women have real powers of choice).[49] However, in Somalia, such emancipatory potential is extremely circumscribed. Here militias that trample both Somali and Western, and traditional and modern cultural values under foot, impose an extremist, deeply anti-intellectual ideology from the barrel of the gun. Thus, they have whipped women for the "modern" transgression of wearing the bra, while they also reject "traditional" Somali forms of dress such as the *diric* and *guntiino* with *garbasaar*.[50] In their eyes, moral womanhood requires not only rejecting anything that is modern *and* Western—an issue about which the nationalist project was deeply ambivalent—but also many of the gender norms associated with the "Somali traditional culture" to which nationalist discourse had turned for legitimization.

There is no doubt that, under the influence of a range of Islamist discourses,[51] gender norms for Somali women have in many aspects narrowed even outside the areas in which Somali Islamist militias are battling it out. However, at the same time, the actual lives of Somali women worldwide have created more space for women's personal agency and choice, in spite of circumstances that are often materially, socially, and psychologically daunting.[52] In recalibrating their own norms of moral womanhood, Somali women both in and outside Somalia will inevitably shape and be shaped by the powerful Islamist and other discourses that try to fashion them in their image.

If gender norms have changed since the collapse of the state, the Somali popular song, the central discursive site in which nationalist modernity and moral womanhood were articulated and contested, has also been transformed.[53] These songs are increasingly produced outside Somalia and disseminated digitally via the Internet, CDs, DVDs, and MP files, and they have survived and have continued to celebrate and grieve over love won or lost. They have also continued to comment on common Somali experiences such as the hardships of the civil war, flight, and the experiences of being refugees in foreign climes, and occasionally comment on political issues, such as support for the self-proclaimed Republic of Somaliland or a call for war against the Ethiopian troops in Somalia. Male and female singers perform a variation of identities in their music videos—with a particularly impressive creative space opened up by Somali- and English-language rappers such as the famous Somali-Canadian artist K'naan.[54] The relations between

men and women (especially young men and women in love) continue to figure prominently in many lyrics, but verbal and visual references to the new
Islamist discourses and the moral womanhood imagined in their image enter the songs in interesting and ambivalent ways. Thus the female singers
of the Kenyan-Somali rap group Waayaha Cusub ("New Times") now usually wear scarves. Moreover, in a song video of late 2006, in which they ful-
minate against the Ethiopian military presence in Somalia (from December
2006 to the end of 2008), the lyrics refer to the duty of "holy war" incumbent on every patriotic Somali, while Falis, the lead female singer, swings
and sways her svelte body against the background of a banner reading
"jihad." In 2010, however, the group came out with a song against the
Islamist al-Shabaab movement, whose militias have taken over a large part
of south-central Somalia, and young Falis was without a headscarf again,
perhaps to protest this movement's authoritarian treatment of women and
disrespect for Somali traditional culture.[55]

As the expressions of a changing youth culture, the new songs continue
to be significant. However, and this is a major shift, the popular songs are no
longer the central—even iconic—site of public discourse they were in the
era 1960–90. This role has now been taken over by the Internet, where hundreds of Somali web sites compete to promote and disseminate the interests
and interpretations of their (often, although not always, clan-identified) tar-
get groups.[56] For the many Somalis who do not have access to the Internet,
this function is fulfilled by Somali-language radio programs such as those of
the BBC, the Voice of America, and the radio stations of neighboring countries such as Djibouti and Kenya, as well as, on a smaller scale, those that
have sprung up in all regions of Somalia.[57] It is here that many of the discursive battles about communal identity, the nature of the state, the role of
Islam and Islamism, and (often implicitly) gender norms are waged.[58]

Notes

1. Margot Badran, *Feminists, Islam, and Nation: Gender and the Making of Modern Egypt* (Princeton, N.J.: Princeton University Press, 1994); Marnia Lazreg, *The Elo-
quence of Silence: Algerian Women in Question* (New York: Routledge, 1994); Deniz
Kandiyoti, ed., *Women, Islam & the State* (Philadelphia: Temple University Press, 1991).

2. Lidwien Kapteijns, "Disintegration of Somalia: A Historiographical Essay," *Bildhaan: An International Journal of Somali Studies* 3 (2003): 11–52.

3. For this book, I transcribed, with the assistance of Maryan Omar Ali, more than
500 songs, of which 120 were transcribed in great detail. Since 1999, I have continued
to study Somali songs as one discourse among many on the violence of the civil war.

4. See Saadia Touval, *Somali Nationalism: International Politics and the Drive for Unity in the Horn of Africa* (Cambridge, Mass.: Harvard University Press, 1963); and Paolo Tripodi, *The Colonial Legacy in Somalia: Rome and Mogadishu—From Colonial Administration to Operation Restore Hope* (New York: St. Martin's Press, 1999).

5. Abdirazak Haji Hussen, "The Somali Crisis: How Did It Happen and Where Do We Go from Here?" public lecture presented at the Somali Institute for Research and Development's Public Forum Series 2004, Boston, May 2, 2004.

6. This was especially true for those based on race and caste.

7. Abdi Samatar, *The State and Rural Transformation in Northern Somalia, 1885–1985* (Madison: University of Wisconsin Press, 1989).

8. See Lidwien Kapteijns and Mursal Farah, "Review of I. M. Lewis, *A Pastoral Democracy: A Study of Pastoralism and Politics among the Northern Somali of the Horn of Africa* (3rd ed., 1999)," *Africa* 4, no. 71 (2001): 719–23; and Lidwien Kapteijns (with Maryan Omar Ali), *Women's Voices in a Man's World: Women and the Pastoral Tradition in Northern Somali Orature, c. 1899–1980* (Portsmouth, N.H.: Heinemann, 1999), 151–57, for a brief analysis of the colonial transformation of Somali kinship. Also see Lidwien Kapteijns, "Women and the Crisis of Communal Identity: The Cultural Construction of Gender in Somali History," in *The Somali Challenge: From Catastrophe to Renewal?* edited by Ahmed I. Samatar (Boulder, Colo.: Lynne Rienner, 1994), 211–31; and Abdi Samatar, "Destruction of State and Society in Somalia: Beyond the Tribal Convention," *Journal of Modern African Studies* 30, no. 4 (1992): 625–41.

9. Donald Donham argues that "to invoke the modern involves a particular rhetorical stance and a way of experiencing time and historicity, with a certain structure of progressive expectation for the future." Constructing views of the "traditional" is, therefore, in his view, intrinsic to modern projects. Donald Donham, "On Being Modern in a Capitalist World: Some Conceptual Issues," in *Critically Modern: Alternatives, Alterities, Anthropologies,* edited by Bruce M. Knauft (Bloomington: Indiana University Press, 2002, 241–57; the quotation here is on 244. For a recent discussion of modernity and nationalism in colonial Sudan, see Heather J. Sharkey, *Living with Colonialism: Nationalism and Culture in the Anglo-Egyptian Sudan* (Berkeley: University of California Press, 2003).

10. For education during the colonial period, see Samatar, *The State*, 59–81; and Lewis, *Modern History,* 97–98, 103, 133, 148–49.

11. Samatar, *The State;* Lewis, *Modern History,* 142–43.

12. For the failures of leadership, see David D. Laitin and Said S. Samatar, *Somalia: Nation in Search of a State* (Boulder, Colo.: Westview Press, 1987); and Ahmed I. Samatar, *Socialist Somalia: Rhetoric & Reality* (London: Zed Books, 1988). For dependence on foreign aid, see Ahmed I. Samatar and Abdi I. Samatar, "The Material Roots of the Suspended Somali State," *Journal of Modern African Studies* 25, no. 4 (1987): 669–90; and Ozay Mehmet, "Effectiveness of Foreign Aid: The Case of Somalia, *Journal of Modern African Studies* 9, no. 2 (1971): 31–47.

13. More research is needed on the group of artists whose creative genius gave shape to this dimension of the Somali nationalist narrative. Kapteijns, *Women's Voices,* 104–6, may overstate the level of formal education of this group and understate the impact of state institutions (e.g., the radio stations of Hargeisa and Mogadishu) in promoting and commissioning socially relevant songwriting. However, artists were certainly urban people who had strong ties to, or roots in, the rural areas and thus served as cultural brokers between the city and the countryside (*miyi iyo magaalo*).

14. Somalia did not have an official Somali orthography until 1972. Even though the massive literacy campaigns that followed this dramatically raised basic literacy levels in city and countryside, Somalia remained in many ways an oral society.

15. For the history of the Somali popular song, see John J. Johnson, *Heellooy, Heelleellooy: The Development of the Genre Heello in Modern Somali Poetry* (Bloomington: Indiana University Press, 1974); and Kapteijns, *Women's Voices,* part two. The label "popular song" or "pop song" is mine, but it is based on the Somali term for the *hees,* or "modern song," which consists of love songs (analyzed by Kapteijns, in *Women's Voices*) and explicitly political songs (analyzed by Johnson, in *Heellooy*). The discourse of *soomaalinimo* and Somali unity informs both genres, but is most explicit in the political songs, so much so that there is a whole subgenre called *waddani* or "patriotic" songs. For the term *hees* and its thematic subdivision, see Maxamed Daahir Afrax, *Fan-Masraxeedka Soomaalida: Raad-raac Taariikheed iyo Faaqidaad Riwaayado Caan-baxay* (published by the author, 1987).

16. Interviews with Faduumo Qasim Hilowle and Ahmed Ismail Hussein Hudeidi, by Ahmed I. Samatar and Lidwien Kapteijns, Saint Paul, July 18 and 20, 2004. The state purposely promoted a national popular culture by creating and financing the radio stations of Mogadishu and Hargeisa and the National Theater in Mogadishu, and paid artists to write songs and plays for these institutions. During the regime of Barre (1969–91), artists increasingly felt the pressure to toe the state's ideological line, but as late as 1989, popular songs epitomized the mood of the people, as in the 1989 song "Land Cruiser," sung by Sado Ali and written by Abdi Muhumed Amin, that blasted the government for spending foreign aid money on land cruisers, while the common inhabitants of the capital had neither electricity nor water.

17. For Somali drama, see Hassan Sheikh Mumin, *Leopard among the Women (Shabeelnaagood),* translated and introduced by B. W. Andrzejewski (London: Oxford University Press, 1974); Afrax, *Fan-Masraxeedka Soomaalida;* and Maxamed Daahir Afrax, "Theatre as a Window on Society: Opposing Influences of Tradition and Modernity in Somali Plays," *Halabuur: Journal for Somali Literature and Culture* 1 and 2 (2007): 74–82.

18. Kelly Askew uses the term "national imaginaries" for "the multiple and often contradictory layers and fragments of ideology that underlie continually shifting conceptions of any given nation." Here, "the nationalist imaginary" stands for the sociocultural dimension of the nation-building project and its impact on notions of Somali public identity. Kelly M. Askew, *Performing the Nation: Swahili Music and Cultural Politics in Tanzania* (Chicago: Chicago University Press, 2002), 273.

19. Said S. Samatar, *Oral Poetry and Somali Nationalism: The Case of Sayyid Mahammad 'Abdille Hasan* (Cambridge: Cambridge University Press, 1982), 56–57. Samatar says this about what nomadic society regarded as its most prestigious genres of oral poetry—precisely the genres that had the greatest influence on the popular song.

20. Samatar, *Oral Poetry,* 58.

21. This was the case in spite of the reification of nomadic tradition that is evident in the popular culture of this period. I have analyzed this previously; see Kapteijns, *Women's Voices,* 151–57. See also Ali Jimale Ahmed, ed., *The Invention of Somalia* (Lawrenceville, N.J.: Red Sea Press, 1995), which diagnoses the problem well but does not do justice to its historical genesis.

22. This is the burden of the second part of Kapteijns, *Women's Voices.* Partha Chatterjee interprets the nationalist cultural project in Asia and Africa slightly differently and

argues that, for example in India, the cultural (sovereignty) project was complete before the political one was undertaken. In Somalia, the cultural project followed the achievement of political independence. Partha Chatterjee, *The Nation and Its Fragments: Colonial and Postcolonial Histories* (Princeton, N.J.: Princeton University Press, 1993), 6.

23. Zeinab Mohamed Jama, "Fighting to Be Heard: Somali Women's Poetry," *African Languages and Cultures* 4, no. 1 (1991): 43–53; and Mariam Muse Boqor, "Somali Women's Roles in the Movement for Independence," oral presentation at the celebration of Somali National Week, Somali Women's and Children's Association, Boston, June 29, 2001. It is precisely because of our limited historical knowledge of Somali women's lives, including their role in the nationalist movement, that I have turned to the songs as a source, if not for women's lives, then at least for discourses about women.

24. Touval, *Somali Nationalism,* 87.

25. See Boqor, "Somali Women's Roles." Compare Badran, *Feminists, Islam, and Nation;* Naomi Chazan, "Gender Perspectives on African States," in *Women and the State in Africa,* edited by Jane L. Parpart and Kathleen A. Staudt (Boulder, Colo.: Lynne Rienner, 1989), 185–201; and Gisela Geisler, "Troubled Sisterhood: Women and Politics in Southern Africa: Case Studies from Zambia, Zimbabwe and Botswana," *African Affairs* 94, no. 377 (1995): 545–78.

26. Lila Abu-Lughod gives as characteristics of modern personhood "a rich inner life and an intense individuality," as well as being "autonomous, bounded, self-activating, [and] verbalizing him/herself." Lila Abu-Lughod, "Modern Subjects: Egyptian Melodrama and Postcolonial Difference," in *Questions of Modernity,* edited by Timothy Mitchell (Minneapolis: University of Minnesota Press, 2000), 87–114; the quotations here are on 94 and 95, respectively. Catherine Lutz and Abu-Lughod argue that such "modern subjects" are also characterized by particular constructions of emotionality, quoting Foucault as arguing that "emotion discourse might represent a privileged site of production of the modern self." Catherine A. Lutz and Lila Abu-Lughod, "Introduction: Emotion, Discourse, and the Politics of Everyday Life," in *Language and the Politics of Emotion,* edited by Catherine A. Lutz and Lila Abu Lughod (Cambridge: Cambridge University Press, 1990), 1–23; the quotation here is on 6.

27. Kapteijns, *Women's Voices,* 111–49.

28. Maryan Muuse, interviewed in Boston, Ramadan (January–February), 2001.

29. Kapteijns, *Women's Voices,* 121–40.

30. Ibid., 141–42, 203.

31. Faduumo and Haydar, a couple of legendary fame, believed to have lived in sixteenth-century Zeila and to have died of love. See Kapteijns, *Women's Voices,* 162.

32. Mumin, *Leopard among the Women.*

33. My translation, but with reference to Mumin, *Leopard among the Women,* 174–77.

34. My translation, but with reference to Mumin, *Leopard among the Women,* 92–95. See also Kapteijns, *Women's Voices,* 144–45.

35. Kapteijns, *Women's Voices,* 201–2.

36. See, e.g., Lata Mani, "Contentious Traditions: The Debate on 'Sati' in Colonial India," in *Recasting Women: Essays in Colonial History,* edited by Kumkum Sangari and Sudesh Vaid (New Delhi: Kali for Women, 1989), 88–126; and Peter Knauss, *The Persistence of Patriarchy: Class, Gender and Ideology in Twentieth-Century Algeria* (New York: Praeger, 1987).

37. Kapteijns, *Women's Voices,* 199–200.

38. Ibid., 200–201.

39. Ibid., 156–57.

40. We do not have a comprehensive history of women during the Barre regime, but see Abdurahman Abdullahi, "Women, Islamists and the Military Regime in Somalia: The Reform of the Family Law and Its Repercussions," unpublished paper; 2007; Somali Women's Democratic Organization, *Women in the SDR* [Somali Democratic Republic]*: An Appraisal of the Progress in the Implementation of the World Plan of Action of the United Nations Decade for Women, 1971–85* (Mogadishu: Somali Women's Democratic Organization, 1985); Samatar, *Socialist Somalia,* esp. 103–7, 113; and Laitin and Samatar, *Somalia,* esp. 86–87, 95.

41. Oral information, Somali community of Boston, 2001.

42. See, e.g., Swanee Hunt and Cristina Posa, "Women Waging Peace," *Foreign Policy* 124 (May–June 2001): 38–47; and Haleh Esfandiari, *Reconstructed Lives: Women and Iran's Islamic Revolution* (Washington, D.C.: Woodrow Wilson Center Press, 1997).

43. Judith Gardner and Judy El Bushra, eds., *Somalia: The Untold Story—The War through the Eyes of Somali Women* (London: Pluto Press, 2004).

44. It has been evident at all major national reconciliation meetings that Somali women also allow themselves to be used as instruments for the sectarian pursuits of their menfolk. See also Matt Bryden and Martina I. Steiner, *Somalia between Peace and War: Somali Women on the Eve of the 21st Century,* African Women for Peace Series (Nairobi: UNIFEM, 1998). Gardner and El-Bushra, *Somalia,* suggest that the women's movement in the (as yet not internationally recognized) Republic of Somaliland appears to be one of the most developed.

45. See, e.g., Paolo Tripodi, *The Colonial Legacy in Somalia.* For a critique of such ahistorical revisionism, see Lidwien Kapteijns, "Review Essay: State and Clan in Somalia," *African Studies Review* 3 (2002): 52–58.

46. For a discussion of the postwar historiography on Somalia, see Kapteijns, "Disintegration."

47. For different kinds of Islamisms (including jihadism), see Alex de Waal, ed., *Islamism and Its Enemies in the Horn of Africa* (Bloomington: Indiana University Press, 2004). For Somalia, see Abdurahman Abdullahi, "Recovering Somalia: The Islamic Factor," paper presented to the Ninth International Congress of Somali Studies, Aalborg University, September 6–7, 2004.

48. For women, the new emphasis on Islam as a marker of moral womanhood was born from the experience of violence, flight, and resettlement in a new and alien context (Boston, participant observation, 2001). See Awa Abdi, "Refugee Camps in Kenya: Where Is the Light?" *Journal of the Anglo-Somali Society* (Spring 2004). For a visually stunning representation of women in the camps, see Fazal Sheikh, *A Camel for the Son* (Gottingen: Steidl, 2001).

49. Compare Salma Ahmed Nageeb, *New Spaces and Old Frontiers: Women, Social Space, and Islamization in Sudan* (Lanham, Mass.: Lexington Books, 2004).

50. Abdi Sheik, "Somali Islamists Whip Women for Wearing Bras," Reuters, October 16, 2009, http://af.reuters.com/article/oddlyEnoughNews/idAFTRE59F1K420091016?sp=true. A *diric* is a loose, untailored dress, usually of very light and beautiful cotton voile, and a *guntiino* is a garment that is tightly wrapped around the body and knotted on top of one shoulder, leaving the other bare. A *garbasaar* is a shawl or wrap worn over

the shoulders and hiding the upper body. These and other forms of dress were considered Somali dress in the nationalist era.

51. In Somalia, Al-Islah al-Islami claims to present an Islamist movement and philosophy that purposefully promotes women's agency and active social roles. See Abdurahman Abdullahi, "Recovering Somalia."

52. See, e.g., Hamdi Mohamed, "Multiple Challenges, Multiple Struggles: A History of Women's Activism in Canada" (PhD diss., University of Ottawa, 2003).

53. The following is provisional, as it is the subject matter of my current research.

54. For K'naan, see www.dustyfoot.com.

55. Waayaha Cusub, "Somalis, Fight and Battle," and "How Amazing al-Shabaab," both available at www.youtube.com, and uploaded respectively on December 16, 2006, and March 17, 2010.

56. Abdisalam M. Issa-Salwe, "The Internet and Somali Diaspora: The Web as a New Means of Expression," *Bildhaan: An International Journal of Somali Studies* 6 (2006): 54–67. According to Salwe, there were more than 400 Somali Web sites as of mid-2004. There are some sites specifically dealing with Islamic perspectives on Somali matters (e.g., www.daralhijrah.com and www.islaax.org), while other sites have sections devoted to religion.

57. See, e.g., the left-hand columns of the home pages of Somali Web sites, e.g., www.hiiraanonline.com and www.wardheernews.com.

58. For an analysis of some such poetic texts published on the Somali Web sites, see Lidwien Kapteijns, "Memory-Making of Mogadishu in Somali Poetry about the Civil War," in *Mediations of Violence in Africa: Fashioning New Futures from Contested Pasts,* edited by Lidwien Kapteijns and Annemiek Richters (Leiden: Brill, 2010).

Chapter 6

Guidelines for the Ideal Muslim Woman: Gender Ideology and Praxis in the Tabligh Jama'at in the Gambia

Marloes Janson

In 1996, when conducting ethnographic field research on female performers in the Gambia, I was surprised by the sight of a few lightweight dome tents on the veranda of a village mosque. The colors of the canvas contrasted sharply with the mud walls of the mosque. Upon inquiry, I learned that these tents had been erected by "white" preachers. Because I was still under the impression that all "whites" were either Europeans or North Americans, I assumed that the tents represented some type of foreign aid action. After a few days, they disappeared, and I forgot about them.

About two years later, I saw a woman covered from head to foot in a

This chapter is based on ethnographic fieldwork conducted between November 2003 and April 2004, and April and June 2005 in the Gambia. The research was funded by a grant from the International Institute for the Study of Islam in the Modern World in Leiden. I wish to thank Margot Badran for asking me to contribute to this volume. I am indebted to her, Kamran Ali, Barbara Cooper, Francesca Declich, Dorothea Schulz, Yoginder Sikand, Abdulkader Tayob, and an anonymous reviewer for comments on earlier versions of this chapter. All errors of course are my own.

black robe at the market. Because I had never seen a woman dressed in this way in the Gambia before, I was curious, and I asked my traveling companion if the woman was a Gambian and to which movement she belonged. He shrugged his shoulders and answered that she must be a "ninja from Saudi."[1] It was then that I learned that, in addition to Europeans and North Americans, Arabs are also referred to as "whites."[2] Believing the woman covered in black to be a Wahhabi,[3] we continued our journey. Once I gained more insight into the Islamic revival in the Gambia, I was able to connect these two seemingly unrelated incidents, both of which reflect the proliferation of the Tabligh Jama'at in the country.

The Tabligh Jama'at is a transnational Islamic missionary movement with origins in the reformist tradition that emerged in northern India in the mid–nineteenth century. Its founder, Mawlana Muhammad Ilyas (1885–1944), believed that Muslims had abandoned the true path of Islam and needed to "return" to the faith to become "authentic" believers. Ilyas strove for a purification of Islam as practiced by individual Muslims through closer adherence to the rules laid down in the *Sunna* (the sayings and practices of the Prophet Muhammad). Over the years, the Tabligh Jama'at expanded into what is probably the largest Islamic movement of contemporary times. It has established a presence in more than one hundred fifty countries throughout the world, and its annual conferences (*ijtima*) in Pakistan and Bangladesh now constitute the second-largest religious gatherings of Muslims after the pilgrimage to Mecca.[4]

Despite the Jama'at's influence on the lives of millions of Muslim men and women worldwide, scholars have paid almost no attention to its growth in Sub-Saharan Africa.[5] One explanation for this indifference is that Sub-Saharan Africa is frequently, but unjustly, seen as the "periphery" of the Muslim world. I focus on the Gambia, which despite its small size has become a flourishing center of Tablighi activities in West Africa during the last decade.[6] Adherents from other African countries regularly assemble in the Gambian city of Serrekunda to exchange ideas on the proper Tablighi method, that is, missionary work aimed at the moral transformation of Muslims.[7]

Within the growing corpus of writings on the Tabligh Jama'at, almost no mention has been made of the women in the movement.[8] This neglect is striking, particularly because in many studies of religious "fundamentalism," women's conduct and appearance are portrayed as emblems of Islam in general.[9] Like most other fundamentalist discourses,[10] the Tabligh Jama'at's moral discourse articulates the ideal gender role for Muslim women as mothers and housewives, with men as breadwinners. As such, it seeks to draw a rigid boundary between the private and public spheres. The role of women is ideally restricted to the realm of the home, while the Gambian branch of the Jama'at demands that, on the contrary, women undertake long-distance missionary tours (which have become the hallmark of the movement worldwide) and deliver public speeches on proper Muslim womanhood. The female followers' public prominence and articulateness challenge the private/public divide. Thus, there appears to be a contradiction between the way femininity is constructed in universal Tablighi ideology and the way it is experienced daily by Gambian women. This chapter explores how Gambian women negotiate this contradiction, and reconcile their gendered Muslim identity with the religious values propagated by the Jama'at's headquarters in South Asia.

As Camillia Fawzi El-Solh and Judy Mabro argue, "The factors which separate or unite the various contemporary discourses on women's 'proper' role in society cannot be adequately understood without gauging to what extent Muslim women themselves participate in these discourses."[11] Taking a similar tack, this chapter aims to depict women not as objects in Tablighi discourse, with its strong emphasis on gender segregation (purdah), but rather as agents in the Islamization process in the Gambia that I have observed during the past decade.[12] In the following pages, the female Tablighis' agency is elucidated in the context of Saba Mahmood's argument about the "docile agent," which suggests that even as women pursue practices and ideals embedded within a tradition that accords them a somewhat submissive status, they create a new form of piety from which they may derive religious empowerment.[13]

Conducting research on the Tabligh Jama'at is quite an undertaking, especially for a non-Muslim female scholar. During my fieldwork, at first I was seen as a spy and an enemy, and the Gambian Tablighis were often reluctant to talk to me. An influential male activist would only be interviewed from behind a curtain.[14] Interviewing male informants became easier when I adopted the Tablighi dress code for women. I was still told time and again, however, that I was not welcome at the Tablighi sessions organized for women and that my name appeared on the organization's "blacklist." But after a few months of perseverance, I was allowed to attend several female learning sessions (*ta'lim*) and to join a missionary tour (*khuruj*) aimed at spreading Tablighi ideology. By participating in these sessions and tour, I gained a better understanding of Tablighi women's endeavors to integrate Islam into their daily lives. I tape-recorded all the *ta'lim* that I attended as well as the sermons delivered during the *khuruj*. Two Tablighi men helped me translate into English whatever was spoken in Mandinka and Arabic during these events.

During my interactions, I had insightful talks with both female and male Tablighi followers. I recorded eight "conversion" stories.[15] "Conversion" here does not refer to the transition from one religion to another but to the embracing of a new form of piety.[16] Yoginder Sikand and Dietrich Reetz remark that the literature on the Jama'at primarily seeks to explicate the movement's fundamental principles, paying little attention to questions of how Tablighi ideology plays out in the lives of individual Muslims and how the Jama'at operates on a daily basis.[17] The conversion stories I recorded provide insight into how doctrine is put into practice. A Tablighi exists in a state of constant interaction with people who engage in different discourses and practices. Information was therefore also obtained from interviews and informal conversations with numerous non-Tablighis.

An account of a *ta'lim* session, a *khuruj,* and a conversion story serves as the starting point of an analysis of the accommodation between Tablighi gender ideology and praxis. Within the limitations inherent to ethnographic research in the Tabligh Jama'at, I cautiously portray Gambian women's involvement in this puritan movement in order to counterbalance the masculine image of "fundamentalist" Muslim movements. But before doing so, I give a brief historical outline of the Jama'at.

The History of the Tabligh Jama'at and Its Rooting in the Gambia

The emergence of the Tabligh Jama'at as a movement for the revival of Islam can be seen as a continuation of a broader trend of Islamic resurgence, which started in India in the wake of the collapse of Muslim power and the consolidation of British rule in the mid–nineteenth century. One manifestation of this trend was the rapid growth of madrassas (religious schools). The Jama'at evolved out of the teachings and practices of the founders of the orthodox Dar-ul 'Ulum madrasa in Deoband, a town near the Indian capital of Delhi. The *'ulama'* (scholars learned in Islamic sciences) affiliated with this school saw themselves as crusaders against Hindu conversion movements and popular expressions of Islam, and they aspired to again bring to life the days of the Prophet Muhammad's companions (*sahaba*).[18]

Mawlana Ilyas was a disciple of the leading Deobandi *'ulama'*, who upon graduation began to teach Muslims about proper Islamic beliefs and practices at mosque-based schools. He soon became disillusioned with this approach, realizing that Islamic schools were producing "religious functionaries" but not zealous preachers who were willing to go from door to door to remind people of the key values and practices of Islam. He then quit his teaching position to begin missionary work through itinerant preaching.[19] This was innovative, in that Ilyas insisted that it was the religious duty of not just a few learned scholars but all Muslims, men and women alike,[20] to carry out Tabligh work. The missionary tours by lay preachers became the hallmark of the Tabligh Jama'at,[21] which was officially established by Ilyas in 1927 in Delhi.

Over the years, the Jama'at has expanded from its international headquarters in India to numerous other countries throughout the world.[22] South Asian missionaries reached West Africa in the early 1960s.[23] As it has developed, the Jama'at has been adapted to numerous local environments, which is reflected in the names by which it is known.[24] In the Gambia, it is called Markaz, which means "center." Markaz does not refer here to the spiritual center of the Muslim world but to a center of *da'wa* (call to Islam) in Bundung, a densely populated neighborhood in Serrekunda, the Gambia's largest city. (Markaz thus refers both to the movement and to the physical structure in Bundung.) In Markaz, men perform their prayers, immerse themselves in constant remembrance of God, listen to sermons, recite the Qur'an, read aloud from the *Faza'il-e-A'maal* (The Merits of Practice)— the most widely read corpus of religious texts in the Jama'at (see below)— talk about the faith, and even spend the night. Markaz is not open to women, but they have their own meeting places, as will be elucidated below.

Worldwide, the supporters of the Tabligh Jama'at are known as Tablighis, but in the Gambian setting they are called Mashalas, as they often exclaim the Arabic expression *"ma sha' allah"* (what God wishes). However, Gambian Tablighis normally do not use this term in referring to themselves, for they see it as having a negative connotation. Many informants told me: "We call ourselves just ordinary Muslims. All we do is follow the footsteps of the prophet." Interestingly, the local Tablighis see themselves as regular Muslims, because they strictly observe what they believe to be the Prophet Muhammad's model, and thus they regard the more "mainstream" Muslims as deviant.[25] Tablighis' observance of the prophet's alleged model is visible in the way they dress and behave. Male adepts can be recognized by their trousers that fall above the ankles, knee-length plain caftans, turbans, and beards,[26] and their wives by their simple full-length black robes, and veils. Other distinguishing features are the bedding and cooking utensils they carry on their backs.[27] Believing that the prophet advocated self-help, they are reluctant to impose on others during their frequent missionary tours and therefore sleep in mosques and cook for themselves. During my field research, it emerged that as a result of their engagement in domestic work, male Tablighis are frequently called "feminine men" by "mainstream" Muslims.[28]

The Gambia's British colonial heritage is one factor that has helped facilitate the spread of Tablighi ideology, which was disseminated mainly by Pakistanis who preached in English (the national language of the Gambia). In Senegal, the neighboring francophone country, the Jama'at is indeed much less popular. This situation is due, probably, not only to the language in which the movement preaches but also to the fact that Sufi brotherhoods are more prominent in Senegal than in the Gambia. Nyang claims the difference in popularity of the brotherhoods in Senegal and the Gambia is connected to their diverse colonial experiences.[29] In Senegal, the pattern of cooperation between rulers and *marabouts* (local Sufi clerics) in colonial times was continued by several contemporary Senegalese leaders, whereas the colonial alienation of Gambian Muslims created conditions that led to the development of Islamic reformism. The appearance of Tablighi preachers coincided with the recent political Islamic resurgence in the Gambia. Captain Yahya Jammeh assumed power in 1994 and invoked Islam to enhance his legitimacy. This provided fresh scope for the creation of a public discourse on Islamic doctrine in the Gambia.[30] As a result, an increasing number of young Gambians in particular seemed to be receptive to a new interpretation of their faith. Thus conditions in the Gambia provided fertile soil for the Tablighi ideology to take root.[31]

The history of the Tabligh Jama'at in the Gambia began with Imam Dukureh, who studied in Saudi Arabia for several years. In the early 1980s, he returned to his native village, Gambisara, a Serahuli settlement in eastern Gambia,[32] and set out to make the villagers more aware of their religion by denouncing their traditional ways of worship. Except for a few likeminded men, the villagers did not embrace his reformist ideas. The agents of change realized that Gambisara was too provincial for Dukureh's innovative ideas, and they built a compound for him in the populous Bundung area of Serrekunda. Dukureh established a small madrasa in the compound, where he instructed his students in Arabic, Islamic studies, and secular subjects like mathematics. When the number of students increased, the school was transferred in the late 1990s to another neighborhood in Serrekunda, where it still exists.

Dukureh found the ideas of a group of itinerant Pakistani preachers congruent with his own beliefs, and he lodged the men in his compound. Over the years, the compound has expanded, and today a two-story building accommodates Pakistani and other visiting preachers disseminating Tablighi ideology. My informants told me that, unlike the early history of the Tabligh Jama'at in the Gambia, these days visiting preachers stay only a short time. In the early 1990s, a mosque was constructed adjacent to Dukureh's compound. According to several informants, this mosque was financed exclusively by the community, which includes rich Serahuli traders. The fact that the Jama'at has its own mosque is exceptional, because most Gambian Muslims belonging to a brotherhood or any other Islamic association pray together with Muslims belonging to other affiliations.[33] The mosque's size is particularly striking. I was told that it can seat two thousand people, an enormous number by Gambian standards, but the actual number of weekly visitors is a few hundred. During the annual conference (*ijtima'*), the mosque attracts more visitors both from the Gambia and abroad.

When Imam Dukureh died in 1999, Markaz no longer had a regular imam. Gambian preachers who have long been involved in the Jama'at now lead the Thursday night and Friday prayers. A small council of "elders" (*shura*) who have long experience with Tabligh work is in charge of Markaz. The council is led by the *amir* (leader). Outgoing preaching groups, from among themselves, elect an *amir* whose orders must be obeyed unquestioningly for the duration of the missionary tour, a recurring event in the Tablighi's life. During subsequent tours, other men are selected as *amir*s.

A striking feature of the Tabligh Jama'at in the Gambia is its popularity among the local African population, particularly the youth of both sexes. In South Africa and in the eastern part of Africa, the Jama'at appeals primarily to Muslims of Indian ancestry.[34] In the Gambia, this group is very small. The Tablighi effort has been adopted primarily by Mandinka (trained by mainly Pakistani preachers), who form the largest ethnic group in the Gambia. Nevertheless, these local Muslims are frequently considered "outsiders" by more "mainstream" Muslims on account of their ideas, practices, and dress code. This applies particularly to the female followers, whom, as we saw above, many Gambians assume to be Saudi Wahhabi women because their faces and bodies are usually completely covered.[35]

The Tabligh Jama'at holds special attraction for middle-class Gambian men and women in their twenties who have a modern, secular education.[36] Elsewhere in Africa, the movement appears to hold greater attraction for middle-aged men.[37] When I asked one of the leading figures in the Gambian Jama'at why it focuses on young people in particular, he addressed me in a direct way: "If you are going to marry, do you prefer a young or an old man? You are young, so you prefer a young husband. The same applies to us. We do not want elderly people; we need youth." "Young" could be interpreted in this context as an awareness of the "real rules" of Islam and a willingness to live according to them. Being "old," by contrast, is equated with being rigid and holding on to customary practices.[38]

The appeal of the Tabligh Jama'at to young men and women may be explained partly by the current economic depression in the Gambia and its drastic social effects, which influence the ways they perceive their lives.[39] In response to the malaise, a growing number of youngsters, primarily in urban areas, invest in Tabligh work. Although they do not receive material rewards, they are assured, they believe, a spiritual reward. Erin Augis argues that in Senegal, socioeconomic and political changes also have spurred youth to create a range of subcultures to address these changes, of which reformist Islam is one.[40]

Although followers of the Tabligh Jama'at are proliferating in the Gambia, especially among young men and women, unlike in South Asia they still form a relatively small group. I estimate their number at a few thousand (less than 1 percent of the Gambian population of approximately 1.5 million), but in the absence of membership records, it is hard to calculate the exact number. Despite its small size, the Jama'at is not an insignificant group in the Gambia, for it is largely responsible for bringing about a broad religious transformation in the society, especially in the celebration of life-cycle rituals such as naming ceremonies and weddings. My informants interpret the quest for "true Islam" as the celebration of these rituals according to the *Sunna*. Thus, for example, the naming ceremony is reduced to its essence: The baby's hair is shaved, it is named, and a ram is sacrificed. All the other activities that customarily take place at naming ceremonies—such as singing, drumming, dancing, spending extravagantly on food, and the intermingling of the sexes—are considered to be *bid'a,* or innovations that deviate from the Prophet Muhammad's path.

In line with the Tabligh Jama'at's stress on austerity, the weddings of its adherents are arranged at little cost. This explains why they are able to marry young (on young people's redefinition of marriage, also see chapter 9 in this volume). Mandinka men generally do not marry until they are at least thirty years old, while many of the male Tablighi activists with whom I worked married in their early twenties. Marrying young was important for my informants, who considered their wedding a major turning point in their search for piety. Because of the movement's success in transforming ritual practice, an Islamic scholar told me he suspected that the Mashalas will "dominate the Gambia within a period of five to ten years and will eventually destroy the country."

Life-cycle events have traditionally been dominated by women in West Africa.[41] By stressing the importance of performing these rituals according to the *Sunna,* the Tabligh Jama'at has eliminated whole arenas of ceremonial life that have always been the prerogative of women.[42] A dedicated Tablighi told me that his wife and her female relatives cried when he decided to celebrate his child's naming ceremony modestly, because this meant that they had lost the opportunity to entertain on a lavish scale. Furthermore, the Jama'at seeks to end established religious practices such as shrine worship, which it considers a form of idolatry. Historically, Gambian women have been actively involved in visiting and praying at shrines.[43] Because of such adaptations, women involved in the Jama'at have lost influence in the ritual domain, but, as will become clear below, they have become more prominent in other areas. Indeed, female Tablighis draw upon their understanding of Islam to gain public space.

The Tabligh Jama'at's Gender Ideology

In the name of Allah, the Benefactor, the Merciful. Allah has created everything on Earth and he selected us, humans, as the best among all his creatures. This implies that we have an important role to play on earth and that we should observe our responsibilities. So that we can have a better understanding of our responsibilities, learning sessions like this are organized. Our main responsibility is to worship Allah and to tell other people about the importance of obeying Allah by worshipping him. We should worship Allah by praying in the right way and at the right time, and by doing *dhikr* [remembrance of God]. You [addressing the female audience] should cover yourself from head to foot when praying. Go out of your houses to remind other people of their religious duties. Tell them to do good things and refrain from doing bad things. Disseminate the little knowledge of Islam you have! We cannot afford to stay indoors; we should go out to invite Muslims to Allah's path. Encourage your husbands to come to the Markaz mosque on Thursday night and exhort your relatives and friends to worship Allah. . . .

Everything you do, you should do with a good intention. Everything you do, you should do for the sake of Allah. Therefore, don't love the world, instead love the hereafter! This is all written down in the *hadith*s [accounts of what the Prophet Muhammad said or did]. You should study the *hadith*s, so that you can instruct other people in the Prophet's words. *Hadith*s are the beauty of Islam. But you should not only read the *hadith*s; you should also practice them. The Prophet has said that we should respect and help each other. The one who supports an elderly woman is like a *mujahid* [one who is performing jihad]. Taking care of women is very important in Islam. The Prophet cared for his she-camels, and therefore women should also be cared for by their husbands. . . .

Another *hadith* explains that wealth does not give one dignity; only fear of Allah can bring about dignity. People like to build big houses, but we do not need them. The Prophet has said that all we need is fear of Allah. Don't fear the police, fear Allah! Those mothers who raise their daughters as God-fearing persons will be protected from hell. Besides treating your children well, you should treat your husband in a good manner. That is the wife's obligation. . . . If you observe Allah's commandments and follow in the Prophet's footsteps you will be rewarded. If you do not obey Allah, you will end up in hell. (extract from a male preacher's address at a female learning session in the Bundung neighborhood of Serrekunda)

Several participants in this female learning session told me that in order to receive religious instruction, women were initially welcomed in the women's wing of the Gambian Tabligh Jama'at's mosque, but because they "disturbed" the sermons with their chatting and later with their cellphones, they were subsequently banned. A middle-aged participant said: "At that time, the mosque was like a public telecenter." Nowadays, special learning sessions, called *ta'lim,* are held for the women involved in the Jama'at every Sunday morning in the houses of female Tablighi activists in and around Serrekunda. These sessions offer an unusual opportunity for women to congregate and to expand their knowledge of Islam.

At the *ta'lim* sessions that I attended, between ten and twenty women were present, most of them dressed in a black *burqa'* (a type of woman's outer garment that covers the body from head to foot). Upon arrival in the hostess's house, they lifted their veils, and when I saw their faces I took them to be in their late twenties. Even the four-year-old daughter of our hostess wore a *hijab* (veil). Some women had taken their babies to the venue, although the Jama'at's central headquarters in South Asia forbids women to take children with them to Tablighi activities. The women with whom I worked complained that their crying babies prevented them from concentrating on the *ta'lim*. They insisted that "we are still learning" and hoped that with time they would become full-fledged missionaries.

The majority of the participants in the *ta'lim* were Gambians, but once I met with a woman from Bangladesh. She told me that the *ta'lim* in her motherland and the Gambia are similar in form and content. Barbara Metcalf and Yoginder Sikand observed women's *ta'lim* in South Asia that seem to be organized in a similar way to the practice in the Gambia. According to Metcalf, the *ta'lim* sessions in India serve as neighborhood learning forums. Like the Gambian *ta'lim,* the sessions described by Sikand focus on the need to engage in Tabligh work, strengthen the faith, improve the practice of Islamic ritual, and bring Islam into women's personal lives.[44]

When the aforementioned *ta'lim* began, the participants seated themselves in a semicircle on a large prayer mat on the floor of their hostess's living room. They listened to a sermon delivered by the male preacher from behind a curtain, so that he could not see the women and they could not see him. The preacher delivered his sermon in Arabic but, because most of the participants did not understand it, he translated his words into Mandinka, the lingua franca of the Gambia. Toward the end of the sermon, which lasted for about one and a half hours, some women laid down on the mat or played with their children. After a communal prayer, the women shook hands with each other and left quickly. This account suggests that women played a fairly passive role during the *ta'lim*: They received the sermon delivered by a male preacher from behind a curtain, some women did not seem to listen attentively, and there was no room for discussion. Nevertheless, the participants emphasized that it was highly important for women to attend these sessions in order to become more knowledgeable about Islam and, consequently, more pious Muslims.

The focus of the *ta'lim* was on how to bring "correct" Islam into the women's lives and on their religious duties. The preacher exhorted his audience to worship God by praying and performing *dhikr* (remembrance of God), to cover their bodies, to be sincere in their acts, to show respect for others and to help them, and to fear God, which can be expressed by observing his commandments closely. In this, the preacher was inspired by the Six Points—*Chhe Baten* in Urdu—which form the foundation of the Tabligh Jama'at and are composed of what are believed to be the basic principles of moral behavior.[45] The Six Points include the article of faith (*kalima*), the five daily prayers (*salat*), knowledge of the principles of Islam (*'ilm*) in order to remember God (*dhikr*), mutual respect (*ikram-i-Muslim*), sincerity of purpose (*ikhlas-i-niyyat*), and sparing time from worldly occupations to devote to missionary work (*tafrigh-i-waqt*). These tenets were explicated by means of *hadith*s in Arabic. In addition to these fundamental principles, which apply to both men and women, typical feminine virtues were stressed in the *ta'lim*. The preacher stated that the ideal Muslim woman covers herself and is a good wife and mother who concentrates her efforts on inculcating religious values in her children and especially her daughters. These traditional female roles are explained in the *Faza'il-e-A'maal* (The Merits of Practice),[46] the standard corpus of Tablighi texts written by Mawlana Zakariyya (1898–1982), one of the chief ideologues of the movement,[47] which offers guidance for everyday life.[48] During the *ta'lim* sessions, the male preacher normally reads from this Islamic manual.

In the "Stories of Sahabah," which is the first text in the *Faza'il-e-A'maal* and emphasizes the strong moral character of the companions of the Prophet Muhammad, the ideal woman is presented as a good (house)wife and mother. It is argued that the "lap of the mother is admitted to be the best field of instruction."[49] Fatima, the prophet's beloved daughter, is described as a hard-working housewife.[50] Zakariyya, the author, comments on the story of Fatima as follows: "Look! This is the life of Rasulullah's [the prophet's] dear daughter. In moderately rich families of our times, the ladies think it below their dignity to attend to domestic work. They need assistance in each and every thing, even in their bathroom! What a difference."[51]

The text goes on to suggest that, based on the example of Asma' bint Yazid Ansari (who reportedly represented a delegation of women that visited the Prophet Muhammad to ask what reward women would receive for their hard work), a woman who carries out her domestic tasks to her husband's satisfaction receives the same reward as men receive for their services to Allah.[52] The author concludes that obedience and good behavior toward the husband is a "very great asset for the women," and will lead them to heaven.[53] These extracts show that the Jama'at turns what it believes to be female duties into religious obligations.

The Tabligh Jama'at's universal goal is to assimilate women to what it perceives to be the normative Islamic standard, and, as a result, the *Faza'il-e-A'maal* strongly emphasizes the importance of the seclusion of women.[54] The home is considered women's rightful place and is imagined to be free from intrusions of the vulgar outside world. Nevertheless, the preacher quoted above encouraged his female audience to leave their houses in order to impart good morals to others. As mentioned above, the female *ta'lim* sessions are not unique to the Gambia, but unlike in South Asia, Gambian women are exhorted to engage actively in missionary tours. At the end of the *ta'lim,* the preacher passed around a sheet of paper for the women to record the names of their husbands and the number of days they intended to go on tour.

The Negotiation of the Jama'at's Gender
Ideology in Daily Praxis

In the literature on South Asia, missionary tours are described as primarily male endeavors. Metcalf argues that although women occasionally accompany their men, this is an exception. Both she and Sikand claim that women are expected to popularize the principles of Tabligh work primarily in the domestic sphere—that is, among their relatives and friends—instead of during missionary tours.[55] However, the Gambian female Tablighi activists told me that they go out with their husbands every two months for a three- to fifteen-day tour. One woman who had already made a forty-day tour was planning to go to Mauritania for another forty days. This indicates that Gambian women are more actively involved in missionary tours than their South Asian counterparts, who go on tour sporadically or not at all. Helen Hardacre's observation that all "fundamentalisms" restrict women's roles in the public sphere does not apply to the Gambian Tabligh Jama'at.[56]

In their outgoing behavior, Gambian female Tablighis not only differ from their South Asian "sisters" but also from women in other *da'wa* and/ or fundamentalist movements.[57] A theme that comes to the fore in Judy Brink and Joan Mencher's insightful volume on women's recent encounters with fundamentalisms in different cultures and religious traditions is a sustained attention to women's religious education.[58] The authors conclude that women derive empowerment from their increased access to religious knowledge. As the different contributions to their volume show, especially Keng-Fong Pang's, female learning sessions like those organized by the Tabligh Jama'at also take place in other contexts.[59] But whereas the pattern of women being instructed to organize their daily conduct in accord with the principles of Islamic fundamentalism and virtuous behavior seems to be common, female activists taking to the streets to disseminate their religious knowledge is certainly not. In South Asia, unlike the Gambia, the term *da'iya* (literally, female bearer of *da'wa*) has the connotation of "teacher" rather than missionary. In the Gambian setting, however, the pedagogical and missionary roles of female Tablighi activists are closely related.

The greater mobility of Gambian female Tablighis points to an apparent contradiction in the Jama'at's discourse on gender as reproduced in the *ta'lim* sessions and the *Faza'il-e-A'maal*: On the one hand, "proper" Muslim women should stay indoors: but on the other, they should involve themselves in Tabligh work, which implies a public role. The conversion story of Aisha, a dedicated female Tablighi activist of thirty years, suggests how Gambian women reconcile their gendered Muslim identity with the religious values propagated by the Jama'at.

I came to know Aisha through a friend of mine whose nephew is an active supporter of the Tabligh Jama'at. Aisha agreed to an interview on the condition that I wear a veil and be accompanied by my friend's nephew and a veiled "sister." She herself was covered from head to foot in a black robe—she even wore gloves and socks—but during the interview, she removed her face veil. I thought the four of us were alone in Aisha's house, but suddenly Aisha's husband, who is an influential person in the organization, intervened from behind a curtain that separated the living room from the bedroom. When she invited him to join us, he refused, saying that he did not want to look at my female companion and me. Nevertheless, the curtain that separated us did not prevent him from giving his opinion. I focus here on Aisha's statements concerning women's involvement in the Jama'at in the Gambia.

In Aisha's opinion, it is of the utmost importance for Muslim women to join missionary tours, which she calls *khuruj,* in order to learn more about their faith. Since she married, she has engaged actively in such tours. She told me that *khuruj* are tours undertaken by a group of about ten Muslims for three, ten, fifteen, or forty days—sometimes even four or six months—with the aim of making other Muslims more aware of their responsibilities toward God and learning more about Islam themselves in the process. She explained: "During *khuruj,* a married couple travels together or as part of a larger group. The men sleep in the local mosque. They ask the people in the village or town visited who is ready for Tabligh work, and their wives stay three nights in the compound of the Muslims who answer in the affirmative. After having spent three nights in the mosque and host compound of the village or town visited, the missionaries continue their tour or return home."

According to Aisha, unlike men, the women engaged in *khuruj* do not go out to invite people to the local mosque. Instead, they ask women from the neighborhood to visit them in their host compound and then teach them to improve their practice of Islamic ritual observances, which uphold gender segregation, by reading *hadith*s aloud. On the basis of these *hadith*s, the women ask the female Tablighi activists for advice on certain issues. During the *khuruj* in which I participated, a young woman asked, for example, whether wearing a nose ring is forbidden in Islam. Another woman remarked that she was not ready to wear the face veil, but one of the female Tablighis who had long been wearing it responded: "Wearing the *niqab* [face veil] is indeed hot; however, it is not as hot as hellfire."

Aisha told me that during the Gambian tours, both male and female Tablighi activists speak in public to remind the listeners of their religious obligations. The practice of women delivering a speech conflicts with the common Islamic idea that the female voice is *'awrat,* a part of the body that needs to be concealed.[60] Again, Gambian women's articulateness differs from women's involvement in Tabligh work in South Asia. According to Sikand,[61] South Asian women activists who are experienced in Tabligh work and well versed in its principles may address other womenfolk on the condition that they take extreme care not to speak in an authoritative tone as if delivering a lecture. Aisha and her counterparts (both male and female), however, used the term *bayan* (the Urdu word for lecture) for speeches delivered by both men and women.

Aisha seemed to recognize the dilemma facing Gambian female Tablighis as public speakers, because she took pains to point out that they may address only female audiences, must let their husbands select the topics of their lectures, and emphasize feminine virtues such as modesty, diffidence, and obedience. She elucidated the topics of women's lectures as follows:

> We talk about how married women should dress, how they should take care of their compounds, how they should perform their domestic chores, and how they should raise their children. Because the woman is responsible for her children's moral upbringing, she must teach them to pronounce *la ilaha illa-llah* [there is no god but Allah] even before they are able to talk. At a young age, she should instruct them in *tajwid* [the correct pronunciation and recitation of the Qur'an]. Furthermore, the mother has to instruct her children in how to dress and behave by telling stories about the children of the Prophet Muhammad's companions. With the help of Allah, the children will grow into devout Muslims. During our *bayan,* we talk about all such topics that give women a stronger faith.

Although their husbands determine the contents of the Tabligh women's *bayan,* they do not fully control these lectures, because questions from the audience often come from a host of unpredictable directions that the husbands do not anticipate. For example, I once attended a *bayan* during which an experienced Tablighi woman talked about Muslim women's ritual observance. Afterward, she was addressed by a young woman from the audience asking whether Islam allows birth control. Unlike women, men select the topics of their speeches themselves. Another difference, which was not mentioned by Aisha, is that while women may only deliver speeches to female audiences, men may address both male and female audiences. As illustrated above, the male speaker must talk from behind a curtain.

According to Aisha, the purpose of *khuruj* is the same for both men and women: to recite the Qur'an and *hadith*s, to perform *dhikr,* to teach, and also to learn. What is important for male as well as female missionaries is to increase their faith; therefore, they are expected to ignore as much as possible worldly concerns during *khuruj.* When they are obliged to engage in the mundane tasks of daily living, they render these acts virtuous by dedicating the intention accompanying them to God.[62] Aisha explained: "Even during cooking we talk only about Allah, the Prophet Muhammad and his companions." She added that a missionary tour is like a "miracle": "So many wonderful things happen during *khuruj.*" These "wonderful things," to which other informants also referred, were spiritual experiences such as sensing personal salvation, gaining heightened religious self-consciousness, encountering the "truth," perceiving divine guidance in one's personal life, and experiencing closeness to God and his prophet.

Although Aisha underscored that the purpose of *khuruj* is similar for both men and women, she was aware of the contradiction between the images of Muslim womanhood projected in the *ta'lim* on the one hand, and women's active involvement in *khuruj* on the other. As a result, she emphasized that their participation should meet certain conditions. First of all, she argued that when setting out on a tour, women should dress strictly according to the *Sunna.* After a discussion with the wife of a Mauritanian Islamic scholar in 1997, Aisha decided to assume the *burqa'.* She explained: "As the Prophet's wives dressed this way, we also have to do it. The best color for the face veil is black, but a green or brown one is also allowed, anything that is not a flashy color. Some women like to embellish their hands with henna. That is the reason why Muslim women should wear gloves. A woman's hands are beautiful, and this beauty is only meant to attract the husband. The same applies to a woman's feet."

Moreover, Aisha told me, only married women are allowed to engage in *khuruj,* and they never travel alone but always in the company of their husbands.[63] Although women become members of the Tabligh Jama'at through their husbands, this does not mean that they do so *only* at their husbands' behest or that they take part in missionary tours solely because of their hus-bands' wishes.[64] I spoke with several female students at the recently founded University of the Gambia who stressed an independent desire to convert to Tablighi ideology. They told me that they wish to marry Tablighi activists, because such men are believed to be serious and to take good care of their wives. Their unveiled contemporaries, by contrast, said they would prefer a "semester" husband: a man who spends most of his time in Europe. To take advantage of the opportunity to find a good husband, the religious students explained, "We do not veil ourselves completely so that our bride-grooms-to-be may notice our beauty and healthy bodies." They intended to become good Tablighi devotees by wearing the *burqa'* after marriage and finding a "decent job" after graduation that would not hinder them from practicing their religion.

A final condition that Aisha mentioned is that, unlike male missionaries, women are not allowed to go on *khuruj* for more than forty days because of their domestic chores and family responsibilities. Although in theory women are allowed to travel for up to forty days, in practice they normally leave their homes for only three days once every two months. Despite these limiting conditions, my informants felt strongly that they had to participate in *khuruj* to acquire religious merit and to achieve a higher level of piety that draws them closer to God. While mentioning limiting conditions re-lated to women's missionary tours, Aisha and other female Tablighi ac-tivists also show how Gambian women are able to adapt Tablighi ideology.

Certain restrictions apply also to Gambian male missionaries. A male Tab-lighi explained that a man may go on *khuruj* only with his wife's permission; and Aisha's husband mentioned that a man may go on a six-month tour only if his wife is able to bear his long absence. Even when women do not form part of a missionary group, they seem to play a crucial role with regard to Tabligh work. The Gambian Jama'at expects women to recruit or to en-courage in men "good Muslim practice," as was illustrated in the previous section. Both male and female Tablighi activists believe that when a husband goes on tour without his wife, the latter will benefit indirectly from it.

The aforementioned demonstrates that Gambian female Tablighi ac-tivists assume a more public role than their South Asian counterparts. Their more visible and vocal presence in public life may be explained partly by local gender relations.[65] Gambian women are used to contributing to house-hold maintenance, and many of them have been generating their own in-come in the informal economy for a long time.[66] Because of worsening eco-nomic hardship, this trend has increased. Working outside the home has become necessary for a growing number of married women in the Gambia, although this conflicts with the Muslim ideal of the husband as the principal provider. Because Gambian women have long been active in the public arena, their participation in outgoing missionary groups seems to be more accepted.

Conclusion

Although the patriarchal Muslim gender ideology, with its prescribed roles of male provider and female domestic caretaker, prevails in all countries where the Tabligh Jama'at has established itself, the movement's conception of proper Islamic womanhood is interpreted differently in different countries. Here I have focused on the Gambia, a country that is a booming center of Tablighi activity. Although the ideal Muslim woman is typically portrayed in the female learning sessions as one who is confined to the house, at the same time these *ta'lim* provide Gambian female Tablighi activists with a new role model that departs from established gender norms.[67]

Unlike in South Asia, where the Tabligh Jama'at originated, the Gambian *ta'lim* exhort married women to leave their homes on missionary tours to instruct female audiences in proper Muslim conduct. In addition to teaching Muslim women, Gambian female Tablighis play a crucial role in recruiting their husbands to missionary work. The Tabligh Jama'at in the Gambia thereby opens up new social and religious space for women, who now appear to have both more knowledge of and a greater say in religious affairs. However, they are not religious authorities in their own right. Their husbands dictate the topics to be discussed in their lectures, and they address only female audiences.

Nevertheless, it emerged during my field research that Gambian female Tablighi activists derive self-esteem and gain the respect of their husbands and fellow Muslims through their new religious agency. Although "mainstream" Muslims frequently told me that they consider the Jama'at's followers to be antisocial and supercilious, because Tablighis tell them (mainstream Muslims) that the ways in which they profess their faith are wrong, at the same time they seemed to harbor secret admiration for the Tablighis' proper ritual observance and the dedication with which they transmit religious values to their children.

The religious agency that Gambian female Tablighis acquire distinguishes them not only from their South Asian counterparts but also from other Gambian Muslim women who do not profess their faith in the public arena and have less knowledge of Islam. Gambian women usually attend a traditional Qur'an school for only a couple of years to learn the basic skills considered necessary to becoming a good wife and mother, such as performing ablutions, praying, and taking care of themselves as proper Muslim women. Some "mainstream" Muslim women complained to me that their fathers kept them "ignorant" of Islam by marrying them off at a young age, thereby limiting their opportunities to enhance their Islamic knowledge.

We may wonder whether Tablighi women's religious agency in the Gambia reflects a conscious, purposeful strategy, or is instead the result of these women's embracing a new form of piety as a means of realizing a virtuous life. Aisha's biographical narrative demonstrates that during their missionary tours, female Tablighi activists embody the movement's notions of proper Islamic womanhood. In the lectures they deliver during their tours, they emphasize traditional "female" virtues such as modesty, obedience, and subservience. From a Western feminist point of view, female Tablighi activists are reinforcing women's submission to men by enacting a patriarchal gender ideology. In traditional feminist scholarship, "agency" has been largely conceptualized in terms of resistance to relations of domination,[68] but female Tablighis do not intend to confront traditional gender norms; instead, they reinforce them to construct a new spiritual and moral identity for themselves.[69]

In this, the female Tablighis are somewhat similar to the women in the Egyptian women's mosque movement described by Mahmood. She argues for a wider notion of agency—beyond resistance to relations of domination— that would encompass women's search for Islamic virtue, even when it reproduces traditional gender ideology.[70] Aisha, like the other female Tablighi activists with whom I worked in the Gambia, chose to strengthen this ideology to acquire religious merit and to achieve a higher level of piety that draws her closer to God. It may be concluded, then, that Gambian female Tablighi activists exercise their new piety in what is not so much a contradiction but rather a dialectic between submission and religious empowerment.[71]

Notes

1. "Ninja" and *kumpo* (a traditional masked dancer) are common, pejorative nicknames for veiled women in the Gambia.

2. Local discourse distinguishes European whites (*toubabs*) from other whites, who are called "Arabs" or *Naar,* which means "fire" in Arabic. The story of the term's ori-

gins is that a group of Arabs came to Senegal from the north, probably Mauritania, and set a village on fire (personal communication with Mara Leichtman, May 2004). What is revealing for what follows is that Indians and Pakistanis are also referred to as whites.

3. A Wahhabi is an adherent of the Saudi Arabian reformist movement of Mohammad Ibn 'Abd al-Wahhab. The Wahhabiyya emerged as an identifiable group in West Africa in the 1940s and early 1950s among the network of both students and merchants who had contacts with the Middle East. See Lansiné Kaba, *The Wahhabiyya: Islamic Reform and Politics in French West Africa* (Evanston, Ill.: Northwestern University Press, 1974).

4. Cf. Mumtaz Ahmad, "Tablighi Jama'at," in *The Oxford Encyclopedia of the Modern Islamic World* 4, edited by John L. Esposito (New York: Oxford University Press, 1995), 165; and Yoginder Sikand, *The Origins and Development of the Tablighi-Jama'at (1920–2000): A Cross-Country Comparative Study* (New Delhi: Orient Longman, 2002), xi.

5. A. Moustapha Diop claims that the Tabligh Jama'at is active from Senegal to Zambia, but, apart from a small number of studies focused on South Africa and Uganda, almost nothing is known about the movement elsewhere in Sub-Saharan Africa. See Diop, "Structuration d'un réseau: La Jamaat Tabligh (Société pour la Propagation de la Foi)," *Revue Européenne des Migrations Internationales* 10, no. 1 (1994), 153. On South Africa, see Ebrahim Moosa, "Worlds 'Apart': Tablighi Jama'at in South Africa under Apartheid, 1963–1993," in *Travellers in Faith: Studies of the* Tablighi Jama'at *as a Transnational Islamic Movement for Faith Renewal,* edited by M. Khalid Masud (Leiden: Brill, 2000), 206–21; Goolam Vahed, "Contesting 'Orthodoxy': The Tablighi-Sunni Conflict among South African Muslims in the 1970s and 1980s," *Journal of Muslim Minority Affairs* 23, no. 2 (2003): 313–34; and Zahraa McDonald, "Constructing a Conservative Identity: The Tabligh Jama'a in Johannesburg," 2004, http://www .general.rau.ac.za/sociology/seminar_series_2005.htm. On Uganda, see Sallie Simba Kayunga, *Islamic Fundamentalism in Uganda: A Case Study of the Tabligh Youth Movement* (Kampala: Centre for Basic Research, 1993); and Abin N. Chande, "Radicalism and Reform in East Africa," in *The History of Islam in Africa,* edited by Nehemia Levtzion and Randall L. Pouwels (Athens: Ohio University Press, 2000), 355–58.

6. This might be explained by the long-standing history of Islam in the Gambia. The Gambia River is one of Africa's most navigable waterways and has historically provided traders easy access to the country's interior, a significant factor in the introduction and growth of Islam. Propelled by jihad (holy war) in the nineteenth century, Islamic beliefs spread rapidly in the Gambia. British colonialist policy further enhanced its spread and consolidation. For quite some time, the Gambia had a higher percentage of Muslim inhabitants than any other West African country. See John S. Trimingham, *Islam in West Africa* (Oxford: Clarendon Press, 1959), 233. Today, more than 90 percent of the Gambian population is Muslim.

7. During the late 1990s, Malian adepts who intended to go on missionary tours were sent by Pakistani preachers to the Gambia to take courses (personal communication with Baz Lecocq, June 2004).

8. Cf. Barbara D. Metcalf, "Women and Men in a Contemporary Pietist Movement: The Case of the Tablighi Jama'at," in *Appropriating Gender: Women's Activism and Politicized Religion in South Asia,* ed. Patricia Jeffery and Amrita Basu (New York: Routledge, 1998); Yoginder Sikand, "Women and the *Tablighi Jama'at,*" *Islam and Christian-Muslim Relations* 10, no. 1 (1999): 41–52 (see also http://www.islaminterfaith

.org/feb2005/article4.htm); and Barbara D. Metcalf, "Tablighi Jama'at and Women," in *Travellers in Faith,* ed. Masud, 44–58. Sikand claims that as a male researcher, he did not have access to female Tablighi respondents and thus his account of female participation in the Jama'at is incomplete ("Women and the *Tablighi Jama'at,*" 41). Metcalf mainly had access to critics of the Jama'at who talked about women a great deal, but from a very one-sided perspective ("Tablighi Jama'at and Women," 44). Attempting to redress the balance, the present chapter pays attention to female Tablighi activists themselves. Further ethnographic research is necessary to provide more insight into their religious beliefs and practices.

9. Although it remains to be seen whether the Tabligh Jama'at is a truly fundamentalist organization—see Barbara D. Metcalf, "'Remaking Ourselves': Islamic Self-Fashioning in a Global Movement of Spiritual Renewal," in *Accounting for Fundamentalisms: The Dynamic Character of Movements,* edited by Martin E. Marty and R. Scott Appleby (Chicago: University of Chicago Press, 1994), 723—it is similar to fundamentalist movements in its literalist interpretation of the Qur'an and *Sunna* and its dedication to restoring "pristine" Islam. See Martin E. Marty and R. Scott Appleby, "Conclusion: An Interim Report of a Hypothetical Family," in *Fundamentalisms Observed,* edited by Martin E. Marty and R. Scott Appleby (Chicago: University of Chicago Press, 1991), 838.

10. E.g., Fatima Mernissi, *Beyond the Veil: Male-Female Dynamics in Modern Muslim Society* (Bloomington: Indiana University Press, 1987); Helen Hardacre, "The Impact of Fundamentalisms on Women, the Family, and Interpersonal Relations," in *Fundamentalisms and Society: Reclaiming the Sciences, the Family, and Education,* edited by Martin E. Marty and R. Scott Appleby (Chicago: Chicago University Press, 1993), 129–50; John S. Hawley and Wayne L. Proudfoot, "Introduction," in *Fundamentalism & Gender,* edited by John S. Hawley (New York: Oxford University Press, 1994), 3–44; Shahin Gerami, *Women and Fundamentalism. Islam and Christianity* (New York: Garland, 1996); John L. Esposito, "Introduction: Women in Islam and Muslim Societies," in *Islam, Gender, and Social Change,* edited by Yvonne Y. Haddad and John L. Esposito (New York: Oxford University Press, 1998), ix–xxviii; Lamia Rustum Shehadeh, *The Idea of Women under Fundamentalist Islam* (Gainesville: University Press of Florida, 2003); and Karin Willemse, "On Globalization and the Bourgeois Family Ideal in Islamist Sudan, a Preliminary Analysis," in *The Gender Question in Globalization: Changing Perspectives and Practice,* edited by Tine Davids and Francien van Driel (Aldershot, U.K.: Ashgate, 2005), 159–78.

11. Camillia Fawzi El-Solh and Judy Mabro, "Introduction: Islam and Muslim Women," in *Muslim Women's Choices. Religious Belief and Social Reality,* edited by Fawzi El-Solh and Mabro (Providence: Berg, 1994), 16.

12. Between 1996 and 2001, I conducted ethnographic field research on the gendered practice of praise singing in the Gambia. This project was funded by a grant from the Centre for Non-Western Studies in Leiden. The research that I conducted between 2003 and 2005 focused on new tendencies in Islam in the Gambia. It was, as mentioned above, funded by a grant from the International Institute for the Study of Islam in the Modern World in Leiden.

13. Saba Mahmood, "Feminist Theory, Embodiment, and the Docile Agent: Some Reflections on the Egyptian Islamic Revival," *Cultural Anthropology* 16, no. 2 (2001) 202–36.

14. "Activist" refers to an individual involved actively in Tabligh work, that is, undertaking missionary tours.

15. For examples of these stories, see Marloes Janson, "Roaming about for God's Sake: The Upsurge of the *Tabligh Jama'at* in The Gambia," *Journal of Religion in Africa* 35, no. 4 (2005): 456–75.

16. I use conversion here in the sense of a "deliberate turning from indifference or from an earlier form of piety to another." See Arthur D. Nock, *Conversion: The Old and the New in Religion from Alexander The Great to Augustine Of Hippo* (Oxford: Clarendon Press, 1933), 7, quoted in Ebrahim Moosa, "Worlds 'Apart'," 208. Signs of Tablighi conversion include the adoption of a new discourse steeped in Islamic metaphor and espousal of an ideal and purist life world with its attendant paraphernalia, such as a dress code; see Moosa, "Worlds 'Apart,'" 214. Interesting in this context is Olivier Roy's definition of Tablighis as "born-again Muslims"; see Olivier Roy, *Globalised Islam: The Search for a New Ummah* (London: Hurst, 2004). Contemporary fundamentalist movements are strongly rooted in the ideology of "renaissance," both as purification and as a return to the purported origins of the faith; see Mamadou Diouf, "Engaging Postcolonial Cultures: African Youth and Public Space," *African Studies Review* 46, no. 1 (2003): 7.

17. Sikand, *Origins and Development of the Tablighi-Jama'at,* 10–12; Dietrich Reetz, "Keeping Busy on the Path of Allah: The Self-Organisation (*Intizam*) of the Tablighi Jama'at," *Oriente Moderno* 8, no. 1 (2004): 295.

18. Cf. M. Khalid Masud, "The Growth and Development of the Tablighi Jama'at in India," in *Travellers in Faith,* ed. Masud, 3–5; Barbara D. Metcalf, *"Traditionalist" Islamic Activism: Deoband, Tablighis, and Talibs* (Leiden: International Institute for the Study of Islam, 2002), 4, 8–9; and Sikand, *Origins and Development of the Tablighi-Jama'at,* 16–17, 66.

19. Ahmad, "Tablighi Jama'at," 166.

20. Here it should be noted that, generally speaking, the Tabligh Jama'at offers women new opportunities by encouraging them to engage in Tabligh work. In this chapter, it is argued that the Gambia seems to be an exceptional case in that its Tablighi women appear to take up this religious duty literally.

21. In this respect, the Jama'at differs largely from many other African fundamentalist movements, which often seek to implement "true" Islam by modernizing religious schooling; see Roman Loimeier, "Patterns and Peculiarities of Islamic Reform in Africa," *Journal of Religion in Africa* 33, no. 3 (2003): 237, 240–41. The Jama'at, on the contrary, sees preaching as the key to "inviting people to Allah's path." Against this background, we have to interpret Roy's argument that "young born-again Muslims do not want to undertake years of study; they want the truth immediately"; Roy, *Globalised Islam,* 169. As a result, Gambian Tablighi activists are frequently criticized as "illiterate" and "immature" preachers. For an overview of non-Tablighis' perceptions of the Tabligh Jama'at in the Gambia, see Janson, "Roaming about for God's Sake"; and Marloes Janson, "Appropriating Islam: The Tensions between 'Traditionalists' and 'Modernists' in the Gambia," *Islam et sociétés au sud du Sahara, nouvelle série* 1 (2007): 61–79.

22. In the literature, it has often been argued that the movement's avoidance of direct political involvement has helped it to increase its influence around the world. Due to its apparently apolitical stance, the Jama'at, unlike Islamist movements, is generally not viewed as a threat by the governments of countries in which it is active.

23. Marc Gaborieau, "The Transformation of Tablighi Jama'at into a Transnational Movement," in *Travellers in Faith,* ed. Masud, 129–31.

24. See Masud, "Growth and Development of the Tablighi Jama'at," 30.

25. See also Roy, *Globalised Islam,* 232. The Tablighis I interviewed frequently accused "mainstream" Muslims of having a distorted knowledge of Islam; the latter, according to them, are misguided and "living upside down." Many informants claimed that of seventy-three denominations in Islam, only one, the Tabligh Jama'at, is destined for paradise.

26. The idea is that if a man's trousers do not touch the ground, they will remain clean and, as a result of this state of purity, his prayers are more likely be answered by God. Furthermore, it is believed that when men wear trousers that fall below the ankles, their ankles and feet will burn in hell. A well-known *hadith* (account of what the Prophet Muhammad said or did) reports that the prophet was displeased with men wearing long garments; see Sahih Bukhari, vol. 4, book 56, no. 692, http://www.usc.edu/dept/ MSA/reference/searchhadith.html. According to my informants, wearing a turban is believed to yield spiritual merit. A female Tablighi activist noted laughingly: "Moreover, the turban beautifies our men."

27. Consequently, backpacks are defined as "*Mashala* bags" in the Gambia. *Mashala* is the emic term for Tablighi activists (see above).

28. See Metcalf, "Tablighi Jama'at and Women," 49–50; and Marloes Janson, "Renegotiating Gender: Changing Moral Practice in the *Tabligh Jama'at* in The Gambia," *Journal for Islamic Studies* 28 (2008), 32–34. In the religious texts read by the Tablighis, men are encouraged to make household duties lighter for their wives, so that the latter may perform their Tablighi duties undisturbed; *Faza'il-e-A'maal,* Six Fundamentals, 38. In South Asia, male Tablighis even use henna to color their beards and apply kohl to their eyes, as this is believed to be *Sunna;* personal communication with Kamran Ali, February 2005.

29. Sulayman S. Nyang, "Islamic Revivalism in West Africa: Historical Perspectives and Recent Development," in *Religious Plurality in Africa: Essays in Honour of John S. Mbiti,* edited by Jacob K. Olupona and Sulayman S. Nyang (Berlin: Mouton de Gruyter, 1993), 244, 252, 267.

30. Cf. Momodou Darboe, "ASR Focus: Islamism in West Africa—Gambia," *African Studies Review* 47, no. 2 (2004): 73–82; Janson, "Appropriating Islam."

31. Another potential explanation for the growth of the Tabligh Jama'at in the Gambia is the influence of the Ahmadiyya Mission since the 1950s; see Humphrey J. Fisher, *Ahmadiyyah: A Study in Contemporary Islam on the West African Coast* (London: Oxford University Press, 1963), 126–29. Both the Tabligh Jama'at and Ahmadiyya originated in India and both are *da'wa* movements, but nonetheless they have very different concepts of Islam. On the basis of Ahmadiyya's belief that the Prophet Muhammad was not the last prophet on Earth, the Tabligh Jama'at in the Gambia rejects the Ahmadiyya Mission. Whether the Jama'at may be interpreted as a countermovement to the Ahmadiyya Mission in the Gambia is a question for future research.

32. The Serahuli have been propagators of Islam, spreading the religion during their trade missions in West Africa.

33. Another exception are the Gambian Ahmadis, who, like the Tablighis, have their own mosques.

34. Cf. Moosa, "Worlds 'Apart,'" 209–10; Vahed, "Contesting 'Orthodoxy,'" 317–18.

35. There are undeniable similarities in ideology and practice between Wahhabis and Tablighis. Consequently, both are referred to as *Sunna moolu* ("*Sunna* people") in local discourse. However, the Wahhabiyya is marked by an outspoken anti-Sufi orientation, while the Tabligh Jama'at borrows from Sufi practices. An example of a Sufi

practice in which also Tablighis engage is *dhikr,* the remembrance of God through recitation of his names. The relation between Sufism and reformism in the Jama'at is a complicated one, about which scholars have made conflicting statements. Ahmad, "Tablighi Jama'at," 165, claims that the Tabligh Jama'at, at least in its initial phase, could be described both as a reinvigorated form of Islamic orthodoxy and as a reformed Sufism, whereas Gaborieau—see Marc Gaborieau, "What Is left of Sufism in Tablīghī Jamā'at?" *Archives de Sciences Sociales des Religions* 135 (2006): 61—defines the Jama'at as a "militant fundamentalist movement." Reetz concludes that typical of activist Islamic movements in South Asia, the Tabligh Jama'at combines the Sufi principles of leadership—which it prefers not to acknowledge publicly—with a reformist message; see Dietrich Reetz, "Sufi Spirituality Fires Reformist Zeal: The Tablighi Jama'at in Today's India and Pakistan," *Archives de Sciences Sociales des Religions* 135 (2006): 33, 47. The Gambian Jama'at not only engages with Wahhabiyya but also has to be studied within a field characterized by competition between various international Muslim nongovernmental organizations and *da'wa* organizations, including the Ahmadiyya (India), Africa Muslims Agency (Kuwait), Islamic Call Organization (Saudi Arabia), World Islamic Call Society (Libya), Munazamat al-Da'wa al-Islamiyya (Sudan), and Muslim Hands (United Kingdom). During the past five years, Salafi-oriented movements have joined the Islamic field in the Gambia. Salafiyya refers to an Islamic reform movement that was founded at the end of the nineteenth century in Egypt.

36. Despite their secular education, many Tablighi activists are more orthodox in their religious observance than Muslims who attended religious school, a characteristic common to adherents of other African fundamentalist movements as well. See Loimeier, "Patterns and Peculiarities," 253–54.

37. A survey in South Africa indicates that the Jama'at holds greater attraction for middle-aged Muslims who for much of their lives have not strictly observed the five pillars of Islam; Moosa, "Worlds 'Apart,'" 212. One explanation is that they have more time, and probably also more money, to devote to Tabligh work.

38. According to Roy, the generational conflict is at the heart of the contemporary Islamic revival; Roy, *Globalised Islam,* 145. As a result, religious practice can be understood as a part of youth culture. See Murray Last, "The Power of Youth, Youth of Power: Notes on the Religions of the Young in Northern Nigeria," in *Les jeunes en Afrique: La politique et la ville,* vol. 2, edited by Hélène d'Almeida-Topor (Paris: L'Harmattan, 1992), 375.

39. The *National Youth Policy Document 1999–2008* shows that the level of youth unemployment is increasing at an alarming rate in the Gambia and estimates that more than 35,000 youths (in a total population of approximately 1.5 million) are now searching for jobs to improve their deteriorated standard of living. As reported by *The Independent* (Banjul), January 10, 2005.

40. Erin J. Augis, "Dakar's Sunnite Women: The Politics of Person" (PhD diss., University of Chicago, 2002), 15, 78. It is often argued that the young (whether college students or the unemployed), having reached a point in life where they question existing society, are more likely to be attracted to fundamentalism. See, e.g., Janet Bauer, "Conclusion: The Mixed Blessings of Women's Fundamentalism. Democratic Impulses in a Patriarchal World," in *Mixed Blessings: Gender and Religious Fundamentalism Cross Culturally,* edited by Judy Brink and Joan Mencher (New York: Routledge, 1997), 231.

41. Saskia Brand, *Mediating Means and Fate: A Socio-Political Analysis of Fertility and Demographic Change in Bamako, Mali* (Leiden: Brill, 2001); Marloes Janson, *The Best Hand Is the Hand That Always Gives: Griottes and Their Profession in Eastern Gambia* (Leiden: Centre for Non-Western Studies, 2002).

42. See Metcalf, "Tablighi Jama'at and Women," 51.

43. See Marloes Janson, "'We Are All the Same, Because We All Worship God': The Controversial Case of a Female Saint in The Gambia," *Africa* 16, no. 2 (2006): 202–36.

44. See Metcalf, "'Remaking Ourselves,'" 716; Sikand, "Women and the *Tablighi Jama'at*," 44–45; and Metcalf, "Tablighi Jama'at and Women," 51. See also Mareike Jule Winkelmann, *"From Behind the Curtain": A Study of a Girls' Madrasa in India* (Amsterdam: Amsterdam University Press, 2005), 56.

45. See Ahmad, "Tablighi Jama'at," 166–67; Masud, "Growth and Development of the Tablighi Jama'at," 21–24; Sikand, *Origins and Development of the Tablighi-Jama'at,* 71–72; Reetz, "Keeping Busy," 295.

46. For South Asian women, the *Bihishti Zewar* (Heavenly Ornaments) by the De-obandi theologian Thanawi is a bedside table book; see Barbara D. Metcalf, *Perfecting Women: Maulana Ashraf 'Ali Thanawi's Bihishti Zewar* (Berkeley: University of California Press, 1990). In the Gambia, however, this book, which intends to provide a basic education for respectable Muslim women, is to my knowledge not available.

47. The English translation of this volume, which was published in the 1950s and is the most widely read text in the Muslim world after the Qur'an, sells for 300 dalasi (about $10) at the Jama'at's mosque and in the market of Serrekunda; see Maulana Muhammad Zakariyya Kandhalvi, *Faza'il-e-A'maal,* revised and improved translation (Lahore: Kutub Khana Faizi, n.d.). Because many Gambians cannot afford this amount, the manual is exchanged between friends.

48. The *Faza'il-e-A'maal* offers guidelines for all conceivable actions: worshipping, dressing, sleeping, eating, drinking, cleaning the teeth, and, according to a young male Tablighi activist, even for such a trivial act as "removing a fly from one's food." These guidelines for everyday life reinforce the movement's cohesiveness, which is an important element in the Tabligh Jama'at's appeal in a country characterized by socio-economic and political instability.

49. *Faza'il-e-A'maal,* "Stories of Sahabah," 174.

50. Ibid., 174–75.

51. Ibid., 175.

52. Ibid., 191.

53. Ibid.

54. Cf. *Faza'il-e-A'maal,* "Muslim Degeneration and Its Only Remedy," 33; Barbara D. Metcalf, "Living Hadith in the Tablighi Jama'at," *Journal of Asian Studies* 52, no. 3 (1993): 592.

55. See Metcalf, "'Remaking Ourselves'," 712; Metcalf, "Tablighi Jama'at and Women," 50; and Sikand, "Women and the *Tablighi Jama'at*," 44. See also Winkelmann, *"From Behind the Curtain,"* 96, 121 n. 1.

56. Hardacre, "Impact of Fundamentalisms." According to Bauer, it is a mistake to think that women in fundamentalism do not venture into the public world. They do not all, however, venture into it as prominently as Gambian female Tablighi activists; Bauer, "Conclusion," 224.

57. As mentioned in note 35, there are also other *da'wa* movements active in the Gambia. But whereas in the Jama'at the focus is on spiritual renewal, the other movements emphasize social welfare. Chanfi Ahmed interprets the widening of the concept of *da'wa* linking moral reform with social welfare as the "Red Cross complex"; see Chanfi Ahmed, "Networks of Islamic NGOs in Sub-Saharan Africa: Bilal Muslim Mission, African Muslim Agency [Direct Aid], and al-Haramayn," *Journal of Eastern African Studies* 3, no. 3 (2009): 426–27. In competition with the Christian Red Cross, contemporary

Muslim organizations feel obliged to provide all kinds of educational services and charity to win Muslims over to their side. Remarkably, except for the Tabligh Jama'at, women do not appear to play a particular role in the other *da'wa* movements.

58. Brink and Mencher, *Mixed Blessings.*

59. Keng-Fong Pang, "Islamic 'Fundamentalism' and Female Empowerment among the Muslims of Hainan Island, People's Republic of China," in *Mixed Blessings,* ed. Brink and Mencher, 41–56. See also Saba Mahmood, *Politics of Piety: The Islamic Revival and the Feminist Subject* (Princeton, N.J.: Princeton University Press, 2005).

60. The prevailing notion is that a woman's voice can nullify an act of worship because it is capable of provoking sexual feelings in men. See Metcalf, "Tablighi Jama'at and Women," 58; and Mahmood, "Politics of Piety," 65.

61. Sikand, "Women and the *Tablighi Jama'at,*" 44.

62. See also Mahmood, "Politics of Piety," 130 n. 20.

63. For the gendering of mission work among Christian missionaries in the Sahel, see Barbara Cooper, *Evangelical Christians in the Muslim Sahel* (Bloomington: Indiana University Press, 2006). Like the Gambian Tablighi women, American Christian missionary women in Niger were going out, which generated a similar contradiction between gender ideology and praxis that confront the Tablighi women. Far from being restrictive, the notion of surrender to God's will and the injunction of female submissiveness tended also in the case of the Christian missionaries, somewhat paradoxically, to open unprecedented and highly responsible roles for women in mission work; ibid., 109. A difference is the way in which the contradiction between gender ideology and praxis has been negotiated by these two categories of missionary women. Although American Christian missionary women are charged with teaching African women how to become good wives to Christian men, they themselves often do not marry, in order to remain faithful to their vocation as missionaries; ibid., 13–14, 111, 302–3. Gambian Tablighi women, by contrast, must be married to set out on missionary tours in order not to lose their position as respectable women.

64. See also Metcalf, "Women and Men," 107.

65. Because the Tabligh Jama'at is a recent phenomenon in the Gambia, and because the women in the movement are still negotiating their gendered Muslim identities, more research on this topic is required.

66. Janson, *Best Hand,* 91; Richard A. Schroeder, "'Gone to their Second Husbands': Marital Metaphors and Conjugal Contracts in the Gambia's Female Garden Sector," in *Readings in Gender in Africa,* edited by Andrea Cornwall (Bloomington and Oxford: Indiana University Press and James Currey, 2005), 111–19.

67. See also Sikand, "Women and the *Tablighi Jama'at,*" 48-49.

68. To illustrate her point of view, Mahmood cites Janice Boddy's work on the North African Zar cult, a widely practiced healing cult that uses Islamic idioms and spirit mediums and is comprised largely of women. Boddy argues that Zar possession serves as "a kind of counter-hegemonic process, . . . a feminine response to hegemonic praxis," and considers it a "means of resisting and setting limits to domination." Janice Boddy, *Wombs and Alien Spirits: Men and Women in the Zar Cult in North Africa* (Madison: University of Wisconsin Press, 1989), 7, 345, quoted by Mahmood, "Feminist Theory," 205–6.

69. Cf. Mahmood, "Feminist Theory," 203, 208; Augis, "Dakar's Sunnite Women," 229.

70. Mahmood, "Feminist Theory."

71. See also Augis, "Dakar's Sunnite Women," 261.

Chapter 7

Titanic in Kano:
Video, Gender, and Islam

Heike Behrend

In the following, I analyze a Hausa remake (2003) by the Nigerian director Farouk Ashu-Brown of the Hollywood film *Titanic* by James Cameron (1998), a cross-cultural remake in which language, cultural traditions, gender constructions, and narrative differ greatly from the "original." In popular criticism as well as academic film studies, remakes have long been seen as a form of plagiarism that makes use in a parasitic way of the original film for commercial interests. Consequently, comparisons of remakes to the "original" often stress the latter's lack of aesthetic quality and other shortcomings. Against this perception of deficiency, which is based on a linear reading of the relationship between original and copy, I instead would like

I would like to thank Margot Badran, Gereon Blaseio, Matthias Krings, Claudia Lie-brand, Katrin Oltmann, Ina Sykora, and Abdalla Uba Adamu for their kind assistance and comments. In addition, I am very grateful to Sean O'Fahey, who invited me to the Program of African Studies at Northwestern University (Evanston) and gave me the chance to discuss some of the themes that are presented in this chapter.

to propose a reading that engages in the complicated and complex exchange relations between the remake and what might better be called the "premake" to reduce and undermine the cultural weight carried by the so-called original. Thus I am not only interested in the processes of reworking and resignifying that remaking a film in a new cultural milieu entails but also in the dialogue between the remake and the premake. From the perspective of the remake, the premake can also be read in a new way.[1]

Although all films (like all texts) are skeins of other films (or texts), remakes make explicit that they copied or borrowed strongly from a previous film. Remakes are conscious repetitions with a difference.[2] They form another attempt "to get it right," and in this way, they undermine the opposition between "original" and "copy."[3] In the following, I not only use the Hausa remake of *Titanic* to discuss the tensions between remake and premake but also to analyze the gender representations in the remake against the background of the Islamist revival in northern Nigeria. In 1999 and the immediately succeeding years, various states in the north of Nigeria, including Kano, introduced codifications of *shari'a* law in the form of new criminal and penal codes. In Kano, as elsewhere, a censorship board was instituted that among other things attempted to control gender representations.

I begin with a short historical account of video as a global medium and its local appropriation in Africa, particularly northern Nigeria. I then analyze the Hausa remake of Cameron's *Titanic* and the local interventions that transformed the film for Hausa audiences, focusing on gender constructions and especially the opposition between married and modern, single, independent women. Finally, I examine local reception of the remake and the issue of censorship and its consequences.

A History of Video Production in Nigeria

Before the advent of local video production in the late 1980s, Nigerians were already consuming films from Hollywood, Bollywood (the Indian film industry based in Bombay, now renamed Mumbai), Hong Kong, and so on, via imported videocassette. These films reached Nigeria mainly through illegal transnational networks of piracy. In Pakistan or the Philippines, they were copied and converted to other formats, such as VHS or CD (or nowadays even DVD), and given subtitles in Chinese, Arabic, and other languages. Then they were shipped, often via Dubai, to Nigeria. These illegal networks, as Brian Larkin has shown, were and are highly efficient. When, for example, a film in Hollywood was launched, it was sold only one week later as a cassette in Nigerian markets—while, for example, people in Europe would have to wait more than two years before they could see the film at a theater and even longer before they could buy the film as a video-cassette or on DVD. Through the medium of video, not only the elite but also poor people were enabled to connect in a new way with the global flow of images, watching these films in video halls (or at home) and so becoming part of a world film community.[4]

The rise of Nigerian video culture at the end of the 1980s has to be seen as part of a worldwide change in the political economy of media. This change came along with the privatization of media production and consumption and the decline of the postcolonial nation-state that also reduced the authority and morale of older state-based media such as television and radio.[5] Though a local celluloid film production never really emerged, "small" media such as video offered new possibilities. Because it required little capital and training, in Nigeria (and Ghana) the production of local videos developed into a real industry. Dramatic features shot directly on video, marketed as cassettes, and sometimes screened for paying audiences or as home videos have become the dominant form of popular culture in Nigeria. Besides American and Indian films, kung fu films, and Egyptian soap operas, Nigerian videos created an enormous arena for local cultural expression and for the reworkings of films from Hollywood and Hong Kong as well as Bollywood.

It was not academic filmmakers, trained at film or art schools in Paris, London, or New York, but young men and a few women, working in traveling theaters or producing so-called popular market literature (i.e., low-priced romantic novels and the like sold in the local market), who took up the new medium and started producing videos, picking up themes and subjects often already in circulation through theater, TV, radio, newspapers, or market literature. Local political affairs, corruption, ritual murders, the magical production of money, witchcraft, occult forces, romantic love, and betrayals were some of the topics that were visualized, sometimes with computer-generated special effects, in these videos. Free from state control, at least initially, the video makers succeeded in opening new public space for the articulation of alternative and subversive points of view.[6] In addition, the new medium started to generate its own critical discourse, for example, in local film magazines and Internet forums.

Hausa Video Production

In the last fifteen years, the video industry of Nigeria has proliferated into different local cultures of video production that can be associated with the nation's three largest ethnic groups—the Yoruba and Igbo in the south, and the Hausa in the north. Northern Nigeria developed its own specific video culture more or less in opposition to that of the south. Though the south is mainly inhabited by Christians, the north has been strongly Islamized, and since 1999 some states have undertaken the implementation of *shari'a*. Though videos produced in the south concentrated on themes such as witch-craft, occult powers, secret societies, and ritual murders, the north favored the genre of melodrama and the topics of matrimonial conflict, passionate love, and betrayal.

In the early 1990s, a group of young men in Kano began to make videos of theater performances and to screen them in video halls. Then, in about 1993, video began to separate itself from theater. Since that time, Kano, lo-cally renamed "Kallywood," has become the center of Hausa video pro-duction.[7] As of 2004, about 175 production companies produced about 350 videos a year. Three of the production companies are owned by women, among them Balaraba Ramat Yakubu, one of the most important female au-thors of Kano market literature.[8] As Abdalla Uba Adamu, the authority on popular video and market literature in Kano, has noted, in the industry's early years (from 1992 until 1997), most Hausa videos were financed by women. Quite a few video directors, such as Hafizu Bello and Aminu Sabo, acknowledged that their mothers sponsored their videos. This is why, Adamu argues, these early videos focused mainly on romantic love and matrimo-nial conflict. By 2000, new independent male producers had emerged and women began to take a lesser role in financing video films.[9]

To gain influence and defend their interests, video makers in northern Nigeria organized themselves into the Arewa (North) Film Producers As-sociation of Nigeria, with a local branch in Kano. Since 2001, this associa-tion has presented an annual Arewa Films Award (modeled on Hollywood's Oscars) for the best Hausa-language video.

The Creation of Gendered Audiences

As mentioned above, the new Hausa video culture connected local people in a new way with the global flow of images that provided the raw material for intertextual reworkings in Hausa videos. Local social, religious, and cultural values mediated the ways through which video as a technology was accepted and shaped the creation of media publics.[10] In the early 1970s, as Brian Larkin has shown, the exhibition of films in Nigerian cinemas was largely restricted to male audiences. During colonial times in Kano, cinemas (along with churches, schools, beer parlors, and dance halls) were established outside the old city, in areas known as *barikis* that became contrary to Hausa moral space. Film watching was associated with alcohol consumption and low-class, mixed-sex activities—pleasures (or sins) in which no respectable person would indulge. For women especially, cinemas were illicit spaces. Women who attended films were seen as *karuwai,* independent women and prostitutes, and their presence, as Larkin explains, "added significantly to the illicit nature of the arena. Sexual availability and sexual activity within the cinema meant that pleasure and desire were to be found both on and off the screen, the erotic pleasures of one context feeding off of the other."[11] Thus, "respectable" Muslim women, who often lived in seclusion, were absent from the male arena of cinema.

The introduction of domestic technologies such as TV and video radically transformed the exclusion of women. Through TV and video, women gained access to the popular culture of films at home. Video not only generated a new public domain; it also opened up what Larkin has called "a privatized female public sphere," in that it allowed women living in seclusion access to films and videos, making available to them what had previously been denied in a male-centered public world.[12] Indian films especially became identified as "women's films" because of their immense popularity among women.[13] It is not by chance that most early Hausa videos were sponsored by women. Forced marriage, love, and betrayal along with co-wife rivalry provide the themes in endless variation in the videos, which strongly appeal to women because, as Abdalla Uba Adamu claims, women especially identify with them.[14] Thus, video created new forms of gendered audiences and spectatorship, not only in relation to fictional dramas but also to religious teachings. Muslims (as well as Christians in the south) increasingly use video and audiocassettes to spread religious messages. For example, *mallams* (religious teachers) in the north have been known to use Qur'anic recitation on audiocassettes imported from Saudi Arabia to help with cases of spirit possession.[15]

The "Indianization" of Kallywood

While borrowing some of the conventions of Hollywood, in the context of the Islamist revival, the Hausa-speaking population of northern Nigeria has increasingly become critical of the Western world and its lifestyle. This is one reason why especially Indian films have become very powerful in Hausa popular culture.[16] Indian films first came to Nigerian cinemas in the 1960s and have increasingly gained popularity. In the 1970s, when state-owned television firms started up, Indian films made their appearance on Hausa television stations on a mass scale. In the 1980s, local businessmen started selling Indian films on cassettes that came to Kano via Dubai. Hindi-language films became so popular that the film plots and narratives were re-told in little booklets of Hausa-language market literature, which again were remediated when broadcast on radio. In addition, Indian film music was taped, translated into Hausa, and sold on audiocassette. A group of Muslim Sufi musicians founded the Society for the Lovers of India in Kano and specialized in converting themes from popular Hindi film songs into Hausa celebrating and glorifying the Prophet Muhammad.[17] In 2003, the first Hausa-Hindi language primer was published—*The Hindi Language Made Easy* —to enable Hausa viewers to learn Hindi and thereby better understand Hindi films. The primer's author confessed that he became deeply interested in learning Hindi from watching thousands of Hindi films and consequently conceived the idea of writing a series of books on the Hindi language.[18]

In the early 1990s, as young video viewers used Indian films as a template for producing their own local videos in the Hausa language and succeeded in building up a local video industry, Hausa video megastars such as Ali Nuhu and Rabi Landiyo were renamed or nicknamed Sha Ruh Khan and Sri Devi, thus assuming the names of their Bollywood equivalents.[19] In addition to the star system, song-and-dance sequences were appropriated from Bollywood films to give expression to emotions, intimacy, and passionate love. Realizing the importance of Indian films in northern Nigeria, Indian film producers reacted, and in 1999 an entire Indian film crew came to Kano to produce a Hausa film, titled *Wasiyya,* in an Indian fashion. Although the film was popular, it was not commercially successful enough to attract further Indian investment.[20] Thus, this fairly long history of Indian film reception, consumption, and adaptation in northern Nigeria led to the "Indianization" of certain aspects of local culture.

Larkin has discussed in detail the complicated ways in which Hausa people see Indian culture as "just like" Hausa culture. For many Hausa women and men, Indian films offer a modernity free of the taint of political and ideological connection with the West. Whereas the West, and especially Western films, are associated with violence, sexual immorality, and materialism, the themes of Hindi films—especially moral values, kinship, family, gender relations, and the tensions between love marriage and arranged marriage and between tradition and modernity—offered various possibilities of identification for Hausa audiences. Thus, from the beginning, Indian films became a model for Hausa video makers, and Indian song-and-dance sequences particularly have been adapted to Hausa videos.[21]

Obviously, global media are not only structured around the dichotomy of "the West and the rest," but here a third space is opened up: Indian films mediating between the reified poles of Hausa Islamic tradition and Western modernity. In addition, Indian films offer Hausa people a cultural foil against other (Christian) Nigerian groups in the south who also watch Indian films but never identified with them as strongly as northern Nigerians. When Hausa video makers, as Larkin has shown, incorporate elements of Indian films into their videos, they are thus engaging in a complicated series of cultural hierarchies both in and outside Nigeria, setting our understanding of the operation of transnational media within more complicated terrain.[22]

Shari'a and Censorship

The local video industry in northern Nigeria did not, however, develop uncontested. Though the locally produced videos that took Indian films as their model became very popular, they also generated a huge controversy in Hausa society over cultural authenticity and un-Islamic and un-Hausa modes of life. As Brian Larkin has stated, the tension arose when styles of love and sexual interaction from Indian films were dramatized in a Hausa context. What could be tolerated while safely confined to the practices of another culture (that was nevertheless similar to Hausa culture) was simply too transgressive when the necessary gap for cultural borrowing was collapsed.[23]

In the wake of the Islamist revival and the introduction of *shari'a*-backed criminal law, Hausa videos were banned in the state of Kano. Shortly afterward, however, the ban was eased and video production continued, but under the watch of a new strict censorship board that included Islamic scholars, who judged each video's conformity with Islamic religious and moral values. The Islamic guardians were especially concerned about gender relations and the maintenance of gender segregation. Thus, since 2001 the representation in videos of women and men touching each other has

been forbidden, and in June 2003, sequences showing men and women dancing together were also prohibited.

Cameron's *Titanic* and Its Premakes

The Hausa remake of James Cameron's *Titanic* offers a unique opportunity
to explore the complicated processes of local appropriation of global image
flows and the interventions made to rework, resignify, and localize images
and gender representations. The remake's director together with his team
became intercultural brokers and mediators who translated and transformed
images, narratives, and plots from one context into another. They had to deal
with the complicated, ambivalent relationship between remake and premake against the background of censorship and Islamist revival.

When the Nigerian director Farouk Ashu-Brown, who converted to Islam
eleven years ago, decided to remake Cameron's *Titanic,* he connected to a
Hollywood production that is itself a remake of other remakes. At least nine
different film versions of the 1912 shipwreck of the *Titanic* exist, including
an Indian remake titled *Mann,* made in Bollywood shortly after Cameron's
1998 film (an adaptation that, unfortunately, I have not yet had a chance to
see). Thus, we have a whole series of films that retell the story of the *Titanic*'s
sinking, creating highly complex relations of intertextuality.

When producing the remake in 2003, the Nigerian director connected to
a Hollywood blockbuster that had tried to outdo previous films in various
ways. Cameron's *Titanic* was the most expensive film ever made (at least in
1998) and was also extremely profitable, with box office returns of $1 bil-
lion. The technical effort was also extraordinary. The luxury liner was rebuilt
in detail, and computer specialists generated special effects that simulated
the shipwreck in a highly realistic way. Cameron's *Titanic* was awarded
eleven Oscars and made its main actors, Kate Winslet and especially Leo-
nardo DiCaprio, global stars. Thus, Cameron's *Titanic* was one of those
mega–Hollywood productions that in a way replicated the hubris that had
led not only to the construction of the *Titanic* but also to its sinking in 1912.[24]

Titanic becomes Nigeria

Like Cameron's *Titanic,* the Hausa remake combines two narratives: the
story of the shipwreck and a love story, a more or less classical "boy meets

girl" story, yet ending in tragedy with the death of the boy. Though all the sequences concerning the ship and the shipwreck are directly copied or, better, pirated from Cameron's film (and from director Renny Harlin's *Deep Blue Sea*), the love story between Jack and Rose is locally refilmed, more or less scene by scene, as the love story between Abdul and Binta, played by two Hausa actors, Ahmed S. Nuhu, already a well-known star in northern Nigeria, and Sadiya Abdu Rano, a newcomer on the video scene. Thus, the Hausa video is a fascinating hybrid construction of images from Cameron's film and those made locally, creating a unique version. Though the parts Farouk Ashu-Brown selected and copied from Cameron are mostly long shots showing the ship or, later, the shipwreck, in contrast, the parts newly produced with local actors are nearly all close-ups, taken from a rather narrow angle to reduce the size of the background and present a seamless montage of the foreign images integrated with the director's own material. Thus, the foreign pirated film material is literally kept at a distance, while the locally produced sequences are brought close. In addition, the copied parts were chosen in such a way that all European passengers as well as the captain, his officers, and staff are excluded, thereby creating an impression that the luxury liner is completely in the hands of Africans. This is achieved by selecting long shots of the ship, so that sailors and passengers are seen only as small dark figures, or scenes in the dark of the engine room, showing, for example, workers with sweating, sooty faces. These carefully selected shots and sequences from Cameron are then juxtaposed with locally made images of, for example, a Hausa captain discussing with an African engineer and an ambitious African shipbuilder the necessity of increasing the ship's speed. The *Titanic,* this monument or icon of Western technical hubris, is thus appropriated and transformed into a ship owned and inhabited by Africans (only). This becomes even more significant when the name *Titanic,* shown a last time before the actual sinking in Cameron's film, appears as *Nigeria* in the Hausa video.

Yet the remake does not only "Africanize" the *Titanic;* it also presents an Afrocentric perspective. Though in Cameron's film no efforts are spared to historicize the costumes and the settings, the sequences produced by Farouk Ashu-Brown transpose the setting as well as the actors into the present. For example, Binta and Abdul are wearing clothes that are fashionable today, T-shirts and jeans. However, while the remake obviously does not care to position the narrative in the past, it nevertheless offers an important historical reference. At the very beginning of the Hausa video, shortly after the credits, a dedication appears, honoring "all the Africans who died when the *Titanic* sank." This dedication evokes the association of the *Titanic* with a slave ship, and with the transatlantic slave trade in which millions of innocent Africans lost their lives. The slave ship, crossing the spaces between Europe, the Americas, Africa, and the Caribbean, has become a central organizing symbol for Afrocentric discourse that powerfully evokes the terror of slavery.[25] Thus, Cameron's *Titanic,* a Hollywood film, is reformulated in a rather subversive way by introducing an Afrocentric perspective reminding viewers of the sacrifices that Africans were forced to make for the sake of capitalist accumulation in Europe as well as America. And it is exactly this Afrocentric perspective that opens up a new view on Cameron's premake by bringing in what is excluded in his film: Africans. (Historical evidence shows that an African family traveled on the *Titanic* to return from Paris via New York to their home in Haiti. Though the woman and two children survived, the man died on the ship.)[26] By referring to this void, the remake makes explicit the omission in Cameron's film—the presence of Africans—thereby criticizing his (naturalized) "white" perspective.

Passionate Love and "Modern Women"

Although, in Cameron's film, the love story between Jack and Rose is told against the background of a radical class divide, the love story between Abdul and Binta shifts the topic to the conflict between arranged and love marriage, thus inscribing a locally intensely debated subject into the video.

For decades in northern Nigeria, a verbal and visual debate has taken place in various local media over what constitutes a married woman. During colonial times, and in particular through Western education, the "free" or "independent" single woman became an icon of modernization that, with the rise of Islamic fundamentalism, was increasingly seen as a challenge to the image of women as mothers and wives associated with Islam and Hausa tradition. Following the emergence of a new class of wealthy traders associated with the Izala movement, female seclusion became more widely practiced and was viewed positively by many women as both an Islamic virtue and a sign of prosperity.[27] Against this background, only married women were seen as respectable, while their negative other, the "independent woman," was identified as a (potential) prostitute (or *karuwai*) whose public mobility became a sign of promiscuity. *Matan zamani* means literally "modern woman" and is used as a euphemism for prostitute.[28]

Thus, with the rise of fundamentalist Islam, divisions among women increased tremendously. By setting themselves apart from *karuwai* and independent women, married women strongly played into the stereotype that presented female sexuality outside marriage as immoral and defined proper behavior for women only in terms of marriage. Because marriage was the accepted norm, independent women were increasingly defined as deviant and became potential scapegoats.[29]

In the Hausa remake, Binta shows all the signs of an independent woman. She is dressed in Western style, wearing jeans and a T-shirt, her face is made up, and she moves freely about the ship. She even visits a disco and dances with Abdul in Western style. Against her parents' will, she dares to choose her lover and have sex with him. Yet in Cameron's film as well as in the Hausa remake, illicit sex is transformed into legitimate sex because both partners declare themselves married. Indeed, after Abdul's death, when Binta among the other survivors is asked for her name, she gives Abdul's name, thereby confirming their marriage.[30] Thus, although their love is conceptualized as transgressive because it transcends class—she is from a wealthy family, while he is poor—and violates parental authority, it nevertheless in both versions accepts cultural rules and the institution of marriage. Binta obviously agrees that a woman's destiny is bound to marriage. In both the remake and the premake, it is only a woman's right to choose her (beloved) husband that is debated.

Arranged Marriage versus Love Marriage

Indeed, within the debate about what constitutes a married woman, another controversy is inscribed. This controversy centers on the role of love between husband and wife and is discussed in various local media. Within the genre of market literature, many novels—frequently written by women—describe the repressive world of arranged marriage.[31] In addition, local videos often feature forced marriage or "forced love" (*soyayyar dole*) as a central theme. Indeed, the Hausa remake of *Titanic* is just one of a whole series of local videos that takes up this subject.

Whereas, according to Abdalla Uba Adamu, Islamic orthodoxy permits forced marriages because the girl is seen as "too young to understand her mind," this is in violation of Islamic teaching, wherein a female's permission is necessary (often given through her official representative, or *walik*) for marriage. In northern Nigeria (as in other regions of Africa), moreover, marriage is not generally founded on love and happiness (of the girl) but instead on the production of children. A relatively radical counterdiscourse questions the institution of arranged marriage and instead demands women's right to choose their husbands on the grounds of a (strange) feeling called love. In many African and European cultures, passionate romantic love has traditionally been regarded as destructive—as a sort of illness and a threat to the social order, and thus to be kept outside marriage. Niklas Luhmann, a German sociologist, has traced what he calls the code of romantic or passionate love as it developed in Europe during the past several centuries. Though in most cultures, for the reasons mentioned above, passionate love and marriage were clearly separated, Europe went its own more-or-less catastrophic way. With the "invention" of "romantic love" and "sexuality" in the eighteenth and nineteenth centuries, love emerged as a sexually based intimacy, which developed into love marriage. However, love marriage remained the privilege of the upper classes. A democratization of the ideal slowly developed in the nineteenth century, as romantic love and intimacy became a necessary compensation for the cold impersonal relations of burgeoning industrial capitalism. Nowadays, expectations of the beloved concerning the fulfillment of the ideal of romantic love have risen to such an extent that the dominant psychological discourse that has forcefully entered everyday life makes a monster of everybody who necessarily fails to fulfill the ideal. Thus, it is not by chance that we Westerners live in a sort of therapy society, in which the attainment of passionate love has become the central goal of life, and yet, when it happens, soon has to be treated by a healing specialist.[32]

In northern Nigeria, the threat of passionate love was counteracted by various social strategies, such as arranged marriage and sexual segregation. Although not a new subject, the ideal of passionate romantic love has gained powerful influence through the widespread consumption of Indian, Western, and lately also Hausa films, and is used by many women to justify their right to choose a husband. Brian Larkin has remarked that women now demand that their husbands act more like lovers in Indian films and men complain that Indian films create female demands that cannot be met.[33]

Passionate Love, Indian Style

Because it is considered to be commercial suicide among Hausa video producers to make a video without Indian-style song-and-dance sequences, as Abdalla Uba Adamu observes,[34] Farouk Ashu-Brown could not fail to include them in his remake of *Titanic*. In Bollywood films, these sequences form main elements of cinematic spectacle. Likewise, they function as a sort of rupture by opening up an often-dreamlike space that at the same time condenses the emotions and makes allusions to romantic love, sexuality, and intimacy.[35]

To uphold—and even surpass—the intensity of emotions between Rose and Jack in Cameron's film and translate them into a Hausa context, Ashu-Brown introduced song-and-dance sequences that closely follow the conventions of Indian films. His film includes three long sequences in which Abdul and Binta—separately and then together—sing and dance in a hybrid Hindi/Hausa fashion, confirming to each other their passionate love. In the second sequence, Binta, against the blue sky with a few white clouds, declares her love for Abdul through a song, opening up an imaginary space of desire and fantasy while at the same time preserving the sexual segregation necessary to Hausa Islamic values. As in Indian films, she changes her surroundings and clothes, for example, from tight jeans and T-shirt to an Indian sari, thus presenting different transcultural images of herself as not only Hausa and modern but also, above all, cosmopolitan.

Against the background of the local debate on Hausa culture and gender, the video of *Titanic* by Farouk Ashu-Brown follows a politics of gender that tries to avoid offensive sexual interaction while at the same time affirming it and so intensifying the play between transgression and conformity. When, for example, Abdul and Binta declare their love to each other, they are each shown in close-ups separated through the montage technique of "shot and countershot," but this separation only intensifies their closeness. And after having consummated their love behind a metallic security door, they reappear and start dancing together in a way that prompted one critic ask how this film could have passed the censors.

Transgression and Male Sacrifice

At the end of the remake, before the *Titanic* finally sinks, Binta and Abdul cling to the back of the ship, their bodies again in close proximity. But all these transgressions, these immoral and forbidden contacts, take place against the background of death. Perhaps the remake passed the censors because punishment follows, with one of the sinners about to freeze in the cold sea. Thus, we have here the classic topic of passionate, romantic love that, because of its asocial, threatening nature, can end only with the death of one of the partners.

It is important to note that in the remake, following Cameron's plot, it is not the woman who is punished by death but the man. Binta, the modern woman, survives and tells her story. This break with the long Western film tradition of female sacrifice reproduced in the Hausa remake also represents a break with the misogynist tradition in Hausa videos of women (but rarely men) often falling sick, going crazy, or dying as punishment for their transgressions.

Local Critics

Although the remake passed the censors, local audiences did not flock to see it. It did not recoup the profits of Cameron's success, but instead was heavily criticized for copying. In addition, the remake raised various questions of cultural authenticity and cultural decline. In a review published on the Internet by the Yahoo group Finafinan Hausa, a critic accused Farouk Ashu-Brown of having stolen not only the title but also twenty-seven sequences from Cameron's *Titanic*. (The critic forgot to count the sequences pirated from *Deep Blue Sea.*) He mocked the director by comparing him to a magpie, which does not lay eggs itself but steals the eggs of other birds. In addition, the critic associated the remake with the Hausa term *wanki,* that is, to wash or to wash out. Thus, remaking was completely stripped of its creative potential and reduced to an act of mere imitation. The director's subversive reworkings of Cameron's premake from an Afrocentric perspective were not at all acknowledged.

Actually, Farouk Ashu-Brown was the first video maker in northern Nigeria to adopt the new technique of copying (and pirating). Though others before him had created remakes by filming local versions of Hollywood or Bollywood premakes that copied them almost scene for scene, he was the first to lift sequences directly from the premake and combine them with locally shot scenes. This original procedure is called *datse* in Hausa, from *datsewa,* meaning "cutting."[36]

However, critical disdain for copying obviously is shared by other intellectuals in Kano as well as various Western film critics who, as I mentioned at the outset of this chapter, see remakes as a form of plagiarism that makes use in a parasitic way of the original film for commercial interests. While upholding the divide between "original" and "copy," they negate the creativity that every act of copying or borrowing implies and fail to acknowledge that every video is a mosaic of other videos. The Nigerian video critic not only faulted the director for stealing but also for polluting Hausa culture. Against the background of the Islamist revival, the hybridity of many locally produced videos in northern Nigeria has come to be seen as a threat to both Hausa culture and Islam. Against borrowings from Hollywood and Bollywood, a reified Hausa culture is upheld and promoted by various intellectuals and religious leaders. The recourse to "authentic" and "traditional" Hausa theater, folk tales, dance, and musical instruments is strongly recommended against the "high acculturative bombardment" of Hindi and Western films.[37] Though the videos that are used for the promotion, propagation, and even preservation of culture and religion are widely accepted, borrowings from southern Nigerian films as well as Western films have been criticized as culturally polluting or poisonous (*gurbatarwa*). Censorship in this context is seen as a sort of sanitization, a form of cleansing to keep the videos in a state of cultural purity.[38]

Some video makers have reacted to censorship and this kind of criticism by redefining their status as author or director in terms of "religious teaching" and moral instruction. One video maker with whom I had the chance to talk in Kano in 2003 related that he had received the plot of his video in a dream, thus connecting to the Islamic tradition of vision and prophesy. He turned the dream into a divine gift that had to be visualized to be communicated to other believers. This filmmaker placed himself at the crossroads of prophesy, modern media, and entertainment.[39] Likewise, he transferred part of his authorship to a religious source outside himself, God or the Prophet Muhammad, thereby transforming the film into a revelation.

Other video makers, however, made use of the strict censorship by consciously transgressing its rules to gain publicity and thereby increase their videos' sales. Although Abdalla Uba Adamu gives the example of one director who was cursed by Muslim scholars, forced into hiding, and later had to apologize and "correct" his video, censorship on the whole has proven to be, it seems, rather counterproductive.[40] In times of fundamentalist revival, when boundaries are tightened, religious and cultural purity are defended, and the temptation to transgress increases, authorship and agency often are transferred to spirits or God. Then it may happen that spirits give expression to what has been excluded and repressed, and what cannot be otherwise said or done. It may not be by chance that unknown spirits recently invaded Kano, took possession of hundreds of schoolgirls, and forced them to dance like actresses in Indian films.[41]

Notes

1. Andrew Horton and Stuart Y. McDougal, "Introduction," in *Play It Again, Sam: Retakes on Remakes,* edited by Andrew Horton and Stuart Y. McDougal (Berkeley: University of California Press, 1998), 1–9; the citation here is on 6.

2. Leo Braudy, "Afterword: Rethinking Remakes," in *Play It Again, Sam,* ed. Horton and McDougal, 326–32; the citation here is on 328.

3. Katrin Oltmann, "Vom *Shop around the Corner* zum 'Global Village' und zurück: Globalization im Hollywood-Remake *You've Got Mail,*" in *Popularisierung und Popularität,* edited by Gereon Blaseio, Hedwig Pompe, and Jens Ruchartz (Cologne: Dumont, 2005).

4. Brian Larkin, "Degrading Images, Distorted Sounds: Nigerian Videos and the Infrastructure of Piracy," *Public Culture* 16, no. 3 (2004): 289–314.

5. Brian Larkin, "Hausa Dramas and the Rise of Video Culture in Nigeria," in *Nigerian Video Films,* edited by Jonathan Haynes (Athens: Ohio University Center for International Studies, 2000), 209–41; the citation here is on 210–11.

6. Ibid., 219.

7. The term "Kallywood" was coined following the example of the Indian film industry in Bombay, which was renamed—with a mixture of contempt as well as admiration—"Bollywood," after Hollywood. Thus a transcontinental genealogy was established with Hollywood as the "hegemonic" founding ancestor. Yet this genealogy allowed Kallywood to refer to Hollywood as well as Bollywood and so to displace the hierarchy inherent in genealogies.

8. Abdalla Uba Adamu, "Parallel Worlds: Reflective Womanism in Balaraba Ramat Yakubu's 'Ina Son Sa Haka,'" *Jenda: A Journal of Culture and African Women Studies* (2003): 1–23.

9. Abdalla Uba Adamu, "Enter the Dragon: Sharia, Popular Culture and Film Censorship in Northern Nigeria," paper presented at Institute of African Studies, University of Cologne, Cologne, November 2004. See also Abdalla Uba Adamu, *Transglobal: Media Flows and African Popular Culture—Revolution and Reaction in Muslim Hausa Popular Culture* (Kano: Visually Ethnographic Productions, 2007).

10. Larkin, "Hausa Dramas," 210–11.

11. Brian Larkin, "The Materiality of Cinema Theaters in Northern Nigeria," in *Media Worlds,* edited by Faye Ginsburg, Lila Abu-Lughod, and Brian Larkin (Berkeley: University of California Press, 2002), 319–36; the quotation here is on 327.

12. Larkin, "Hausa Dramas," 227.

13. Brian Larkin, "Indian Films and Nigerian Lovers: Media and the Creation of Parallel Modernities," *Africa* 67, no. 3 (1997): 406–40; the quotation here is on 424.

14. Adamu, "Enter the Dragon."

15. Conerly Carol Casey, "Medicines for Madness: Suffering, Disability and the Identification of Enemies in Northern Nigeria" (PhD diss., University of California, 1997), 101.

16. The films that are produced in Bollywood and then exported are mostly Hindi films, thus excluding, for example, Tamil, and so are not representative of the entire Indian population.

17. Abdalla Uba Adamu, *"The Song Remains the Same": Media Parenting and the Construction of Media Identities in Northern Nigeria Muslim Hausa Home Videos* (Kano: Center for Hausa Cultural Studies, n.d.). See also Malami Buba and Graham Furniss,

"Youth Culture, Bandiri, and the Continuing Legitimacy Debate in Sokoto Town," *Journal of African Cultural Studies* 12, no. 1 (1999): 27–46; and Brian Larkin, "Bandiri Music, Globalization and Urban Experience in Nigeria," *Cahiers d'Etudes Africaines* 168 (2002): 739–62.

18. Adamu, *"Song Remains the Same,"* 17ff.

19. Ibid., 20.

20. Ibid., 24.

21. Larkin, "Indian Films."

22. Brian Larkin, "Itineraries of Indian Cinema: African Videos, Bollywood and Global Media," in *Multiculturalism, Postcoloniality and Transnational Media,* edited by Ella Shohat and Robert Stam (New Brunswick, N.J.: Rutgers University Press, 2003), 170–92; the citation here is on 172f.

23. Larkin, "Bandiri Music," 751.

24. Claudia Liebrand and Franziska Schössler, "Und die schönste Frau ist DiCaprio: Gender-Konzepte in James Camerons Film Titanic," in *Geschlechterkonstruktionen in Sprache, Literatur und Gesellschaft,* edited by Elisabeth Cheauré, Ortrud Gutjahr, and Claudia Schmidt (Freiburg: Rombach, 2002), 137–51.

25. Paul Gilroy, *The Black Atlantic: Modernity and Double Consciousness* (London: Verso, 1993), 4.

26. See the Web site of the Titanic Historical Society, www.titanichistoricalsociety .org.

27. Barbara M. Cooper, *Marriage in Marad: Gender and Culture in Hausa Society in Niger* (Portsmouth, N.H., and Oxford: Heinemann and James Currey, 1997), 134.

28. Ibid., 184.

29. Ibid., 190; also see 171.

30. According to Abdalla Uba Adamu, a Muslim Hausa woman is not required to change her name after marriage. Yet modern state bureaucracy requires a surname for passports, registration cards, etc. This is why many modern women adopt their husband's name after marriage while more "traditional" women retain their father's name (personal communication with the author).

31. Adamu, "Parallel Worlds," 1.

32. Niklas Luhmann, *Liebe als Passion Zur Codierung von Intimität* (Frankfurt: Suhrkamp, 1994). See also Heike Behrend, "Love à la Hollywood and Bombay in Kenyan Studio Photography," *Paideuma* 44 (1998): 139–53.

33. Larkin, "Indian Films," 424ff.

34. Adamu, *"Song Remains the Same,"* 10.

35. Tejaswini Ganti, "'And Yet My Heart Is Still Indian': The Bombay Film Industry and the (H)Indianization of Hollywood," in *Media Worlds,* ed. Ginsburg, Abu-Lughod, and Larkin, 281–300.

36. Ibid., 25.

37. Ibid., 32.

38. Dul Johnson, "Culture and Art in Hausa Video Films," in *Nigerian Video Films,* edited by Jonathan Haynes (Athens: Ohio University Center for International Studies, 2000), 200–208; the citation here is on 202.

39. Birgit Meyer, "Visions of Blood, Sex and Money: Fantasy Spaces in Popular Ghanaian Cinema," *Visual Anthropology* 16, no. 1 (2003): 15–41; the citation here is on 18.

40. Adamu, "Enter the Dragon."

41. Casey, "Medicines for Madness," 71.

Chapter 8

Shari'a Activism and *Zina* in Nigeria in the Era of *Hudud*

Margot Badran

In 1999, the year of the return to democracy in Nigeria after years of military dictatorship, the contender for the governorship of Zamfara, the state with the highest poverty and lowest literacy in the north, pledged to incorporate *hudud,* or Islamic laws of crime and punishment, into statutory law. This move was billed as a "return to the *shari'a.*" By 2002, twelve out of thirty-six states had instituted codified *hudud* laws (hereafter, simply *hudud* laws). Under these laws, sex outside marriage, or *zina,* was criminalized, and for the guilty could bring the ultimate penalty of death by stoning, while

This chapter was originally published in *Global Empowerment of Women: Responses to Globalization and Politicized Religions,* edited by Carolyn Elliot (New York: Routledge, 2007), and is reprinted here by permission of the publisher. It is a pleasure for me to express my thanks at the outset for the various kinds of support that made this research both possible and enriching. I am grateful to the Fulbright New Century Scholars program for inviting me to be part of the cohort of scholars in 2003–4 around the theme of global women's empowerment. I thank Aisha Imam for facilitating my affiliation with Baobab during the course of my project and members with whom I corresponded and amputations were prescribed for crimes of theft.[1] Human rights activists and feminist activists in Nigeria, who had seen the disastrous effects of *hudud* in other countries over the past decades, worried that women and the poor would fall victim to these laws.[2]

As feared, it was not long before women were accused of *zina* (adultery) and brought before *shari'a* courts. In what became two high-profile cases, Safiyatu Husseini of Sokoto and Amina Lawal of Katsina, both from northern states with Muslim-majority populations, were summarily convicted and sentenced to death by stoning in the lower *shari'a* courts. These quickly became high-profile cases, locally and globally. It did not escape attention that it was women—and, more precisely, poor women—who were brought before the law, while the men involved simply absconded. Nigerian women activists, Muslims and non-Muslims alike, together with some male supporters, immediately swung into action. Through their nongovernmental organizations, Baobab for Women's Human Rights and the Women's Rights and Protection Association (WRAPA), activists offered the two women legal assistance, and simultaneously mounted wide publicity campaigns. The accused were eventually acquitted in higher *shari'a* courts of appeal in their respective states—Safiyatu Husseini in 2002, and Amina Lawal in 2003—as a result of a scrupulous application of *fiqh* (Islamic jurisprudence). Thus, it was within the Islamic legal system that the women were both convicted and acquitted following the strenuous work of Nigerian activists. However, Westerners who protested through petitions and via the media—until Nigerian activists asked them to desist as their support be-

met in person. I am grateful to Habu Muhammad, whom I met when he was a Fulbright scholar at the Program of African Studies in Northwestern University and who was very helpful in introducing me to people in Kano, where he teaches at Bayero University in the Department of Political Science. I am grateful to Haruna Wakili, director of Mambaya House, and Ismaila Zango, deputy director, and professors at Bayero University for their warm welcome and help during my stay in Kano. I thank Hamidu Bobboyi, then director of Arewa House, for the hospitality he extended, and Aisha Lamu and her husband, Sheikh Lemu, for having me as their guest in Minna. I thank my colleague and friend Muhammad Sane Umar for our many conversations, both in Evanston and in Jos, where he was most helpful during my stay, as was Philip Ostien of the University of Jos. I thank all the women with whom I had extended interview-conversations for sharing their knowledge and for their candor and wit. They are at the center of this work. In this final moment as I write this note, I wish to thank Carolyn Elliot, who was a superb leader of the New Century Scholar group and who right up to the final editing of the volume in which this was first published was helpful to all of us. I appreciate the keen eye she brought to my chapter.

came counterproductive, especially when laced with expressions of Islamophobia—took credit for the victory as a triumph of (Western) secular discourse. Yet this is not to suggest that the intensive glare of the global media, from the West and other parts of the world, was without positive influence.

The campaigns women mounted to see justice done for Amina Lawal and Safiyatu Husseini, through organizing legal teams to defend their rights before higher *shari'a* courts, along with the public advocacy and debates that they stimulated, constitute a stunning manifestation of Islamic feminism at work. Did this activism and its positive outcomes provoke or further enhance Islamic feminist consciousness, that is, the awareness of the Qur'an-based rights of women as *insan* (human beings)? Did the successful campaigns catalyze intensified longer-term debates in Nigeria about issues of gender justice and social justice that mobilized Islamic discourse to empower Muslim women and erode the oppressive treatment of women in the name of Islam? Seeking answers to such questions, I went to Nigeria early in 2005 to meet women and engage with them in conversations, participate in local gatherings, and carry out interviews. I describe this research in greater detail below.[3]

In this chapter, I observe how women's activism concerning the *zina* cases made salient contributions to the ongoing project of articulating and implementing Islamic feminism in Nigeria. The Nigerian experience forms an important part of the global Islamic feminist story. Muslim women in various locations move in strikingly parallel ways, as well as along divergent paths and in different time frames, in elaborating and activating Islamic feminism.

Before "the Return" to *Shari'a*

Starting in the late 1970s, and especially from the 1980s, two diametrically opposed discourses on women and gender were generated by Muslims and circulated transnationally and nationally. The first one, which was initially spread mainly by men as Islamists or advocates of political Islam, also called Islamic fundamentalists, was a patriarchal discourse in the language of Islam, supporting male domination and the protection of women in a system of unequal gender rights and laying stress on women's family roles. The other was a gender-egalitarian discourse articulated by Muslim women as feminists and human rights advocates that stressed women's rights and public roles in the multiple and intersecting discourses of Islamic modernism, and (Muslims') secular feminism/s, human rights, and democracy.

The 1990s saw the appearance of the new Islamic feminist discourse, referred to above, based on women scholars' new Qur'anic interpretation articulating the full equality of women and men across the public-private spectrum. This Islamic feminist discourse, backed by the new exegetical work, elaborated a more radical notion of gender equality than Muslim women's secular feminisms, which had typically acquiesced in the notion of equity or balanced gender roles in the private or family sphere. The early secular feminist movements in Muslim-majority societies, which first arose in the early twentieth century, fighting battles on multiple fronts, found it easier to make headway pushing for full equality in the public sphere. They accepted the new Islamic modernist approaches to ameliorating injustices in the family through pushing for optimal performance of gender-differentiated roles.[4] It would take time for the societal changes and higher levels of training needed to enable women to embark on a more radical interpretation on their own, as happened toward the end of the twentieth century. By the turn of the twenty-first century, the patriarchal and egalitarian discourses on women and gender within Islam and their respective proponents were on a high-stakes collision course.

From the early 1980s, Muslim women living in different parts of the globe, joined by some non-Muslims, began to consolidate a transnational feminist / human rights culture in the network called Women Living Under Muslim Laws (WLUML), which began informally when Algerian women objected to not being consulted about the draft for a new Muslim family law in Algeria. Since it was formally established in 1984, WLUML has engaged in advocacy and lobbying work on questions of laws and their implementation, issuing alerts and circulating petitions on behalf of women suffering victimization. It undertook a long-tem project gathering data on laws and women's experience in Muslim societies around the world that resulted in the publication of *Knowing Our Rights: Women, Family, Laws and Customs in the Muslim World* in 2003, which had appeared in a third edition by December 2006.[5] The women who began WLUML were (secular) feminists and human rights advocates who used international discourses, and who familiarized themselves with the various legal discourses, including religious jurisprudence, found in the societies where they operated. And with the development of the Islamic feminist discourse in the 1990s, they accessed its insights and methods as well.[6]

As Muslim women were consolidating this transnational feminist network culture, the transnational movement of political Islam was spreading globally. Islamism, which had begun to surface in parts of the Muslim world in the 1970s, made its appearance in northern Nigeria toward the end of that decade through a group called Jama'atu Izalat al-Bid'a wa Iqamat al-Sunna (Society for the Eradication of Innovation and the Establishment of Tradition), which was known as Izala.[7] The Izala movement has been called neo-fundamentalist because it did not challenge the state (like such fundamentalist movements as the Egyptian-founded Muslim Brothers), but rather civil society and especially Sufi trends, advocating legal reform (or a return to Islamic laws). At the core of Izala's reformist project was spreading its own brand of Islamic education, and to that end it created Islamic schools throughout the north to teach religious subjects, along with what in Nigeria are called Western subjects (and are elsewhere often called modern subjects), to males and females alike. An unintentional result of these neofundamentalists' mission of teaching the religious sciences and the Arabic language was to open the way for questioning Izala's reactionary patriarchal attitude toward Islam. A young woman with whom I spoke after she had completed studies in an Izala-run school went on to give women lessons in religion in her home, where she introduced them to a gender-egalitarian approach to Islam. While operating as an outspoken feminist education activist—and she is not shy about claiming this label—she continued her Islamic religious studies at the university.[8]

During this same period, Nigerian women were creating their own associations and spearheading their own educational initiatives. In 1985, Muslim women from around the country with ties to the Muslim Sisters Organization and other Islamic associations came together to establish the Federation of Muslim Women's Associations of Nigeria (FOMWAN), with Aisha Lemu as its first head or *amira.* Its main purpose was to provide schooling for Muslim girls in a curriculum that combined Islamic and Western subjects. Although FOMWAN laid stress on education and an overall religious formation, it also provided health training and services in its various outreach programs. This grassroots association celebrated its twentieth anniversary in 2005 at a large conference in the nation's capital, Abuja.[9] Its current head is the activist, writer, and journalist Bilkisu Yusuf.

Nigerian women, including both Muslims and Christians together, were also forming human rights and women's rights organizations in the 1990s. I mention, as examples, the two organizations that came to the rescue of the women accused in the two *zina* cases. Baobab for Women's Human Rights was established in 1996 under the leadership of Ayesha Imam, a founding member of WLUML.[10] Although autonomous, the organization has ties with WLUML. Three years later, in 1999, the year the first *hudud* laws were announced, WRAPA was founded, with activist Saudatu Mahdi assuming the position of secretary-general. Human rights and feminist activists employed multiple discourses, seeing human rights, democracy, and progressive religious discourse as mutually reinforcing women's rights and human rights, as well as gender justice and social justice. Muslim women operating more fully within an Islamic framework, such as the FOMWAN women, and those functioning within multiple frameworks, such as Baobab and WRAPA members, were not adversarial, but rather their focus and their projects differed.

From talking with women from both groups, it appears that around the turn of the twenty-first century—and especially in the aftermath of the *zina* cases—these two groups were converging more and more in their concerns about issues of women, state, and society. The problematic verdicts issued by the lower *shari'a* courts in the *zina* cases and the impressive backing by women activists from Baobab and WRAPA through the mobilization of *fiqh* readings have galvanized women across a broad spectrum in support of a common quest for gender justice and social justice in the aftermath of the instituting of *hudud* laws.

Islamic Feminism

Islamic feminism is a global discourse that is continually fed by the local reality, while the global discourse likewise animates the local. In the 1990s, a new feminist paradigm in the language of Islam caught the attention of Muslim women, themselves feminists, in different locations, who, often unbeknown to each other, started to call it Islamic feminism. They were noticing and naming a feminist discourse and practice grounded in rereadings of the Qur'an, seeking rights and justice for women—and for men—in the totality of their existence. Women interpreters enunciated two key concepts of Islamic feminism—gender equality and social justice—which are fundamental ideals that were to be applied in everyday life across the public-private continuum.[11]

Islamic feminism, with its paramount grounding in religious discourse, did not reject or replace what has been known as Muslims' secular feminism/s expressed in the discourses of Islamic modernism, secular nationalism, and humanitarian and—later—human rights. Islamic feminism elaborated the principle of gender equality as part and parcel of all equalities within Islamic discourse as its paramount discourse. It can be seen as building upon and extending the Islamic modernist strand of Muslims' multivocal secular feminism.[12] The African American scholar Amina Wadud, in her book *Qur'an and Woman: Reading the Sacred Text from a Woman's Perspective,* elaborated the notions of gender equality and social justice, and made clear their necessary intersection.[13] Her work has provided powerful support in the form of strong Islamic argumentation in the struggle for the implementation of equality and justice across lines of race, gender, and class.

Patriarchal ideas articulated in the language of Islam have subverted the practice of gender equality and social justice that the Qur'an puts forward. The Pakistani American Asma Barlas faced the problem head-on when she defined patriarchy and unmasked its invidious work in eroding the notion and practice of the Qur'anic equality of human beings (*insan*), irrespective of their physical attributes (anatomy, skin color, etc.) and various socially constructed differences. Removing the structures of inequality that patriarchy sustains is fundamental to the project of understanding and practicing equality.

Barlas's *"Believing Women": Unreading Patriarchal Interpretations of the Qur'an,* the outcome of work begun in the 1990s, was published in 2002.[14] Other scholars concerned about inequitable or problematical laws enacted in the name of Islam turned their attention to the Islamic jurisprudence (*fiqh*) derived from interpretations of the Qur'an and other sources such as *hadith* (the sayings and deeds attributed to the Prophet Muhammad). Ziba Mir-Hosseini, a London-based scholar from Iran, scrutinized *fiqh* and its application in the enacting of Muslim personal status codes, which are also called family laws.[15] These codes, claiming firm grounding in Islamic jurisprudence support a patriarchal family structure.

Complicating the reform of *fiqh*-backed laws, commonly called *"shari'a* laws" and often simply, "the *shari'a"* (as the elision of *fiqh* and *shari'a* as divinely guided "path" illustrates), is the widely held belief that to alter the Muslim personal status or family laws is to tamper with the sacred. This has long been an effective way to inhibit people from engaging in critiques of *fiqh* and attempts to recast *fiqh*-based laws. This is not to say, however, that there have not been serious and sustained movements by feminists to reform *fiqh*-based Muslim family law, nor that some successes have not been achieved.[16]

Islamic feminists have taken pains to make the distinction between the *shari'a* as the path discerned from the Qur'an that Muslims are exhorted to follow in life (*shari'a* as divine inspiration and guiding principles) and so-called *shari'a* law(s) (laws deriving from understandings of *fiqh* that are man-made, and therefore open to questioning and change). The *shari'a,* as "the path" indicated in the scripture as the word of God, is sacred; but it needs to be ascertained through human effort. By stressing the distinction between man-made law(s) and the divine path, Islamic feminists strive to remove an obstacle in the way of those who feared—indeed, were encouraged to fear—that they might be challenging divine law if they questioned *fiqh* and the laws deriving from it.[17]

Shari'a as Path and as Politics

In Nigeria, with the politicization of the *shari'a,* the distinction between *shari'a* as "the path" and *shari'a* as man-made law was expediently kept blurred by states that came to be called the "*shari'a* states" after instituting *hudud* laws and declaring "a return to the *shari'a.*"[18] Although the label "*shari'a* states" was originally conferred by non-Muslims to refer to states that had instituted *hudud* laws, and was then taken up by the media, it was soon brandished by the so-called *shari'a* states themselves as if in confirmation of their self-arrogated task to reestablish the *shari'a.*

It is important to note parenthetically that the notion of a "*shari'a* state" as a state within a sovereign state is peculiar to Nigeria. A "*shari'a* state" should not be confused with a sovereign "Islamic state," which declares its Constitution and all its laws to be based on the *shari'a.* Unlike in the self-styled Islamic states, the notion of the "*shari'a* state" in Nigeria simply pivoted around the institution of *hudud* laws, a law-and-order approach to Islam.

By making the claim and igniting hope for a new "coming" of *shari'a* to be ushered in through the "gate of *hudud,*" state authorities set themselves on a course they did not chart. In short, they misread the politics. The rapid and zealous implementation of *hudud* witnessed by the condemnations of the two poor women in the *zina* cases flung open a Pandora's box of confusions and contractions swirling around "the *shari'a*" and actions taken in its name, and vividly linked two kinds of oppressions: that of women and the poor. Thus, with the explosion of the two *zina* cases on the scene, women who came to the rescue of their condemned sisters put forward another definition of *shari'a* and opened up a fresh look at *fiqh.*

Hudud

Hudud have remained traditionally operative, but they were never codified in Saudi Arabia. Long surpassed by secular statutory laws in most Muslim societies, *hudud* were reinstated in codified form in the late 1970s and early 1980s in Iran, Pakistan, and Sudan with the imposition of Islamist regimes.[19] The imposition of *hudud* elicited strong opposition among women both inside and outside these countries. Women as human rights activists and secular feminists in Pakistan through Shirgat Gah (which began as a women's resource center in 1975 with ties to WLUML) and through the Women's Action Forum (created in 1981) have fought the abuses perpetrated against women through aggressive campaigns of public protest and exposure, and letter-writing and petition campaigns—and continue to do so today, with a certain amount of success.[20] Meanwhile, Iranian women at home and in the diaspora have mounted wide vigorous protests on behalf of women victimized under *hudud* laws. The network called Nisa Meydaan (Women's Field), which includes such long-term activists and lawyers as Shirin Ebadi and Mihrangaz Kar, as well as many scholars such as Ziba Mir-Hosseini and Val Moghadam, is currently engaged in a vigorous transnational initiative called the "Stop Stoning Forever Campaign."[21] Pakistani and Iranian activists have made extensive use of the WLUML network in support of women condemned under *hudud* laws, and to expose and discuss the laws per se. And when *hudud* laws were proclaimed in Nigeria, local women activists—who had gained exposure to the workings of *hudud* laws in other countries and had supported the causes of women victimized under these laws—were well experienced, well networked, and poised to act.

Two *Zina* Cases in Nigeria

The women-headed defense teams composed primarily of women lawyers, along with specialists in jurisprudence and Arabists, that were assembled by Baobab and WRAPA appealed the cases of Safiyatu Husseini and Amina Lawal in the higher *shari'a* courts. The *shari'a* court system (both the lower and higher courts) had only been accustomed to hearing personal status cases (or cased related to family law and inheritance) since the early nineteenth century, when *hudud* (which previously had never been codified in Nigeria, although they were practiced in what were called "*qadis'* courts") had been outlawed under the British. With independence in the 1960s, a national criminal code was enacted. Close and routine familiarity with Islamic jurisprudence concerning *hudud* was lacking, along with a recent history of precedents.

In appealing the cases, the women-headed defense teams laid out details of *fiqh* demonstrating the stringent requirements of evidence and strict pro-

cedures that needed to be followed in *hudud* cases to protect the cause of
justice. The cases, which resulted in acquittals, constituted an impressive
public display of "learning through legal action," or "walking through *fiqh.*"
The acquittals were a triumph of the principles of Islamic equality and justice over patriarchal inequities. To date, there have been no more convictions for *zina,* and accordingly no capital punishment has been carried out.
Although capital punishment is on the books in the Federation of Nigeria,
its implementation has fallen into abeyance.[22]

Whereas classical *fiqh* (consolidated during the formation of the major
schools of jurisprudence in the ninth and tenth centuries) shored up a patriarchal model of the family, classical jurisprudence took a strikingly gender-
egalitarian approach to crime and punishment. Requirements of evidence
and procedures were to be strictly applied to both women and men. It
has been suggested that the penalty of death by stoning for those guilty of
zina was prescribed for both sexes, and it was so onerous that the punishment was meant to act as a deterrent, not a weapon to be easily wielded—
especially against the vulnerable. It rankled when judges in the lower
shari'a courts handed down quick verdicts of guilty to the two women accused of *zina* while the men involved were never brought before the courts,
and that the convicted were poor women. It clearly did not signal the advent of social justice that the state-directed "return to the *shari'a*" had prom-
ised. People linked oppression against women and oppression of the poor.
They began to insist that social and economic justice should prevail as part
of living by the *shari'a* before *hudud* laws might be introduced.

The cooperation between Muslim and Christian women in the *zina* cases
occasioned a strengthening of transcommunal activism in support of justice
and equality in Nigeria. Backing the cause of justice in the *shari'a* courts
was not of necessity linked to a religious identity or faith position, as the
support of Nigerian Christian activists acting on behalf of their endangered
Nigerian and Muslim sisters illustrated. The activists shared common understandings of justice and equality, irrespective of their religious affiliations. This has seldom been noticed, as observers have been quick to circu-
late instances of interreligious strife rather than transreligious cooperation,
especially on issues of women and gender.[23]

Nigerian Muslim Women's Narratives

To understand the long-term impact of the activism centering on the two
zina cases and the support initiated by women as part of the elaboration of

the project of Islamic feminism, I spoke with women in the Muslim-majority states of northern Nigeria, where *hudud* laws were in force, as well as with women in the Middle Belt, where Muslims were not in the majority and *hudud* laws were nonexistent. To get the views of those living in states without *hudud,* I conducted a total of fifty interviews in February and March 2004 in six of the twelve states in the north with *hudud* laws—Kano, Katsina, Sokoto, Kaduna, Niger State, and Zamfara—as well in Plateau State in the Middle Belt, where Muslims and Christians are roughly equal in number.[24] The overall mix of persons with whom I talked included, along with a preponderance of Muslim women, some men and a few Christians, whom I met more by chance than by design.

My interlocutors—as I prefer to call them, because the interviews resembled conversations with a vibrant give-and-take—were middle-class women living and working in major cities. They included activists, academics, lawyers, journalists, writers, teachers, government employees, and some students. They represented mainly two generations: (1) those in their midforties and fifties, including, at the outer limit, some in their sixties who brought some historical depth to the current debates; and (2) those in their thirties, more or less. Their views inform the core of this chapter. A few encounters with students in their twenties pointed to preoccupations of a third generation that would form an intriguing new project.

During the period of my research, I participated in two conferences, at which I had interactions with Muslims and Christians, and with women and men: the Conference on Christian-Muslim Relations in Zamfara in March 2005, and the Conference on Promoting Women's Rights through Shari'ah in Northern Nigeria, sponsored by the Centre for Islamic Legal Studies at Ahmadu Bello University in Zaria.[25] On an earlier visit to Nigeria, I had participated in the International Conference on the Implementation of Shari'ah in a Democracy: The Nigerian Experience, held in Abuja. My presentation, "Ongoing Tafsir on Men and Women in Islam: Constructions and Practices of Democracy and Social Justice"—in which I spoke about Islamic feminist discourse, mainly focusing on Amina Wadud and Asma Barlas—exposed me to the passions and perils the subject evokes.[26] These experiences in public forums were instructive and helpful in contextualizing my more private discussions with women.

I am careful in this chapter, as always, to make the distinction between Islamic feminism as a named discourse and Islamic feminist as an assumed identity. In my encounters in northern Nigeria and the Middle Belt, I did not find reference made to Islamic feminism as an explicit discourse, nor did I find persons who called themselves Islamic feminists. Moreover, I discov-

ered that the terms "feminism" and "feminist" were not in general circulation, and that they were highly controversial, so to use such terms publicly
would have been provocative and counterproductive. I did, however, find
what I recognized as Islamic feminist questions, concerns, ideas, and forms
of activism. In speaking of "Islamic feminism" or "Islamic feminists" in
Nigeria, I thus use these terms in a purely analytical sense, to be able to
place the ideas and experience of Nigerians in the context of the global phenomenon of Islamic feminism and to discuss Nigerian expressions of
Islamic feminism and their important transnational and national contributions. To protect their privacy, I do not identify women by name. However,
I do quote some of their words to give readers direct access to their expres-
sive voices. All the women whom I quote are activists, and thus I identify
them simply by profession.

Women and ("the Return to") *Shari'a*

You have to know *shari'a* before you can implement it. We thought that
because of the enormous protection that Islam gives women, that this is
what would obtain. Muslim women thought the *shari'a* states would give
us this. [But] It was like we were at the receiving end. This issue of adultery and sentencing only women to death, even the manner in which it
was done, made us feel that the *shari'a* was against women, which is not
true. We feel maybe because it is a male-dominated society and because
of selfish reasons that women only are at the receiving end. (professor)[27]

We are not quarreling with the *shari'a* as a concept, but we are quarreling with the implementation. Regarding our men: Why is it for you
shari'a implementation is about women being "proper"? If we are going
to get what the *shari'a* stands for, then we will be better off. We are going to hold you accountable. We are going to say the *shari'a* should be
implemented with social justice. (professor)

Men hijack the *shari'a* to the detriment of women. (professor)

If the rich get off and the poor "get the *shari'a* on them," there will def-
initely be a problem. (student)

If we practice *shari'a,* people will live in peace because some will not
acquire too much wealth while others live in poverty. If the *shari'a* is

practiced as it should be, there will be more space for women in the society. (professor)

During the time of the two *zina* cases, women's attention was riveted on *hudud;* but in the aftermath of the acquittals, attention shifted to a broader discussion of the *shari'a* as a whole.[28] Some two years after the second acquittal, the subject of the *shari'a* kept coming up in my conversations with women. Women, as the above quotations indicate, repeatedly spoke of how the male-defined (and/or the "state-defined") *shari'a* was constructed and deployed to the detriment of women and the poor. They expressed no doubt that this was a contradiction of the Qur'anic message. The *zina* cases were a wrenching example for women of the willingness to make scapegoats of women and poor people. Women pointed out publicly (as, increasingly, men did as well) that within the context of Islam, *hudud* should only be put in force in a society where the social and economic well-being of all categories of people prevail; only then is it possible that justice might be served under *hudud.*

Concerning the state-announced "return to *shari'a,*" women repeated that the *shari'a* had always been integral to Muslim life in Nigeria and important in their own lives. What was significant now was how the *shari'a* was understood by Muslims: to what were they were "returning"? During conversations, women showed that they had a firm idea of how patriarchal thinking had intruded into the egalitarian message of the Qur'an, thereby skewing understanding and practice of the *shari'a.* The women repeatedly insisted that access to formal training in religion should be widespread among women so that they could understand the *shari'a* for themselves and be part of its broader articulation and practice.

Many women confided that they were not in favor of *hudud,* and certainly not under conditions in which social and economic justice did not prevail; but in the face of a fait accompli, with *hudud* laws now in place, they would continue their vigilant struggle for justice within the existing legal framework. Women thus did not choose to contest the laws as such, but rather their applications. They also did not address head-on the question of the broader idea of a state-backed *shari'a.* This was a wise tactic—and probably their only real option, for women, as they told me, had far less public space to debate and dissent than men. In a conference on comparative perspectives on *shari'a* in Nigeria at the University of Jos in January 2004, when Abdullahi an-Na'im, a renowned Sudanese scholar of law and Islamic jurisprudence, argued against the notion of a state-backed *shari'a,* he was met with an explosive outcry.[29]

Women found space—or more space—to confront discrimination and injustice to women in the context of the *shari'a* court than in the public societal arena at large. It was in the context of the courts that women brought different knowledge and understanding to bear. This was a stunning case of women's activism as Islamic knowledge production. It did not escape public attention that it was women who had taken the initiative in coming to the defense of the accused, who were also women. Women assembled the defense teams that were made up mainly (but not only) of women lawyers and specialists, who successfully took the cases of the condemned women to the higher *shari'a* courts, where men only presided. Thus, women's voices were heard through their legal defense teams in the context of the *shari'a* court system, where their solidly *fiqh*-backed arguments won the day. This underscored the notion of women as human beings (*insan*) capable of defending justice, and not simply a category in need of protection or as a group of weak, deficient, and vulnerable human beings.

The usurpation of the right within the Nigerian common law system for women to act as judges—and, indeed, within an Islamic system (for it is patriarchal convention rather than Islamic jurisprudence that prevents women from being judges)—leaves the adjudication of criminal cases in the *shari'a* courts solely in the hands of men. In certain other Muslim societies, such as Iran, Sudan, and Morocco, women have been able to act as judges. And more recently, as a result of the persistence of Muslim women's feminist activist struggle, women in Egypt have been allowed to be judges.[30] The legal activism on the part of Nigerian women demonstrated that women were quicker than most men to support—and to rally support for—the vulnerable and victimized. Through their activism, women not only saved other women from further victimization but also served as examples of empowerment to their sisters.

It was also widely apparent that as Nigerians, Muslim and Christian women worked together in the defense of their fellow citizens. One Muslim said: "I am a human rights activist. I believe in human rights because Islam has a charter. I am working with other human rights organizations because in the end we are all Nigerian. [I struggle] if my right is denied, the same with my Christian counterpart, so we are all working for human rights, but I have guidance from my religion concerning what human rights is." Another Muslim activist woman said of the Christian supporters: "The Christians did not come out as Christians but as women." I have noted elsewhere that among the binaries Islamic feminism breaks down is opposition between Muslims and non-Muslims, as well as between the secular and the religious.

The Need for New Interpretation

We are looking beyond old interpretations and static ways of doing things, and at the need to engage with today. What will happen if Muslim women are not carried along as things are developing? The Qur'an gives women space, the right to participation, consultation. There is a tendency to use the cultural perspective to belittle women, to deny the consultation of women, making them irrelevant when it comes to decisionmaking, making them virtual minors who cannot take decisions, who need to have others take decisions for them. Are men addressing all the issues we want them to address? Aren't women best placed to examine things from a woman's perspective? (writer)

A problem with a lot of the *tafsir* is that it has been done centuries back. They were mainly made by scholars who had never encountered another culture so that they were operating with an understanding only of their own people. Because, in Islam, knowledge is a vibrant thing, ideally it should be a continuous looking at what others have done and adding to it, not just closing down and saying that's it. (professor)

Until now, the question of *ijtihad* [independent reasoning in approach to religious texts] has been kept silent. It has not been made public. (professor)

In conversations, women repeatedly stressed the need for women themselves to interpret the Qur'an and *fiqh,* the core project of Islamic feminism. The two *zina* cases made dramatically clear the need for gender-sensitive readings of religious sources. Some women who have been university professors since the 1980s explained that two decades ago, they had pointed to the need for women to engage in religious interpretation. They find themselves reiterating this today. The idea that women could read the Qur'an and other religious texts for themselves remains highly threatening to most people, especially because it could lead to the assumption of authority in religious matters on the part of women. A younger activist claimed that the trials of the two women "sensitized people to do research. The trials aroused their curiosity." She insisted that "the debates help in enlightening individuals and to push them to find out for themselves what *shari'a* entails."

A young woman professor declared quite simply: "Patriarchal ideas are presented as Islamic. You read the Qur'an and find most of what they are preaching is not in the Qur'an." She repeated a point that several other women made about the lack of public space in which they can debate issues of women and Islam. She confided: "You [women] risk being called Western, radical, or even having a fatwa put on you." Speaking not only of women, she continued: "Our people are now beginning to perceive the heavy dose of religious prescription they are given and that at the same time [understand that] those dispensing it are not applying it to themselves." This is an example of the disenchantment I heard voiced a few years down the road from the state-heralded "return to the *shari'a*" in the wake of the *zina* cases. Women and the poor had became the touchstone of society's protracted wait for justice.

How does one take the analysis into public space and make it operative? Repeatedly, women spoke about the problem of being ostracized if they were too outspoken in public about their views on "sensitive issues" such as women and the *shari'a*. I heard the term "no-go area" often in relation to controversial subjects, and I was plainly told that men have far more leeway to dissent in public than women. Although women have greater freedom to speak out in the contexts of universities and certain nongovernmental organizations, they are still more constrained than men. One activist and former university professor said: "It is a social precept that Islam does not allow women to question, to condemn." Another professor and activist exclaimed: "Until now, the question of *ijithad,* or critical intellectual inquiry into religious sources, has been kept silent. It has not been made public."

Recuperating a Local Female Tradition
of Scholarship and Authority

Claiming a line of scholarly women within the Islamic tradition is important for contemporaries in establishing legitimacy and authority as females within the field of religious learning. Compiling histories of Muslim women of the past as models and inspiration for present-day women is integral to the project of Muslim women's feminisms. The genre of the biographical dictionary holds a central place in Islamic scholarship. The Pakistani activists and Shirgat Gah members Farida Shaheed and Aisha Shaheed made a recent contribution to this genre when they published *Great Ancestors: Women Asserting Their Rights in Muslim Contexts,*[31] which includes an essay on the illustrious Nigerian woman Nana Asma'u.[32]

Muslim women in Nigeria today who are not finding it easy to occupy a place within the ranks of *'ulama'* (Islamic scholars) as Qur'anic interpreters or specialists in *fiqh* and other Islamic sciences can claim Nana Asma'u (1793–1864) as a revered female ancestor and renowned Islamic scholar and teacher to claim legitimacy for the work of contemporary women as religious scholars. Nana Asma'u (as Mack discusses in chapter 1), who came from a family of women and men who were religious scholars, was the daughter of Usman dan Fodio, the leader of the religious revival and founder of the Sokoto Caliphate.[33] She is well known for playing a key role in the spread of the Islamic revival, and especially in the education of women.

FOMWAN dedicated the cover story, "Muslim Women Scholars," in its journal *The Muslim Woman* in celebration of its twentieth anniversary in 2005 to promote the education, including religious education, of women.[34] Sa'idiyya Umar, a FOMWAN member and the director of the Center for Hausa Studies at Usmanu Danfodiyo University in Sokoto, sees in the Yantaru movement that Nana Asma'u led, bringing schooling in religion and other subjects to women in villages far and wide, a model that FOMWAN continues today in its mission to provide religious formation and education for Muslim women throughout the country.[35] Laying claim to her past, Asma'u Joda, an activist and member of Baobab, asserted: "In my Fulani community, women have for centuries had a long tradition of being religious scholars. Asma'u, daughter of Usman dan Fodio, was appointed in charge of religious affairs by her brother Muhammad Bello." She insisted: "We have to reread our histories."[36]

Claiming a Depatriarchalized Islam

It was evident in private conversations among women that the recent trials had triggered renewed debates about gender equality and social justice as principles found in the Qur'an but lacking in society, indicating an accelerated impatience with the lack of delivery of promises that the acclaimed "return to the *shari'a*" held out and the kind of oppression that can come with so-called law reform. The debates and activism around the *zina* cases produced a heightened Islamic feminist consciousness. They led to a clash of consciousnesses in Nigeria between the Islamic feminist consciousness and the Islamist or neofundamentalist consciousness. They represented very different approaches to the *shari'a* and to the law. The challenge for women is how to move from analysis to action in the arena of the community and society at large, and not in the restricted atmosphere of the *shari'a* courts. How can women construct a functioning, depatriarchalized Islam?

In Nigeria as elsewhere, Islamic feminism, by whatever name, is a work in progress. Nigerian Muslim women are aware of the dilemma and the challenge of moving themselves and their culture beyond patriarchy claiming to be Islamic into the space where an egalitarian Islam is operative. From what I observed in Nigeria, it seems that a process is now under way that cannot be reversed. It also appears that the road to a depatriachalized Islam there, as elsewhere, will be long and full of perils. However, the Nigerian success story in the *zina* cases and the debates about Islam and the *shari'a,* and about equality and justice, form a salient chapter in the local and global Islamic feminist narrative.

Notes

1. For a stunning analysis of *zina* and contextualization of *hudud,* see Charmaine Pereira, "Zina and Transgressive Heterosexuality in Northern Nigeria," available at www.feministafrica.org.

2. The network Women Living under Muslim Laws has circulated a huge amount of information on women suffering under *hudud* laws, as have women's associations in different countries where *hudud* laws are in effect, such as Iran and Pakistan.

3. I wrote about my encounters in an article titled "Liberties of the Faithful," *al-Ahram Weekly,* May 19–25, 2005, which has been republished in a slightly different form: Margot Badran, *Feminism beyond East and West: New Gender Talk and Practice in Global Islam* (New Delhi: Global Media Publications, 2006), 67–76.

4. See, e.g., Margot Badran, *Feminists, Islam, and Nation: Gender and the Making of Modern Egypt* (Princeton, N.J.: Princeton University Press, 1995).

5. See "Women Living under Muslim Laws," *Knowing Our Rights: Women, Family, Laws and Customs in the Muslim World,* 3rd ed. (London: Women Living Under Muslim Laws, 2006), http://www.wluml.org/sites/wluml.org/files/import/english/pubs/pdf/knowing%20our%20rights/kor_2006_en.pdf.

6. On WLUML, see Farida Shaheed (one of its founding members), "Networking for Change: The Role of Women's Groups in Initiating Dialogue on Women's Issues," in *Faith and Freedom,* edited by Mahnaz Afkhami (Syracuse: Syracuse University Press, 1995); and Valentine Moghadam, *Globalizing Women: Transnational Feminist Networks* (Baltimore: Johns Hopkins University Press, 2005).

7. Sanusi Lamido Sanusi, "Fundamentalist Groups and the Nigerian Legal System: Some Reflections," available at www.whrnet.org, provides telling insights into the movement and its implications. For a detailed study of the Izala movement, see Ousmane Kane, *Muslim Modernity in Postcolonial Nigeria: The Society for the Removal of Innovation and Reinstatement of Tradition* (Leiden: Brill, 2003). The reader will note two different translations of this group; in the text, I have preferred to use the one provided by Sanusi.

8. Muhammad Sane Umar discusses this young woman (preserving her anonymity) in "Mass Islamic Education and Emergence of Female 'Ulema' in Northern Nigeria: Background, Trends, and Consequences," in *The Transmission of Learning in Islamic Africa,* edited by Scott S. Reese (Leiden: Brill, 2004).

9. For a self-profiled history of FOMWAN and its present structure and work, see *FOMWAN: Twenty Years of Service to Islam* (Abuja: n.p., 2005). It is now under the leadership of its fifth head or *amira,* Bilkisu Yusuf.

10. *Baobab for Women's Human Rights and Sharia Implementation in Nigeria: The Journey So Far* (Lagos: Baobab, 2003).

11. I looked at Islamic feminism in two talks in Cairo, "Islamic Feminism: What's in a Name?" in 2002 and "Islamic Feminism Revisited" in 2006. Both can be found on the Web site of *al-Ahram Weekly* (www.ahram.org.eg/weekly), where they were originally published, and in Badran, *Feminism beyond East and West,* 23–42.

12. I have discussed the confluences of Muslim women's secular feminisms in "Locating Feminisms: The Collapse of Secular and Religious Discourses in the Muslim Mashriq," *Agenda* (South African feminist journal; special 50th issue on African feminisms) 59 (2001): 41–57; and "Between Secular Feminism and Islamic Feminism: Reflections on the Middle East and Beyond," *Journal of Middle East Women's Studies,* inaugural issue (January 2005): 6–28.

13. Amina Wadud, *Qur'an and Woman: Reading the Sacred Text from a Woman's Perspective* (New York: Oxford University Press, 1999).

14. Asma Barlas, *"Believing Women": Unreading Patriarchal Interpretations of the Qur'an* (Austin: University of Texas Press, 2002).

15. Ziba Mir-Hosseini, *The Religious Debate in Contemporary Iran* (Princeton, N.J.: Princeton University Press, 1999); Ziba Mir-Hosseini, *Marriage on Trial: A Study of Family Law, Iran and Morocco* (New York: I. B. Tauris, 2000).

16. The most recent example is the reform of the Moroccan Mudawana in 2004, which is now the most progressive *shari'a*-backed Muslim family law. The earliest feminist efforts to reform Muslim personal status law go back to early-twentieth-century Egypt, where the battle has been sustained but the gains minimal.

17. For a concise clarification of this, see Ziba Mir-Hosseini, "Muslim Women's Quest for Equality: Between Islamic Law and Feminism," *Critical Inquiry* (Summer 2006): 629–45.

18. On "the return to the *shari'a*" in Nigeria, see *Comparative Perspectives on the Shari'ah in Nigeria,* edited by Philip Ostien, Jámila M. Nasir, and Franz Kogelmann (Ibadan: Spectrum Books, 2005).

19. For a general exposition of *hudud,* see Cherif Bassiouni, ed., *The Islamic Criminal Justice System* (London: Oceana, 1980).

20. See Khawar Mumtaz and Farida Shaheed, *Women of Pakistan: Two Steps Forward, One Step Backward?* (Karachi: Zed Books, 1987); Anita Weiss, "Implications of the Islamization Program for Women," in *Islamic Reassertion in Pakistan: The Application of Islamic Laws in a Modern State,* edited by Anita Weiss (Syracuse: Syracuse University Press, 1986); and Anita Weiss, "Women's Action Forum," in *The Oxford Encyclopedia of the Modern Islamic World* (New York: Oxford University Press, 1995), vol. 4, 346–48. Shahla Haeri deals with the *hudud* and Islamization process initiated by the state; Shahla Haeri, *No Shame for the Sun: Lives of Professional Pakistani Women* (Syracuse: Syracuse University Press, 2002).

21. See www.meydaan.org and Soheila Vahdati, "Stop Stonings in Iran, But Don't Confuse the Issue," *Women's eNews,* January 4, 2007.

22. I am grateful to Richard Joseph and Ndubisi Obiorah for confirmation of this.

23. On transcommunal cooperation, see Ayesha Imam, "Fighting the Political (Ab)Use of Religion in Nigeria: BAOBAB for Women's Human Rights, Allies, and Others," in

Fundamentalism: Warning Signs, Law, Media and Resistances, edited by Ayesha Imam, Jenny Morgan, and Nira Yuval-Davis (London: Women Living Under Muslim Laws, 2004), available at www.wluml.org.

24. I had originally wanted to speak with women of more modest backgrounds from villages as well as major cities, but for a number of reasons this proved totally beyond my reach.

25. At the Conference on Christian-Muslim Relations, I was invited to give a presentation and encouraged to be an active participant. I received an invitation from the organizers to attend the Conference on Promoting Women's Rights through Shari'ah in Northern Nigeria, where I was strictly an observer in the plenary sessions, although I contributed in the breakout session. At the first conference, in Zamfara, women and men intermixed in the sittings; at the Kaduna conference, women and men were arranged in parallel groups in the hall.

26. This paper provoked both critical and favorable response, more the former than the latter.

27. From here on, I display quotations from Muslim women interviewed and simply designate their professions. All the activists I interviewed are women from various professions. I include quotations as the words of the women are pithy and powerful. Purely summarizing their thoughts and arguments does not convey the same force.

28. Though my focus is on the debates as I gleaned them through interviews, conversations, group discussions, and at conferences, there has been much written in the press and learned publications. FOMWAN dedicated a special issue of *The Muslim Woman* (8, 2003) to the theme: Sharia Implementation in Nigeria. In keeping with FOMWAN's education mission, stress is laid on the importance of education in understanding and living by the *shari'a.*

29. See Abdullahi an-Na'im, "The Future of *Shari'ah* and the Debate in Northern Nigeria," in *Comparative Perspectives on the Shari'ah in Nigeria,* ed. Ostien, Nasir, and Kogelmann, 327–57.

30. This adverse effect of the enactment of *hudud* has yet to be widely noticed. A woman lawyer, activist, and daughter of a former grand *qadi* said in an interview: "If a woman can adjudicate under common law, I do not see any reason why she cannot do so as well under *shari'a* law."

31. Farida Shaheed and Aisha Shaheed, *Great Ancestors: Women Asserting Their Rights in Muslim Contexts* (Lahore: Shirgat Gah, 2004).

32. "Nana Asma'u (1795–1865)," in ibid., chap. 4, "Women at the Cross-roads: The Nineteenth Century," 51–54.

33. For an analysis of Asma'u's scholarly work, poetry, etc., within the context of Muslim intellectual and political life, see chapter 1 of this volume, by Beverly Mack. For the first full-length biography, see Jean Boyd, *The Caliph's Sister: Nana Asma'u, 1793–1865, Teacher, Poet, and Islamic Leader* (London: Frank Cass, 1989); and on her oeuvre, see Jean Boyd and Beverly Mack, eds., *The Collected Works of Nana Asma'u bint Shehu Usman dan Fodio 1793–1864* (East Lansing: Michigan State University Press, 1997).

34. "Muslim Women Scholars," *The Muslim Woman* 9 (2005).

35. "Nana Asma'u the Great Scholar," *The Muslim Woman* 9 (2005).

36. Interview with Yoginder Sikand, available at www.islaminterfaith.org.

Part III

Shari'a, Family Law, and Activism

Chapter 9

Women and Men Put Islamic Law to Their Own Use: Monogamy versus Secret Marriage in Mauritania

Corinne Fortier

In recent years, several Muslim countries have instituted significant legislative reforms, especially with respect to marriage and divorce. In Mauritania, the government introduced the first personal status code in 2001. This code recognizes women's right to monogamy. But this code has not brought about a sociojuridical revolution, because these rights have long been recognized and enforced in the Moorish society of Mauritania.[1] They are juridically and religiously legitimized in the classic Maliki legal texts that govern Moorish juridical practice. The right to monogamy is found in the classical texts of Islamic law (*shari'a*), which form the legal basis of this society.

Moorish women did not wait for the introduction of a personal status code that guaranteed their right to monogamy. The situation of Moorish women in this regard is different from that of Moroccan women, who in 2004 gained the right to monogamy through the reform of the family code, the Mudawana, which permits a woman to add a clause to her marriage contract giving her the right to divorce if her husband takes another wife. Un-

213

like women elsewhere in Africa and the Middle East, Moorish women in Mauritania have traditionally contracted monogamous marriages. However, their ostensibly monogamous marriages have been undercut by the widespread practice of secret marriage engaged in by men. In this chapter, I look at both monogamy and secret marriage.

The Practical Application of Islamic Jurisprudence (*Fiqh*)

Moorish women in Mauritania function in a unique sociocultural context. Mauritanian Moorish society, made up of speakers of Hassaniyya, a dialect of Arabic, is culturally highly homogenous. This region was first Islamized by the Almoravids, who introduced the Maliki school of jurisprudence in the eleventh century.

Moorish society is made up of Bedouin tribes, many of which are now sedentary and concentrated mainly in the capital city of Nouakchott. Nevertheless, their members generally do not have recourse to state tribunals to arbitrate their lawsuits, which are thus settled internally, sometimes by a local *qadi*. If the French colonization of Mauritania modified the local political landscape, it did not fundamentally change the local judicial structure, especially in the area of the family, where reference to Islamic jurisprudence remained primary.

The Mauritanian code of the family of 2001, based on Islamic jurisprudence, is in conformity with the classical Islamic texts used locally, while it also takes into account conventional social practice in Moorish society. The Moors have habitually used Maliki texts as their legal basis.[2] These include the *Risala* of al-Qayrawani (tenth century), the *Mukhtasar* of Khalîl (fourteenth century), and the *'Asmiyya* of Ibn 'Asim (fourteenth century).

Moorish judicial practice, which has long recognized women's right to monogamy, contradicts the widespread notion that a society's use of classical Islamic judicial sources must necessarily be detrimental to women. This belief underestimates the importance of the social context in which these texts are used. My research shows that knowledge of these sources as well as local gender relations are the main determining factors of both the use made of the legal texts and their application in social practice.

The Moorish population displays a familiarity with religious texts.[3] In addition to showing an awareness of the subtleties of Maliki jurisprudence,

Moorish society reveals a grasp of *usul al-fiqh,* or the foundations of jurisprudence; that is, they demonstrate an understanding of how *fiqh* is constructed and applied. Knowledge of the letter of the law, and the spirit of the law, facilitates the application of the texts in daily life in a dynamic and enlightened manner.

Moorish society is a nomadic entity in which oral memorization is highly developed, especially in the area of religious knowledge, which is greatly valued.[4] In general, men from the *maraboutic* tribes (*zwaya*) in Mauritania have more knowledge of Islamic jurisprudence than men from warrior (*hassan*) or tributary tribes (*znaga*), or men who are blacksmiths (*m'allmin*), bards (*iggawan*), or former slaves (*haratin*). However, the legal codes related to the obligations of daily life are known through oral tradition by all members of society, including the women, as well as by specialists in Islamic jurisprudence, who are called for only in cases of litigation.

It is neither necessary, nor indeed customary, to engage a judge (*qadi*) to effect the legal-religious marriage ceremony, which essentially involves agreeing to the contract (*'aqd*) before the marriage feast. The only case where a judge might be present is when the marriage involves a member of a *maraboutic* tribe, and if a *qadi* is a member of the family and proposes to seal the union with a written contract. Otherwise, the marriage contract is purely oral. Because testimony by witnesses (*'udul*) serves as legal proof in Islamic jurisprudence, the oral nature of the marriage contract does not diminish its legally binding character.[5]

In Mauritania, boys and girls do not have equal access to learning. Traditionally, girls and boys attended Qur'anic schools, where they mainly learned by rote verses of the Qur'an necessary for prayers. Literate women remain the exception in Mauritania; however, women play an important role in the oral transmission of the history of the Prophet Muhammad (*sira*) to their children. Mothers also instill in their daughters an awareness of their religious rights, especially with respect to monogamy.

Moorish women display an understanding, passed down orally from mother to daughter, of certain principles and provisions of *fiqh* as understood in the Maliki school, that enables them to take initiatives to protect their wishes and interests when contracting and dissolving a marriage. Their ability to claim these rights does not owe to the influence of any local feminist movement but to a careful balancing of their knowledge of the relevant Islamic law related to marriage and of their culture's social realities. Most Moorish women are unaware of the existence of a feminist movement within Islam or in the West. However, they can be seen as engaging in every-day acts of feminism or "everyday feminism," as Margot Badran calls it,[6] without the label or necessarily a "feminist consciousness."

In Moorish society, women know how to assert themselves in dealings with men. It is indeed easier for women to make their voices heard in a so-ciety, like the Moorish one, in which segregation by gender is not absolute and where women are not threatened by physical violence from men than in a society in which women are totally excluded from discussion and where the threat of confrontation and coercion by men hangs over them. In Moor-ish society, women participate in discussions with their husbands. Men also respect an ancient code of Arab chivalry (*futuwwa*) called *muruwwa,* which commends courtly behavior toward women.[7]

Moorish women know how to exploit the social importance of their rights to monogamy, supported as they are by their own families. One must re-member that in Mauritania tension between men and women exists within the context of an equally important structural tension between families united by marriage. This double tension is evident when a marriage contract is drawn up and two groups confront one another: the women of the family of the fu-ture wife, and the men of the family of the future husband. It is the mother of the girl, accompanied by her female relatives, who demands of the father and other male relatives of the prospective husband that the monogamy clause be included. The right to monogamy in Moorish society must be renegotiated for each marriage. This shows the fragility of this right, which must be defended from generation to generation by women, lest it be denied by men.

The Clause (*Shart*) of Monogamy

According to conventional readings, the Qur'an (4:3) allows a man to take four wives as long as they are treated equally (*al-'adl fi al-mu'amala*): "Marry such women as seem good to you, two, three, four; but if you fear you will not be equitable, then only one, or what your right hands own; so it is likelier you will not be partial."[8] Against this right granted to men by the Qur'an, the most sacred reference source for Muslims, Moorish women assert their dignity as women though their refusal of polygamy. This claim to dignity is transformed into law by the fact that Moorish women impose monogamy in their marriage contract.

Monogamy is a long tradition in Mauritania. Moorish women, in con-trast to women in many other African Muslim communities, especially in the Sub-Saharan region, will only accept polygamy in exceptional cases, such as being married to the head of a Sufi brotherhood (*shaykh*) who is felt to be blessed with *baraka* (blessings). In 1999, the tradition of monogamy was challenged by an isolated Islamist movement, comprising not only men but also women who agreed to be married as a second wife in order "to set an example." However, this movement met with little enthusiasm in Moorish society and did not survive.

How can we explain the institution of monogamy in Moorish society? Moors' traditional mode of life linked to nomadism might appear to explain this practice. But I do not find this explanation very satisfying. The Bedouin lifestyle does not necessarily imply monogamy, as evidenced by the existence of polygamous Bedouin communities in, for example, Egypt and Arabia. The more likely explanation is related to the position of women in Moorish society. For example, divorced Moorish women—like those in the Tuareg society of Algeria, Mali, or Niger—can easily remarry, in contrast to women in North African and Middle Eastern societies that place a high value on women's virginity. The remarriage of Moorish women—even three to five times nowadays—is not only widespread but is also perceived favorably as an indication of a woman's charm and femininity.[9]

Moorish women know how to use the subtleties of Islamic jurisprudence to legally enforce their insistence on monogamy. One method is to include it as a condition (*shart*) in the marriage contract. The husband must respect this condition, or the marriage may be dissolved by the women by means of *faskh*. Islamic jurisprudence permits the addition of clauses (*shurut*) to the marriage contract that are related to the reciprocal rights and obligations of the spouses.[10]

Maliki jurists allow two categories of additional clauses to the marriage contract, both of which are compatible with the laws governing marriage. The first is restricted to clauses stipulating the obligations within marriage, for example, the husband's financial responsibility for the wife and abstention from any mistreatment. These conditions are nevertheless rarely insisted upon, because they are already stipulated in the legal act of marriage in Maliki Islam, and are therefore considered to be redundant.

The second category of clauses allowed in Maliki jurisprudence are those that, while compatible with the general laws pertaining to marriage, nonetheless modify the normal rights and responsibilities of the spouses. The frequently invoked condition in Moorish marriage stipulating that the husband not take another wife is part of this category of clauses; if he violates this clause, the woman will have the right to a divorce.

This stipulation is embedded in the phrase "neither preceding nor following" (*la sabiqata wa la lahiqata*). The term "preceding" indicates that if the man is already married, he must repudiate his wife. This condition applies to both official wives and unofficial wives. In Moorish society, however, as mentioned above, outside official marriage there exists another form of marriage called "secret marriage" (*as-sirriyya*), with which I shall deal in the second half of this chapter. Thus the implicit formula "neither preceding nor following" is sometimes replaced by a more explicit formula: "He will not marry someone else or practice secret marriage" (*la tizawaj 'aliha wa la yatasarra*).

When a marriage is contracted, the mother of the bride, accompanied by middle-aged female relatives, requests on behalf of her daughter, who is absent for reasons of modesty, that the clause prohibiting polygamy be added to the contract. This request is made in front of a group of men that includes the older notables of the community as well as the father or guardian (*wali*) of the bride and the father or representative (*wakil*) of the groom, who is also absent for reasons of modesty. In addition to showing the oppositional relationship between the two families, this ceremony most fundamentally reveals the power relations between the sexes.[11]

The acceptance of this clause by men is characteristic of a society where masculine identity is not defined by control over women and their autonomy but rather by a kind treatment of women and a recognition of their rights. In Moorish society, it would be inappropriate for a man to refuse this clause, because his agreement to it is a measure of his respect for his wife. However, in practice, the husband will not accept the clause of monogamy unless the mother, who presents the request in the name of her daughter, agrees to a reduction in the bridewealth (*sadaq* or *mahr*). Women, therefore, must buy this right from men; only by giving up a part of their marriage compensation will they persuade men to surrender their right to marry more than one woman.

The condition of monogamy in the marriage contract is found in other Muslim societies as well as in Kabyle society in Algeria.[12] A similar clause was used by certain Jews of Morocco, because polygamy was also authorized within certain limits by Talmudic law.[13] It is not clear in these other instances whether acceptance of this clause was also accompanied by a reduction of the bridewealth. In the Moorish practice, it is the bridewealth that allows the woman to negotiate certain rights. This is in accordance with the spirit of Islamic jurisprudence.

Other Marriage Clauses

In the past in Mauritania, when Moorish men took part in long-distance caravan trade, the mother of the future bride would impose a second condition on the marriage: The husband could travel only for a certain period of time, generally a year. This condition is in part foreseen in the marriage contract, because Maliki jurisprudence allows a woman whose husband has not been to the conjugal home for two years to ask for a dissolution of the marriage.[14] Another condition related to the question of marital fidelity appears to have existed in the past, although it seems to have been rarely imposed, stipulating that a husband is not allowed to leave his home during the night.[15]

Although exceptional, a condition concerning the couple's mode of residence may also be stipulated. In Moorish society, the couple generally lives in the encampment of the husband's family. This may also be the residence of the wife's family if the spouses are near cousins. When required by the husband's professional activities, the couple might not live near the husband's family. In addition, a woman may demand that her husband live near her parents. This condition, however—referred to as "the corner post of the tent" (*ajamj al-khalva*)—is exceedingly rare.

Because it is highly unusual for a man to accept this condition, which would insult his honor, it remains exceptional and is used instead as a dissuading clause imposed by families that do not want to give their daughters in marriage to other tribes. The *maraboutic* tribe of the Idaw'ali from the oasis of Tijikja in the Tagant region, for example, used this clause at the beginning of the twentieth century to avoid the transfer of their palm groves to strangers through the marriage of their daughters to men from other tribes.[16] The condition is also imposed in certain cases, especially when the wife is the only female child and wishes to stay near her parents in order to help them in their old age.

Some may theorize that the practice of a married couple living close to the wife's parents is of Berber origin and is opposed to the practice of a married couple living close to the husband's parents, as is the rule in Arab society. The Berber expression (*znaga*) used to denote the practice in *Hassaniyya* points toward this conclusion. In addition, in certain Berber regions like the Kabyle region of Algeria, a woman may stipulate in her marriage contract that she will continue to reside with her mother and father; if her husband refuses to join her, she may reclaim her liberty after asking the *qadi* to certify that the clause was not respected.[17]

But it is not satisfactory to oppose Berber cultural practices to Arab practices; this clause, for instance, can be found in other cultural contexts that contain no Berber influence, such as Iran.[18] Extending the field of comparison to non-Maghreb Muslim societies underlines the irrelevance of a supposedly explanatory dualistic opposition that systematically attributes certain ethnographic features common to North African societies to either "Berber" or, by default, "Arab" influence.

To what extent is the husband bound by the clauses added to the marriage contract? According to Islamic jurisprudence, stipulations that do not contradict the law are legally binding.[19] In addition, the Arabic axiom "The condition takes precedence over the law" (*shart yaghlab al-hukum*) seems to be especially applicable to marriage contracts. The Prophet Muhammad is said to have insisted on following the conditions agreed to in the marriage contract. According to one *hadith,* "Conditions that must be respected above all are those that are related to marriage."[20]

Although, for certain Sunni jurists, stipulations of this type added to a marriage contract are reprehensible (*makruh*), they are nevertheless acceptable if the husband submits to them of his own accord.[21] In Moorish society, the only conditions the husband is legally obligated to uphold are those that are compensated for by a reduction in the bridewealth, such as the condition insisting on monogamy. He is not bound by those imposed without financial compensation, as is shown by the term used to designate such a clause: "unrealized [literally "absent"] clause" (*shart al-maffrud*).

"Secret Marriage" (*As-Sirriyya*)

The nomadic lifestyle may be seen as encouraging secret marriage among Moorish men who clandestinely marry women in different places. If most men accept women's demand for monogamy, they also engage in the practice of secret and clandestine polygamy. Men in Moorish society also know how to take advantage of the ambiguities of the law, which enable them to circumvent women's demands for monogamy—to which they agreed—by entering into multiple marriages secretly.

Secret marriage in Mauritania is called *sirriyya,* an Arabic word for "secret." Secret marriage is not legally recognized in the personal status code recently enacted by the Mauritanian government, doubtless because of the taboo associated with this form of marriage, because of disagreement regarding its religious legality, and because in recent years its prevalence has decreased.

In Mauritania, secret marriage is a long-standing practice linked to the constant movement of Moorish men far from their encampments, whether to graze their herds or for commercial reasons. In the past, commercial movement was part of the caravan trade; today, many men may own a small shop in another African country. It was not uncommon, therefore, for a man to have secret wives he regularly visited in a number of different places. The clandestine nature of these marriages was made possible in Mauritania by the geographic distance between wives. But the practice of secret marriage appears to be declining in Mauritania, because the end of nomadism and the trans-Saharan trade have made the prolonged absence of men more rare.

Other societies practice similar forms of secret marriage.[22] Moorish secret marriage, in my view, may be compared with the customary marriage (*'urfi*) practiced in Egypt or even the temporary marriage (*mut'a*) widespread among Shi'i, especially in Iran. In the following, I seek to place secret marriage in a comparative context through a systematic examination of phenomena observed in Moorish society as they relate to those observed in other societies.

One of the major differences between secret marriage and official marriage (*zawaj* or *nikah*) in Muslim societies where both are practiced consists of the fact that the first concerns two individuals but the second involves two families in addition to two individuals.[23] Also, a woman united with a man in a secret marriage does not have the right to support from the husband (*nafaqa*)—which is, in principle, guaranteed in an official marriage—or the social recognition granted a legitimate wife. In addition, if she has children, proof of their paternity depends entirely on the goodwill of their father.

Secret marriage is less restrictive for the man than official marriage, because he is not bound by the duty of *nafaqa* for his secret wife, although in Moorish society the man usually does offer her a few gifts. The minimal economic investment involved in secret marriage, because men are not obliged to provide support or housing as they are for an official wife, is the reason that in Egypt married men prefer secret marriage to polygamous marriage.[24] The rise in *'urfi* marriages in Egypt in recent years is widely attributed to the high cost of state-sanctioned, socially recognized marriage; many young people resort to it as an alternative to de facto polygamous unions.[25] As a result, while Egyptians use *'urfi* marriage to avoid the financial burden of polygamy, Moors contract secret marriages instead of polygamous marriages, which are practically forbidden. Unlike in Egypt,[26] polygamy in Mauritania, though not regulated by state law, is not widely practiced and indeed began to decline early in the twentieth century. Polygamous marriages in Egypt are highly frowned upon.

The religious ceremony for secret marriage in Mauritania is the same as that for official marriage, except that the condition of monogamy is never demanded by a woman accepting this type of marriage. The woman, having in most cases been married before, is no longer subject to the matrimonial constraints imposed by her father. Because her father does not attend the marriage ceremony, the groom may participate in person rather than through a representative, as is the custom for reasons of modesty when his future father-in-law is present.

The marriage takes place in private, in the presence of the couple and two witnesses (*'udul*), who agree to keep the union secret. These witnesses are generally trusted relatives or friends of the man, or people passing through who are completely indifferent to the union. A third man pronounces the legal formula, which states the names of the two partners, the amount of the brideprice, and the first verse of the Qur'an (*al-fatiha*).

This is the final step of the marriage ceremony, because in contrast to an official marriage, a secret marriage is never followed by a ceremony (*'ars*) that would make it public. For it is the lavish ceremony attended by many guests that makes a couple's union official; even their sexual union as the consummation of the marriage usually occurs at the time of this ceremony. Without such a ceremony, there is no public recognition of secret marriage, although it is sanctioned by a certain legal recognition within the framework of Islamic jurisprudence.

Given the absence of a public ceremony, Moorish secret marriage is comparable both to *fatiha* marriage, practiced in Morocco,[27] and to ambulant marriage (*al-zawaj al-misyar*), practiced in the Nadj region of Saudi Arabia,[28] and which has spread to other countries in the Gulf and elsewhere, including Egypt.[29] It is also in some respects comparable to *mut'a* marriage, practiced in Iran.[30] In Shi'i jurisprudence, the procedure is much simpler than for the other rites, because there is no need for two witnesses.[31]

Because of its secret nature, this form of marriage in Mauritania is theoretically different from *'urfi* marriage in Egypt, which requires publicity.[32] But in practice, secret marriage in Mauritania is also similar in certain ways to *'urfi* marriage in Egypt, which is usually conducted in great secrecy because only two witnesses sign the paper that serves as sole evidence of the marriage.[33] Because *'urfi* marriages resemble secret marriages, the distinction made by some Egyptian theologians (*'ulama'*) between the former, considered to be legal, and the latter, equated with adultery,[34] seems in reality of little significance.

The issue of secrecy (*sirr*) is also the most problematic one for Maliki jurists. Theoretically, secret marriage (*nikah as-sirr*) is invalid in Maliki jurisprudence because of the very fact that it remains secret. On this point, Ibn 'Asim, a jurist from the end of the fourteenth century, argued: "One should avoid contracting a marriage in secret, even by asking the witnesses to keep the silence. The annulment of such a contract is obligatory."[35] Nevertheless, Maliki jurists do not unanimously agree that secrecy should render a marriage void.[36] The same can be said of Moorish jurists, one of whom argues: "If, after contracting a marriage, one keeps it secret, this does not render it invalid; one should be wary of the apparent meaning of the texts."[37] Therefore, a number of rulings (*hukum*) by Moorish jurists recognize this type of marriage as valid, arguing that because it requires witnesses, it is not in fact "secret."

The Functions of Secret Marriage

The common denominator in these various forms of parallel marriage—Moorish secret marriage, Iranian *mut'a* marriage, Saudi ambulant marriage,[38] and even Egyptian *'urfi* marriage—is that they permit a man to have legitimate sexual relations with a woman other than his wife and without her knowledge. Historically in Mauritania, because the secret was generally well guarded, the marriage was often revealed only if the husband had a child with his secret wife. In most cases, the "official" wife would not insist on a divorce, as permitted by the "neither preceding nor following" clause, but instead would ask her husband to repudiate what to her was an intruder but to her husband was a legal additional wife. More generally, secret marriage in Mauritania, like *'urfi* marriage in Egypt[39] or ambulant marriage (*misyar*) in Saudi Arabia,[40] is entered into by men who want to have legitimate sexual relations with a woman outside of marriage. Thus, in this case, these forms of marriage resemble pleasure marriage (*zawaj al-mut'a*) which is allowed by Shi'is but proscribed by Sunnis[41] even though it can be practiced by Sunnis in Lebanon.[42]

However, in the case of Moorish secret marriage or *'urfi* marriage in Egypt, a specific time limit is not set in the marriage contract, as it is in the case of *mu'ta* marriage, also called temporary marriage (*mu'aqqat*), or in ambulant marriage (*misyar*). In the *mu'ta* marriage or the *misyar* marriage there is no need for divorce because the contract expires with the lapse of its duration.[43]

The question of ending a secret marriage is treated differently in various societies. In Moorish society a secret marriage can be dissolved in the same way it was contracted, without ceremony and upon the woman's as well as the man's initiative. In Morocco *fatiha* marriage is also terminated without divorce, often on the husband's initiative.[44] However, in Egypt, most likely because of the gender relations peculiar to this society, and given the fact that *'urfi* marriage sometimes has a more public character, divorce pronounced by the man is required in order to end the marriage, or else the woman risks spending her life unable to remarry.[45]

Another reason for a Moorish man to enter into a secret marriage is the absence of progeny. In Mauritania, generally when a man cannot have children with his wife, he will choose to contract a secret marriage with a woman of his choice, usually of inferior social status such as a descendant of a slave (*hartaniyya*), rather than repudiating his wife and remarrying. In this way he hopes to have children whose paternity will be connected to him by the legal act of the secret marriage. Because the secret marriage is considered by the Moorish jurists to be legal, a child born from this union is legally recognized as legitimate.

The husband's decision to take a secret wife in order to produce children may be made with his official wife's agreement, as she would prefer this arrangement to repudiation. Secretly marrying other women is therefore often a way for a man to increase his progeny, and therefore his social influence. In this case Moorish secret marriage is distinguished from pleasure marriage (*mut'a*), in which procreation is not the aim. Nevertheless, men in Iran sometimes contract a *mut'a* marriage to increase their progeny or to produce sons if their official marriage has yielded only girls.[46]

In Mauritania, the reasons that lead women to accept marriage as a secret wife are either emotional or economic, as the brideprice represents some financial gain for the woman or for her family. Secret marriages, therefore, involve primarily women of inferior social status. In the same way, women who accept *'urfi* marriage in Egypt[47] or *mut'a* marriage in Iran[48] are usually in difficult socioeconomic situations. When Moorish marriage involves a young woman still under her father's authority, it is often her family that forces her to contract a secret marriage with a wealthy man for economic reasons. This situation is found also in Egypt, where extremely poor women are forced by their fathers to contract *'urfi* marriages with rich men from the Gulf.[49]

In Mauritania, if the marriage is not in order to procreate, it can also involve women of noble classes who are widowed or divorced. When the secret marriage is not meant to produce children and a pregnancy results, the woman cannot establish the paternity of the child if the legal-religious marriage ceremony (*'aqd*) took place in the presence of witnesses she does not know. In this case, only a woman who had a written contract drawn up at the time of her secret marriage can oblige the man to recognize the child as his own.

As is the case with secret marriage in Mauritania, establishing the paternity of a child born from a *fatiha* union in Morocco, a *mut'a* union in Iran, or an *'urfi* union in Egypt presents problems, because recognition of paternity in Islamic jurisprudence depends on prior recognition of the marriage. In Morocco, because legal proof is lacking, the fate of the woman in a *fatiha* marriage and that of her children depend on the goodwill of the man.[50] The situation is quite similar in Iran, because a contract of *mut'a* marriage requires no witnesses or registration; however, it is difficult to prove the identity of the child's father.[51] In Egypt, it is also the man's prerogative to recognize or reject the child, and to honor or conceal the written proof of the marriage.[52] However, according to the new Egyptian personal status code, along with classic evidence such as the contract, witnesses, and letters, a judge may now order proof by DNA test.[53]

But recently the practice of secret marriage in Mauritania has declined among married men. Now that divorce has become commonplace, men today are less hesitant to repudiate their wives and remarry the woman of their choice. In addition, secret marriage, which was traditionally the prerogative of married men desirous of sidestepping women's demand for monogamy, now involves a different category of men: young unmarried men. In practice, secret marriage is used by young people as a means of legalizing premarital sexual relations. This new kind of secret marriage creates a new problem in that it takes place without the consent of the girl's family. According to Maliki jurisprudence, it is illegal for a young woman to marry without her legal guardian (*wali*), and the practice is condemned in Mauritania.

A similar situation exists in Egypt, where *'urfi* marriage has recently spread among students.[54] But the reason is different, because in Egypt the *'urfi* couples want to marry conventionally but lack either the financial resources or familial approval.[55] This marriage is condemned by Egyptian theologians for the same reason as in Mauritania: the absence of a woman's guardian.[56] Another reason put forth by the Egyptian *'ulama'* in condemning this kind of marriage concerns the worthiness of the witnesses (*'udul*), but this argument seems less fundamental than the preceding one because it could just as easily be advanced to condemn secret marriages contracted by married men.

Conclusion

This study shows that although religious sources, chiefly the Qur'an and the *hadith* as well as *fiqh,* serve as the foundation of social and religious organization for various Muslim societies, how these sources are put to use is often tied to local custom, as shown by the insistence on monogamy in Moorish society. This method of adapting Islamic jurisprudence by integrating specific practices of the society does not contradict the spirit of the law.

In addition, this study has shown that different groups, especially different gender groups whose interests may diverge, can legally use the subtleties or ambiguities of Islamic jurisprudence to make their wishes prevail, even when they may be contradictory. Thus Islamic jurisprudence is variously understood and permits the coexistence of divergent rights, as shown in the case of men's right to polygamy authorized in the Qur'an and the Islamically recognized right of a woman to demand monogamy in the marriage contract. Finally, it is clear that the corpus of Islamic jurisprudence, as it has been constituted since its origins, grants a rather large margin of freedom to the members of Muslim societies who refer to it, allowing them room to negotiate within its bounds.

Furthermore, Islamic jurisprudence is not fixed but is actually the source of numerous debates among the jurists themselves. Their disputes over the understanding of a term may have major legal consequences, as seen in the discussion of the secret nature of a marriage that takes place before witnesses. This argument can be used to render legal a type of marriage that was not a priori allowed in the foundational sources of Maliki jurisprudence.

Juridical debates regarding its legitimacy notwithstanding, secret marriage does exist, with slight variations and different terminology, in several Muslim societies. If, in Moorish society, secret marriage allows men to realize their desire for polygamy, it also allows them in other societies where polygamy is more accepted to have sexual relations with one or with several women without incurring certain obligations of marriage such as financial support of the wife (*nafaqa*) and the duties of paternity.

The detailed study of monogamy or of secret marriage has also shown how the material goods constituting the wife's brideprice and those contributing to her support are central to the process of male appropriation of women's sexuality. This process of appropriation of the female body as well as of her progeny, though relative in secret marriage, is absolute in official marriage.

In Muslim societies, as in other societies, the bridewealth given to a woman's family by her future husband and the support it is intended to ensure are the necessary conditions for acquiring control over her sexuality—sexuality being understood also in the sense of procreation. Indeed, in many societies, including Western ones, an exchange of goods typically precedes the sexual exploitation of a woman's body, both within and outside the conjugal context (e.g., in seduction or even prostitution). The endurance of such practices in culturally diverse societies proves that the woman's body is considered a potentially alienable entity, whether in a legal and familial context such as marriage or in a more informal and individual one such as seduction or prostitution.[57] These social practices obviously pose the important and universal issue of male presumption of the alienable nature of the female body.

Notes

1. In Mauritania, alongside the arabophone Moorish society, one finds Halpulaaren and Soninke communities. I conducted intensive fieldwork in different regions of Mauritania, in the desert (*bâdiyya*) and in the capital city Nouakchott, for eighteen months from 1996 to 1998, living with families and interacting with both men and women of different ages, social statuses, and tribal origins. On the Mauritanian status code in 2001, and the role of bridewealth in women's divorce or *khul'*, see C. Fortier, "Le droit au divorce des femmes Maures du point de vue du droit musulman (*khul'*)," *Maghreb Review: La Mauritanie contemporaine—Enjeux de mémoire et nouvelles identités* 35, nos. 1–2 (edited by Pierre Bonte et Sébastien Boulay) (2010): 179–93. And for a comparaison with *khul'* in Egypt, see C. Fortier, "Le droit au divorce des femmes (*khul'*) en islam: Pratiques différentielles en Mauritanie et en Égypte," in *Droit et Cultures: Actualités du droit musulman—Genre, filiation et bioéthique* 59, no. 1 (edited by Corinne Fortier) (2010): 55–82.

2. On the subject of legal texts known and taught in Mauritania, see C. Fortier, "Mémorisation et audition: L'enseignement coranique chez les Maures de Mauritanie," *Islam et sociétés au Sud du Sahara* 11 (November 1997): 85–105. On an elementary level, the first work of Islamic jurisprudence studied in the Qur'anic school is *al-Akhdari* (Algeria, sixteenth century). Then comes *Ibn 'Ashir* (Morocco, seventeenth century), in which the first chapter treats dogma (*'aqida*); the second, law (*fiqh*); and the third, mysticism (*tasawwuf*). Also, girls are initiated to a slim collection of *hadith* (*ahadith*), called *Dala'il al-khayrat* (Les voies menant aux bonnes oeuvres), of al-Djazuli (Morocco, fifteenth century). Between the ages of ten and fifteen years, students first study the *Risala*

of al-Qayrawânî (Tunisia, tenth century). Then, between the ages of fifteen and twenty, they study the *Mukhtasar* of Khalîl (Egypt, fourteenth century) and, after age twenty, the *'Asmiyya* of Ibn 'Asim (Andalousia, the end of the fourteenth and beginning of the fifteenth centuries). Next, more profound legal works are gradually added to this corpus, such as that of az-Zaqqaq (Morocco, sixteenth century), as well as commentaries (*shuruh*) on fundamental legal texts. The explanations of *Ibn 'Ashir* frequently consulted are those of Mayyara (Morocco, seventeenth century) and in Chinguetti (Adrar), those of Ahmad Bashir wuld Hanshi, a learned Moor of the nineteenth century belonging to the Laghlal tribe. In Mauritania, the best-known commentaries of *Khalil* are those of ad-Dasuqi (Egypt, the end of the eighteenth and beginning of the nineteenth centuries), 'Abdal al-Baqi (Egypt, seventeenth century), al-Hattab (Libya, sixteenth century), al-Bannani (Morocco, eighteenth century), Ibn Ghazi (Egypt, fifteenth century), al-Mawwaq (Andalousia, fifteenth century), and at-Tata'i (Egypt, sixteenth century).

3. On this subject, see C. Fortier, "Soumission, pragmatisme et légalisme en islam," *Topique,* no. 85, *Les Spiritualités* (2003): 145–61.

4. In Moorish society, Islamic scholarship is still highly valued, although in some milieus money is becoming even more important. An ignorant person sets out to acquire knowledge from one who knows more, rather than remaining ignorant or pretending to know. Unfortunately, this attitude is not always shared by certain members of other Muslim societies, who are considered well versed in Islam though their knowledge of it is, in reality, fragmentary and rigid, a situation contributing sometimes to perpetuating false ideas and even a certain obscurantism.

5. This is also the case in other Muslim countries where the administration is more developed than in Mauritania: "Formal procedures of registration have generally been legislated in Muslim states, but do not necessarily affect the validity of marriage or divorce not so registered, in deference to the continuing currency of the 'classical rules.'" E. Fawzy, "Muslim Personal Status Law in Egypt: The Current Situation and Possibilities of Reform through International Initiatives," in *Women's Rights and Islamic Family Law: Perspectives on Reform,* edited by L. Welchman (London: Zed Books, 2004), 16–91; the quotation here is on 9.

6. This expression is Margot Badran's (personal correspondence).

7. Concerning the courtly tradition in Arab culture, see B. Farès, *L'Honneur chez les Arabes avant l'Islam* (Paris: Maisonneuve, 1932). This ancient Arab value has been adopted by Islam: "*Muruwwa* is the sister of the faith" (*muruwwa akhtu din*). For more details on the courtly tradition of the Moors, see C. Fortier, "Épreuves d'amour en Mauritanie," *L'Autre: Cliniques, cultures et sociétés* 4, no. 2 (2003): 239–52.

8. A. J. Arberry, trans., *The Koran Interpreted* (London: George Allen and Unwin, 1980), 100.

9. For more details on this subject, see C. Fortier, "Séduction, jalousie et défi entre hommes: Chorégraphie des affects et des corps dans la société maure," in *Corps et affects,* edited by F. Héritier and M. Xanthakou (Paris: Odile Jacob, 2004), 217–34.

10. R. Charles, *Le Droit musulman,* Collection *Que sais-je?* no. 702 (Paris: PUF, 1956), 50.

11. I have shown elsewhere the extent to which the festive marriage ceremony that follows the legal-religious one is a performance of the power relations between sexes; see C. Fortier, "Le rituel matrimonial maure ou la mise en scène des rapports sociaux de sexe," *Awal* 23 (April 2001): 51–73. After Evans Pritchard, I use the term "bridewealth" to underline the social and economic dimension of the exchange between two families,

and the term "brideprice" when this exchange concerns strictly two individuals. Evans Pritchard, "An Alternative Term for 'Bride-Price,'" *Man* 31, 1931: 36–39. About the role of the bridewealth in Muslim jurisprudence, see C. Fortier, "Le droit musulman en pratique: Genre, filiation et bioéthique," in *Droit et Cultures: Actualités du droit musulman—Genre, filiation et bioéthique* 59, no. 1 (edited by Corinne Fortier) (2010): 11–38.

12. For Kabyle society, see J.-P. Charnay, *La vie musulmane en Algérie, d'après la jurisprudence de la première moitié du XXè siècle* (Paris: PUF, Collection Quadrige, 1965), 44. Margot Badran notes that writing particular stipulations into marriage contracts, such as monogamy, occurred in urban society in late-nineteenth-century Egypt but was not common. See *Harem Years: The Memoirs of an Egyptian Feminist, Huda Shaarawi,* translated and introduced by Margot Badran (New York: Feminist Press, 1987), 142 n. 23.

13. H. Zafrani, *Deux mille ans de vie juive au Maroc* (Paris: Maisonneuve & Larose, 1998), 81.

14. Charles, *Le Droit musulman,* 52.

15. This condition seems to have been quite rare, however, for I had not heard of it until coming across a reference to such a clause in a manuscript from the ancient city of Chinguetti (dated 1900–1901 CE) in the possession of a family from the *maraboutic* Laghlal tribe.

16. A. Ould Khalifa, *La Région du Tagant en Mauritanie* (Paris: Karthala, 1998), 205.

17. Charnay, *La vie musulmane en Algérie,* 46.

18. In Iran, it is possible for the woman to add a clause of residence in the marriage contract, but not of monogamy: "For example, a woman may insert a clause in her marriage contract requiring that she not be taken out of her place of residence. On the other hand, a woman cannot legally demand that her husband refrain from marrying a second wife while still married to her. This condition, the *'ulama'* claim, is against the explicit Qur'anic text that allows a man to make contracts of permanent marriage with four women simultaneously." S. Haeri, *Law of Desire: Temporary Marriage in Shi'i Iran* (Syracuse: Syracuse University Press, 1989), 38.

19. Charles, *Le Droit musulman,* 50.

20. A. D. Eldjazaïri, *La Voie du musulman,* trans. M. Chakroun, 3 vols. (Paris: Maison d'Ennour, 1996), vol. 3, 91. *Hadith* are sayings of the Prophet Muhammad, and also his deeds, as well as the words or deeds of the prophet's companions that were not contradicted by him. All these items constitute the *Sunna,* the second source of reference for Muslims after the Qur'an. It is well known that many *hadith* in circulation are of questionable provenance.

21. M. Ibn 'Asim, *'Asmiyya,* translated by L. Bercher (Algiers: Institut d'Études Orientales-Faculté des Lettres d'Alger, 1958), 304 n. 311.

22. Citing the Talmud, Patai writes that this form of marriage was legal "among the Jews of Babylonia in the third century," and that "even sages and rabbis when visiting in another town used to practice this custom" (quoted by Haeri, *Law of Desire,* 219 n. 2).

23. From this point of view, Moorish secret marriage is indeed comparable to the Shi'i *mut'a* marriage: "Although both types of Shi'i marriage involve the exchange of some form of valuables, in the case of a contract of permanent marriage the stress is on its symbolic exchange and long-term reciprocities, whereas temporary marriage rests on immediate exchange and the commercial aspects of the contract." Haeri, *Law of Desire,* 65.

24. G. Shahine, "Illegitimate, Illegal or Just Ill-Advised?" *Al-Ahram Weekly Online* (Cairo), February 18–24, 1999.

25. S. Jabarti, "A Happy *Misyar* Union," *Arab News,* June 5, 2005.

26. Recent statistics provided by the National Center for Sociological and Criminological Research show that within three years of a marriage, nearly 25 percent of Egyptian husbands take a second wife. R. Leila, "Polygamous duplicity," *Al-Ahram Weekly Online,* Cairo, February 26–March 3, 2004.

27. Ziba Mir-Hosseini, *Marriage on Trial: A Study of Family Law, Iran and Morocco* (New York: I. B. Tauris, 2000), 171.

28. Oussama Arabi, *Studies in Modern Islamic Jurisprudence* (The Hague: Kluwer Law International, 2001), 147.

29. Jabarti, "Happy *Misyar* Union."

30. Haeri, *Law of Desire,* 33.

31. Mir-Hosseini, *Marriage on Trial,* 168.

32. Fawzy, "Muslim Personal Status Law," 42.

33. An *'urfi* marriage that takes place without the presence of a judge is not registered with the authorities. Shahine, "Illegitimate, Illegal or Just Ill-Advised?"

34. Ibid.

35. Ibn 'Asim, *'Asmiyya,* 59.

36. L. Bercher, who provides commentary on the *'Asmiyya,* gives more detail on this subject. See Ibn 'Asim, *'Asmiyya,* 303 n. 308. According to him, the prevailing opinion is that this marriage is no longer annullable if a certain time has passed since its consummation.

37. This opinion reported by Ould Bah is that of the jurist Muḥâmmad wuld Aḥmad Yawra, of the very *maraboutic* family the Ahal-al-'Aqil of the Awlad Dayman tribe of the region of Trarza. Ould Bah, *La Littérature juridique et l'évolution du malikisme en Mauritanie* (Tunis: Faculté des Lettres et Sciences humaines, Université de Tunis, 1981), 107.

38. On this subject, see Arabi, *Studies in Modern Islamic Jurisprudence,* 147–61.

39. M. Tadros, "Secretly Yours," *Al-Ahram Weekly Online,* May 27–June 2, 1999.

40. As Jabarti explains, "Some Gulf discussions speak of *misyaf*—summer marriage—enacted during the typical extended vacations which Saudis take abroad. To avoid illegitimate sex—sex outside of marriage—these short-term marriages are negotiated during trips abroad." Jabarti, "Happy *Misyar* Union."

41. Haeri gives the arguments advanced by the Sunni theologians in refusing to legalize temporary marriage, which is accepted by the Shi'i: "Anchoring their reasoning on the same sources, the Shi'i and Sunni *'ulama'* emerge with completely different interpretations and rationales for the Qur'anic commandments and the Prophet's Tradition. The Sunnis claim that the Qur'anic reference to *mut'a* was canceled by several subsequent verses in the Qur'an itself, namely, the *suras* of the Believers (23:5–6), Divorce (65:4) and Woman (4:3). . . . Accordingly, the Sunnis argue that *mut'a* is not marriage, because intercourse is lawful only within the confines of permanent marriage or slave ownership (Q4:3, 23:6). *Mut'a* of women, they say, is neither a form of marriage, *nikah,* nor slave ownership, *milk-i yamin.* Therefore, it is forbidden. No provisions, the Sunni argument continues, exist for inheritance for the *mut'a* spouses (Q4:12); that the *'idda* of *mut'a* is undetermined since its duration is not specified in the Qur'an; and that consequently the status of children in this form of sexual union is unclear. Moreover, the Sunni *'ulama'* maintain, since the number of *mut'a* wives a man can simultaneously

marry is unlimited, and since there is no divorce in *mut'a* union, therefore, the custom of *mut'a* of women has been canceled in the Qur'an itself." Haeri, *Law of Desire,* 61–62.

42. Jabarti, "Happy *Misyar* Union."

43. Jabarti specifies that *misyar* marriages "are really are quite similar to *'urfi* marriages except that the bride knows it will end at a particular time." Jabarti, "Happy *Misyar* Union."

44. Mir-Hosseini, *Marriage on Trial,* 173.

45. Shahine, "Illegitimate, Illegal or Just Ill-Advised?"

46. Haeri, *Law of Desire,* 173.

47. Y. Fathi, "Patrimony Blues," *Al-Ahram Weekly Online,* Cairo, June 16–22, 2005.

48. "*Mut'a* is what woman has to accept, because of her social disabilities, for example her age, not being a virgin, or coming from a lower social class." Mir-Hosseini, *Marriage on Trial,* 219 n. 3.

49. Fathi, "Patrimony Blues."

50. Sometimes this refusal to recognize the child and the secret marriage that produced it occurs with the complicity of the man's family who has housed the couple but at a later date hopes that their son will be officially engaged to another woman. Mir-Hosseini, *Marriage on Trial,* 172–73.

51. Haeri, *Law of Desire,* 55.

52. "According to the most recent statistics released by the Ministry of Justice, there are at least 12,000 paternity cases currently in the courts. Legal analysts estimate that 70 to 90 percent of those cases are the result of *'urfi* marriages." Shahine, "Illegitimate, Illegal or Just Ill-Advised?"

53. Fathi, "Patrimony Blues."

54. Secret marriages between young unmarrieds have been in practice since the 1960s in Somalia, where they are called in Somalian *khubdbo-shireed.* N. Farah, *Secrets* (Paris: Le Serpent à Plumes, 1998), 349.

55. Jabarti, "Happy *Misyar* Union."

56. Tadros, "Secretly Yours."

57. On this subject, see C. Pateman, *The Sexual Contract* (Cambridge: Polity Press, 1988).

Chapter 10

Islam, Gender, and Democracy in Morocco: The Making of the Mudawana Reform

Julie E. Pruzan-Jørgensen

The adoption of a new family law in 2004 was a landslide event for Moroccan women and an outstanding improvement in Muslim women's family rights. According to the new Mudawana,[1] as the law is called, Moroccan women are no longer regarded as inferior but are now formally equal to their husbands within the family. The law has also improved women's access to divorce and ability to choose when and whom to marry.[2] But this dramatic change did not occur overnight. It only happened after long confrontations between liberal women's organizations, Islamist organizations, and representatives of patriarchy and the monarchy over the role and interpretation of women's rights and Islam in Morocco.

The chapter is primarily based on forty-eight formal interviews conducted during extensive fieldwork in Morocco in 2004 and 2005. The informants were selected on the basis of their personal involvement in the Mudawana reform process from various positions and vantage points. They included numerous civil society actors, politicians (including former and present members of the government), judges, lawyers, *'ulama'* (Islamic scholars),

233

adoul (Islamic notaries), and members of the royal Mudawana Commission, as well as academics and journalists who followed the process closely.
In the interviews, informants were asked to narrate the Mudawana reform
process from their own perspective by pointing out what they saw as its
main events, actors, and significance.[3]

When asked about the political significance of the Mudawana reform,
many informants highlighted the close connection between the reform and
the so-called democratic transition; that is, the introduction of political reforms ameliorating the harsh authoritarianism of the regime, begun by King
Hassan II in the late 1990s and continued by his son and successor, Mohammed VI. Yet most studies of Moroccan family law have not considered
this democratic significance,[4] or have simply assumed that the enhancement
of women's rights equals democratization per se.[5]

But does an increase in Muslim women's family rights automatically entail democratization? This chapter aims to challenge this assumption while
highlighting the need for a specific and careful analysis of the overall political significance of struggles for women's rights in the Islamic world.
More specifically, I contend that while the expansion of Muslim women's
family rights reflects political *liberalization,* we should be very careful
about assuming that such developments are necessarily reflective of the
much more comprehensive processes of political *democratization.*

The following pages will thus take us through the story of the heated political process that ultimately resulted in Morocco's recent Mudawana reform in order to highlight its political and possibly democratic significance.
However, I start out by briefly clarifying my understanding of "political liberalization" and "democratization."

Political Liberalization versus Democratization

Political liberalization involves an expansion of public space through the
recognition and protection of civil and political *rights and liberties.* It is a
mix of reversible policy and social changes, which redefine and extend
rights and liberties to individuals or collectives. Typical examples of political liberalization are increased freedom of movement, speech, and voluntary association.[6]

However, political liberalization does not necessarily entail a change of
the fundamental rules of the political game.[7] This, in contrast, is what de-

mocratization does. Democratization has two dimensions. One concerns citizens; the other concerns their rulers. With regard to citizens, democratization implies that individuals are granted the right to be treated as equals with respect to the making of collective choices, and entails an expansion of political participation in such a way as to provide citizens with a degree of real and meaningful *collective control over public policy.* The other dimension of democracy concerns the ruling elites, for whom democratization entails *accountability to all members of the polity.* Democratization thus requires not only the rights of individuals to participate in and influence political decisions; it also requires that these decisions matter, that they concern the ruling structures and make ruling elites accountable. In other words, democratization is ultimately about changing the fundamental rules of the political game by enhancing the citizens' means of participating in collective decisionmaking and controlling their rulers while also making regimes accountable to this control.[8]

Political liberalization and democratization thus respectively entail enhanced rights and freedoms of individuals and collectives on one hand, and increasing popular control and participation as well as accountability of rulers on the other. Furthermore, and of significance for the analysis that concerns us here, authoritarian rulers may promote political liberalization not in order to democratize but instead based on a "belief that by opening up certain spaces for individual and group action, they can relieve various pressures and obtain needed information and support without altering the structure of authority, that is, without becoming accountable to the citizenry for their actions or subjecting their claim to rule to fair and competitive elections."[9] In other words, political liberalization measures may be initiated without necessarily leading to democratization, which would entail more substantial changes in the very foundations and structures of a given political regime. And they may even be part of a more or less consciously orchestrated regime strategy to liberalize in order *not* to democratize.[10] With these clarifications in mind, let us turn to the story of the Mudawana reform to gain a sense of its political significance.

The Mudawana

The Mudawana was established in the years immediately following Moroccan independence from France and Spain in 1956. Until then, there was no common family legislation but a mix of local customary law and the law

of the colonial rulers. For the new Moroccan leaders, the establishment of
a common personal status code for all Moroccans was of strong symbolic
importance because it served to unify the divided postcolonial nation under
the banner of Islam,[11] and under the guidance of the Moroccan king in his
capacity as *amir al-mu'minin* (commander of the faithful).[12]

The new personal status code was very comprehensive. It was elaborated
upon recommendations from a royal advisory commission of *'ulama'*.[13]
The legendary independence hero Allal al Fassi attempted to introduce certain modern innovations,[14] but the final Mudawana ended up as a rather
strict and conservative codification of Islamic family law based on the jurisprudence of the Maliki school.[15]

The codification was an integral element of the intense postcolonial competition for power between King Mohamed V and the political parties. In
essence, Mohamed V allowed the conservative forces among the *'ulama'*
to decide on a strict and patriarchal interpretation of *shari'a* in exchange for
their recognition of his authority as king and *amir al-mu'minin*. With this
concession, the king not only managed to secure important support from the
religious authorities; he also profited indirectly from the legal codification
of a hierarchical and patriarchal family structure that strengthened his role
as the ultimate authoritarian and protective father figure in Morocco.[16]
Thus, the new Mudawana both reflected and consolidated patriarchy and
did so in Islamic language. And it was inextricably linked to the overall political structures in Morocco, as its codification was central to the establishment and legitimation of the newly independent Moroccan autocracy.

Challenging Patriarchy, Islam, and Autocracy

The ensuing decades were characterized by modernization and social
change, notably in the bigger cities, where Moroccan women increasingly
received education and participated in the workforce. For many of these
women, the gap between their status in the public and private spheres was
incomprehensible and unacceptable. Despite earning advanced degrees and
sharing important responsibilities at work, they were still treated as dependent minors within the family. Accordingly, women increasingly raised
their voices and called for a change of the Mudawana, especially within the
leftist opposition parties.[17]

However, the 1970s and 1980s, known as the "years of lead," were also
years of harsh political repression. King Hassan II, who had inherited the

throne from his father in 1961, was a powerful autocratic ruler who ruthlessly repressed the left-wing opposition through imprisonment and mysterious "disappearances." Thus, while a number of the left-wing opposition parties professed to be concerned with women's rights and conditions, the "women's issue" in practice remained subordinated to other concerns. In this context, getting women's rights onto the political agenda was extremely difficult. Over the years, a number of women came to realize that if they wanted to promote women's rights, they would have to do so from a position outside the political party structure, given that the parties were too preoccupied with the overall fight for democracy and human rights.

This was the backdrop for the emergence, throughout the late 1980s and the beginning of the 1990s, of a number of new Moroccan women's organizations. The first and most important were the Association Démocratique des Femmes du Maroc (ADFM; Democratic Association of Moroccan Women), established in 1985, and the Union de l'Action Féminine (UAF; Union of Feminine Action), established in 1987 by a group of women who had previously known great success with the publication of a monthly women's magazine, *Tamania mars* (meaning "March 8," International Women's Day). The following years saw a proliferation of other organizations, among them notably the Ligue Démocratique pour les Droits de la Femme (LDDF; Democratic League for Women's Rights).

Despite differences in political affiliation and outlook, the majority of these liberal women's organizations shared a number of general characteristics. They were based in Rabat or Casablanca; they had ties to one of the oppositional left-wing parties; their leadership was mainly composed of well-educated, middle-class urban women; and they were working, among other things, for reform of the Mudawana. Furthermore, the majority of these organizations used a rights-based approach. In this, they found tremendous moral and financial international support, stemming largely from the United Nations Decade for Women (1974–85) and its aftermath, particularly the adoption of the Convention on the Elimination of Discrimination against Women. This UN framework provided a useful legal and political framework, a huge international network, financial support (especially from UNIFEM), and, not least, substantial legitimacy and leverage vis-à-vis the Moroccan authorities, who were increasingly forced to develop national gender strategies.[18]

The fight of the new liberal women's organizations to put women's rights on the public agenda remained an uphill battle during the so-called years of lead. They faced a patriarchal society in which their inferior family status was both rooted in tradition and religiously codified and legitimated in the

Mudawana. Demanding a change in their status thus meant confronting both patriarchal tradition and conservative interpretations of Islam. Furthermore, these new women's organizations *also* had to navigate in a repressive autocracy, with limited room for free expression and organization. In other words, the newborn liberal women's organizations had entered an extremely complex and challenging arena where they were simultaneously confronting patriarchy, conservative interpretations of Islam, *and* autocracy.

Political Liberalization

During the early 1990s, Hassan II came under increasing pressure to soften the authoritarian character of the state. After the fall of the Berlin Wall, international attention focused on human rights and democratization and inspired the creation (and regime acceptance) of a number of Moroccan human rights organizations. Meanwhile, the already desperate social situation, with alarming rates of poverty, unemployment, and illiteracy, was aggravated by economic liberalization measures undertaken to comply with the Structural Adjustment Programme mandated by the International Monetary Fund. This put further pressure on Hassan II to muster political support. The combined influence of these and other both internal and external forces gradually pushed Hassan II to ease repression and introduce a controlled process of political liberalization. In the 1990s, Morocco ratified a number of international human rights conventions,[19] established a consultative council on human rights, and introduced a reference to the Universal Declaration of Human Rights in its revised Constitution, which nevertheless continued to vest full executive power in the Moroccan king and *amir al-mu'minin,* commander of the faithful.[20]

This process of liberalization also led to increased tolerance of the Islamist movement.[21] In return for its recognition of the religious legitimacy of the king as *amir al-mu'minin,* the moderate Islamist organization *Harakat al-Islâh wa at-Tawhid* (Movement for Reform and Unity, MUR)[22] was slowly allowed onto the formal political scene and was permitted to participate in parliamentary elections for the first time in 1997.[23] However, alleged attempts by the Palace to also convince Morocco's most prominent Islamist dissident, the charismatic Shaykh Abdessalam Yassin, leader of the more spiritually oriented *Jama'a al-Adl wa-l-Ihsan* (Justice and Spirituality), to recognize the legitimacy of the Palace did not succeed.[24] Although Justice and Spirituality remained officially banned, it was increasingly tolerated by the Palace.

The Liberal Women's Movement Strikes

The liberal women's movement seized the opportunity presented by the process of gradual political liberalization. In March 1992, the UAF launched a petition aimed at collecting 1 million signatures for a reform of the Mudawana. They did so referring to the new human rights discourse of the regime and stressing the lack of consistency between the inferiority of women in the Mudawana and their status as full citizens granted by the Constitution. They further legitimated their demands by referring to women's universal rights as defined in the international human rights framework. Their campaign was influenced by the insights and experiences they had gained through the publication since 1983 of *Tamania mars,* which had created a new public platform for discussions on and especially by women. Under the leadership of its charismatic leader, Latifa Jbabdi, the UAF's campaign became a large collective endeavor backed by most of the existing liberal women's and human rights organizations that united in support of the petition. A liberal Moroccan women's movement was born.[25]

Meanwhile, the campaign was met with strident criticism. Some of the most fervent critiques were voiced by a number of prominent *'ulama'.* However, the Islamist organizations, notably the MUR (Unity and Reform), also protested against the petition, issuing *fatawa* (religious rulings) against the campaign and even accusing its organizers of apostasy and of being Western lackeys. Although the main voices of criticism were male, especially because only men had the authority to speak out as *'ulama',* a number of female Islamist activists likewise attacked the petition from inside the Islamist movement.

After months of strong and sometimes violent confrontations, King Hassan II decided to intervene. In September 1992, he addressed an audience of women, including representatives of the liberal women's organizations. Although this was in itself a positive and novel step, his speech was both very authoritarian and patriarchal. He addressed the women as his "daughter" (*ma fille*), professing to understand their demands, while stressing that the issue was not to be dealt with politically because it came directly under his prerogatives as commander of the faithful.[26] He then nominated an advisory commission, which was given a mandate to look into and propose changes to the Mudawana. The commission, composed mainly of conservative *'ulama'* or male religious scholars, subsequently presented a number of recommendations, based on which Hassan II announced a slightly modified Mudawana in his capacity as commander of the faithful.[27]

The changes introduced by this first timid reform in 1993 were limited. Among the most important were that women now had to consent in writing to marriage; a woman whose father was deceased could now conclude her marriage without a *wilaya* (male matrimonial guardianship); and a husband could no longer repudiate his wife without telling her, as repudiation now had to be authorized by a religious judge (*qadi*) in the presence of both spouses. With regard to polygamy, it became obligatory that both existing and future wives be informed of each other's existence; existing wives were given the right to ask for divorce; and, most important, a judge was given the right to forbid polygamy if he feared the wives would not be treated justly.[28] However, the code still enshrined a conservative and patriarchal interpretation of women's status and role within the family, for it retained the fundamental philosophy and principles of the old Mudawana.

Accordingly, the reform was praised and welcomed by many of those who had opposed the campaign of the liberal women's movement, for whom the timid reform was a great disappointment. Even more so, as the king's intervention seemed to have checked the momentum created through their campaign.[29] They nevertheless saw it as a small victory that the whole issue was no longer taboo. The Mudawana had become a law that *could* be changed, despite its foundation in Islamic law.[30]

Returning to our concern with the overall political implications of the reform process, we must consider why Hassan II stepped in. What was the overall political significance of his intervention, specifically with regard to democratization? Upon first glance, the significance seems positive. Women's family rights were improved by law (albeit modestly) after years of activism by a growing liberal women's movement, which had managed to put a controversial and sensitive issue on the public agenda despite lacking formal political support and despite patriarchal and autocratic resistance. However, upon close scrutiny, a less positive reading emerges. For one thing, the king's intervention essentially confirmed the patriarchal nature of the code. Furthermore, as pointed out by many informants from the liberal women's movement, the king had managed to co-opt their agenda, thus weakening an emerging new force from civil society. In so doing, he had also managed to reassert—and monopolize—his religious authority as *amir al mu'minin,* thus limiting action and religious interpretation by other voices in society. And finally, the limited reform seems to have provided Hassan II, at a relatively small cost, with a means of promoting an image of the Moroccan regime as liberalizing before an external audience eager to see such changes in advance of the 1995 world conference on women's rights in Beijing.

The "Democratic Transition"

In the period after the first limited Mudawana reform, the disappointed liberal women's organizations mainly concentrated on practical work, notably on establishing a number of emergency centers for women in need. These centers strengthened their awareness and knowledge of the lives of ordinary Moroccan women. It is noteworthy how this more concrete, practical work of the women's organizations in many ways resembled that of the Islamist organizations, who had gained much of their popularity and insights through local community work.

Meanwhile, important developments took place within the Islamist movement, where members of the MUR prepared to participate for the first time ever in the upcoming parliamentary elections in 1997. In parallel, women activists within the Islamist organizations also became increasingly assertive and active. Much of this activism had been spurred by the UAF's petition and the liberal women activists' somewhat monopolistic discourse on "what Moroccan women want." This discourse provoked many Islamist women activists to increasingly engage in and promote a counterdiscourse on women's rights based on an Islamic framework. During the resistance to the UAF's petition campaign, these activists had remained "hidden" within the major male-led organizations. But now they increasingly insisted on establishing their own platforms and discourse. In 1994, activists from the MUR founded a new women's organization, the Organization for the Renewal of Women's Awareness (ORWA). And in 1998, a separate women's section was established within Justice and Spirituality under the leadership of Shaykh Yassin's articulate daughter, Nadia. Thus, while the liberal women's movement drew important lessons from the Islamist movement concerning the importance of proximity and of providing concrete social services, Islamist women's organizations in turn saw the importance of establishing independent and visible organizational platforms and employing a rights-based discourse to promote their cause—and to counter the liberal women's claims. In this way, the emergence and maturation of the opposing liberal and Islamist women's organizations were, to a certain extent, mutually constitutive.[31]

But changes were not only occurring within the various women's organizations. In 1996, the non-Islamist opposition parties—notably the left-
wing Union Socialiste des Forces Populaires (USFP; Socialist Union of
Popular Forces) and Parti du Progrès et du Socialisme (PPS; Party of
Progress and Socialism) and the more national-conservative Istiqlal—
voted in support of a constitutional revision, hence signaling their implicit
acceptance of the rules of the political game, including the vast constitutional prerogatives of the king.[32] This acceptance seemingly paid out, as
the longtime opposition leader Abderrahmane Youssoufi of the socialist
USFP was appointed prime minister of a broad coalition government after
the parliamentary elections of 1997. Meanwhile, the king also used his prerogatives to personally name four key so-called ministers of sovereignty.[33]
Despite these royal nominations, the new government was known as
gouvernement d'alternance" (i.e., the government of alternation) and was
widely perceived as marking a major turning point in Morocco's transition
to democracy.[34]

The National Action Plan

The liberal women's organizations welcomed Youssoufi's speech of investiture, in which he gave a clear priority to improving women's conditions in Morocco. Among the first tasks of the new *alternance* government
was the finalization of the *Plan d'action national pour l'intégration de la
femme au développement (PANIFD;* National Action Plan for the Integration of Women in Development), in compliance with Morocco's obligations to the UN Convention on the Elimination of Discrimination against
Women.[35] The new secretary of state for employment, social protection,
family, and children, Said Saadi of the formerly Communist PPS party,
gathered a committee of experts,[36] and organized a number of consultative
workshops and seminars financed by the World Bank.

The *PANIFD* was presented to the public in March 1999. It concentrated
on four areas of intervention to increase the role of women in Moroccan
development: education, reproductive health, women's integration in economic development, and the strengthening of women's legal, political, and
institutional capacities and power.[37] Its primary frame of reference was human rights as defined in the international conventions to which Morocco
adheres. Meanwhile, the *PANIFD* also stressed the necessity of reconcil-

ing international human rights and Islamic frames of reference and thus also made references to Islamic legal tradition. These references were made, however, to a modernist and thus controversial interpretation of Islamic law.[38] Some of the recommendations of the *PANIFD* specifically necessitated a reform of the Mudawana. Among other things, the plan proposed raising the minimum age of marriage for girls from fifteen to eighteen years, suppressing the obligatory matrimonial tutorship (*wilaya*), abolishing repudiation, and introducing divorce by the courts as the only means of terminating a marriage contract. Finally, it also proposed the abolition of polygamy, with all exceptions contingent on the agreement of both the first wife and a judge.[39]

As had been the case after the 1992 Mudawana reform petition, the recommendations concerning the Mudawana were vehemently criticized by various political actors over the following months. Among the first to criticize the *PANIFD* was a prominent member of Saadi's own government, Alaoui M'Daghri, minister of Islamic affairs and endowments (*habous*) and one of four so-called ministers of sovereignty directly appointed by the king. The *PANIFD* was also criticized by the League of 'Ulama,' by the MUR, and by the Parti de la Justice et du Développement (PJD; Justice and Development Party). They argued that the *PANIFD* was a threat to Islam and to the Moroccan nation, family, and traditions. They also accused Saadi and the liberal women's organizations of being Western footmen, while specifically accusing Saadi of insufficient consultation with the Ministry of Islamic Affairs and Endowments, the *'ulama'*, and the Islamist parties and organizations. They also accused him of disrespecting democratic procedures by trying to force the *PANIFD* on the government by presenting it publicly without a prior intergovernmental vote.[40]

But it was not only the *PANIFD*'s opponents who manifested their opinion in the public sphere. Those in favor of the plan also united their forces in two big networks, which assembled the majority of liberal women's organizations, human rights organizations, some of the bigger trade unions, and most left-wing parties.[41]

In this way, the debate over the *PANIFD* came to mark a turning point not only with regard to women's rights but also with regard to the role and visibility of civil society in Morocco. The debate then became the platform for a broad societal discussion between increasingly strong and professional organizations of *'ulama'* and Islamists, as well as liberal women's and human rights organizations.

The Social Earthquake

Hassan II died in June 1999 and left the throne to his son, Mohamed VI. He quickly proclaimed his intentions both to strengthen the general process of political liberalization and specifically to see a strengthening of women's position in society.[42] He demonstrated the latter by appointing the first-ever female royal adviser, Zoulikha Naciri; in his private life, his marriage to a brilliant and educated wife stood in marked contrast to the preference of his ancestors, whose wives had lived in secluded harems. Meanwhile, the heated debate over the *PANIFD* continued. It reached a dramatic climax on March 12, 2000.

In Rabat, a long-planned Moroccan contribution to an international women's millennium march "against violence and poverty" turned into a demonstration in support of the controversial *PANIFD*. According to one of the organizers, more than sixty different organizations participated, among them various liberal women's organizations such as the ADFM, the UAF, and the LDDF, but the march also assembled activists from human rights organizations, trade unions, and the left-wing political parties. It is estimated that somewhere between forty thousand and a hundred thousand participants marched in the streets of Rabat on behalf of Moroccan women's rights and the *PANIFD*.[43]

Meanwhile, in Casablanca, a quickly organized counterdemonstration "for the preservation of Islam and the fight against moral dissolution" mobilized a massive following. Although the police estimated the participation at sixty thousand, the organizers claimed they had assembled half a million participants. The French newspaper *Le Monde* reported an estimate of a hundred thousand to two hundred thousand participants. This demonstration was highly significant in at least three ways. For one thing, its size, organization, and discipline came as a strong public manifestation of the strength and popularity of the Islamist movement. Second, the demonstration was significant for its broad following, as it attracted representatives from many institutions and political parties, including members of the government coalition. Their participation in the march against the *PANIFD* clearly underscored the profound disagreements on the issue within the government as well as the lack of strength and discipline among the leadership of the parties in the *alternance* government.

Third, the strong female presence at the Casablanca demonstration was significant. Headed by front figures from the Islamist women's sections such as Nadia Yassin (the president of the women's section of Justice and

Spirituality) and Bassima Hakkaoui (the president of ORWA, the women's organization affiliated with the MUR and the PJD), a large number of women, most of them veiled, marched in a neatly organized, separate women's section. Their protest was not directed against the idea of the reform of women's situation as such, but it was specifically directed against the *PANIFD*'s proposed reform of the Mudawana, which to them represented both secularization and Westernization. Their protest was also directed against the manner in which the *PANIFD* had been elaborated. According to a key female PJD activist, "I participated—and I am a feminist activist. I defend women, the family, man. . . . The plan was not the result of a national dialogue. It expressed the points of view of an elite, of a political party [the PPS], which intended to make changes without respecting the specificity of this people. . . . There were more than a million participants—of whom the majority defended the rights of women. We worked in women's organizations—against the plan, for the rights of women. . . . The plan neglected women's associations, even other political parties."

The massive female participation in both the Rabat and Casablanca demonstrations clearly illustrates that the conflict was *not* simply one that opposed Moroccan women against Moroccan men. Neither was it a question of Islam versus rights, because the large majority of demonstrators in both Rabat and Casablanca made their demands within frameworks that included references to rights and to Islam. Rather, what differed was their *interpretation* of rights and of Islam. The discussions about the *PANIFD* and the proposal of a Mudawana reform had become the main arena of confrontation for two broad societal visions that were concerned with far more than the Mudawana issue. They had become symbolic of the vast societal divide over the interpretation of Islam and the roles of tradition and modernity.

Two opposing visions of the character and development of Moroccan society in general, and the role and interpretation of Islam in particular, were clashing in what many informants have alluded to as the "societal earthquake." The march in Rabat signified a modernization project that placed the individual and her rights as defined in international conventions—such as the UN Convention on the Elimination of Discrimination against Women—at the forefront, while invoking a modernist interpretation of Islam. In contrast, the march in Casablanca emphasized the necessity of promoting women's rights from within Islam and of reconciling women's rights with "tradition," thus making changes "the Moroccan way."

Although this conflict of interpretation was at the forefront of the two demonstrations, other agendas were seemingly also in play. For instance, informants from Justice and Spirituality have stressed that their "hearts were in Rabat" but that they marched in Casablanca in order to signal to the *makhzen*[44] that they would not accept empty reforms or not being taken into account. Meanwhile, paradoxically, informants from various liberal women's organizations have stressed that the Casablanca march was also meant as an internal show of force by authoritarian elements of the *makhzen,* which allegedly were behind the impressively swift and well-organized mass gathering in Casablanca in order to display its power.

At any rate, with respect to our overall interest in the democratic features of the reform process, the extent and openness of these virulent public reactions are very important. For one thing, the staging of two peaceful mass demonstrations articulating diverging opinions on an immensely controversial domestic issue constituted an unprecedented phenomenon in Moroccan political history. Furthermore, the many and varied public reactions to a government proposal from a diverse and lively civil society were clear indicators of a more open public sphere in Morocco.[45] The participation of the Islamist organizations, notably the officially banned Justice and Spirituality, was particularly unprecedented, signaling both the new public activism of the Islamist movement in Morocco and increased toleration by the regime.[46] Finally, the sizable involvement of Moroccan women in both demonstrations testified to women's increasing participation and importance in the public sphere.[47]

The Politicians Give Up . . .

However, March 12, 2000, had also amply illustrated the weakness of the parties in the *alternance* government. After the Casablanca demonstration, Prime Minister Youssoufi began to back away from the controversial *PANIFD.* In September 2000, he initiated a government reshuffle in which Saadi lost his seat. The controversial author of the infamous *PANIFD* had become too much of a burden for the *alternance* government, despite its initial ambition to improve women's conditions. But the firing of Saadi was not enough to calm the fierce criticism of the *PANIFD,* which had become a major liability for Youssoufi. In the following spring, after a failed attempt to resolve the issue through a government commission, he finally gave up on reforming the Mudawana and left it to the king to arbitrate.

Youssoufi's decision to abandon the *PANIFD* struck a divisive blow to the liberal women's movement. To some organizations, such as the ADFM and the LDDF, it not only represented a setback for the *PANIFD* itself but also threatened to dash the hopes for democratization that had been born with the *alternance* government. Others, such as the UAF, saw Youssoufi's decision to leave the issue for royal arbitration in a more positive light, as the best possible solution in view of the staunch resistance to the *PANIFD*. Meanwhile, the majority of the *PANIFD*'s opponents welcomed arbitration by the king as commander of the faithful as the only legitimate and acceptable way to proceed. In terms of democratization, the development was very significant. By the spring of 2001, after an unprecedented broad and free societal debate, an elected government supported by various civil society organizations gave up legislating and left it to the king to rule. The *alternance* experience had suffered a fatal blow.

. . . and the King Steps In

In April 2001, Mohammed VI announced that, in line with tradition, he would establish a commission to advise him on a revision of the Mudawana. In a novel move, he named three women to the sixteen-member commission, which like previous commissions was dominated by *'ulama'*. The three women were Zour el Hour (a judge and future president of the country's biggest family tribunal in Casablanca), Rahma Bourquia (a professor of sociology and future president of the university at Mohamedia), and Nouzha Guessous (a professor of pharmacology).[48] During its thirty months of existence, the commission received about eighty delegations from various organizations and groups of interest.

Meanwhile, a process of intensive lobbying redynamized the liberal women's movement, as the main organizations decided to unite in a new "network of spring" aimed at influencing the commission and public opinion. A remarkable feature of the discourse of the network was its reliance on Islamic arguments, often assisted by *'ulama'* performing modernist *ijtihan* (independent critical thinking). Although some of the activists within the network had also previously included references to Islam in their arguments, the degree to which these now colored their discourse vis-à-vis the advisory commission was quite marked. In this way, the members of the liberal women's movement adopted a conscious strategy of challenging their opponents on their own turf—religion.

Meanwhile, their opponents also made great efforts to mobilize and articulate their views vis-à-vis the advisory commission in order to ensure a limited reform that would not alter the fundamental principles of the exist-

ing Mudawana, notably its foundation in *shari'a*. In addition to the commission, the Islamist movement actively lobbied the public; the ORWA, for
instance, elaborated a comprehensive alternative Mudawana reform proposal, which it presented to the commission.[49]

While the commission worked, parliamentary elections took place in
September 2002, but they did not yield a clear majority. The king ultimately
decided to ignore all the elected political candidates and appointed the busi-
nessman Driss Jettou as the new prime minister in charge of a broad-based
government that also included several other technocrats. This move aptly
reflected the ambiguity of the democratic transition in Morocco. Despite
relatively free and fair elections, the king used his prerogatives to disregard
the popularly elected politicians in his appointment of a new prime minister.[50] Meanwhile, the elections were important in terms of women's representation, as 10 percent of the parliamentary seats had for the first time been
reserved for women. This led to a remarkable addition of female parliamentarians, including six from the PJD, among them Bassima Hakkaoui,
the first ORWA president.

Soon after the investiture of the new government, Morocco experienced
its first major terrorist attack. On May 16, 2003, a group of youth inspired
by the Salafia Jihadia and allegedly affiliated with al Qaeda committed coordinated suicide attacks on various Westernized locations in Casablanca
that cost more than forty lives. The attacks were a huge shock to the Moroccan populace, which could no longer claim to live in a stable and peaceful haven in Islamic harmony under the divine guidance of the commander
of the faithful. The immediate aftermath was characterized by severe questioning and criticism of the role of Islamist ideology in Morocco, and for a
while the legal existence of PJD as a political party was seriously threatened. The PJD survived by swiftly and radically moderating its official discourse and replacing the most controversial figures in its leadership.

The Reform

Finally, in October 2003, while the Islamist movement was still weakened,
Mohamed VI decided to present the key religious elements of a new and
far-reaching Mudawana reform.[51] Husbands and wives were now to become equal partners in the family; women were to gain easier access to divorce by the courts and would no longer need male tutors to marry; their
minimum marital age was to be raised from fifteen to eighteen years; and

spouses were henceforth to be permitted to share goods acquired during their marriage upon its dissolution. The symbolically significant issue of polygamy was also settled; a husband's right to polygamy would remain theoretically intact—but was subjected to very strict conditions so as to render it almost impossible in practice.[52]

The king's reform thus went very far. It also resembled the recommendations in Saadi's plan. There were, however, a number of stark differences between the two, primarily of a formal and symbolic character. Most notably, the sovereign carefully argued solely within an Islamic framework, making extensive use of *ijtihad,* while not making references to international conventions or obligations.

In contrast to his father's reform in 1993, Mohamed VI also chose to involve the democratically elected representatives of the nation not only in the ratification but also in the making of the revised law. While the king as *amir al mu'minin* had already settled the most controversial religious aspects, he left it up to the parliamentarians to decide on various aspects concerning the new law's implementation. They did so over the following months, after which the Parliament subsequently voted unanimously for the new family law, which went into force in early February 2004. Hence, after a long and tumultuous political reform process, a new and substantially revised family law radically strengthened Moroccan women's rights within the family.

The extent of the king's reform proposal came as a great surprise to the majority of Moroccans. It was nevertheless quite well received among the vast majority of activists, including those who had been most strongly opposed to the *PANIFD.* This is not surprising, because the continuing restriction of free speech and criticism of the monarchy in Morocco means that most actors will praise any ruling once it has been pronounced by the Moroccan king and *amir al mu'minin.* Nevertheless, it seems that the king had in fact managed to find a formula satisfactory to most of those involved, as most could claim that they had come out as "winners" from the reform process.

The liberal women's movement praised the extent of the proposed reforms, which went further than most of them had ever hoped. The new law included the majority of recommendations from Saadi's plan, with a few noticeable exceptions, such as the retaining of the controversial institutions of repudiation and polygamy, the practice of which had, however, been substantially hampered. According to a key figure in the ADFM, "the principal advance was that it abolished the matrimonial tutelage. *That* is what has destabilized the established order, the patriarchy: namely, giving women the legal capacity to marry on their own."

Meanwhile, the king's reform also received praise from Islamist activists. Informants from the PJD and ORWA maintain that it was a victory for them that the new law remained (solely) based on *shari'a* and thus respected both religion and Moroccan tradition. They also point out that the law was based on advice from *'ulama'* and involved arbitration by the *amir al mu'minin,* whereas adoption of the *PANIFD* would have represented a break from Moroccan religion and tradition. Nadia Yassin and the women's section of Justice and Spirituality also welcomed the new law. According to my informants, their movement had never been against a revision of the Mudawana as such, but had rather stressed the necessity both of reliance on *shari'a* and of linking Islamic reform to more profound political changes.

However, other segments of the former opponents to the *PANIFD* seemed less eager to praise the new law—namely, the majority of traditional patriarchal authorities such as the *'ulama', adoul,* and judges. Whereas the Islamists could rightly claim to have won something (respect for *shari'a,* royal arbitration, etc.), these actors had lost considerable influence and terrain. Despite the new law's continued foundation in *shari'a* and the important role accorded to *'ulama'* within the royal advisory commission, the law was a setback for patriarchy, both because it enhanced women's rights and because it reassigned certain responsibilities from *'ulama'* and *adoul* to newly established family courts and secular judges.[53]

As we have seen, the political process that ultimately resulted in the Mudawana reform took place within and contributed to a wider process of political liberalization. But was it also part of and an indicator of a process of democratization, implying an increase in collective participation in decisionmaking and of the accountability of those in power? I suggest that the various elements signaling a democratic significance of the Mudawana reform may be summarized in two overall arguments—one about "substance" and one about "process."

The Substance Argument: The Mudawana Reform as an Intrinsic Part of Democratization

Many informants, notably liberal women's activists, argued that the Mudawana reform was in itself an intrinsic and necessary part of the democratic transition in Morocco, because democratization starts at home, in the family, the basic unit of society. As long as girls are brought up to see themselves as inferior to men, they will never be able to participate fully in public life. Put another way, unless all citizens enjoy equal rights in the private sphere, there can be no democracy in the public sphere. In the words of a key UAF activist: "For the women, the question of women was a new democratic issue that differed from others in that it was not only an institutional, but a societal issue. And thus, the democratic battle had to involve / be based on society itself. . . . One could not make democratic changes without women, without female citizens." Or, to use Valentine Moghadam's term, a *gendered* democracy in which women *participate* on equal terms with their male relatives necessarily starts with equality at home.[54]

Assessing the validity of this claim obviously hinges on one's understanding of "democracy." If one employs, as Moghadam does, a broad-based understanding of democracy, including not only political structures but also the extent to which citizens feel empowered and motivated to participate, it obviously follows that the new Moroccan family law is a significant indicator of democratization.

However, sticking to the more common usage for and understanding of democratization—namely, changing the fundamental rules of the political game by enhancing citizen involvement in and control over political decisionmaking, and the accountability of their rulers—the substance argument given here is not convincing.

Although the new Moroccan family law unmistakably extends new and important rights to Moroccan women, these rights do not necessarily enhance the participation in and control over political decisionmaking of ordinary Moroccans, be they men or women, nor do they increase the accountability of their rulers. Moroccan women have been empowered in the private sphere, and this *may* eventually have a spillover effect in the public sphere, if they use this new power and position to increase collective decisionmaking and the accountability of their rulers. But there is no guarantee that this will happen. And unless or until it does, it would be incorrect to equate the Mudawana reform with democratization.[55] Thus, although the promotion of Moroccan women's rights in the new Mudawana certainly is an important liberalization measure and has much significance with respect to Moroccan women's position in the private sphere, these new rights are complementary to but not in themselves sufficient evidence of democratization in Morocco.

The Process Argument: The Mudawana Reform Process as an Indicator of Democracy

Whereas the above argument focuses on the significance of the new law itself, other arguments in my interviews indicated that elements of the political *process* preceding the reform were indicators of democratization, namely, the respective roles during the process of *the Moroccan Parliament* and of *civil society* which I discuss in turn.

Many informants saw the involvement of Parliament in the Mudawana reform process as an indicator of democratization. For the first time, a Moroccan king and *amir al-mu'minin* had allowed the elected representatives of the Moroccan people to legislate on family law, thereby strengthening the executive role of the parliamentarians and indicating growth in collective control over decisionmaking and in the king's accountability to his subjects. But this argument fails to hold up when subjected to further scrutiny. For one thing, even before the involvement of Parliament in the Mudawana reform, the authority and legitimacy of not only the parties of the *alternance* government but also of the entire parliamentary structure were substantially undermined when Youssoufi abandoned the *PANIFD* and left it for the king to arbitrate.

Furthermore, the process illustrated the weakness of the democratically elected government. Despite the existence of many and varied political parties and relatively free and fair parliamentary elections, the main political base of power still resides in and is controlled by the Palace. The reform process did not change this. On the contrary, a key ingredient in Youssoufi's and Saadi's failure to promote the *PANIFD* was the strong resistance they met from within the ranks of government, especially the Palace-appointed minister of Islamic affairs and endowments (one of the so-called ministers of sovereignty), Alaoui M'Daghri. And finally, the involvement of Parliament did not signify an increase in the king's accountability and only a very limited strengthening of collective decisionmaking, because the popularly elected parliamentarians were not given a mandate to discuss the new law as such. Rather, with regard to all the controversial, religious issues, they were only given the "right" to rubberstamp what the king had already decided. Hence, what was left for "collective decisionmaking" were only a number of rather insignificant details concerning the practical application of the new family law.[56]

Thus, the involvement of the Moroccan Parliament in the Mudawana reform process does not seem to indicate a process of democratization. In fact, parliamentary involvement may first and foremost have served to legitimate what the king had already decided by implicating the "representatives" of the nation.[57] Rather than indicating democratization, it may thus have served to strengthen the legitimacy and authority of the Moroccan king and commander of the faithful.

The Mudawana reform process also featured a lively civil society, which played an important political role through increasingly professionalized lobbying and agenda setting. Furthermore, this civil society activism was characterized by increasing diversity, as evidenced by the participation of both liberal and Islamist activists who had traditionally been excluded from the public sphere. This novel and impressive strength, diversity, and professionalization of Moroccan civil society certainly constituted a clear and important indicator of political liberalization, as individuals and collectives obtained and used new freedoms and rights to organize and speak out. But did this new participation of civil society during the Mudawana reform process also indicate democratization—that is, increased collective control and ruler accountability?

Again, I do not think so. In fact, and most paradoxically, the strong civil society participation may rather have served to further undermine the traditional political parties and the parliamentary structure, and hence set back further the prospects for democratization in Morocco. What happened throughout the historical reform process was that the liberal women's demands were increasingly separated from the agenda of the "prodemocratic" political parties, and thus "depoliticized,"[58] in the sense that the Mudawana debate increasingly took place outside Parliament, thus further marginalizing both the institution and its already weak political parties.[59] Though it was influential in pushing for a Moroccan family law and the promotion of women's rights, civil society may in this sense have actually decreased rather than heightened the prospects for Moroccan democratization. However, this weakening of political parties was not true for all. While the PJD may have been at least momentarily weakened throughout the process due to external events (namely, the terrorist acts of May 16, 2003), the party seems to have gained considerable strength from its participation in the Mudawana reform process as a responsible yet involved political actor, while retaining strong affiliations with other members of civil society (notably the MUR and ORWA).

How about the agenda setting of both the liberal women's movement and their Islamist adversaries—was it an indication of democratization? The liberal women's movement managed to force the Mudawana reform issue onto the public agenda and to influence decisionmakers. Meanwhile, the ability of their Islamist opponents (in liaison with their allies within the state apparatus, notably the minister of Islamic affairs and leading *'ulama'*) to counter these demands was equally noteworthy. But was this influence a sign of democratization? Yet again, keeping to our understanding of democratization as signifying increased collective control and regime accountability, I find no justification for interpreting this influence as a sign of democratization, because the reform was, after all, ultimately based on an authoritarian decision made by the powerful Moroccan king.

However, over the long term, the rich learning experience of the diverse civil society activists may very well prove to have been significant for future political developments in Morocco, including democratization. This also holds true with respect to popular mobilization, where the liberal women's movement seems to have learned the importance of popular outreach and mobilization after the successful mass mobilization of the Islamist movement in Casablanca in 2000, while the Islamist movement seems to have learned the importance of making separate women's organizations and employing a rights-based discourse when promoting their arguments.

To summarize the role of civil society, the Mudawana reform process was characterized by the growing importance of civil society and was a clear indicator of political liberalization. Meanwhile, the significance of civil society involvement as a sign of democratization is more difficult to assess. All in all, however, it would seem that this involvement did not significantly increase collective control and regime accountability, as the reform process remained subject to control by the monarchy, despite elements of public agenda setting and consultation. That said, the experiences gained by civil society during the process may potentially provide the basis and impetus for a new push for democratization in Morocco.

Conclusion

The Mudawana reform was an extremely important development in terms of the formal improvement of Moroccan women's rights within the family. Furthermore, the reform process opened the public sphere to the participation of new political actors, such as liberal women's organizations and Islamist organizations, including Islamist women's organizations. As such, the process clearly increased the recognition and protection of civil and political *liberties and freedom* and can be considered a process of substantial political liberalization. Meanwhile, if we understand democratization to entail the enhancement of popular political control and the accountability of rulers, neither the substance of the new Mudawana nor the political processes that led to it can be considered clear indicators of democratization. Paradoxically, the Mudawana reform process may even have strengthened the liberalizing but still profoundly authoritarian Moroccan monarchy, whose legitimacy and authority appear to have been bolstered by its shrewd manipulation of the tumultuous Mudawana reform process.

Let me conclude with two final observations on the Mudawana reform and the rich political process that preceded it. First of all, the political process that preceded the recent Mudawana reform clearly illustrates the necessity of understanding and studying family law reforms as processes of not only religious and/or social but also general political significance. We have seen how Moroccan women who fought for a revision of their personal status had to do so on three fronts, confronting simultaneously patriarchal patterns of tradition and authority, conservative interpretations of Islam, *and* an autocratic, albeit liberalizing, regime.

Second, the Moroccan reform process also illustrates the importance of avoiding oversimplified representations of Islam and women's rights as ultimately opposing and irreconcilable. As the Moroccan story shows, rather than being a question of one or the other, the main issue may concern conflicting *interpretations* of Islam and of women's rights. In other words, Islam may not per se be a barrier to improving women's rights. Rather, the main obstacles to reform can be profound societal disagreements over the *interpretation* of family law—and over who has the right to make such interpretations. Thus, though it is obviously necessary to view critically the apparent consensus on the Moroccan king's reform, given his authoritarian position, the reform process nevertheless indicates that it may indeed be possible to reconcile the promotion of women's rights with Islam. In some societies, which are deeply imbued with Islamic values and tradition, the way toward reform and rights promotion may be by and through Islam, not against it.

Notes

1. "Mudawana" literally means "collection" or "code of laws." It is also the title of one of the most famous law books of the Maliki school, namely, Sahnun's *Al-Mudawwana al-kubra*.

2. For a detailed presentation of the content of the revised Mudawana, see Malika Benradi, "Genre et droit de la famille: Les droits des femmes dans la Moudawana—de la révision de 1993 á la réforme de 2003," in *Féminin, Masculin: La marche vers l'égalité au Maroc 1993–2003,* edited by Mohamed Mouaqit (Fez: Friedrich Ebert Stiftung, 2004), 71–77.

3. The interviews were conducted for my PhD thesis, which besides forty-eight formal interviews also relies on a large number of more informal interviews and personal observations as well as various official Moroccan documents, press, and publication of

various civil society and scholar-activists on the subject. For a full presentation, see Julie Pruzan-Jørgensen, "Liberalizing Autocracy at Work: Intra-oppositional Dynamics and Regime Legitimation during the Moudawana Reform Process" (PhD thesis, University of Copenhagen, 2009). I am deeply indebted to my informants for their willingness to share their memories and analysis of the process during often long and repeated interviews.

4. There are, however, a few exceptions; notably, see Jean-Phillippe Bras, "La réforme du code de la famille au Maroc et en Algérie: Quelles avancées pour la démocratie?" *Critique Internationale* 37 (October–December 2007): 93–125. Other essays that have looked at the reform from a political (but not democracy) perspective include Rabéa Naciri, "La Moudawwana et sa réforme: Le rôle de l'Etat," in *La réforme du droit de la famille: Cinquante années de débats—Études et analyses, Prologues: Revue maghrébine du livre* 3, special issue, edited by Mohamed Mouaqit (2002): 40; Léon Buskens, "Recent Debates on Family Law in Morocco: Islamic Law as Politics in an Emerging Public Sphere," *Islamic Law and Society* 10, no. 1 (2003): 70–131; Alain Roussillon, "Réformer la Moudawana: Statut et conditions des Marocaines," *Maghreb-Machrek* 179 (Spring 2004): 79–99; Zakia Salime, "Between Islamism and Feminism: New Political Transformations and Movements in Morocco" (PhD diss., University of Illinois at Urbana-Champaign, 2005); and Katja Elliott Zvan, "Reforming the Moroccan Personal Status Code: A Revolution for Whom?" *Mediterranean Politics* 14, no. 2 (July 2009): 213–27.

5. E.g., see Fatima Sadiqi and Moha Ennaji, "The Feminization of Public Space: Women's Activism, the Family Law, and Social Change in Morocco," *Journal of Middle East Women's Studies* 2, no. 2 (2006): 86–114.

6. On political liberalization and democratization in the Arab world, see Rex Brynen, Bahgat Korany, and Paul Noble, "Introduction: Theoretical Perspectives on Arab Liberalization and Democratization," in *Theoretical Perspectives on Arab Liberalization and Democratization,* (Boulder, Colo.: Lynne Rienner, 1995), 3. For a general introduction, see the seminal work by Juan J. Linz and Alfred Stepan, *Problems of Democratic Transition and Consolidation: Southern Europe, South America, and Post-Communist Europe* (Baltimore: Johns Hopkins University Press, 1996), 3–15; and Guillermo O'Donnell and Philippe C. Schmitter, *Transitions from Authoritarian Rule: Tentative Conclusions about Uncertain Democracies* (Baltimore: Johns Hopkins University Press, 1986), 7.

7. Marina Ottaway, *Democracy Challenged: The Rise of Semi-Authoritarianism* (Washington, D.C.: Carnegie Endowment for International Peace, 2003), 9; Daniel Brumberg, "Liberalization versus Democracy: Understanding Arab Political Reform," in *Uncharted Journey: Promoting Democracy in the Middle East,* edited by Thomas Carothers and Marina Ottaway (Washington, D.C.: Carnegie Endowment for International Peace, 2005), 15–36.

8. O'Donnell and Schmitter, *Transitions from Authoritarian Rule,* 7–8. See also Brynen, Korany, and Noble, "Introduction," 3.

9. O'Donnell and Schmitter, *Transitions from Authoritarian Rule,* 9.

10. Ottaway, *Democracy Challenged,* 3–9.

11. Islamic family law has unusually strong symbolic significance in Morocco, because it was instrumentalized during the French protectorate as part of a divide-and-rule strategy of playing the Arab and Amazigh (or Berber) ethnic groups off one other. See

Mounia Charrad, *States and Women's Rights: The Making of Postcolonial Tunisia, Algeria and Morocco* (Berkeley: University of California Press, 2001), 103–13, 139–42.

12. Article 19 of the Moroccan Constitution grants the Moroccan king extensive prerogatives both as ruler of the nation and as its highest religious authority—i.e., *amir al-mu'minin,* or commander of the faithful. See Mohamed Tozy, *Monarchie et Islam Politique au Maroc,* 2nd ed. (Paris: Presses de la Fondation Nationale des Science Politiques, 1999); and John Waterbury, *The Commander of the Faithful: The Moroccan Political Elite—A Study in Segments Politics* (New York: Columbia University Press, 1970).

13. Hans-Georg Ebert, "Das neue Personalstatus Marokkos: Normen, Methoden und Problemfelder," *Orient* 46, no. 4 (2005): 613–15.

14. Allal al Fassi was the leader of the independence party *Istiqlal,* which played a key role in the Moroccan fight for independence. For a discussion of the internal commission disagreements, see Mohammed El Ayadi, "La femme dans le débat intellectuel au Maroc," in *La réforme du droit de la famille,* ed. Mouaqit, 10.

15. The Maliki school, one of four main schools (or *madhab*) of Islamic law, is predominant in North Africa; see Charrad, *States and Women's Rights,* 31–50. For a general introduction to Muslim family law, see John L. Esposito, *Women in Muslim Family Law* (Syracuse: Syracuse University Press, 1982).

16. Naciri, "Moudawwana," 42–45. See also Fatima Mernissi, "État et Planification Nationale," in *Portraits de Femmes,* edited by Mohamed Alahyane (Casablanca: Éditions Le Fennec, 1987). For a general presentation of the patterns of authority of the Moroccan ruler, see Abdellah Hammoudi, *Master and Disciple: The Cultural Foundations of Moroccan Authoritarianism* (Chicago: University of Chicago Press, 1997).

17. Mohamed Janjar, "Émergence de la société civile au Maroc: Le cas du mouvement associatif féminine," in *La Société Civile au Maroc: L'Emergence de Nouveaux Acteurs de Développement,* edited by Maria-Angels Roque (Barcelona: Publisud/Sochepress, 2005), 110–11.

18. Despite the many similarities among these new women's organizations, it has been very difficult for me to decide what to label them. Although "the Moroccan women's movement" seems an obvious choice, and is in fact used both by the groups themselves and most of the Moroccan media, this label misleadingly implies a monolithic, unified movement representative of *all* Moroccan women. While I do think it appropriate to speak of a Moroccan women's movement, it is far more diverse, because it notably includes significant contributions from various Islamist women's activists and organizations, with very divergent views, as we shall see. An alternative might be to characterize these organizations as part of "the modernist movement"—as this is how many of them also see and depict themselves. But I also find this term problematic, as it suggests that this group alone represents modernity, and obscures the modern features of many of their "opponents," notably among the Islamist organizations. The term "secular" also seems inappropriate, because it often carries negative, antireligious connotations in Morocco. The same is true of the term "feminist," which is often employed by their adversaries but not the majority of activists themselves, because of its perceived antinational, antireligious, antimale, and pro-Western connotations. I have thus opted to characterize the above organizations as "liberal," because this term seems less monolithic as well as less tainted, and because it highlights their rights-based frame of reference. Finally, it should be highlighted that these considerations of terminology not only are a question of presentation but do in fact point to one of the key is-

sues at stake in the reform of the Mudawana, namely, the importance of and fundamental disagreements over the appropriate frame of reference for understanding women's rights.

19. Notably, see the Convention on the Elimination of Discrimination against Women, which was ratified by Morocco in 1993 (with reservations).

20. See Benradi, "Genre et droit de la famille," 39.

21. The Islamist movement is dominated by two currents, which have followed markedly different itineraries over the past decades, not least in their attitudes vis-à-vis the regime and in their demands for reforms. Al-Islah wa-l-Tajdid (Reform and Renewal) had its roots in the radical Shabiba Islamiyaa (Islamic Youth), but developed over the years into accepting and approaching the regime. In 1996, it was transformed into Harakat al-Islâh wa-at-Tawhid (Movement of Unity and Reform, also known as MUR). The movement has increasingly been allowed to enter the formal political scene. It was allowed to participate in the parliamentary elections in 1997 via attaching itself to an existing political party, the Mouvement Populaire Démocratique et Constitutionnel (MPDC), which then was no more than an empty shell organized around its old *zaïm,* Abdelkrim Al-Khatib. In 1998, it was allowed to establish Morocco's first legal Islamist party, Hizb al-Adala w-al-Tanmia (Party for Justice and Development). In contrast, Al-Adl wa-l-Ihsan (Justice and Spirituality), remains a forbidden, largely social-spiritual movement. Meanwhile, it is considered to have a much greater following and to constitute the potentially strongest political challenger to the Moroccan regime, whose legitimacy it has never fully accepted. See Tozy, *Monarchie;* Malika Zeghal, *Les Islamistes marocains: Le défi à la monarchie* (Casablanca: Éditions Le Fennec, 2005); Michael J. Willis, "Between Alternance and the Makhzen: At-Tawhid wa Al-Islah's Entry into Moroccan Politics," *Journal of North African Studies* 4, no. 3 (1999): 45–80; and Michael J. Willis, "Morocco's Islamists and the Legislative Elections of 2002: The Strange Case of the Party That Did Not Want to Win," *Mediterranean Politics* 9, no. 1 (2004), 53–81.

22. In fact, in 1997, the organization was still called Harakat al-Islâh w-at-Tajdid (Reform and Renewal). Only upon its integration into parliamentary life (where its political wing was eventually to become the Hizb al Adala wa-l-Tanmia, or Party of Justice and Development), the organization changed its name to its present name, Harakat al-Islâh wa-at-Tawhid (Movement for Reform and Unity, MUR). I have, however, for reasons of simplicity, decided to refer to it as the MUR throughout the text.

23. In fact, they were first allowed to participate via integrating another already existing party (the MPDC). Only after the 1997 elections were they allowed to form their own independent party, the present-day Hizb Al-Adala w-Al-Tanmia, or Party of Justice and Development).

24. The name of the organization is often translated as Justice and Charity. However, I refer to it *as Justice and Spirituality,* as this is the translation used and preferred by my Adl wa-l-Ihsan informants.

25. I see the collective activity in support of the UAF petition as indicating a turning point in the history of the liberal women's movement inasmuch as it represented the first major collective endeavor and a new offensive strategy in the public sphere. Other studies date the birth of the Moroccan (liberal) women's movement differently. Fatima Sadiqi and Moha Ennaji, for instance, focus on the publication in 1946 by the Akhawat al-Safaa (Sisters of Purity) association of the Istiqlal party of a number of demands as

"the first 'public' voice of the Moroccan feminist movement," Sadiqi and Ennaji, "Feminization of Public Space." Other authors see the creation in 1983 of the women's magazine *Tamania mars* as decisive; see Salime, *Between Islamism and Feminism,* 54.

26. Benradi, "Genre et droit de la famille," 15.

27. El Ayadi, "La femme dans le débat intellectuel."

28. Benradi, "Genre et droit de la famille," 35–38.

29. Bruce Maddy-Weitzman, "Women, Islam, and the Moroccan State: The Struggle over the Personal Status Law," *Middle East Journal* 59, no. 3 (2005): 393–410.

30. Many informants stressed how the issue had become "desacralized," implying that the Mudawana had become a law that could be both spoken about and changed just like any other law.

31. See Salime, *Between Islamism and Feminism,* for further discussion of these intricate and co-constitutive interrelations between the liberal (or "feminist," in Salime's terminology) and Islamist women's movements.

32. Myriam Catusse and Frédéric Vairel, "'Ni tout à fait le même ni tout à fait un autre': Métamorphoses et continuité du régime marocain," *Maghreb-Machrek* 175 (Spring 2003): 76.

33. Among these four "ministers of sovereignty," one was to play a key role in the Mudawana reform process, namely the minister of religious affairs and Islamic endowments (*habous*), Alaoui M'Daghri, who was known for his conservative interpretations of Islam; see Zeghal, *Islamistes marocains,* 242.

34. Catusse and Vairel, "'Ni tout à fait le même,'" 80.

35. The work to elaborate an Action Plan had already been initiated under the previous government under the then–minister for national solidarity, Zoulikha Nasri, who was later to be appointed the first female royal adviser.

36. Two prominent members of the ADFM, Rabéa Naciri and Amina Lemrini, were employed by Saadi as consultants in their respective professional capacities.

37. Moroccan State Secretariat for Employment, Social Protection, Family, and Children, *Plan d'action national pour l'intégration de la femme au développement* (hereafter *PANIFD*) (Rabat: Moroccan State Secretariat for Employment, Social Protection, Family and Children, 1999), 3–4 (the page numbers refer here and in the following to the electronic copy of the *PANIFD* provided by the Centre Marocain d'Information, de Documentation et d'Études sur la Femme).

38. The plan stressed the necessity of following an Islamic legal tradition capable of taking social changes and demands of democracy into consideration, that is, the critical and innovative Islamic legal tradition based on *ijtihad* and the *maqasid*s. See *PANIFD,* paragraph 50 (p. 39).

39. *PANIFD,* 76.

40. For detailed descriptions of their critique, see El Ayadi, "La femme dans le débat intellectuel," 17–19.

41. The key division between the two networks was the question of whether to involve the political parties. Though the former refused to do so, the latter was open to partisan political participation. Despite this and other points of disagreement, the two networks did collaborate.

42. See http://www.map.co.ma/mapfr/info_fr/sm_discours_parlement.htm.

43. Jean-Pierre Tuquoi, "Au Maroc, les Islamistes gagnent du terrain face aux partisans de la modernité," *Le Monde* (Paris), March 14, 2000.

44. *Makhzen* literally means "treasury." The origin of this connotation stems from precolonial days, when the sultanate was never in full control of the entire country and there were ongoing fights for securing taxes for the treasury between the *bled-al-Makhzen* and the *bled-as-siba* (the dissident tribes). Since independence, the term has been used rather broadly to designate the system of government, the state apparatus, and the intricate network of royal alliances, as well as referring to the principle of authority in Morocco, which is based on allegiances and submission. In the following, I refer to the Makhzan as the clientilist networks of privilege surrounding the Palace. For more details, see Tozy, *Monarchie,* 43.

45. See Buskens, "Recent Debates on Family Law in Morocco," for a discussion of the concept of public sphere in a Moroccan context.

46. Zeghal, *Islamistes marocains,* 11.

47. Sadiqi and Ennaji refer to the increasing "feminization" of the public sphere, but only with respect to the increasing influence of the Moroccan liberal women's movement (which they describe as "feminist"). If one is to describe the Moroccan public sphere as increasingly "feminized," one might also include the important participation of various Islamist women activists, such as Nadia Yassin, thus also highlighting the complexities of the Moroccan women's movement. See Sadiqi and Ennaji, "Feminization of Public Space."

48. None of the women members of the commission had formal affiliations to any women's organization, but Rahma Bourquia and Nouzha Guessous were affiliated with the left-wing PPS and USFP parties, respectively.

49. Organisation du renouveau de la prise de conscience féminine, *Le code de statut personnel: Revendications et propositions,* booklet presented to the royal Mudawana Commission.

50. Catusse and Vairel, "'Ni tout à fait le même,'" 83.

51. He spoke at the opening session of Parliament. Besides the fact that the opening of Parliament is an important day in Morocco, it may also have influenced the timing of the royal speech that French president Jacques Chirac was in the country for a three-day visit, thus ensuring the presence in Morocco of numerous foreign media.

52. For details, see Benradi, "Genre et droit de la famille," 71–77.

53. While the new law thus increases the importance of secular judges in family matters, many of the bastions of Moroccan patriarchy and tradition seem unofficially opposed to the new Mudawana, as evidenced by the considerable barriers to its implementation in the legal system in the form of delays, lack of homogenous rulings, misuse of the possibilities for exception, etc. See Global Rights, http://www.globalrights.org/site/PageServer?pagename=www_mid_index_64; or the yearly reports issued by the LDDF. See also Sadiqi and Ennaji, "Feminization of Public Space," 109.

54. See Valentine Moghadam, "The Gender of Democracy: The Link between Women's Rights and Democratization in the Middle East," *Arab Reform Bulletin* 2, no. 7 (2004): 2–3. See also Nikki R. Keddie, "A Woman's Place: Democratization in the Middle East," *Current History* 103, no. 669 (January 2004): 25.

55. For a general discussion on the relationship between democratization and the promotion of women's rights, see Marina Ottaway, "The Limits of Women's Rights," in *Uncharted Journey,* ed. Carothers and Ottaway, 115–30.

56. This point is underlined by the frequency with which my informants dated the new law to October 2003—i.e., the date of the king's speech—rather than February 2004, when it entered into force.

57. Mohamed Mouaqit, "Genre, développement et égalité: Synthèse," in *Féminin, Masculin,* ed. Mouaqit, 286.

58. According to Abdeslam Maghraoui, this "depolitization" of parliamentary politics is a general phenomenon in the politics of postindependent Morocco; see Abdeslam Maghraoui, "Depolitization in Morocco," *Journal of Democracy* 13, no. 4 (2002): 24–32.

59. For a general discussion of the dynamics of civil society and political parties in Morocco, see James Sater, "The Dynamics of State and Civil Society in Morocco," *Journal of North African Studies* 7, no. 3 (2002): 101–18.

Chapter 11

Family Law Reform in Mali: Contentious Debates and Elusive Outcomes

Benjamin F. Soares

In this chapter, I am concerned with understanding the recent efforts to re-form the laws in the Republic of Mali governing marriage and inheritance, what is usually referred to as the *code de la famille,* that is, the family code. Since the advent of multiparty elections in the *laïc* or secular state of Mali in the early 1990s, prominent members of the Malian government and civil servants, Malian women's rights activists, secular nongovernmental organizations (NGOs), and international and bilateral donors have all made considerable efforts to promote various social reforms, including the advance-

This chapter is dedicated to the memory of Professor Gerti Hesseling. It draws in part on various periods of field research in Mali between 1992 and 2005, as well as brief visits in June 2009 and January 2010. I am grateful to Northwestern University's Melville J. Herskovits Library of Africana Studies for its collection of Malian newspapers and to Margot Badran, Barbara Cooper, Rosa De Jorio, Moussa Djiré, Gerti Hesseling, Roman Loimeier, Brinkley Messick, and Rebecca Shereikis for comments on drafts of the chapter. An earlier version of the chapter was published in *Die Welt des Islams,* volume 49 (2009), and is used here with the permission of Brill.

ment of women's rights and the promotion of gender equality, particularly through changes in the family code.

Despite such efforts, at the time of writing, the proposed reforms had still not been made into law. Though some, including both Malians and Western observers, have attributed the lack of reform of the family code to the increased influence of "Islamists" and/or to religiously conservative Muslims in Mali, here I draw on historical research and some recent ethnography to propose an alternative reading of the lack of institutional law reform in Mali. As I argue, the wide gap between Malian civil law relating to the family and the lived experiences and social practices of many Malians, who are overwhelmingly Muslim, has become even more apparent in this era of political liberalization and promotion of global human rights discourses. This has helped to make such proposed social reforms as the advancement of women's rights and family law reform even more contentious.

The Legal Realm

The Malian state, like the French colonial state that it replaced, is a *laïc* or secular state, which at least in theory means that the state does not intervene in matters of religion. Even though the Malian state, like most other contemporary states, uses largely European-derived codes of law, legal pluralism is an important, though little-studied, feature of the society.[1] This legal pluralism has varied over time, from place to place, and between the country's different ethnic, social, and linguistic groups. Alongside European-derived Malian state law, there is a diversity of normative orders and legal principles, which are operative but often rather difficult for outside observers (and even some Malians) to apprehend, let alone unpack. Throughout the country, there are various methods and means for conflict resolution and management, including so-called traditional institutions, some of which are local and/or regional in scope and influence. Many Malians regularly seek out local leaders such as village heads (*chefs*) and/or religious leaders (Muslim, Christian, "traditional," or "animist") to assist in conflict resolution. Such "traditional" extrajudicial means of managing conflict often play a prominent role for the many Malians who very rarely approach state judicial institutions—and particularly courts.

Malians from nearly all ethnic groups and all religious backgrounds (Muslim, Christian, "animist") also make reference to what is usually called "custom"—here frequently using the vernacular term *laada,* from the Arabic *'adat* (literally, "custom")—in the conduct of their social lives and affairs. Such "custom" is quite often given ethnic qualifiers, such as Bambara, Dogon, or Fulani (or Peul) custom, and is not unrelated to French colonial efforts to codify such "custom" as *coutumiers juridiques* or customary law.[2] In contemporary Malian courts, assessors (*assesseurs*) serve as experts on the "customs" of various ethnic groups, providing in principle such information to assist judges in making legal decisions, particularly in land tenure disputes and questions related to the inheritance of land.[3] Paradoxically, some of what assessors consider and promote as "custom" is actually derived from principles or notions of Islamic jurisprudence (*fiqh*) and may diverge from actual social practice.

In addition to invoking "custom," many Malian Muslims also invoke various principles that they deem Islamic in the conduct of their social lives. In some of Mali's vernacular languages, the term *shari'a* (e.g., *sàriya* in Bambara or *sariya* in Fulfulde, two of Mali's main lingua francas) is often used to refer to law, as well as what is deemed more generally correct practice (however interpreted). Many Malian Muslims also regularly refer to and apply Islamic legal principles, many of which are derived from the Maliki school of *fiqh* that has historically been the predominant school of Islamic jurisprudence in West Africa.

Although many contemporary observers, wittingly or unwittingly adopting the colonial view on law, tend to collapse "custom" and *fiqh,* sometimes even referring to the two indiscriminately as "custom," as Malian state law (see below) and the courts mentioned above do, it is quite clear that the application of principles from *fiqh* has had a very long history in this region.[4] Moreover, the use of *fiqh* has been in no way confined to a limited number of predominantly Muslim urban centers, as some have recently asserted.[5] For centuries, Muslim religious specialists in the broader region have studied some of the standard legal texts of the Maliki school of jurisprudence, including, most notably, the major legal compendium, the *Mukhtasar* of Khalil b. Ishaq (d. fourteenth century), and also Ibn Abi Zayd al-Qayrawani's tenth-century conspectus, *al-Risala.*[6] Such knowledge of Islamic jurisprudence and the Maliki school in particular was long the preserve of Muslim scholarly elites and those to whom they transmitted such basic Islamic knowledge. In addition to the rules of worship (Arabic, *'ibadat*) as elaborated in such texts of jurisprudence, it is particularly in those areas directly related to the family—such as marriage, divorce, and inheritance—that many Muslims in Mali have ordinarily interpreted and applied and often continue to apply Islamic legal principles in their social lives. In

certain places in the country, some Muslim religious leaders continue to ap-
point experts in Islamic jurisprudence, locally called *qadis*, to whom they
turn for counsel and advice. Ordinary Malian Muslims regularly consult
such persons knowledgeable about Islam (and Islamic jurisprudence) to ensure that their actions and practices are in accordance with Islamic principles. Many Malians who invoke *fiqh* do so sometimes rather self-consciously
but often without much reflection, given how Islamic legal principles inform many groups' social practices and daily lives, as well as their culture,
in the anthropological sense.[7]

There is historical and ethnological evidence to suggest that even some
historically non-Muslim groups in the region have long employed legal
principles in such matters as marriage and inheritance that resemble those
of their Muslim neighbors.[8] However, since the colonial period, many non-
Muslims in Mali have embraced Islam.[9] Along with the spread of knowledge about Islam and Islamic religious practices, there has been a con-
comitant spread of knowledge and use of *fiqh* among many Malians in the
twentieth century. Though one can see the wider use of principles of *fiqh* in
many areas of social life, it is particularly apparent in the areas of marriage
and inheritance among the significant number of people who have converted to Islam in recent decades.

However, one should not understand the increased reliance and application of Islamic legal principles as a simple, straightforward process of Muslims merely setting out to apply immutable Islamic principles or as an inevitable process of unilinear Islamization. Barbara Cooper has quite
convincingly argued that in neighboring Niger, "the preference for codified
law among French [colonial] administrators tended to shift the legal discourse of the region not towards the Napoleonic code but rather towards the
Maliki law [*fiqh*] already available as a resource."[10] Early in the twentieth
century, such processes were under way during colonial rule in what is
present-day Mali.[11] As more people became Muslims, reliance on certain
basic principles of *fiqh* intensified. Rather than assuming such a shift to be
evidence of the inevitable telos of the development of Islam in Africa,[12] one
should understood it within the larger context of the major socioeconomic
transformations that have led to an expansion of a new sphere of activities
in colonial and postcolonial Mali.[13] It was within such a new sphere that
Muslims adopted more standardized ways of being Muslim, including ritual daily prayer and regular fasting during the month of Ramadan.[14]

At the same time, such standardized ways of being Muslim also included
some of the many rules and principles of Islamic jurisprudence, which

people were beginning to learn and to apply in their own lives and those of their kin. In some cases, certain Muslim scholars and preachers actively sought to encourage people, including recent converts to Islam, to give up a whole range of practices that they deemed un-Islamic. These included various practices related to marriage, divorce, and widowhood, which converts to Islam were encouraged to renounce in order to conform more closely to "correct" Islamic principles usually derived from *fiqh*—what was often called *shari'a* in the vernacular.

In recent decades, the basic knowledge of Maliki jurisprudence that was once the preserve of Muslim scholarly elites has become much more widespread in Mali through a number of new channels. The modern Islamic educational institutions, madrasas (private schools for fee-paying students that provide an Islamic education alongside secular subjects), which have flourished in urban Mali, have been an important means for the transmission of knowledge of Islamic jurisprudence.[15] Indeed, all madrasas include at least some basic Islamic jurisprudence, almost always from the Maliki school, in the curriculum.[16] In addition, various Muslim activists and preachers have also sought to diffuse such knowledge to ordinary Malian Muslims, for example, via the mass media and particularly through some of the new Islamic programming that has become popular on the many private radio stations, including Islamic radio stations, which have opened since media liberalization in the 1990s.

Despite very low levels of literacy in Mali, the print media have also been important in the transmission of knowledge of Islamic jurisprudence in the country. Inexpensive editions of the standard legal texts of the Maliki school in the original Arabic and sometimes in French (Mali's official language, and the language of instruction in state schools) are readily available in Islamic bookshops and are used in teaching, for self-study, and as reference books for preachers who give public sermons.[17] In addition, there are also very basic texts of Islamic jurisprudence in French translation available in the form of inexpensive pamphlets that are very popular with the growing French-language reading public, which has been increasingly interested in learning more about Islam and its "correct" practice. In a recent development, print media about Islam in Bambara, Mali's most important lingua franca, have become more widely available. For example, the relatively young modernist Malian imam, Modibo Jara [or Diarra] (b. 1957), who has undertaken the task of translating many basic Islamic texts from Arabic into Bambara, has also translated a simplified version of al-Akhdari's short basic primer of law relating to Muslim worship (*'ibadat*) from the sixteenth century into Bambara, as well as Ibn Abi Zayd's much more voluminous *al-Risala*.[18] Such Islamic books in the vernacular are also available for sale in the country's Islamic bookshops, and the short and inexpensive texts are quite popular with the expanding Bambara-language reading public.[19]

Given the legally pluralistic nature of Malian society today, many Malians regularly apply rules and principles from "custom" and/or Islamic jurisprudence that not infrequently conflict with postcolonial Malian legislation.[20] Such legal discrepancies are readily apparent in the area of land tenure,[21] as well as in family law. In the case of marriage, many couples in Mali who marry—and an overwhelming majority in rural areas—never register their marriages ("religious ceremonies" in the language of Malian civil law) with the state. In other words, their marital unions are not recognized as civil marriages. For some Malians (both Muslims and non-Muslims), not having a civil marriage has long been and remains a form of resistance to the state and its institutions. Moreover, many Malians live far from the government offices where they are supposed to register their civil marriages.

However, many Malians do in fact officially register their marriages. As Rosa De Jorio has convincingly argued, "the motivation behind the choice of a civil marriage is to some extent pragmatic—it is a contract that facilitates the resolution of legal issues (e.g., facilitating a woman's access to her husband's pension and custody issues) and is related to people's specific entanglements with state institutions."[22] In fact, the vast majority of Malians who do have civil marriages are urban dwellers and include those who depend on the state for their salaries, such as civil servants, as well as other salaried employees, who require proof of civil marriage for such social benefits as family allowances (*allocations familiales*), as well as to ensure dependents' rights to pensions, insurance claims, and so forth. Much inheritance of property (both fixed and movable) in Mali is handled according to rules of Islamic jurisprudence, "customary" law, or some combination of these, and such inheritance transactions frequently occur without any recourse to state courts.[23]

As noted, in the past few decades, Malian society has become increasingly Islamized. One consequence of this increased Islamization has been that Islamic legal principles derived from *fiqh* have become part of lived practice for many Malians, as well as a point of reference with great symbolic import. In this way, Islamic legal principles, however interpreted and applied, have a palpable presence in the society. But in the postcolonial secular Malian state, Islamic jurisprudence is clearly not on an equal footing with Malian law. Indeed, some Malian jurists even seem to treat Islamic jurisprudence—which many Malian Muslim scholars continue to study, teach, and apply—with disdain.

Gender and the Law

The idea that men and women are equal is a principle that has been firmly grounded in postcolonial Malian law since shortly after independence. In fact, successive Malian governments have reaffirmed this principle, for example, in the 1960 and 1974 constitutions and, more recently, in the era of political liberalization and multiparty democracy since the early 1990s. Although the equality of men and women is explicitly stated in Mali's 1992 Constitution,[24] existing Malian state laws relating to marriage do not always treat men and women as equals. It is striking (but generally unremarked upon) how some of these existing Malian laws are very close—sometimes nearly identical—to some of the rules of Islamic jurisprudence, particularly those of the Maliki school long applied here, as the following examples suggest.[25]

In the 1962 *Code du mariage et de la tutelle* (hereafter the 1962 code), which remains in effect today, article 34 stipulates that the husband is considered the head of the family (*chef de famille*). He is responsible for household expenses (*les charges du ménage*) and chooses the place of residence where his wife is "obligated" to live.[26] This is all in accordance with the standard texts of Maliki jurisprudence used in Mali, as is the requirement that two witnesses be present for a marriage to be legally valid (article 21). In a major departure from Islamic jurisprudence, permission from a guardian (*wali* in Arabic) is not required for a woman to marry. Interestingly, the 1962 code cites bridewealth (*la dot*) and marriage gifts (*les présents en vue du mariage*) that might be required "by custom" (*lorsqu'ils sont exigés par la coutume*) (article 3), which implies that "custom" also encompasses *fiqh;* in Islamic jurisprudence, bridewealth (Arabic, *sadaq* or *mahr*) is actually required for a marriage to be valid. In Mali, the particularities of bridewealth and the gifts exchanged before marriage are indeed subject to "custom," as well as to local and regional conventions that have changed considerably even in the past few decades.[27] In contrast to Maliki jurisprudence but in keeping with historical and contemporary marriage practice in Mali, the 1962 code states that the bridewealth and presents for a young girl (*jeune fille*) are double those for an adult woman (*femme*) (article 3), who may presumably be divorced or widowed.[28] In contrast to Maliki jurisprudence, where only a minimum is set for bridewealth, the 1962 code—most likely

reflecting the first postindependence government's socialist proclivities—
set maximum total amounts for bridewealth and presents together, which
have long been ignored and flouted.

Despite Malian women's associations' proposals to abolish polygyny in
the late colonial period,[29] the 1962 *Code du mariage et de la tutelle* allows
for civil marriages to be either monogamous or polygynous (and to be determined as such by the marriage partners at the time of marriage).[30] In accordance with Islamic jurisprudence, the 1962 code indicates that a Malian
woman may only be married to one person at a time, while a husband may
legally have up to four wives. However, unlike the Qur'anic injunction that
the husband should treat his wives equally (see Q 4:3), there is no such
stipulation in the 1962 code. But the 1962 code (article 58) did outlaw the
husband's ability to repudiate his wife—*talaq* in Islamic jurisprudence—
at the time a major achievement of Malian women's rights activists.[31] A
divorce can only be granted if one of the spouses is wronged (e.g., through
adultery, abuse, or neglect), and the guilty party (husband or wife) is required, as needed and if possible, to pay alimony (*pension alimentaire*)
(article 82).[32] The 1962 code indicates that a divorced woman must wait
three months before remarrying (article 80), and a widowed woman must
wait four months and ten days (article 101). Here, the authors of the Malian
law code have simply applied the concept of *'idda* from Islamic jurisprudence. This is the period of time that a woman (divorced or widowed)
must wait before remarrying in order to determine, first, whether she is
pregnant and then paternity and the rights of the child to maintenance
(*nafaqa*) and eventually inheritance.[33] In accordance with the general
rules of Islamic jurisprudence, male children inherit twice the amount al-
lotted to female children. However, in a departure from general *fiqh* principles, where the father and his patriline retain rights over any children, a
widow has custody over her children (article 103).[34] In addition, if the
woman is the wronged party in a divorce, she also retains custody of the
children (article 86).

Although the 1962 code outlawed forced marriage (article 2), many
Malian commentators have pointed to some other problematical sections of
this code that clearly discriminate against women.[35] Although this code
states that "spouses owe each other mutual respect, fidelity, help, and aid"
(*les époux se doivent mutuellement respect, fidélité, secours et assistance*)
(article 32), the preceding sentence in the same article of the law unambiguously states that a woman "owes . . . obedience to her spouse" (*doit . . .*

obéissance à son époux), who in turn owes her "protection" (article 32). In addition, the 1962 code set the minimum age for marriage at fifteen years for women and eighteen for men.

Given the extent to which some of these existing Malian laws discriminate against women, it is not surprising that many Malians, and not only women's rights activists, have advocated law reform. In fact, since the early 1990s, there have been some important changes to Malian law affecting women. For many years, Malian women complained that article 38 of the 1962 code stipulated that a woman could not engage in her own commercial activities without her husband's permission. This article of the code directly contravened many Malian women's socially accepted prerogative to have an independent income, which many earn via their own trading activities. However, in 1992, a new commercial law code (Law 92-002, August 27, 1992) abrogated such restrictions on women's independent commercial activities.[36] Similarly, in Malian law, salaried women—whether married or single—have historically been taxed at a higher rate than salaried men. The reasoning seemed to be that because men (unlike women) were assumed to have dependents (wives and children), their rate of taxation should be lower. However, in 1992, the state adjusted the tax rules to alleviate the extra fiscal burden on salaried women,[37] many of whom indeed have their own dependents. These specific changes to commercial and tax law proved to be rather uncontroversial, and they were made soon after Alpha Oumar Konaré began his first term as the country's first democratically elected president. Before considering actual attempts to reform the family law, which has been much more controversial, it is instructive to consider the broader social context within which Malian women find themselves.

The Social Context

Many Malian women's life experiences are a stark reminder of some of the difficulties—and inequalities—they often face.[38] Here, I briefly consider some of these difficulties, which relate directly to those areas of the proposed reforms to the family law. Although the following examples suggest that the reform of family law would seem to be imperative for advancing Malian women's rights, a major complicating factor is, as noted above, that the majority of Malians' marriages are not registered and therefore are not legally recognized.

First, there are the manifold problems associated with arranged marriages. Though the 1962 code states that marriage must be by mutual consent, there continue to be many marriages of underage girls and sometimes against the wishes of one or both marriage partners. Such arranged marriages are often a real problem in contemporary Mali. I do not say this because arranged marriages are so jarring to Western middle-class sensibilities, as recent debates in Europe over Muslim immigrants and their marriage partners clearly suggest.[39] Rather, I do so because many Malians, men and women alike, regularly point to marriages in which one or both parties did not consent. In fact, I know many Malians whose parents or elders arranged for them to marry a partner whom they did not like, sometimes did not know, and may have never even seen before the day of the wedding. Such arranged or forced marriages happen especially, though not exclusively, in rural areas. Contrary to what Western middle-class observers might expect, these arranged marriages are sometimes quite stable and durable. To understand this, it is important to note that Malians generally think of marriage as the bringing together of kin groups, rather than simply an affair of individuals.[40] Some arranged marriages in Mali are between members of kin groups who might be cousins (or more distantly related kin), as is the case among other groups of Muslims elsewhere in the world. Though such factors may contribute to the stability and durability of a particular marriage, they can also become obstacles to the dissolution of an unhappy marriage.

Indeed, I know of several couples who have been quite simply miserable and have attempted to end their marriages. But ending a marriage one's elders has arranged is often difficult, not least when married couples live in the same household as the husband's parents, as they frequently do in Mali. However unhappy a married couple or one of the marriage partners might be, many Malians are reluctant to allow a marriage to end because this might adversely affect the relationship between the two kin groups united through it. In one particularly poignant case, a mother-in-law told her daughter-in-law who wanted a divorce that she should accept that there would never be a divorce in their family. She emphasized that her daughter-in-law would die in the marriage her kin (including her own mother-in-law) had arranged for her when she was in her early teens.

Although the 1962 code also outlawed the husband's ability to repudiate his wife, this kind of divorce is still widespread in Mali. In practice, such a repudiation can take different forms (whether irrevocable or not), and many Malian Muslim scholars readily point to the texts of Islamic jurisprudence where the rules for *talaq* are listed. Many Malian women, whose marriages are unhappy or unstable, fear that they might be repudiated at any moment. In the early 1990s, a Muslim woman, the poor and illiterate daughter of a village imam, asked me to write a letter in French to her husband to ask him whether he had actually repudiated her. The woman was particularly eager to know the status of her marriage. If she had been repudiated (as she suspected and seemed to hope), she also sought written proof of the repudiation. Such proof—forthcoming only at the whim of her husband—would allow her to marry another man. The woman was all too aware that to enter into a new marriage without tangible proof of divorce was potentially quite risky for her, for religious, legal, and social reasons.

Mali has long had rather high rates of internal and external migration, which have placed particular strains on marriage.[41] In many cases, the migrant's wife and children remain behind with his family while the migrant goes off in search of work. Women whose husbands may be absent for several years often worry about their future. But such women very rarely ask for or initiate a divorce, even though Maliki jurisprudence, and even some "customs," give women the right to a divorce if abandoned. A popular Muslim preacher on the radio in Bamako recently advised women to wait at least four years (and possibly as long as ten years) before seeking divorce from an absent husband.[42] In any case, Malian women are especially reluctant to ask for a divorce when they have children. This is because the husband and his kin generally have custody rights after the children reach a certain age of maturity. In addition, a woman who may be waiting for a husband to return after being away two or three years, and perhaps even longer, usually cannot object if her husband married another wife while he was away. One of Mali's most prominent Muslim clerics once told me that migrants' wives left in the village are only human and sometimes have sexual relations with other men. For him, this was a compelling reason to make divorce more easily attainable for women, though he readily noted that there was considerable resistance to such an idea.

Although women's sexual needs are recognized in Islamic jurisprudence, the situation is considerably less straightforward in practice. A Malian woman I know whose husband was away for many years became pregnant by another man. No one publicly discussed the woman's extramarital affair or pregnancy until she died from complications of a clandestine abortion, which is illegal in Mali. After her death, many people expressed sympathy for the woman and seemed to blame her husband for what had happened. As I have heard Malians point out, when a long-absent husband returns to his wife, she cannot refuse him sexual relations, even if she fears contracting a sexually transmitted disease. There are many cases of Malian migrants who, after having lived for periods elsewhere in Africa, returned and, possibly unknowingly, infected their wives with HIV/AIDS before dying.

It would be a mistake to assume that it is only poor and uneducated Malian women who face such problems. A well-known Muslim cleric and Sufi *shaykh* I know married the highly educated daughter of one of his followers, a prominent, senior civil servant and community political leader in Bamako, the Malian capital. Although the woman had initially refused to marry someone she considered an undesirable marriage partner—an old man and a Muslim cleric to boot—she eventually agreed to the alliance, which her father had eagerly sought. Upon marriage, the woman became the Muslim cleric's fourth wife. But not long after their wedding, the woman and her husband disagreed over domestic arrangements. When she refused to live in the Muslim cleric's small village (where his other three wives and many children lived), he simply divorced her and proceeded to marry the much younger woman who had worked as a servant in their household. Everyone said the Muslim cleric's act of making the poor and uneducated servant his new replacement wife was his way of "punishing" his disobedient fourth wife. The divorced woman had no recourse whatsoever, and she returned to live in her paternal kin's household. The incident caused considerable consternation and embarrassment to her father and some of his kin, who blamed the woman for the failure of the marriage.

Although anthropologists have long pointed to the many tensions within polygynous households,[43] the nature of existing family law is such that tensions can frequently turn into outright conflict. Many men who entered a civil marriage with their first wife under the 1962 code often obtain only a "religious marriage" for their subsequent marriage(s).[44] In some cases, the husband does not even inform his first wife that he has married another woman or women. As many Malians report, it is a common occurrence that upon the husband's death, the wife with whom he contracted a civil marriage and their children can use legal means to expel the other wife or wives and children from the family home they may share. The woman recognized by law as the man's wife and her children can also make claims to inheritance, to the detriment of the other members of the polygynous family. Thus, civil law can trump Islamic jurisprudence. Current Malian law also offers little protection to those wives who have not contracted civil marriages. In fact, the law does not recognize these women as wives but rather sees them as concubines or mistresses. In addition, if a husband refuses to support the children from such a "religious marriage," it is difficult for the mother of the children to appeal to the state for intervention.[45]

Although space limitations prevent me from addressing in detail the many other difficulties Malian women face,[46] Malian law, as noted above, states that a wife is supposed to be obedient to her husband. Many Malians assert that this is part of their "customs" and/or "traditions." Many also state that a wife's obedience to her husband is "Islamic," and some even insist that this principle is enshrined in the Qur'an.[47] As one might imagine, this issue has caused considerable contention in Mali; one of the more frequently cited problems is the insistence of many a husband that his permission is required for his wife to work outside the home or to attend public meetings or gatherings.

The Proposed Reforms

Since the political liberalization of the early 1990s, there has been an impetus for various social reforms in Mali, coming both from within the country and from the so-called international community. An important centerpiece of such reforms has been the advancement of women's rights and promotion of gender equality. Some of Mali's major donors, multilateral institutions, and various NGOs operating in the country—particularly those affiliated with the Malian NGO umbrella group, Coordination des Associations et ONG Féminines (Coordinating Group for Women's Associations and NGOs)—have promoted such social reforms, which they have sometimes linked directly to the major political and economic reforms and liberalization in the country. The specific efforts to improve women's status and to reform the family code in Mali have also been part of a much larger project of legal reform that important bilateral donors to Mali such as Canada and the Netherlands have supported and funded.

Beginning shortly after Mali's first multiparty elections in 1993, the government of President Alpha Oumar Konaré pursued an ambitious reform agenda, and, as noted above, succeeded in changing at least some laws adversely affecting women. The president's wife, Adam Konaré Ba, a prominent historian and outspoken advocate of women's rights, actively promoted women's rights and regularly intervened in public discussions about the need for reform during her husband's two five-year terms as president. In 1993, Konaré Ba published a detailed and lengthy biographical dictionary of prominent Malian women in which she identified and outlined some of the major impediments, including legal impediments, to gender equality in Mali.[48]

By the time of the United Nations' Fourth World Conference on Women, in Beijing in 1995, the Malian government seemed particularly committed to the reform of family law. Some women's rights activists, however, have criticized the government for not acting quickly enough to promote women's rights. After the Beijing conference, which the Malian government had supported and endorsed, the government demonstrated its considerable commitment to the promotion of women's rights, not least at the institutional level.[49] In 1997, the Malian government turned the Commissariat à la Promotion Féminine (Commissariat for the Promotion of Women) into a new ministry, the Ministry for the Promotion of Women, Children, and the Family. In 1999, the government also created a special division of this ministry, the Direction Nationale de la Promotion de la Femme (National Office for the Promotion of Women), which sought to advance women's rights. From the beginning, the reform of the family code was an important, indeed central, part of efforts to promote women's rights and gender equality.

Efforts to draft new legislation related to family law in line with the UN's Beijing Conference Platform for Action and the recommendations from the subsequent special session of the UN General Assembly in 2000, which the Malian government had also supported and endorsed, took several years.[50] The reform process included public meetings throughout the country, the so-called *concertations régionales* (regional consultations), that were designed to inform the public about the government's intentions and, ostensibly, seek the public's input.[51] The Malian government also worked closely with various NGOs and international donors on public educational campaigns about women's rights, which included the use of the expanding private radio sector, as well as national television. During this time, many Malian women's rights activists were intervening in public debates about women's rights, and prominent members of NGOs promoting women's rights—often in concert with the Ministry for the Promotion of Women, Children, and the Family—used the new private radio stations as well as their access to journalists at the many new newspapers to promote their agenda of reform of the family code.[52] Throughout, there was much public discussion about the particulars of the proposed legislation and sometimes quite heated debate.

In line with international legal conventions to which Mali was a signatory, the specific proposed reforms to the family code sought to make women and men equal in marriage and inheritance. Some of the most important features of the proposed legislation included raising the minimum legal age for girls to marry to eighteen (i.e., to be the same as the minimum legal age for men), eliminating the so-called obedience clause, and making men and women equal in matters of inheritance. Though the process of passing the reforms was ostensibly designed as a participatory democratic exercise, it is clear that key members of the Ministry for the Promotion of Women, Children, and the Family saw it as an almost inevitable process about which Malians needed to be educated. In remarks about the long process of getting the reforms implemented, the minister, Mme Diarra Afoussatou Thiéro, characterized it as a necessary "social pedagogical exercise" for Malian citizens, whom many Malian civil servants seemed to assume would be pliant and docile.[53]

In 2002, late in his second (and final) five-year term, President Konaré formally presented the legal texts to reform the family code (as well as separate legal texts to outlaw the practice of excision, or female genital mutilation) to the National Assembly. Some believed that as the outgoing president, Konaré wanted these reforms to be part of his legacy as a respected statesman. Cynical observers noted that it was one of his last attempts to impress the international community, and the West in particular, while he looked for his next job, which would eventually be chairman of the Commission of the African Union. Faced with considerable public criticism of the proposed reforms, Konaré's government withdrew the draft legislation only a few weeks after having introduced it to the National Assembly for consideration. In doing so, Konaré seemed to have effectively abandoned the reform efforts, at least during his tenure as president. Amadou Toumani Touré, Konaré's successor, who was elected in 2002 (and reelected for a second term in 2007), and key members of his government have expressed commitment to the reform of the family code very much along the same lines that Konaré and his government had proposed. However, since President Touré was elected in 2002, there seem to have been almost no serious efforts to reform the law, that is, until well into his second term.[54]

After President Konaré hastily withdrew the draft legislation in 2002, proponents of the family law reform package immediately (and somewhat too conveniently) blamed "Islamists" for its failure.[55] Indeed, some characterized its failure as another "victory of the Islamists" over Konaré and his ambitious reform agenda.[56] It is, however, disingenuous to label all opponents of the reform package as Islamists or even as simply conservatives. In its attempt to reform family law, the Malian government seems to have seriously misjudged the widespread and popular opposition of ordinary Malian Muslims.

In his capacity as the president of the Ligue malienne des imams et érudits pour la solidarité islamique (LIMAMA; Malian League of Imams and Scholars for Islamic Solidarity), an organization of imams and Muslim preachers, Balla Kallé addressed an open letter to President Konaré in which he objected to the proposed changes, stating that they clearly and unambiguously violated Islamic precepts. Before his death in 2009, Kallé was one of the country's most prominent Muslim religious leaders. A member of a celebrated lineage of Muslim religious specialists, he was imam of the main Friday mosque in central Bamako. Coming from such an eminent religious personality, Kallé's sharp rebuke of President Konaré had maximum effect. In a general statement in his letter, Kallé wrote:

> The imams and [Muslim] scholars of Mali, who are the natural leaders of the Muslim community, reject the text in question [the proposed reforms to the family code], until it is revised. . . . It is useful to recall that the preoccupation of the Muslim community continues to be and remains the strict respect of the precepts of the Holy Qur'an and the traditions of the Prophet Muhammad [the *Sunna*] (peace be upon him). It is not possible for a Muslim to support a text that violates these precepts.[57]

After several Islamic associations in Bamako called for demonstrations against the president and the proposed law reform, the government held a series of meetings with members of the Haut conseil islamique (High Islamic Council), the new organization that the Malian government hoped would serve as the main interlocutor with the country's Muslims. Upon learning of the deep dissatisfaction with the proposed reforms and facing the possibility of large demonstrations, Konaré's government withdrew the proposed reforms from consideration.

However, Imam Balla Kallé was only among the most well known of the many Muslim religious leaders who objected to the proposed reforms. Some of the major proposed changes to the family law included the elimination of the obedience clause, the rescinding of the husband's prerogative to choose the married couple's place of residence, and inheritance matters, all of which were said to contravene Islamic law.[58] Much of the vocal opposition to the reforms came from male Muslims, who have become more visible and audible in the broader public sphere over the last decade. Some of the public critics of the proposed reforms had rather predictable objections. In some cases, it is not an exaggeration to say that opposition was quite simply reactionary. Here I am thinking of one Muslim intellectual's pamphlet on "gender," written in response to the public debate about reform. The author, Yacoub Doucouré, the well-known founder and director of a modern Islamic lycée (high school) in the regional capital of Sikasso, tells us that Islam liberated "pagan" women, giving them all the rights they need.[59] In his pamphlet, he actually argues for limiting Muslim women's rights even further and restricting their activities outside the home in ways that are reminiscent of conservative Muslim countries such as Saudi Arabia. It is worth emphasizing, however, that these are very much minority views in Mali (see below).

Some of the other public critics of the family law reforms suggested that the government's proposed changes were merely a continuation of its pursuit of Western-inspired social agendas that were not compatible with Islam or most Malians' Muslim identity. Employing what has become standard anti-Western rhetoric, one of the more eloquent of these critics was Mahmoud Dicko, the current president of the Haut conseil islamique, who condemned the proposed reforms as simply another instance of the "sociocultural mimicry [*mimétisme socioculturel*] that drains the reference points for our [Muslim] identity."[60] Such views are similar to recent critiques of globalization in the Arab world, Indonesia, and elsewhere.[61]

Although some of the public critics of the proposed reforms might be characterized as Islamists, most, including Imam Balla Kallé, were decidedly not. It is also entirely too facile to dismiss ordinary critics of the planned legislation as simply conservative and reactionary. In fact, the picture is rather more complicated. Restricting Muslim women's rights even further is not endorsed by many Muslim clerics in Mali and certainly not by the most influential in the country. In fact, I have heard prominent Malian Muslim clerics say that it is absurd to think that Malian women's public activities could be as restricted as they are elsewhere in the Muslim world. I would even go so far as to argue that there is an emerging consensus in Mali about advancing women's rights, which public educational campaigns and public debates have certainly helped to promote. Many Malians today would agree that forced marriage should not be permitted, which is not to say that it does not persist in many places in the country, particularly in rural areas. Many would also agree that teenage girls should not be forced to leave school to marry. Moreover, many recognize that women need to have more rights within marriage. As I have noted, some Muslim clerics have recently been involved in new efforts to educate the public about women's rights to divorce. The Muslim cleric mentioned above who was concerned about abandoned wives began to give sermons recommending that if a woman's husband is absent for more than six months, she should be allowed to divorce and remarry as she sees fit.

For many Malians, one of the most serious problems with the proposed reforms was that religious marriage would still not be legally recognized.[62] In the existing 1962 family code, marriage is actually defined as "secular" (*laïc*) (article 1), and the proposed reforms would not have changed this. The fact that existing law does not recognize the validity of "religious ceremonies" that may precede civil marriage (article 6 of the 1962 code) has been a source of considerable controversy in Mali. The 1962 code even goes so far as to state that any religious official (*ministre d'un culte*) who conducts "religious ceremonies" preceding a civil marriage will be subject to a fine (article 6).[63] Though Muslims in Mali are often divided in their opinions over many different religious (not to mention political) issues, they have been united over the question of so-called religious marriage. It is highly significant that Muslims who might disagree vehemently over such issues as correct religious practice, theology, or leadership of the Muslim community have been nearly unanimous in the demand that religious marriages be legally recognized. The idea that a marriage conducted according to the rules of Islamic jurisprudence can be deemed illegitimate is deeply offensive to many Malians. As noted above, most marriages in the country are religious marriages that have not been registered with the state. In the public discussions and debates about the reform of family law, the question of legal recognition of religious marriage was to become a major point of contention.

The issue was by no means new. In the early 1990s, during the first session of the newly democratically elected National Assembly, the opposition party leader Mountaga Tall of the Congrès National d'Initiative Démocratique (National Congress for Democratic Initiative) tried without success to have the assembly pass a law officially recognizing so-called religious marriage.[64] At the time, many ordinary Malian Muslims supported his initiative. However, as a member of the opposition in the assembly, Tall stood no chance of passing his proposed legislation. Moreover, prominent Malian women's rights activists argued that legally recognizing religious marriage would necessarily restrict women's rights, and secular critics accused Tall, a descendant of the nineteenth-century Muslim conqueror and ruler of the region, of courting "Islamists" in the country. However, during subsequent public debates about family law reform, Malians repeatedly raised the issue of the legal status of religious marriage and pointed to Tall's initial proposal.

The Response of Muslim Activists

One of the most interesting subsequent developments was how Islamic associations, including women's Islamic associations, and individual Muslim activists who sometimes disagree on many religious and political issues became united in their call for the official recognition of religious marriages. After the government withdrew its proposed legislative changes to the family code in 2002, various leaders of Malian Islamic associations eventually tried to devise a system of official "Muslim marriage" certificates. It seems that Muslim activists from some of the leading Islamic associations wanted to try to force the Malian government to recognize the marriages of most Muslims in the country. This new activism on the part of Muslims qua Muslims followed from the political liberalization of the 1990s and the expansion of the public sphere.[65] Indeed, Muslims intervening in the public debate sometimes made considerable effort to advance political and social agendas at odds with those of the secular state. Many of these Muslim activists, like their secular counterparts, frequently talked about their rights as Malian citizens and sometimes even invoked what they called their "Islamic citizenship" (*citoyenneté islamique*), however vague such a formulation might be.[66]

Although some of these new Muslim activists were women, including members of the Union nationale des femmes musulmanes (UNAFEM; National Union of Muslim Women), it is striking that the vast majority who joined the public debate were (and are) men. Some Muslim women activists participated in the drafting of documents related to the proposed changes to the family code.[67] However, similar to what Annelies Moors has found in the debates over family law in Palestine,[68] Muslim women activists were largely silent in the Malian debates. But the presence and the "politics of presence" of such Muslim women activists in the public sphere were highly significant.[69] When Muslim women activists appeared at some public gatherings, they were often dressed in plain, loose-fitting monochromatic robes—that is, clothing far removed from the dominant aesthetic styles for most women in urban Mali. Even more striking, some of these women wore the face veil, which is worn only very rarely by women in Mali.[70] Their dress (and silence) seemed to index them as the exact opposites of the secular women's rights activists who have been so prominent (and vocal) in recent public debates in Mali.

Various leaders of the country's new Islamic associations took the initiative and tried to mobilize leading Muslim religious leaders and organizations in support of legalizing what they called the "Islamic marriage certificate" (*acte de mariage islamique*), which they set about drafting. In support of such marriage certificates, proponents pointed to the long history of Islam in Mali and the fact that some Muslims had regularly used such written religious marriage contracts in the past, particularly in the country's historic centers of Islamic learning. Indeed, as one prominent imam noted, there are many such marriage contracts in the Arabic manuscript collection of the Ahmed Baba Center in Timbuktu.[71] Some Muslim activists, including certain individuals who had studied in North Africa, made reference to the institution of "professional witnesses" (Arabic, *'udul*)—that is, those government-appointed persons required in order for a marriage to be considered valid—in Morocco and other places in North Africa. They seemed to be demanding the same sort of legal recognition from the secular Malian state. Their efforts to have religious marriage officially recognized, which received extensive media coverage, had considerable popular support.[72]

Although LIMAMA, the organization of imams and preachers, was the Islamic association that took the main initiative, many Muslim religious leaders affiliated with different and rival organizations readily endorsed LIMAMA's proposal for state recognition of "Muslim marriage." In 2004, following various meetings of members of Islamic associations in Bamako, LIMAMA invited Malians to a public meeting at the main Friday mosque in central Bamako, where they unveiled their new Islamic marriage certificate. Some of Bamako's most prominent Muslim leaders and heads of Islamic associations attended—including the government-sponsored national Islamic organization founded in the 1980s, the Association malienne pour l'unité et le progrès de l'Islam (AMUPI; Malian Association for the Unity and Progress of Islam); the newer Haut conseil islamique, which includes representatives from the country's most important Islamic associations; and members of UNAFEM. At the meeting, speakers asked imams to complete the new Muslim marriage "certificates" (written in both French and Arabic) at their mosques when couples were married.

In addition to LIMAMA, at least three of the country's most active Islamic associations, AMUPI, and the Muslim reformist association, the Association Islamique pour le salut (Islamic Salvation Association, known as AISLAM), devised their own marriage certificates. Almost immediately, imams in mosques in Bamako began issuing such marriage certificates and officially recording marriages, which many had never done in the past. The language of these marriage certificates indicates that their authors are attempting to make these new marriage contracts conform to classical Islamic marriage contracts, while also incorporating some new language that signals the importance of women's rights as well as more modernist conceptions of conjugal life. If one considers the marriage certificate AMUPI prepared, this is particularly clear:

> At the mosque of MaliMag [the oldest and most important reformist mosque in central Bamako], the marriage between . . . has been celebrated following the prescriptions of Islamic law [*loi islamique*]. In exchange for bridewealth [*une dot*] paid to the woman, the amount of which had been set by mutual agreement. The representative of the husband asked for the young girl [*sic;* presumably never married] in marriage; and the representative of the young girl accepted and, in accordance with the powers that her matrimonial guardian [*tuteur matrimonial*] has on her coming from God Most High, [he] gave the young girl in marriage and delivered her into the hands of the husband for good treatment [*bon traitement*].[73]

In addition to the husband's "good" or "proper" treatment of his wife (though its particulars are left unspecified), the AMUPI contract stipulates that the marrying couple listen attentively to advice from the imam about how to make their marriage last.[74]

If, at first, it seemed that the Malian government might permit these marriage certificates to be used, their legality was almost immediately called into question.[75] Not long after imams began delivering the new marriage certificates, representatives of the Malian government stated that they were not legally valid. The minister for territorial administration, who is also in charge of "religious affairs," eventually told the Haut conseil islamique to ask the Islamic associations to stop issuing the new religious marriage certificates. The government then sent a letter to the Islamic associations requesting that they stop issuing the marriage certificates, noting that it first wanted to work to revise the proposed family law texts and bring them to a vote in the National Assembly. The Islamic associations complied with the government's request. Although there seemed to be more support for the principle of official recognition of religious marriages, possibly even from the government, some leaders of Islamic associations complained that the government did not seem genuinely committed to legalizing religious marriages.[76] In the meantime, the Malian state still does not confer legitimacy on the vast majority of Malians' marriages that are not civil marriages. At the same time, the state seems unwilling to cede any legal power to Muslim clerics within the realm of family law.

Conclusion

Although it would be unwise to try to predict the ultimate outcome of the attempt to reform family law in Mali, it is clear that many Malians would welcome some degree of reform. In fact, many ordinary Malian Muslims, including some Muslim clerics who were vocal opponents of the government's proposed changes in 2002, regularly cite the need for change in some areas of family law in ways not unlike the government's proposed reforms. As the recent, far-reaching reforms in Morocco in 2004 indicate, such reforms in a country like Mali cannot be entirely ruled out.[77] In Mali, on the one hand, the secular state seems very reluctant to make many concessions to Muslim clerics who would like to have the marriages they contract legally recognized. On the other hand, a vocal contingent of Muslim activists demands that "Islamic law" be central to any such reforms. But there is a diversity of "Islamic" perspectives on women's rights in Mali.[78] If the state does recognize religious marriages, calls for the legalization of the full gambit of classical Maliki legal principles related to marriage, including repudiation, which earlier generations of Malian women's activists fought to have legally banned, could possibly follow. It is difficult to imagine that the Malian women's rights activists who have fought so hard for previous reforms and changes in the law would accede to any such demands. The dramatic spread of Islamic legal principles in the country over the past several decades and the enduring symbolic importance of "Islam" to so many Malians almost seem to guarantee that any attempts to reform the law will be fraught with contradictions. The secular Malian state—its relative weaknesses notwithstanding—has sought to retain its prerogatives in the realm of law and has thus far not been willing to loosen its hold on matters of family law. The result has been a failure to reform family law, with the status quo ante persisting. It should, however, be clear from this discussion that the debates and controversies over family law reforms cannot be understood simply as the inevitable outcome of the opposition of "conservatives" (or "Islamists") to those committed to advancing women's and global human rights. Although the ultimate outcome of any proposed reforms in Mali remains uncertain, contentious debates over family law and such social reforms as the promotion of women's rights will undoubtedly continue for some time.

Notes

Since this essay was first conceived and then subsequently completed, there have been important developments around family law reform in Mali. In May 2009, the Malian Conseil des Ministres adopted reforms to the family code similar to those that President Alpha Oumar Konaré had proposed in 2002, and in August 2009 the National Assembly subsequently voted overwhelmingly to approve them. Faced with considerable public opposition and large organized demonstrations, President Amadou Toumani Touré did not promulgate the law and instead returned the proposed reforms to the National Assembly for reconsideration. It is now unclear whether any such reforms will be made into law during President Touré's second term. Indeed, it is unlikely such law reforms could be adopted without amendments. Many doubt that the promulgation of such laws is even possible, at least for the time being, given the size of the public demonstrations against the reforms led in part by Mahmoud Dicko, the current president of the Haut conseil islamique. It is interesting to note that many Malians think that the new and seemingly sudden impetus for reform came from outside Mali, particularly from various donors and nongovernmental organizations working in the country. Some reform advocates have also criticized the government for failing to sufficiently educate the public about the latest proposed reforms and their merits and how with little warning on the eve of the month of Ramadan it had the National Assembly swiftly vote on the law reforms. Here some commentators have pointed to the Malian state's weakness and its possible ineptness.

1. On legal pluralism in this region, see, for the early colonial period, Richard L. Roberts, *Litigants and Households: African Disputes and Colonial Courts in the French Soudan, 1895–1912,* Social History of Africa Series (Portsmouth, N.H.: Heinemann, 2005); as well as the collection of essays that focuses on issues of land tenure in contemporary Mali in *Le droit en Afrique: Expériences locales et droit étatique au Mali,* edited by Gerti Hesseling, Moussa Djiré, and Barbara Oomen (Paris and Leiden: Karthala and Afrika-Studiecentrum, 2005).

2. See the colonial attempt to codify such "custom" in what is present-day Mali in *Coutumiers Juridiques de l'Afrique Occidentale Française,* vol. 2, *Soudan* (Paris: Larose, 1939).

3. Maaike De Langen, *Les assesseurs et la justice, configurations du droit et de la coutume dans les conflits fonciers à Douentza, Mali, rapport d'une recherche de terrain* (Leiden: Van Vollenhoven Institute, 2001).

4. See the important work on *fiqh* in the region by John Hunwick, *Sharia in Songhay: The Replies of al-Maghili to the Questions of Askia al-Hajj Muhammad,* Fontes historiae Africanae 5 (London: Oxford University Press for British Academy, 1985). Cf. Dorothea E. Schulz, "Sharia en nationaal recht in Mali," in *Sharia en nationaal recht in twaalf moslimlanden,* edited by J. M. Otto, A. J. Dekker, and L. J. van Soest-Zuurdeeg (Amsterdam: Amsterdam University Press, 2006), 335–55, which presents a superficial understanding of the history of Islam and Islamic jurisprudence in Mali that is often factually incorrect.

5. See, e.g., Dorothea E. Schulz, "Political Factions, Ideological Fictions: The Controversy over Family Law Reform in Democratic Mali," *Islamic Law and Society* 10, no. 1 (2003): 132–64.

6. On Islamic education in Mali, see Bintou Sanankoua and Louis Brenner, eds., *L'enseignement islamique au Mali* (Bamako: Éditions Jamana, 1991); Seydou Cissé,

L'enseignement islamique en Afrique noire (Paris: L'Harmattan, 1992); and Louis Brenner, *Controlling Knowledge: Religion, Power and Schooling in a West African Muslim Society* (Bloomington: Indiana University Press, 2001).

7. See Benjamin F. Soares, "Notes on the Anthropological Study of Islam and Muslim Societies in Africa," *Culture & Religion* 1, no. 2 (2000): 277–85.

8. See, e.g., the discussion of Bambara "customary law" given by Alfred Aubert, "Coutume Bambara (cercle de Bougouni)," in *Coutumiers Juridiques,* vol. 2, *Soudan,* 1–126.

9. See Robert Launay and Benjamin F. Soares, "The Formation of an 'Islamic Sphere' in French Colonial West Africa," *Economy and Society* 28, no. 4 (1999): 497–519; Maria Grosz-Ngaté, "Memory, Power, and Performance in the Construction of Muslim Identity," *PoLAR: Political and Legal Anthropology Review* 25, no. 2 (2002): 5–20; and Benjamin F. Soares, "Islam and Public Piety in Mali," in *Public Islam and the Common Good,* edited by Armando Salvatore and Dale F. Eickelman (Leiden: Brill, 2004), 205–26.

10. Barbara M. Cooper, *Marriage in Maradi: Gender and Culture in a Hausa Society in Niger, 1900–1989* (Portsmouth, N.H.: Heinemann, 1997), 38–39.

11. See Rebecca Shereikis, "From Law to Custom: The Shifting Legal Status of Muslim *Originaires* in Kayes and Medine, 1903–13," *Journal of African History* 42 (2001): 261–83; and Rebecca Shereikis, "Customized Courts: French Colonial Legal Institutions in Kayes, French Soudan, c. 1880–c. 1913" (PhD diss., Northwestern University, 2003); and Roberts, *Litigants and Households.*

12. Cf. Humphrey J. Fisher, "The Juggernaut's Apologia: Conversion to Islam in Black Africa," *Africa* 55, no. 2 (1985): 153–73.

13. See Launay and Soares, "Formation of an 'Islamic Sphere.'"

14. See Soares, "Islam and Public Piety"; and Benjamin F. Soares, "Islam in Mali in the Neoliberal Era," *African Affairs* 105 (2006): 77–95.

15. On madrasas in Mali, see Brenner, *Controlling Knowledge.*

16. See Oumar Kane, "L'enseignement islamique dans les médersas du Mali," in *L'enseignement islamique au Mali,* ed. Sanankoua and Brenner.

17. On public sermons in colonial and postcolonial Mali, see Soares, "Islam and Public Piety"; and Benjamin F. Soares, *Islam and the Prayer Economy: History and Authority in a Malian Town* (Edinburgh and Ann Arbor: Edinburgh University Press and University of Michigan Press, 2005).

18. For an analysis of Modibo Jara's writings, see Francesco Zappa, "Écrire l'Islam en bambara: Lieux, réseaux et enjeux de l'entreprise d'al-Hâjj Modibo Diarra," *Archives des Sciences Sociales des Religions,* 147 (2009): 167–86; and Francesco Zappa, "L'islamizzazione della lingua bambara in Mali: Tra pubblicistica scritta e letteratura orale," *Rivista degli Studi Orientali* 77, supplemento no. 2 (2004): 39–86.

19. Although it is difficult to quantify the Bambara-language reading public, it seems to have been growing.

20. See Hesseling, Djiré, and Oomen, *Le droit en Afrique.*

21. Ibid.

22. Rosa De Jorio, "When Is 'Married' Married? Multiple Marriage Avenues in Urban Mali," *Mande Studies* 4 (2002): 31–44; the quotation here is on 33.

23. However, as Hesseling, Djiré, and Oomen indicate in *Le droit en Afrique,* many people do go to courts over land tenure disputes.

24. "Tous les Maliens naissent et demeurent libres et égaux en droits et en devoirs. Toute discrimination fondée sur l'origine sociale, la couleur, la langue, la race, le sexe, la religion et l'opinion politique est prohibée." 1992 Mali Constitution, art. 2. See http://www.justicemali.org/index.php?option=com_content&view=article&id=102&It emid=56.

25. Cf. Elmahmoud Soumeïlou, *L'influence du droit musulman sur le code du mariage et de la tutelle en République du Mali, mémoire de fin d'études* (Bamako: ENA, 1985).

26. See http://www.justicemali.org/index.php?option=com_content&view=article &id=102&Itemid=56.

27. On changes in bridewealth and marriage in rural Mali, see Maria Grosz-Ngaté, "Monetization of Bridewealth and the Abandonment of 'Kin Roads' to Marriage in Sana, Mali," *American Ethnologist* 15, no. 3 (1988): 501–14. For urban Mali, see Richard Marcoux, Mouhamadou Gueye, and Mamaou Kani Konaté, "La nuptialité: Entrée en union et types de célébration à Bamako," in *L'insertion urbaine à Bamako,* edited by Dieudonné Ouédraogo and Victor Piché (Paris: Karthala, 1995), 117–44; Saskia Brand, *Mediating Means and Fate: A Socio-Political Analysis of Fertility and Demographic Change in Bamako, Mali* (Leiden: Brill, 2001); and De Jorio, "When Is 'Married' Married?" See also the work of the demographer Solène Lardoux, "Polygyny, First Marriage and Fertility in Senegal and Mali" (PhD diss., University of Pennsylvania, 2004).

28. In this way, the 1962 code seems to translate the distinction between virgin and nonvirgin in *fiqh* but makes no explicit reference to virginity.

29. See Rosa De Jorio, "Female Elites, Women's Formal Associations, and Political Practices in Urban Mali (West Africa)" (PhD diss., University of Illinois, 1997).

30. On the history of Malian women's associations and their shaping of post-colonial family law, see De Jorio, "Female Elites."

31. See De Jorio, "Female Elites."

32. In this way, divorce by mutual agreement (or "no-fault divorce") is not possible under the 1962 code.

33. For a discussion of how the *'idda* for widows is interpreted in Mali, see Soares, "Notes on the Anthropological Study of Islam."

34. "Après la dissolution du mariage par la mort de l'un des époux, la tutelle des enfants mineurs et non émancipés appartient de plein droit au survivant des père et mère."

35. See Adam Konaré Ba, *Dictionnaire des femmes célèbres du Mali (des temps mythico-légendaires au 26 mars 1991) précédé d'une analyse sur le rôle et l'image de la femme dans l'histoire du Mali* (Bamako: Éditions Jamana, 1993), 58–61.

36. United Nations, *Convention sur l'élimination de toutes les formes de discrimination à l'égard des femmes* (CEDAW/C/MLI/2-5), Mali, March 25, 2004, 13, 60, http://www.wildaf-ao.org/fr/IMG/pdf/Mali_rapport_CEDEF_FR.pdf.

37. Ibid.

38. See the engaging ethnography from urban Mali given by De Jorio, "Female Elites"; and Brand, *Mediating Means.*

39. See, e.g., Unni Wikan, *Generous Betrayal: Politics of Culture in the New Europe* (Chicago: University of Chicago Press, 2002); and the rather pointed critique of such "cultural essentialism" and "cultural anxiety" in Europe by R. D. Grillo, "Cultural Essentialism and Cultural Anxiety," *Anthropological Theory* 3, no. 2 (2003): 157-173.

40. Grosz-Ngaté, "Monetization of Bridewealth"; and De Jorio, "When Is 'Married' Married?"

41. On the long history of migration in this region, see François Manchuelle, *Willing Migrants: Soninke Labor Diasporas, 1848–1960* (Athens: Ohio University Press, 1997).

42. See, e.g., Sidiki Doumbia, "La situation des femmes délaissées: La loi islamique juge de façon différente," *Les Echos,* August 25, 2006.

43. For Mali, see Brand, *Mediating Means.*

44. As Iman Ngondo a Pitshandenge notes, this is a much broader problem in many African countries where only monogamy is legally recognized. See her "Marriage Law in Sub-Saharan Africa," in *Nuptiality in Sub-Saharan Africa: Contemporary Anthropological and Demographic Perspectives,* edited by Caroline Bledsoe and Gilles Pison (Oxford: Clarendon Press, 1994), 117–29.

45. The mother can bring a lawsuit in the name of her child or children. However, more frequently, the mother appeals to kin and religious leaders or to civil servants working, for example, with the Brigade pour la protection de l'enfant et des moeurs, who often attempt to mediate between the woman and the father of her children. See Maïmouna Coulibaly, "Vie en concubinage: Une union au détriment de la femme," *Les Echos,* June 24, 2005.

46. For other examples, see the Malian women's magazine *Muso: La magazine des femmes* at www.musow.com.

47. Some point to specific passages in the Qur'an, the most important being sura 4, verse 34.

48. Konaré Ba, *Dictionnaire;* see also Marijke Van den Engel and Gerti Hesseling, "Women and Law in Mali," in *Kinship Structures and Enterprising Actors: Anthropological Essays on Development,* edited by J. A. Andersson and M. Breusers (Wageningen: Ponsen & Looijen, 2001), 299–316.

49. However, there were many other efforts and activities to promote women. See Rosa De Jorio, "Gendered Museum, Guided He(tour)topias: Women and Social Memory in Mali," *PoLAR: Political and Legal Anthropology Review* 25, no. 2 (2002): 50–72, for a discussion of the new Malian women's museum.

50. For a broader discussion of such reforms and their ties to other economic and political reforms—democratization and liberalization—in the country, see Soares, "Islam in Mali."

51. On such "democratic" experiments in Mali, see Susanna D. Wing, "Questioning the State: Constitutionalism and the Malian Éspace d'interpellation démocratique," *Democratization* 9, no. 2 (2002): 121–47.

52. See Ministère de la Promotion de la Femme, de l'Enfant et de la Famille, *Situation des femmes au Mali cinq ans après la conférence de Beijing,* Rapport National, March 2000, http://www.justicemali.org/doc013.htm.

53. See Alexis Kalambry, "Droit de la famille: La synthèse est lá," *Les Echos,* September 12, 2001.

54. In 2009 a new set of proposed reforms was presented to the National Assembly. Like the earlier ones, the 2009 proposed reforms have also triggered considerable opposition culminating in a mass rally in a Bamako football stadium. These recent developments are summarized in the unnumbered note at the top of page 285.

55. Cf. Schulz, who writes about vague "conservative forces"; see Schulz, "Political Factions," 157. See also Susanna D. Wing, "L'État de droit confronté au pluralisme juridique: L'exemple des droits de la femme au Mali et au Bénin," in *Gouverner les so-*

ciétés africaines: acteurs et institutions, edited by Patrick Quantin (Paris: Karthala, 2005), 247–62; and Bintou Sanankoua, "Femmes du Mali," *Esprit* 317 (August–September 2005): 212–18.

56. C. H. Sylla, "Code de la famille et excision: La dernière victoire des islamistes sur Alpha," *Le Républicain,* June 10, 2002.

57. Boukary Daou, "Code de la famille et excision: Les musulmans disent non à Alpha," *Le Républicain,* June 5, 2002.

58. These and some of the other objections are listed by AMUPI and UNAFEM [Union nationale des femmes musulmanes], *Guide sur femme, famille et Islam* (Bamako: AMUPI and UNAFEM, 2002), http://www.mpfef.gov.ml/Guide_sur_Femme_Famille_Islam.pdf. See also Schulz, "Political Factions."

59. Yacoub Doucouré, "Genre et religion: Repères sur les rapports de genre dans la société islamique," photocopied pamphlet, 2002.

60. El Hadj Mahmoud Dicko, "Declaration du Collectif des Associations Islamiques du Mali," *Info-Matin,* May 7, 2001.

61. See Mark LeVine, "Globalization in the MENA and Europe: Culture, Economy and the Public Sphere in a Transnational Context," *Journal of Muslim Minority Affairs* 26 (2005): 145–70.

62. See B. S. Diarra, "Nouveau code des personnes et de la famille: Les associations islamiques s'interrogent," *Aurore,* May 30, 2002.

63. "Tout ministre d'un culte qui procédera aux cérémonies religieuses d'un mariage sans qu'il ait été justifié d'un acte constatant la célébration civile de ce mariage délivré par l'officier de l'état civil, sera puni d'une amende de 5.000 à 30.000 francs." See http://www.justicemali.org/index.php?option=com_content&view=article&id=102&Itemid=56.

64. Mountaga Tall's role is discussed by Laya Diarra and Tiémoko Traoré, "Légalisation du mariage religieux au Mali," *Soir de Bamako,* July 29, 2005.

65. See Soares, *Islam and the Prayer Economy;* and Benjamin F. Soares and Réne Otayek, eds., *Islam and Muslim Politics in Africa* (New York: Palgrave Macmillan, 2007).

66. See AMUPI and UNAFEM, *Guide sur femme, famille et Islam.*

67. Ibid.

68. Annelies Moors, "Representing Family Law Debates in Palestine: Gender and the Politics of Presence," in *Religion, Media, and the Public Sphere,* edited by Birgit Meyer and Annelies Moors (Bloomington: Indiana University Press, 2006), 115–31.

69. Ibid.; for neighboring Niger, see Ousseina Alidou and Hassana Alidou, "Women, Religion, and the Discourses of Legal Ideology in Niger Republic," *Africa Today* 54, no. 3 (2008): 21–36.

70. In fact, the presence of such women so attired seemed so newsworthy that one of Mali's newspapers featured a large photo of such women alongside a feature article on "Islamic marriage." See Sékouba Samaké, "Campagne pour la législation du mariage islamique: Présentation de la première mouture," *Info-Matin,* September 20, 2004.

71. Sékouba Samaké, "Campagne pour la législation du mariage islamique."

72. This is interesting to compare with Senegal where a small "lobby" has sought to reform family law. See Marie Brossier, "Les débats sur le droit de la famille au Sénégal," *Politique africaine* 96 (2004): 78–98.

73. Quoted in B. Touré, "Mariage: Que valent les certificats délivrés par les mosquées?" *L'Essor,* January 8, 2005. The text in French: "A la mosquée de MaliMag,

il a été célébré, suivant les prescriptions de la loi islamique, le mariage entre. . . . Moyennant une dot payable à la femme dont le montant a été fixé d'un commun accord. Le représentant du mari a demandé la jeune fille en mariage ; et le représentant de la jeune fille a accepté et a donné la jeune fille en mariage selon les pouvoirs que son tuteur matrimonial a sur elle venant de Dieu le Très Haut et l'a remis entre les mains du mari pour un bon traitement."

74. Chiaka Doumbia, "Mariage musulman: Plus comme avant!" *Le Challenger,* May 16, 2005.

75. See Touré, "Mariage"; and Youssouf Zégué Coulibaly, "Le mariage religieux: légalisé ou autorisé?" *Nouvel Horizon,* August 24, 2005.

76. See Fatoumata Dicko, "L'état malien interdit l'acte de mariage religieux," *Aurore,* March 27, 2006.

77. See the thoughtful assessment of the family law reforms in Morocco given by Jamila Bargach, "An Ambiguous Discourse of Rights: The 2004 Family Law Reform in Morocco," *Hawwa* 3, no. 2 (2005): 245–66.

78. See Rosa De Jorio, "Between Dialogue and Contestation: Gender, Islam, and the Challenges of a Malian Public Sphere," *Journal of the Royal Anthropological Institute* 15 (2009): S95–S111.

Chapter 12

Legal Recognition of Muslim Marriages in South Africa

Rashida Manjoo

South Africa's history of colonization and apartheid included discriminatory laws, policies, and practices based on factors including race, sex, gender, culture, and religion. The goal was to create a system of legal, social,
and economic separation of the country's people. By contrast, in postapartheid South Africa, many diverse people coexist in harmony, despite
differences stemming from culture, race, religion, and the like. The Constitution of South Africa Act 108 of 1996 (hereafter, the Constitution) is
viewed by many as an ideal model for multicultural democratic contexts,
wherein the right to equality exists along with the right to culture, tradition,
and religion. In this constitutional context, South Africa has been described
as a unitary, multicultural, secular democracy that protects individual liberty and freedom through a Bill of Rights, with applicability to both the state
and individuals. The new Constitution's mandate is transformative justice,

An earlier version of this chapter was presented in 2003 at the conference of the International Association of Law Libraries in Cape Town.

which requires positive measures to redress historical injustices and the consequences of past discriminatory laws and policies. The foundational values of the Constitution are nonsexism, nonracism, the right to dignity, and the right to substantive equality.

Under apartheid, despite the limited recognition or nonrecognition of other forms of law by the state, there had been widespread observance of both religious laws and African customary laws. During both the colonial and the apartheid eras, there was limited state recognition and codification of these customary laws. With respect to Islamic laws and jurisprudence, there was no recognition at all by the state. Marriages conducted according to Muslim rites were refused legal recognition on the grounds that they were potentially polygamous, and hence repugnant to good public policy, as defined by the white minority ruling class. Such marriages have been denied civil law status and benefits under many laws, including the Marriage Act 25 of 1961, the Divorce Act 70 of 1979, the Intestate Succession Act 81 of 1987, and the Maintenance of Surviving Spouses Act 27 of 1990. The courts have been used by some people (mainly those with knowledge and resources) to seek relief against discrimination and disadvantage arising from the nonrecognition of their marriages. Cases that have been brought to court include claims for spousal benefits and support, inheritance claims, and actions related to the determination of the legitimacy of children born of marriages conducted under Muslim rites.

During the apartheid era, judgments rendered by the courts clearly reflected an intolerance of diversity, and also the imposition of values of the white minority ruling class on all South Africans. Since 1994, however, the courts have been bound by the spirit, ethos, and values of the new Constitution, which as noted above is based on human dignity, freedom, and equality. Hence, subsequent judgments have reflected these new values and have illustrated a rejection of the values articulated in the apartheid-era judgments. A limitation of the judgments in the postapartheid era is that they reflect a focus on the rights and obligations created by the existence of a de facto monogamous Muslim marriage. Unfortunately, the courts have not addressed the issue of polygynous marriages, nor have they recognized Muslim marriages as valid. The legal recognition of religious marriages requires legislation to be passed, and this is a function of the legislature. Hence the courts are careful not to overstep their authority by creating a new law that recognizes religious marriages. This would be a violation of the separation-of-powers principle that is enshrined in the Constitution, wherein the executive, the legislature, and the judiciary have different prescribed powers.

Muslims, who constitute approximately 1.5 percent of the population (numbering about 600,000), have been present in South Africa for more than three hundred years.[1] Their origins, interpretation of Islam, and everyday practices are diverse. They do not constitute a homogenous group, with one approach to personal status or family issues within an Islamic framework. There is no uniform system of personal status laws, either at the formal state level or at the informal community level. In some Muslim communities, the judicial and social welfare divisions of the local *'ulama'* (Muslim clergy) councils informally provide services in the family law area. The dispute resolution function, which is performed by these councils in the Muslim family law arena, is based on their own subjective interpretations of religious laws and jurisprudence. Thus, matters of marriage, divorce, custody, succession, and so on are sometimes resolved by these bodies. There is no empirical research on how widespread the use of such forums has been, and also in which geographic region of the country such usage is most prevalent. However, on the basis of data from one province in particular (the Western Cape), generalizations have been made about the wider use of such forums.[2]

The administration of Muslim Personal Laws (MPLs) by the judicial and welfare sections of the clergy bodies has been widely criticized. The Commission on Gender Equality (CGE), an independent constitutional body, has been involved in numerous activities relating to the problems experienced by women in their interactions with the clergy, along with problems arising from the legal nonrecognition of Muslim marriages. Complaints received by the CGE about the handling of family law matters by the clergy revolve around issues relating to divorce, polygyny, spousal and child support, domestic violence, and the like. Complaints received by the CGE also clearly indicate that the implementation and practice of religious law, as presently understood and practiced, has resulted in tensions and conflicts between women's right to equality and the right to religious freedom. Numerous complaints indicate a discriminatory and male-biased approach to such issues.

In spite of this situation, clergy groups have made persistent efforts, both during and since apartheid, to have the MPLs recognized by the state. The political changes of the 1990s saw the issue of the MPLs become part of larger political discussions about a new, nondiscriminatory, nonracist, nonsexist democratic South Africa. The remedial efforts of the current democratic government are visible in the area of both African customary law and the MPLs. In this chapter, I confine myself to the legal reform efforts being made with respect to the recognition of Muslim marriages. The following

sections examine the applicable legal framework, give an overview of the
legal reform effort, and analyze selected provisions of the proposed draft
law recognizing Muslim marriages.

The Legal Framework

Both the interim Constitution of 1993 and the final Constitution of the Republic of South Africa of 1996 contain a Bill of Rights that guarantees many
rights and freedoms, including the freedom of conscience, religion, opinion, and belief. The freedom of religion and belief guarantee includes both
the right to hold a religious belief and to express such a belief in practice.
Section 9 of the Constitution of 1996 recognizes the right to equality as a
core value, and it is formulated both as a mandate for equal treatment and
as a prohibition against unfair discrimination on many grounds, including
gender, sex, religion, conscience, and belief. The right to dignity (as stated
in section 10) has also been used by the Constitutional Court to protect the
family and family life. Section 15 (3) permits the state to enact legislation
enabling the recognition and practice of any religious, personal law, and
family law system and to recognize marriages concluded under any tradition or system of religious, personal, or family law, subject to such laws being consistent with other provisions of the Constitution. This latter condition means that any laws passed as permitted by Section 15 (3) must comply
with the rights and freedoms that are guaranteed in the Bill of Rights, given
that the Constitution is the supreme law of the land. Section 31 states that
all people have the right to enjoy their culture, practice their religion, and
use their language, and also to form, join, and maintain cultural, religious,
and linguistic associations in a manner in keeping with the Bill of Rights.

The Promotion of Equality and Prevention of Unfair Discrimination Act
4 of 2000 (in section 8), forbids customary, religious, or other practices that
would impair the dignity of women and undermine equality between
women and men and forbids any policy or conduct that would unfairly limit
women's access to land rights, finances, or other resources. This legislation
explicitly forbids systems that would prevent and/or disadvantage women
from inheriting family property. International and foreign law must also be
taken into account by courts when interpreting the Constitution. This involves consideration of both South Africa's obligations under international
law and jurisprudence from other countries. South Africa has ratified, without reservations, the United Nations Convention on the Elimination of All

Forms of Discrimination against Women. Article 16 of the convention deals with marriage and family life and the duty of a state to take all necessary steps to end discrimination against women in those areas. This is thus an obligation that the South African government cannot ignore in its quest to recognize religious marriages.

It is apparent from this description that the South African political and legislative framework is more than adequate to protect both individual and group rights. It is also clear that as a secular, multicultural society with a long history of oppression and discrimination, the framework attempts to accord respect and dignity to different cultures and religions. At the same time, it promotes and protects the human rights of all women. The rights to equality, human dignity, and freedom are guaranteed by the Constitution, and religious, cultural, and traditional laws must respect such rights in both content and implementation. In the following section, I set out recent legal reform efforts aimed at the recognition of Muslim marriages.

The Efforts of the South African Law Reform Commission

The South African Law Reform Commission (SALRC) is a statutory body appointed by Parliament, which had in the 1980s and early 1990s considered the status of the Muslim Personal Laws. In 1996, it reconsidered this project with a particular focus on the recognition of Muslim marriages. Due to concerns raised in the past about the representativeness of the SALRC project committee on this issue and also to the procedures it followed, a new project committee was recommended and subsequently appointed by Parliament in 1999, following a more transparent nominating process. Its mandate was to investigate Islamic marriages and related matters. The committee published an issue paper identifying the issues and problems with respect to Islamic marriages in May 2000, and in December 2001, it published a discussion paper with a draft bill. After collecting responses from the general public, the committee released a revised bill in October 2002. The final report and a substantially amended draft Muslim Marriages Bill were released in July 2003 and were submitted to the minister of justice, but as of 2008, they had not yet been submitted to Parliament. The parliamentary process requires that a member of the executive (in this instance, the minister of justice) present legislation to Parliament for consideration and further public consultation before the enactment of laws.

The SALRC has encountered widespread criticism, including accusations that it has accorded preferential treatment to the clergy. The project committee has insisted that the draft bill of 2003 is supported by the majority of the community—despite the fact that it has been notified that the consultation process was flawed; that many women are unaware that the bill codifies religious law (as opposed to merely recognizing Muslim marriages); and that many of its provisions are contested, given the different schools of interpretation of Islamic law.

The preamble of the Muslim Marriages Bill 2003 sets out the objectives it seeks to achieve, which include the establishment of provisions for the recognition and registration of Muslim marriages; specification of the status and capacity of spouses in Muslim marriages; regulation of the proprietary consequences of Muslim marriages; regulation of the termination of Muslim marriages and the consequences thereof; provision for the making of regulations; and provision for matters connected therewith. In the following subsections, I discuss selected provisions of the bill.

Section 1: Definition and Interpretation of the Act

With respect to divorce, section 1 of the bill delineates several different forms, including revocable or irrevocable *talaq, faskh,* and *khula. Talaq* is defined as the unilateral pronouncement of divorce articulated by a male spouse; *faskh* as a decree of dissolution of marriage on any grounds or basis permitted by Islamic law and by application by either party to the marriage; and *khula* as the dissolution of a marriage at the wife's behest and on terms agreed to by both parties. A distinguishing feature of *khul'* is that under this system, a wife renounces all financial claims on her husband, especially any unpaid *mahr* (the dowry a husband gives his wife), in order to obtain a divorce.

Section 2: Application of This Act

According to section 2 of the bill, this law would apply to Muslim marriages entered into after the commencement of this act where the parties have chosen to be bound by its provisions, as well as to marriages entered into previously, unless the parties elect to seek an exemption. It would also apply in instances where parties are already married under civil law and now elect to have the provisions of the act apply to their marriage.

Section 3: Status and Capacity of Spouses in Muslim Marriages

Section 3 of the bill states that a wife and husband in a Muslim marriage are equal in human dignity and have equal legal capacity and financial independence. Both parties thus have the capacity to own and acquire assets and to dispose of them, to enter into contracts, and to litigate in their own names. This provision is of course in accordance with Islamic law and also the Constitution of South Africa.

Section 5: Requirements for a Valid Muslim Marriage

The requirements of section 5 of the bill include consent—that is, both parties must consent to the marriage (a woman does not need to consent through a representative)—the presence of witnesses, as required by Islamic law (although this section does not mandate that the witnesses must be male); and that both parties have reached the minimum marriage age of eighteen years.

Section 6: Registration of Muslim Marriages

According to section 6 of the bill, marriages entered into before the commencement of the act (except those parties who have elected not to be bound by its provisions) must be registered in the prescribed manner within a period of two years or within a time period determined by the minister of justice. Marriages entered into after the commencement of the act (where parties choose to be bound by its provisions) must be registered at the time of the conclusion of the marriage. Section 6 (3) places obligations on the marriage officer (i.e., the state-accredited individual who conducts the marriage ceremony) to inform the parties that they are entitled to conclude a contract of their own choice regulating their marital regime, including a standard contract. The officer has to present the parties with examples of such contracts, and he or she must ensure that the parties understand the registration procedures.

Section 8: Proprietary Consequences

Under the terms of section 8 of the bill, a Muslim marriage is considered a marriage out of community of property excluding the accrual system, unless the parties agree to contract into another proprietary system and do so in a prenuptial contract (called an antenuptial contract in South Africa). The consequences of a marriage out of community of property excluding the accrual system is that each party retains those assets that they bring into the marriage and also those assets that they acquire over the duration of the marriage. A prenuptial contract must be registered in the Deeds Registry. This section also allows for spouses in a Muslim marriage regulated by the act to jointly apply to court for leave to change their matrimonial property system.

The bill also recognizes and attempts to regulate polygynous marriages. In instances where a husband is in more than one marriage, the law requires that all parties having a sufficient interest in the matter, especially the existing wives (both religious and civil law wives), must be named in, and notified of, any court proceedings relating to a change in marriage contracts. It includes a provision that a husband in a Muslim marriage who intends to contract another Muslim marriage must seek court approval. The court must grant the approval if it is satisfied that the husband will be able to maintain equality between the spouses, as prescribed by the Qur'an. The language in this section does not specify what factors the court must consider to establish whether equality can be maintained. In terms of normal judicial practice, interpretation is at the discretion of the judge, with reference to the relevant laws, and in this instance also with reference to any applicable Qur'anic injunctions. The court may make an order terminating the existing matrimonial property regime and also ordering the immediate division of the estate. All persons with an interest in the matter, in particular the existing wives, must be joined in the proceedings, that is, be cited as parties in the application papers. A husband who enters into a second marriage without the required court order may be subject to a fine not exceeding 20,000 rand ($3,400). Furthermore, it is an offense for a marriage officer to register a second marriage unless the order of court is furnished by the husband before the registration of the subsequent marriage.

Section 9: Termination of Marriages

Section 9 of the bill makes reference to existing civil law legislation to assist the process of terminating marriages, subject to the grounds and procedures permitted by Islamic law. The section sets out the process governing the different forms of termination, including the time frames for registration of a *talaq* and procedures for *khul'*. This section also deals with the procedures for the division of assets; the custody, access, and maintenance of children; and the issue of a conciliatory gift.

Section 11: Custody of and Access to Minor Children

Section 11 of the bill attempts to introduce the norms of existing legislation as well as those of Islamic law. The bill attempts to be sensitive to the constitutional protection of children and also to the applicable provisions of Islamic law. Hence, in custody and access disputes, courts are required to consider the best interests of the child, Islamic laws, and also any report from the Office of the Family Advocate (a statutory body that investigates provisions related to children in divorce matters).

Section 12: Maintenance

Section 12 of the bill also attempts to integrate existing civil law and Islamic law. The husband is obliged to maintain his wife during the duration of the Muslim marriage, and the father is obliged to maintain his children until they become self-supporting (there is no specific age mentioned in the legislation). Maintenance of a child includes the provision of food, clothing, separate accommodation, medical care, and education. Upon dissolution by divorce of a Muslim marriage, the husband is obliged to maintain the wife for the mandatory *'idda* period (i.e., the mandatory waiting period during which a woman in a Muslim marriage may not remarry). This period is applicable to both widows and divorcees, and its duration depends on the period necessary to establish pregnancy (usually three menstrual cycles). The husband is also obliged to remunerate the wife where she has custody of the children, including providing a separate residence, and providing remuneration for breastfeeding for two years from the birth of the child.

Section 13: Compulsory Mediation

Section 13 of the bill requires mediation as a first step toward the dissolution of a marriage. This can be conducted by any accredited mediation agency. Parties to a mediation agreement may apply to a court to have their agreement be made an order of the court, that is, a legally binding agreement.

Section 14: Arbitration

According to section 14 of the bill, the spouses in a Muslim marriage may refer a dispute to an arbitrator, and the provisions of the Arbitration Act shall apply. The Arbitration Act is currently used in South Africa largely to resolve commercial disputes, and it is unclear how it will be used in family law disputes by accredited arbitrators. Courts are not bound by arbitration awards and can thus entertain disputes anew.

Section 15: Courts and Assessors

Section 15 of the bill proposes that if a dispute is referred to court, a Muslim judge must be appointed as presiding officer, failing which a Muslim lawyer of at least ten years' standing will be appointed instead. Also, the court is to be assisted by two Muslim assessors (appointed by the minister of justice), who shall have the requisite knowledge of Islamic law.

Section 17: Unopposed Proceedings

According to section 17 of the bill, in unopposed matters or matters where the parties have drawn up a settlement agreement, a Muslim judge shall sit without assessors. The reasoning is that in the absence of disputes, the judge will not require input from any additional experts in making the decision to grant the divorce.

An Analysis of the Draft Bill

The recognition of Muslim marriages requires legislative intervention, and the proposed Muslim Marriages Bill of 2003, as set out above, is but one attempt to resolve the discrimination and disadvantages that have been suffered by members of the Muslim community. Since 1994, the courts have attempted to ameliorate the constitutional violations that have resulted from the nonrecognition of Muslim marriages. Unfortunately, these remedies have not included the legal recognition of such marriages. As discussed above, this is a task that must be undertaken by the legislature and not the judiciary. The analysis that follows is based on my interpretation of the bill and my understanding of the constitutional obligations that are owed to all citizens of South Africa. It is not based on expertise related to religious laws, jurisprudence, and practices but on an understanding that the norms and values underpinning Islamic laws and jurisprudence are also embodied in the Constitution.

The Muslim Marriages Bill raises many constitutional concerns, including provisions related to the codification of religious laws in a secular multicultural democracy; the scope of application of such laws; potential violations of women's equality rights, both intergroup and intragroup; and issues related to the achievement of both individual and group equality. The South African Constitution does not mandate strict separation of religion and state; instead, the practice by the different organs of state has been to avoid "entanglement" with religion. Unfortunately, the bill violates this practice, thereby also violating the doctrine of the separation of religion and the state that exists in many secular democracies.

The bill also violates the constitutional guarantee of freedom of religion and belief, both in terms of the interpretations of religious law as found within the codified provisions and also in the provisions relating to state enforcement of such provisions. It is apparent that the bill represents a compromise to meet constitutional guarantees, and hence it includes provisions from the different schools of Islam. This is problematic for many, because it assumes a common understanding of the Muslim Personal Laws and also assumes that the Muslim community in South Africa is homogenous. The imposition of one version of religious law on all Muslims is viewed by many as a violation of their constitutional rights, for it empowers the state to enforce and control the manner in which people choose to practice their religion and express their faith and belief. Furthermore, the bill may be viewed as undermining the autonomy of religious institutions.

In terms of equality between the citizens of a nation-state, the codification of a religious system that privileges one religious group in a secular democracy may be viewed as violating the equality rights of other groups. This is particularly relevant to the South African context, where there are other religious groups whose marriages are not recognized. Additionally, the provisions related to the appointment of Muslim judges and assessors to hear disputes brought by Muslim litigants could also be interpreted as privileging one sector of society and thus violating the same standard of equality for all citizens. Worse still, they may be seen as a potentially divisive factor in a country with a history of divisions. The reality in South Africa is one where all judges are bound by the dictates of the Constitution, and they are expected to be guided by this in their decisionmaking, even if the litigants are of a different race, sex, cultural, or religious group.

Further, with respect to intragroup equality norms, the bill advocates different rules and procedures for people bound by the Muslim Marriages Bill. It treats the proprietary consequences of marriage, divorce rules and procedures, the maintenance of spouses, and the custody of and access to children differently from the handling of such issues under the civil marriage system. One example of this relates to civil law marriages, which are automatically in community of property, whereas marriages under this bill will be automatically out of community of property. As discussed above, the consequences of a marriage out of community of property excluding the accrual system are that each party retains the assets that he or she brings to the marriage as well as those acquired during the marriage. This effectively works to the disadvantage of the spouse who does not work outside the home and who also might not inherit family assets. The provisions related to compulsory mediation and arbitration are also problematic, based both on equality arguments and on the fact that they ignore the reality of unequal power relations in many marriages. Furthermore, compulsory mediation is a contradiction in terms, given that mediation by its very nature is a voluntary process agreed to by both parties, who choose a neutral third party as a mediator.

In terms of individual rights to gender equality, many believe that the current practice of Muslim Personal Laws cannot be reconciled with the constitutional guarantee of substantive gender equality. They see this bill as further entrenching the existing de facto inequalities that many Muslim women experience through the implementation and practices of Islamic law. This view is borne out by the provisions on issues related to property, spousal support, 'idda, divorce rules and procedures, and polygyny. For example, the proviso relating to postdivorce/postdeath waiting periods may be seen as a violation of gender equality, given that it is a mandatory obligation imposed on Muslim women only. It is also viewed as illogical because the purpose is to ascertain the paternity of a child who may be born to a woman after the death of her husband or the dissolution of a marriage. With technology today, this can be established in a fairly short time, and hence the specific time provision in the bill does not make sense. This acontextual approach to the codification of religious laws is seen as ignoring time, place, and scientific developments in the world today. It is also seen as conservative, backward looking, and harmful to both the individual and the religion.

Another example of potential violation of individual equality rights relates to those provisions in the bill that recognize and sanction the practice of polygyny, while at the same time providing some legislative protective measures. This raises two crucial issues in the context of the enshrined right to equality, both in general terms and with regard to sexual equality. The bill does not specify a woman's right to enter multiple marriages, which begs the question of whether the right to religion is overriding the right to equality in this instance. The bill also ignores the economic factors and unequal power relationships that force women into polygynous marriages. By legislating to regulate polygyny through the courts, this inequality/discrimination defect is not necessarily remedied. Further, there is no requirement for the wife's consent before her husband contracts a subsequent marriage. Debates have ensued as to whether court regulation of polygyny is practically possible, under modern social and economic conditions, and also whether men will follow the prescribed court process—particularly in a context where the state's right to intervene in the religious domain is not widely accepted.

Conclusion

In light of the above-mentioned problems, the Parliamentary Office of the Commission on Gender Equality decided, after numerous interventions, to exercise its mandate and draft a secular law that recognizes all religious marriages. This draft legislation is a generic law of general application and thus does not codify any aspects of any religion. The CGE legislation was tabled with the relevant state officials in 2005, but as of 2008 it had still not been disclosed to the public. The lack of attention to the crucial constitutional issue of discrimination against the Muslim community is of concern to many. There are ongoing discussions among lawyers about launching a constitutional court challenge to force the legislature to redress the constitutional violation resulting from nonrecognition of religious marriages.

As noted above, the reality is that South Africa is a secular country that has constitutionally enshrined the rights to freedom of religion, belief, conscience, and opinion. In this context, the protection of minority group rights, whether based on religion or culture, is constitutionally guaranteed in broad terms. The question of how to interpret such a constitutional guarantee has also now been clear since the seminal *Bhe* case was decided by the Constitutional Court in 1994. The *Bhe* case concerned the resolution of a conflict between gender equality rights and cultural rights. The issue facing the court involved the inheritance rights of girls under African customary law. The court in this case struck down the discriminatory customary law practice, which precluded women and girls from inheriting family property. This judgment clearly affirmed that where equality rights clash with rights to culture, the equality right will override the right to culture. On the basis of this judgment, one may infer that the same approach will be adopted when a clash arises between equality rights and religious rights. Generally, cases since 1994 have articulated the preeminent values of equality and dignity in the new South African society.

It is clear that the protection of minority group rights does not include a right to a personal status legal system that conflicts with the Constitution's fundamental protection of the principle and practice of the equality of all citizens. Also, it is clear that the courts will not sanction an unconstitutional system that violates individual rights. Hopefully, when appropriate draft legislation finally reaches the legislature, the substantive equality rights of women will trump archaic and discriminatory provisions that violate women's rights to both equality and religion.

Notes

1. See Ebrahim Moosa, "Prospects for Muslim Law in South Africa: A History and Recent Developments," *Yearbook of Islamic and Middle Eastern Law* 3 (1996): 134–37.

2. See Somaya Abdullah, "Multicultural Social Interventions and Nation-Building in South Africa: The Role of Islamic Counselling and Psychotherapy" (PhD diss., University of Cape Town, 2002).

Glossary

(Terms in Arabic and words in other languages used in Africa)

'adat. Custom.

'ajami. Non-Arab speaker of Arabic; non-Arabic languages written in Arabic script, such as Hausa.

'alim. Male religious scholar.

'alima. Female religious scholar.

amir. Lit. Arabic, prince; used here to indicate the head of a religious organization.

'amir al-mu'minin. Commander of the Faithful, a title held by the King of Morocco.

amira. Lit. Arabic, princess; used here to indicate the head of a religious organization.

asbab al-nuzul. Occasions of revelation of the Qur'an.

asl. Origin or foundation.

'awrat. Lit. Arabic, genitals, that part of the body that should be covered.

305

bayan. Lit. Arabic, statement or declaration; used in Gambia as lecture citing the Qur'an and *hadith.*

brassage sahélien. Blending of cultures from North Africa and the so-called sub-Saharan Africa.

burqa'. Loose all-enveloping garment worn by women; term commonly used in Afghanistan and South Asia.

da'iya Female missionary; also used in Gambia for teacher.

darb. Striking or beating.

da'wa. Invitation or call to Islam.

dhaqan. Somali for culture.

dhikr. Ceremonial recitation of the names of God.

diin. Somali for religion (Arabic *din*).

diric. Loose-fitting, sleeveless dress of fine cotton, worn with a petticoat as underskirt (Somali).

faskh. Anullment of marriage by judicial decree issued by religious authorities.

fatwa. Nonbinding religious opinion (pl. *fatawa*).

fiqh. Islamic jurisprudence.

fuqaha. Jurists (sing. *faqih*).

garbasaar. Shawl or shoulder wrap (Somali).

guntiino. Woman's garment consisting of a length of cloth wrapped around the body and tied on the left shoulder (Somali).

habous. Islamic endowments, Moroccan usage (standard Arabic *awqaf*).

hadith. Recorded saying and/or deed attributed to the Prophet Muhammad.

haj. Pilgrimage to Mecca.

hijab. Covering of the head and body, often refers simply to covering the head and hair.

hees or *heello.* Somali term for the literary genre of song.

hudud. Criminal laws based on a reading of Islamic jurisprudence (*fiqh*).

'ibadat. Religious rituals.

'idda. Waiting period for a woman following divorce or death of a husband before she can remarry.

ijtihad. Independent critical reading of religious sources.

ijtima'. Lit. Arabic, meeting; used in Gambia for annual conference of the Tablighis.

ikhlas-i-niyyat. Sincerity of purpose (Mandinka).

ikram-i-muslim. Respect for a Muslim (Mandinka).

'ilm. Knowledge or science.

imam. Leader of prayer.

insan. Human being.

islaannimo. Muslim identity, an identity emphasizing 'Muslim-ness' (compare withis *soomaalinimo*).

isnad. Chain of transmission of *hadiths.*

jihad. Lit. Arabic, exertion or struggle; often glossed in West as "holy war."

kalima. Lit. Arabic, word used in Gambia as article of faith.

karuwai. Female or male prostitute in Hausa.

khul'. A woman-initiated divorce to be granted by a *qadi* (religious judge) in which the woman renounces all financial claims on her husband.

khuruj. Missionary tour.

kuble or *kulle.* Seclusion, in Hausa.

lakkwal. French-introduced schools in Niger in Hausa and Zarma languages.

laada. "Custom" in vernacular in Mali, from the Arabic word *'adat.*

madrasa. Lit. Arabic, a school. In many non-Arabic-speaking Muslim communities it refers to a religious school where the Qur'an and Arabic are taught. In Niger it has been used to signify a modernized (often bilingual Arabic-French) school.

Maghreb. The western flank of northern Africa from Libya to Morocco.

mahr. The dower the husband gives the wife.

makaranta. Traditional Qur'anic school in Hausa.

makhzen. Lit., storehouse or treasure; commonly used in Morocco to refer to the clientilist networks of privilege surrounding the palace.

malam. Male religious teacher (*malama,* female religious teacher) in Hausa.

Mandinka. Majority ethnic group in the Gambia; also the name of the language spoken by them.

marabout. Sufi holy man, usage in North and West Africa.

markaz. "Center" or headquarters, referring to the Tabligh Jama'at's mosque (Gambia).

mashalas. Term used in Gambia for a Tablighi, derived from the Arabic *ma sha' allah* (what God wishes).

masrax. Somali for 'theater.'

matran zamani. Modern woman in Hausa, colloquial for prostitute.

Mudawana. Name of the Moroccan personal status code; lit., collection of laws.

mujahid. One who engaged in *jihad* or mental and moral struggle.

muqqaddamat. Female religious authority, Hausa.

muruwwa. Chivalry in Hassaniyaa (Mauretania).

nafaqa. Support due a wife and children, and a divorced woman.

niqab. Face veil.

qadi. Lit. Arabic, judge, often refers to religious judge.

qawwamun. Men as "protectors and maintainers" of women (Qur'anic term).

riwayyad. Play or theatrical production in Somali.

sadaq. (See also *mahr*) dower the husband gives the wife.

sahaba. Friends of the Prophet Muhammad.

salat. Prayer.

shari'a. The path a Muslim should follow as discerned from the Qur'an, often used to indicate "Islamic law," which would more precisely be referred to as Islamic jurisprudence.

shart. Condition that can be added to a contract.

shaykh. Male religious leader.

shaykha. Female religious leader.

shura. Consultation.

sirriyya. Secret.

soomaalinimo. Somali identity or 'Somali-ness.'

Sunna. The example seen through the words and deeds of the Prophet Muhammad.

tafrigh-i-waqt. Taking time from worldly occupations to participate in missionary work, used by Tablighis in Gambia.

tafsir. Exegesis (plural, *tafasir*).

tajwid. Art of reciting the Qur'an.

talaq. Divorce or repudiation by a husband of his wife.

ta'lim. Education or learning.

tamsir. Religious commentaries in Hausa.

ta'sil. Foundationalism.

tatrib. Ecstasy.

'udul. Trustworthy individuals qualified to testify according to Islamic jurisprudence; also Islamic notaries.

'ulama'. Religious scholars.

umma. Muslim community.

'urf. Custom.

'usul al-fiqh. Foundations of Islamic jurisprudence.

wa'azi. Admonition, warning, counseling in Hausa.

wali. Legal guardian or legal "tutor."

zawaj al-mut'a. Temporary marriage allowed in Shi 'i Islam.

zina. Adultery.

Contributors

Ousseina D. Alidou is an associate professor of linguistics, gender, and cultural studies in the Department of African, Middle Eastern, and South Asian Languages and Literatures and Comparative Literature at Rutgers University, where she also directs the Center for African Studies and is an affiliated graduate faculty member of the Department of Anthropology and the Department of Women's and Gender Studies. Her research focuses on gender, discourse, and literacy practices in Afro-Islamic societies. Her books include *Engaging Modernity: Muslim Women and the Politics of Agency in Postcolonial Niger* (University of Wisconsin Press, 2005); *Post-Conflict Reconstruction in Africa* (World Press, 2006); and *A Thousand Flowers: Social Struggles against Structural Adjustment in African Universities* (World Press, 2000). She has also published numerous journal articles on Afro-Islamic women's contributions to oral and written literatures in francophone Africa. She received her PhD in theoretical linguistics from Indiana University–Bloomington in 1997.

Margot Badran, a historian of the Middle East and Islamic societies and a specialist in gender studies, is a senior fellow at the Center for Muslim-Christian Understanding at Georgetown University and a senior scholar at the Woodrow Wilson International Center for Scholars. From 2003 to 2004, she was preceptor at the Institute for the Study of Islamic Thought in Africa and Edith Kreeger Wolf Distinguished Visiting Professor in the Department of Religion at Northwestern University. Among her books are *Feminism in Islam: Secular and Religious Convergences* (Oneworld Publications, 2009), which *Choice* has included on its list of outstanding books for 2010; *Feminism beyond East and West: New Gender Talk and Practice in Global Islam* (Global Media Publications, 2006); and *Feminists, Islam, and Nation: Gender and the Making of Modern Egypt* (Princeton University Press, 1995), which was translated into Arabic as *Raidat al-Harakat al-Niswiyya al-Misriyya wa al-Islam wa al-Watan* (2000). In addition, she was coeditor of *Opening the Gates: A Century of Arab Feminist Writing* (with miriam cooke; Indiana University Press, 1990; new, expanded edition, 2004); and the translator, editor, and introducer of *Harem Years: The Memoirs of an Egyptian Feminist, Huda Shaarawi* (Feminist Press, 1987). She also writes on issues of women, gender, and feminism in Islam and Muslim societies for the *Al Ahram Weekly* in Cairo and other newspapers.

Heike Behrend is a professor of anthropology at the Institute of African Studies of the University of Cologne. She has conducted intensive research in Kenya, Uganda, Ghana, and Nigeria; currently, she is studying media in Africa (photography and video) and is continuing to investigate the relationship between religious change, violence, and war in Uganda. She has been a visiting professor at the École des Hautes Études en Sciences Sociales in Paris, the Program of African Studies at Northwestern University in Evanston, and the University of Florida in Gainesville. In 2007, she was a senior research fellow at the Internationales Forschungszentrum Kulturwissenschaften in Vienna. In 2010, she was a visiting professor at the Tokyo University of Foreign Studies. She has published extensively on technical media in Africa, religion, and war, and recently has studied the Catholic Church in western Uganda, resulting in a book that will be published soon by James Currey in Oxford.

Corinne Fortier is an anthropologist associated with the Laboratoire d'Anthropologie Sociale (Social Anthropology Laboratory) of the Collège de France and the Centre National de la Recherche Scientifique (National Center for Scientific Research), both in Paris. She has conducted field research in Algeria, Egypt, and Mauritania, and has studied Islamic scriptural sources related to body, gender, misfortune, and the transmission of knowledge. Her research interests in France include gender, sexuality, and filiation, especially with respect to medically assisted procreation, prostitution, or transidentity. She received the Bronze Medal of the National Center for Scientific Research in 2005. She recently edited an issue of the journal *Droit et Cultures* (vol. 59, no. 1, 2010) on current issues in Islamic jurisprudence, including gender, descent, and bioethics.

Marloes Janson is a researcher at the Zentrum Moderner Orient (Centre for Modern Oriental Studies) in Berlin. Currently, her research focuses on youth participation, especially of female youth, in the Tabligh Jama'at in the Gambia and on Chrislam, a religious organization fusing Christian and Muslim beliefs and practices in Lagos, Nigeria. She has previously conducted research on griottes, oral traditions, local forms of Islamic expression, and religious reform in the Gambia and Senegal. Her publications include *The Best Hand Is the Hand That Always Gives: Griottes and Their Profession in Eastern Gambia* (CNWS Publications, 2002). Her book *Young, Modern and Muslim: The Tabligh Jama'at in the Gambia* is forthcoming. In 2009, she was a visiting professor at Brandeis University. She received a PhD in cultural anthropology from Leiden University in 2002.

Lidwien Kapteijns is Kendall-Hodder Professor of History at Wellesley College, where she teaches African and Middle Eastern history. Her current research focuses on Somali popular culture as mediation of civil war violence. She has published widely on Sudanese and Somali history and has, in this context, translated and published a number of Arabic- and Somali-language sources. Her book *Women's Voices in a Man's World: Women and the Pastoral Tradition in Northern Somali Orature, c. 1899–1980* (Greenwood/Heinemann, 1999) analyzes both Somali folklore texts and Somali popular songs in the period since independence. Her most recent book is the coedited volume *African Mediations of Violence: Fashioning New Futures from Contested Pasts* (with Annemiek Richters; Brill, 2010), which includes her chapter "Making Memories of Mogadishu in Somali Poetry about the Civil War."

Beverly B. Mack is a professor of African studies in the Department of African and African American Studies and a courtesy professor of religious studies at the University of Kansas, where she teaches courses on women and Islam, Muslim women's autobiography, African women writers, and Islamic (Sufi) literature. She has conducted extended field research in Kano, Nigeria, and Fez, Morocco, as well as additional research in Ghana, Côte d'Ivoire, and Guinea-Conakry. Her extensive publications on African literature and Muslim women's lives in West Africa include *Hausa Women in the Twentieth Century* (coedited with Catherine Coles; University of Wisconsin Press, 1990); *The Collected Works of Nana Asma'u, Daughter of Shehu Usman dan Fodiyo, 1793–1864* (coedited with Jean Boyd; Michigan State University Press, 1997); *One Woman's Jihad: Nana Asma'u, Scholar and Scribe* (with Jean Boyd; Indiana University Press, 2001); and *Muslim Women Sing: Hausa Popular Song* (Indiana University Press, 2004). She is currently working on a book about Muslim women scholars in Nigeria and Morocco.

Rashida Manjoo is the United Nations' special rapporteur on violence against women, its causes, and consequences. She holds a professorship in the Department of Public Law at the University of Cape Town. She has also served as the Des Lee Distinguished Visiting Professor at Webster University, where she has taught courses in human rights with a particular focus on women's human rights and also transitional justice. She was the Eleanor Roosevelt Fellow with the Human Rights Program at Harvard Law School (2006–7) and also a clinical instructor in the program in 2005–6. She is an advocate in the High Court of South Africa and a former commissioner of the Commission on Gender Equality. She was associated with the Law, Race, and Gender Research Unit at the University of Cape Town and at the University of Natal, Durban, where she was involved in social context training for judges and lawyers. She is the founder of the Gender Unit at the Law Clinic at the University of Natal and the Domestic Violence Assistance Program at the Durban Magistrates Court. She is a member of the International Coalition for Women's Human Rights in Conflict Situations and of the Women Living Under Muslim Laws Network. She was an active member of the Women's Caucus for Gender Justice in the International Criminal Court and remains an Advisory Board member of the Women's Initiative for Gender Justice.

Julie E. Pruzan-Jørgensen is a project researcher at the Danish Institute for International Studies and is currently affiliated with l'Institut d'Études de l'Islam et des Sociétés du Monde Musulman of l'École des Hautes Études en Sciences Sociales in Paris. Her research focuses on the interlinkages between Islam, gender, and politics in North Africa and the Middle East. She received her PhD from the University of Copenhagen in 2010. Her dissertation probed the relationship between processes of political liberalization and authoritarian resilience based on an in-depth case study of the Moroccan family law reform. Her publications thus far have mainly focused on developments in Morocco, but she is currently engaged in a broader, comparative study of women's activism within the main Islamist organizations in Egypt, Jordan, and Morocco.

Raja Rhouni is assistant professor in the Department of English Literature and Cultural Studies of the Faculty of Letters and Human Sciences at Chouaib Doukkali University in El Jadida, Morocco. In 2006 and 2007, she served as a fellow of the multidisciplinary research program "Europe in the Middle East: The Middle East in Europe," sponsored by the Berlin-Brandenburgische Akademie der Wissenschaften, the Fritz Thyssen Foundation, and the Wissenschaftskolleg zu Berlin. Her project focused on an Islamic feminist critical hermeneutic of the Qur'an. Her recent book is *Secular and "Islamic Feminist" Critiques in the Work of Fatima Mernissi* (Brill, 2010). She received her PhD in cultural and development studies from Mohammad V University in Rabat in 2005.

Sa'diyya Shaikh, a South African, is currently a senior lecturer in the Department of Religious Studies at the University of Cape Town. She works at the intersection of Islamic studies and gender studies, pursuing a special interest in Sufism and its implications for Islamic feminism and feminist theory. She has just completed a manuscript on gender and sexuality in the works of a thirteenth-century Andalusian Sufi thinker, Ibn Arabi. She is also involved in an empirical research project on sexuality, marriage, and reproductive choices among South African Muslim women. Her research interests and publications cover issues of Muslim women and gender violence; feminist approaches to *ahadith* and Qur'anic exegesis; contraception and abortion in Islam; theoretical debates on Islam and feminism; Sufism, gender, and Islamic law; and "Engaged Sufism." She received her PhD in religion from Temple University, Philadelphia.

Benjamin F. Soares, an anthropologist, is a senior research fellow at the Afrika-Studiecentrum in Leiden. He has conducted research in Mali, Nigeria, and Senegal, as well as among West African Muslims living in France. He has held fellowships at the University of Chicago and the École des Hautes Études en Sciences Sociales in Paris and has taught at Northwestern University, the University of Chicago, and the University of Sussex. His publications include *Islam and the Prayer Economy: History and Authority in a Malian Town* (University of Michigan Press and Edinburgh University Press, 2005); the coedited collections, both with René Otayek, *Islam and Muslim Politics in Africa* (Palgrave Macmillan, 2007) and *Islam, Etat et société en Afrique* (Karthala, 2008); *Muslim-Christian Encounters in Africa* (Brill, 2006); and the coedited volume *Islam, Politics, Anthropology* (with Filippo Osella; Wiley-Blackwell, 2010).

Index

Abu Bakr, Omaima, 4
Abuja, 195
Abu-Lughod, Lila, 125
Abu-Zayd, Nasr Hamid, 6, 72, 77–78, 82–83
Adamu, Abdalla Uba, 176–77, 183–84, 187
Addis Ababa, 3
'Adl wa al-Ihssan, al-, 71
adultery. See *zina*
African Gender Institute (University of Cape Town), 3
African Training and Research Center for Women (Addis Ababa), 3
agency, 187; women's, 41, 43, 90, 110, 139, 149, 164–65
Ahl al-Hadith, 83
Ahmed, Leila, 76

Ahmed Baba Center (Timbuktu), 282
ajami (non-Arabic texts written in Arabic scripts), 44–46, 63–64
Akhdari, Al, 267
Algeria, 20, 194, 217–19
Alidou, Ousseina, 2, 5, 6
amir al-mu'minin (commander of the faithful, Morocco), 236, 238, 240, 249–50, 252
An-Naim, Abdullahi, 71, 203
Ansari, Asma' bint Yazid, 158
apartheid, 12, 291–92
Arabic, 19–20, 23–27, 31, 45, 64, 150, 152, 157–58, 174, 267, 282
Arabs, 42, 92, 97, 148, 217
Arewa Film Producers Association of Nigeria, 176
Arkoun, Muhammad, 6, 74, 83–84

315